Ireland, 1641

Manchester University Press

Series editors

DAVID EDWARDS & MICHEÁL Ó SIOCHRÚ

Already published

The plantation of Ulster: Ideology and practice
Micheál Ó Siochrú and Éamonn Ó Ciardha (eds)

Ireland, 1641

Contexts and reactions

Edited by
MICHEÁL Ó SIOCHRÚ
&
JANE OHLMEYER

Manchester University Press

Copyright © Manchester University Press 2013

While copyright in the volume as a whole is vested in Manchester University Press, copyright in individual chapters belongs to their respective authors, and no chapter may be reproduced wholly or in part without the express permission in writing of both author and publisher.

Published by Manchester University Press
Altrincham Street, Manchester M1 7JA, UK
www.manchesteruniversitypress.co.uk

British Library Cataloguing-in-Publication Data is available

Library of Congress Cataloging-in-Publication Data is available

ISBN 978 0 7190 9726 3 *paperback*

First published by Manchester University Press in hardback 2013

This paperback edition first published 2015

The publisher has no responsibility for the persistence or accuracy of URLs for any external or third-party internet websites referred to in this book, and does not guarantee that any content on such websites is, or will remain, accurate or appropriate.

Printed by Lightning Source

This volume is dedicated to John Morrill,
a great colleague and true friend of Irish history

Contents

List of figures   *page* ix

List of contributors   xi

Series editors' preface   xv

Acknowledgements   xvii

1   Introduction – 1641: fresh contexts and perspectives   1
    Jane Ohlmeyer & Micheál Ó Siochrú

2   Early modern violence from memory to history:
    a historiographical essay   17
    Ethan H. Shagan

3   The '1641 massacres'   37
    Aidan Clarke

4   1641 in a colonial context   52
    Nicholas Canny

5   Towards a cultural geography of the 1641 rising/rebellion   71
    William J. Smyth

6   Out of the blue? Provincial unrest in Ireland before 1641   95
    David Edwards

7   News from Ireland: Catalan, Portuguese and
    Castilian pamphlets on the Confederate War in Ireland   115
    Hiram Morgan

8   Performative violence and the politics of violence
    in the 1641 depositions   134
    John Walter

9   Atrocities in the Thirty Years War   153
    Peter H. Wilson

10 Why remember terror? Memories of violence in the
    Dutch Revolt   176
    Erika Kuijpers & Judith Pollmann

11 Language and conflict in the French Wars of Religion   197
    Mark Greengrass

12 How to make a successful plantation: colonial experiment
    in America   219
    Karen Ordahl Kupperman

13 An Irish Black Legend? 1641 and the Iberian Atlantic   236
    Igor Pérez Tostado

14 Afterword – Settler colonies, ethno-religious violence
    and historical documentation: comparative reflections
    on Southeast Asia and Ireland   254
    Ben Kiernan

Index   274

List of figures

1 Distribution of a range of atrocities and events, as reported
in the 1641 depositions   *page* 73
2 Summary of the percentage distribution of 'killings/murders'
per barony, as reported in the 1641 depositions   77
3 Geographical expansion of urban foundations from the
medieval period with particular reference to the late sixteenth
and the first half of seventeenth century Ireland   82
4 Distribution of Irish colleges on the continent and Irish writing
in Latin in Europe as a whole (c.1550–1700)   85

Contributors

Nicholas Canny is a Member of the Scientific Council of the European Research Council, and Professor Emeritus of History at the National University of Ireland, Galway, where he served as Founding Director of the Moore Institute for Research in the Humanities, 2000–11. He was President of the Royal Academy 2008–11. An expert on early modern history broadly defined, he edited the first volume of *The Oxford History of the British Empire* (1998) and, with Philip D. Morgan, *The Oxford Handbook of the Atlantic World, c.1450–c.1850* (2011). His major book is *Making Ireland British, 1580–1650* (Oxford, 2001).

Aidan Clarke is emeritus Erasmus Smith's Professor of Modern History, Trinity College Dublin. He is a former Vice-Provost of the College and past president of the Royal Irish Academy. He has published extensively on early modern Ireland, with a particular focus on the crisis of the mid-seventeenth century. His most important publications include *The Old English in Ireland, 1625–42* (1966, 2nd edn, 2000) and *Prelude to Restoration in Ireland: The end of the Commonwealth, 1659–1660* (1999). He is currently general editor of the 1641 Depositions Project, which will be published in twelve volumes by the Irish Manuscript Commission.

David Edwards is Senior Lecturer in the Department of History, University College Cork, and a Director of the Irish Manuscripts Commission. His books include *The Ormond Lordship in County Kilkenny, 1515–1642: The Rise and Fall of Butler feudal power* (2003), *Age of Atrocity: Violence and Political Conflict in Early Modern Ireland* (editor, 2007). Collaborating with Keith Sidwell, he recently completed an edition and translation of Dermot O'Meara's *Ormonius* (1615), published by Brepols in 2012.

Mark Greengrass is Emeritus Professor of early-modern history from the University of Sheffield and currently Senior External Fellow at the

Albert-Ludwigs Universität Freiburg im Breisgau. He has researched and published extensively on early modern French history and recently completed volume five of the *Penguin History of Europe* (*The Fortune of the Gods: Europe Reformed, 1517–1648*). He is currently working on the history of 'communication politics' in late Renaissance France, investigating the significance of libels, slander and rumour, as well as the circulation of news.

Ben Kiernan is the Whitney Griswold Professor of History and founding Director of the Genocide Studies Program at Yale University (www.yale.edu/gsp). He is the author of *The Pol Pot Regime: Race, Power and Genocide in Cambodia under the Khmer Rouge, 1975–1979* (1996), *Genocide and Resistance in Southeast Asia: Documentation, Denial, and Justice in Cambodia and East Timor* (2007) and the award-winning *Blood and Soil: A World History of Genocide and Extermination from Sparta to Darfur* (2007). He has also published over a hundred scholarly articles on Cambodian history, Southeast Asia, and the global history of genocide.

Erika Kuijpers is the author of *Migrantenstad. Immigratie en sociale verhoudingen in 17e-eeuws Amsterdam* (2005). She has published on the history of migration, literacy and late medieval labour markets. She is currently researching personal memories of the Dutch Revolt in the context of the VICI research project 'Tales of the revolt: memory, oblivion and identity in the low countries, 1566–1700', funded by NWO (Netherlands Organisation for Scientific Research), on which more information can be found at www.earlymodernmemory.org.

Karen Kupperman is Silver Professor of History at New York University. Her scholarship focuses on the early modern Atlantic world, particularly contacts and ventures between Europe and America and the ways that participants interpreted each other. Her edition of Richard Ligon's *True and Exact History of the Island of Barbadoes* (1657, 1673) was published by Hackett Books in 2011 and her book *The Early Modern Atlantic World* was published by Oxford University Press in 2012. She is currently studying music as a mode of communication and the link between music and universal language schemes.

Hiram Morgan teaches at University College Cork. He is the author of *Tyrone's Rebellion: The Outbreak of the Nine Years War in Tudor Ireland* (1993) and has edited a number of volumes, including *Political Ideology in Ireland, 1541–1641* (1999), *Information, Media and Power through the Ages* (2001) and *The Battle of Kinsale* (2004). He was a founder and co-editor of *History Ireland*, Ireland's illustrated history magazine. He is currently working on a biography of Hugh O'Neill, earl of Tyrone, for publication by the Royal Irish Academy.

Jane Ohlmeyer is Erasmus Smith's Professor of Modern History and Vice-President for Global Relations at Trinity College, Dublin. She has published widely on a number of themes in early modern Irish and British history. Her books include *Civil War and Restoration in the Three Stuart Kingdoms* (1993); *Ireland from Independence to Occupation, 1641–1660* (editor, 1995); *Political Thought in Seventeenth-Century Ireland* (editor, 2000); and *Making Ireland English: The Irish Aristocracy in the Seventeenth-Century* (2012). She was also one of the Principal Investigators on the 1641 Depositions Project.

Micheál Ó Siochrú is Associate Professor of History at Trinity College Dublin. He is author of numerous books and articles on seventeenth-century Ireland, including *Confederate Ireland 1642–1649: A constitutional and political analysis* (2nd edn, 2008) *God's Executioner: Oliver Cromwell and the Conquest of Ireland* (2nd edn, 2009). As one of the principal investigators on the 1641 Depositions Project, he recently completed the online publication of the collection with colleagues at Aberdeen and Cambridge, and is currently working on a new edition of Oliver Cromwell's letters and papers for Oxford University Press.

Judith Pollmann is Professor of Early Modern Dutch history at Leiden University in the Netherlands. She has published widely on the religious history and political culture of the Low Countries. Her latest book is *Catholic Identity and the Revolt of the Netherlands, 1520–1635* (2011). She is the director of the VICI research project 'Tales of the revolt: memory, oblivion and identity in the Low Countries, 1566–1700', funded by NWO (Netherlands Organisation for Scientific Research), on which more information can be found at www.earlymodernmemory.org.

Ethan Shagan is Professor of History and Director of the Center for British Studies at the University of California, Berkeley. His publications include *Popular Politics and the English Reformation* (2003); an edited volume entitled *Catholics and the 'Protestant Nation': Religious Politics and Identity in Early Modern England* (2005); and most recently *The Rule of Moderation: Violence, Religion and the Politics of Restraint in Early Modern England* (2011).

William J Smyth is Emeritus Professor of Geography at University College Cork. His research interests lie in the cultural and historical geography of Ireland and the Atlantic World. Co-editor of *Common Ground: Essays on the Historical Geography of Ireland* (1988), he is the author of the new introduction to Séamus Pender's *A Census of Ireland c.1659* (2002) and the award-winning *Map-making, Landscapes and Memory: A Geography of Colonial and Early Modern Ireland c.1530–1750* (2006). With John Crowley and Michael Murphy, he edited an *Atlas of the Great Irish Famine* published by Cork University Press in 2012.

Igor Pérez Tostado lectures at the Pablo de Olavide University in Seville. His primary research is on Irish–Spanish–British relations in the early modern period, both in Europe and the Atlantic. His books include *Irish Influence at the Court of Spain in the Seventeenth Century* (2008) and, with Enrique García Hernán, *Irlanda y el Atlántico Ibérico: movilización, participación e intercambio cultural* (2010). He is currently working on a monograph on the Irish in the Spanish Caribbean.

John Walter is Professor of History at the University of Essex. He is the author of *Understanding Popular Violence in the English Revolution* (RHS Whitfield Prize, 1999), *Crowds and Popular Politics in Early Modern England* (2006) as well as the editor (with Roger Schofield) of *Famine, Disease and the Social Order in Early Modern Society* (1989) and (with Michael Braddick) of *Negotiating Power in Early Modern Society: Order, Hierarchy and Subordination in Britain and Ireland* (2001).

Peter H. Wilson is GF Grant Professor of History at the University of Hull, having worked previously at Sunderland and Newcastle universities. He has written or edited fifteen books on European history including *Europe's Tragedy: A History of the Thirty Years War* (2009) which received the Distinguished Book Award from the Society for Military History in 2011.

Series editors' preface

The study of early modern Irish History has experienced something of a renaissance since the 1990s, with the publication of a number of major monographs, examining developments in Ireland during the sixteenth and seventeenth centuries from a variety of different perspectives. Nonetheless, these works still tend to group around traditional topics in political or military history and significant gaps remain. The idea behind this new series is to identify key themes for exploration and thereby set the agenda for future research. Manchester University Press, a leading academic press with a strong record of publishing Irish-related material, is the ideal home for this venture.

This second volume in the series focuses on a key episode in early modern Irish history, the 1641 rebellion, but from a unique global perspective. Despite a veritable glut of publications on 1641 of late, none thus far have attempted to examine events in a broader European, Atlantic or colonial perspective. In addition to leading historians of Ireland and England, the contributors to this volume include experts on the Thirty Years War in Germany, the French Wars of Religion and the Dutch Revolt, as well as the Spanish and English Atlantic worlds and Southeast Asia in the early modern period. Their work provides a series of fascinating comparisons and contrasts, as the study of Ireland in 1641 moves from the realm of memory to history.

Acknowledgements

This collection of essays derives from an international conference held in Trinity College Dublin (23–25 October 2009) on the theme of 'Plantation and reaction: The 1641 rebellion'. Many of the papers were presented at this conference or were delivered at the Ninth Lewis Glucksman Memorial Symposium on 'War and atrocity: the 1641 depositions' (22 October 2010), which was hosted by the Trinity Long Room Hub, or at the Trinity Department of History's 'Early Modern Research Seminar'. A particular highlight was Aidan Clarke's lecture, which he delivered to a packed house at Dublin Castle on 23 October 2009. It was made possible thanks to the genersoity of the Office of Public Works and Dublin City Council and especially the City Manager, John Tierney. We are deeply grateful to our fellow contributors, the co-organisers and the audiences at these events for participating in them with such enthusiasm.

This volume is very much part of the wider '1641 Depositions Project', which began in 2006 when the Irish Research Council for the Humanities and Social Sciences awarded Jane Ohlmeyer a Government of Ireland Major Research Project Grant (€247,000) for the digitisation, transcription and online publication of the depositions relating to Ulster. The following year the Arts and Humanities Research Council awarded Micheál Ó Siochrú, then at the University of Aberdeen, and John Morrill, Cambridge University, a grant of €650,000 to do likewise for the three other provinces. Micheál Ó Siochrú moved to Trinity later that year and Tom Bartlett took over as the AHRC Principal Investigator in Aberdeen. Trinity College Dublin provided additional funding for conservation. We are deeply grateful to these bodies for funding the 1641 Project, together with this collection of essays and other major events – the 2009 conference, other colloquia at Trinity, Aberdeen and Cambridge and a major exhibition in the Long Room.

The 1641 Depositions Project began in October 2007 and ended in October 2010 on time, within budget and over specification. All of the depositions are now freely available online http://1641.tcd.ie. Much of the credit for this achievement must go to the 'core' team of transcribers, Annaleigh Margey, Edda Frankot and Elaine Murphy, and to Aidan Clarke, who is the general editor of the project. Their commitment, good humour and hard work was deeply appreciated. They helped to make this project the success it is.

We would also like to thank the former Trinity Provost, Dr John Hegarty, the former Dean of Research, Dr David Lloyd, and our colleagues in the Communications Office, in High Performance Computing, in the Trinity Long Room Hub, and in the School of Histories and Humanities, especially the History Department, for their support and goodwill. In all over 50 archivists, computer scientists, conservators, historians, historical geographers, linguists and literary scholars became involved in the project, and the fact that a cross word was rarely exchanged is a tribute to their collective enthusiasm for it. Throughout we worked closely with Brian Donovan and Eneclann, who digitised the depositions, and with our colleagues in the Library, especially, Robin Adams, the former College Librarian, Bernard Meehan, College Archivist, Susie Bioletti, Head of Conservation and Tim Keefe, Head of Digital Resources and Imaging Services. Colleagues from Trinity's School of Computer Science, especially Shay Lawless and Vinnie Wade, played an increasingly important role in the project as did IBM LanguageWare, especially D.J. McCloskey and Marie Wallace. Eamon Darcy and Felicity O'Mahony helped to curate a wonderful exhibition (October 2010–April 2011) in the Long Room, 'Ireland in Turmoil', which allowed us to show case the depositions and related materials. Elaine Murphy and Ciaran Wallace worked with a small army of History graduate students as they normalised the spelling of names and matched seventeenth-century placenames with their modern equivalent. We are also deeply grateful to Barbara Fennell, who led the AHRC-funded 'Language and linguistic evidence in the 1641 depositions' (2010–11), and her team, especially Mark Sweetman, for their support.

Producing a volume like this always takes longer than one might wish. We would like to thank Manchester University Press for their professionalism, and Ian Campbell who worked as sub-editor, standardising the footnotes. They and our fellow contributors have been a delight to work with and we have truly appreciated their patience and good humour.

Jane Ohlmeyer and Micheál Ó Siochrú
Trinity College Dublin

Introduction
1641: fresh contexts and perspectives

JANE OHLMEYER & MICHEÁL Ó SIOCHRÚ

On 22 October 1641, a rebellion in Ireland triggered the onset of a decade of civil war, invasion and conquest. The colonial authorities thwarted an attempt to seize Dublin castle, but could not prevent Catholic insurgents from capturing strategic strongholds in Ulster. Over the winter of 1641 and spring of 1642, the rebellion spread to engulf the rest of the country. The rising was accompanied by incidents of extreme violence as Catholics attacked, robbed and murdered their Protestant neighbours. The Protestants retaliated with indiscriminate attacks on the Catholic civilian population during one of the most brutal periods of sectarian violence in Irish history. The total number of men, women and children who lost their lives during the initial months of the rebellion or subsequent war will never be known, yet more people died during the course of the 1640s and 1650s than in the rebellion of 1798 or in the civil wars of the twentieth century. Proportionally, the conflict resulted in a greater demographic catastrophe than the potato famine of the 1840s, with the population loss estimated at over 20%.[1]

In late December 1641, as Protestant refugees poured into the city of Dublin, the colonial administration commissioned eight clergymen, including Dr Henry Jones, dean of Clogher, to collect witness statements from the traumatised settlers. In January 1642, as the rebellion intensified, the authorities extended the scope of the commission to include allegations of murders and massacres. In March, they appointed a sub-commission to take similar statements in Munster. The outcome was thousands of sworn testimonies, compiled according to a set format, listing the name, address, social status and/or occupation of each deponent, along with a description of material losses, and, where possible, information on those responsible.[2]

The bulk of the statements were taken in 1642–43, but the Commission for Despoiled Protestants continued its work until September 1647. Initially intended as a straightforward record of material losses, Irish Protestants quickly recognised the propaganda value of these testimonies. Throughout the 1640s, Henry Jones and his colleagues skilfully exploited the harrowing accounts of death and destruction to construct a seemingly irrefutable case for the re-conquest of Ireland by Protestant forces from England. At the end of the war in Ireland in 1652, the commissioners of the newly established High Courts of Justice, including the ubiquitous Henry Jones, made systematic use of the original testimonies from 1641 to 1642, alongside supplementary evidence that they themselves collected throughout Ireland, to condemn hundreds of people to death for their alleged involvement in the murder of Protestants.[3]

From the restoration of Charles II in 1660, the depositions emerged as a central component in one of the most protracted and bitter of Irish historical controversies. Catholic apologists repeatedly dismissed the collection as hopelessly biased, and as providing wildly exaggerated figures for the numbers of Protestants killed in 1641, while ignoring atrocities against Catholics. Irish Protestants, however, insisted that the testimonies, taken under oath, provided inconvertible evidence of a general massacre of settlers.[4] In 1741, on the one-hundredth anniversary of the Ulster rising, John Stearne, the bishop of Clogher, presented the entire collection to Trinity College Dublin, where it remains to this day. The college bound the 19,000 manuscript pages into thirty-one volumes, divided on a county-by-county basis.[5] In addition to the original statements taken by Henry Jones and his colleagues, the clerk of the commission, Thomas Waring, made a large number of copies in the mid-1640s. The collection also includes similar testimonies by Munster Protestants, taken in 1642–43 by an English cleric, Philip Bysse, examinations conducted for the High Courts of Justice between 1652 and 1654 and a variety of miscellaneous documents.[6]

This manuscript collection is indispensable to the study of seventeenth-century Ireland, providing the only detailed narrative of events during the crucial early months of the rebellion, albeit only from a Protestant perspective. The depositions are also legal documents and certain information was standard to each one. The name and address of the deponent was always recorded and in many instances the occupation and age of the deponent was also noted. If capable of writing, the deponent usually signed their statement or left a mark if they were unable to sign. The depositions record the names of over 90,000 victims, assailants, bystanders and observers, and include references to every county, parish and barony in Ireland.

The deposition of Lady Ann Butler, sworn on 7 September 1642, was typical in many respects. She began her testimony by explaining who she was and what she had lost.

The La Dame Ann Butler wife vnto Sir Thomas Butler of Rath healin in the County *of Catherlagh knight and Barr{onet} of Carlow* duly sworne and examined deposeth that since about st patricks day last & since shee hath beene *was* robed and deprived of her lands rents goods and chattells to the vallues following, by means of this rebellion In sheepe Cowes oxen yong *cattle* and ould, In breeding mares sadle mares catch horses, Geldings, and other Cattle.[7]

Her laundry-like list of losses amounted to the staggering figure of £4,906, the equivalent of a small fortune today. Lady Ann then went on to identify who had committed these outrages, men whom she clearly knew well, and detailed how they had burned and pillaged her home. She explained that she and her family were then taken to Kilkenny under restraint, constantly threatened with torture and death because 'they weare ranke puritan protestants'.

Having graphically related her own experiences, Lady Ann recounted those of an English woman, Jane Jones, who had allegedly been an eye-witness to a particularly harrowing incident that involved the violent murder of newly born twins.

Jane jones said she . . . had seene to [the] number of 35 English goinge to exicution and that shee had seene[t]hem when they wea[re exe]cuted, [their bodyes] espos[ed to devour]ing [Ravens and] not soe mu[ch as a bur]iall. Another English woman who was nuly deliuered of two childeren in one birth they violently compelled her in her greate payne and siknesse to rise from her childbed and tooke the infant that was left aliue and dash[ed] his braines against the stones and after thrue him into the riuer of [the] Barrow: and the deponent one day hauing a peece of sammon to dyner on Mr Bryan Cauonoghs *wife* being with her: shee *the said Mrs Reanall* refused to eate any parte o[f] the samon and being demanded the reason shee said she would not [eate] any ffish that came out of the Barrow because shee had seene s[everall] infants bodyes and other carkases taken [of the] [Eng]lish taken vp in [the weares].

Lady Ann then concluded her deposition with an account of her incarceration in Kilkenny and the refusal of the insurgents to help her 'because shee *& her family* weare protestants and would not turne to masse'.[8] This extraordinary narrative, combines eye-witness and hear-say accounts, fact and fiction, thus allowing us to recapture the experiences of an ordinary woman as she and her family struggled with conflict, fear and trauma following the outbreak of the 1641 rebellion.

The 1641 depositions form a 'single-purpose' archive. Ben Kiernan, an expert on the history of genocide in Southeast Asia, notes in this volume that 'single-purpose archives by definition do not record the full context . . . Thus, what the archives don't tell us is as important as what they do.'[9] In the case of Ireland, no comparable body of evidence survives to record Catholic losses over the winter of 1641–42 or the massacres that the Catholic community suffered at the hands of government forces. The witness accounts are clearly biased and some commentators suggest that the depositions constitute the most controversial documents in Irish history.[10] Propagandists, politicians and historians have all clearly exploited the depositions at different times, principally to justify their implacable hostility towards Irish nationalism or the Catholic religion, and the controversy surrounding them has never been satisfactorily resolved. In fact, the 1641 'massacres', like the siege of Derry (1688), King William's victory at the Boyne (1690) and the battle of the Somme (1916), have played a key role in creating and sustaining a collective Protestant/ British identity. In some circles, the seventeenth century is still alive in public memory like few other places in the modern world, but with the easing of sectarian tensions in the twenty-first century, seventeenth-century Ireland may finally be passing from memory into history.[11]

THE 1641 DEPOSITIONS PROJECT

The graphic and sectarian content of the 1641 depositions helps explain why attempts by the Irish Manuscripts Commission to publish them in the 1930s failed. A letter, dating from October 1935, from the Stationer's Office to the president of the Irish Manuscripts Commission acknowledged that the censor 'could not interrupt the Commission in its publication programme', but 'we can visualise the mild uproar which will follow the appearance of the more gruesome of the depositions. Anything savouring of selection would probably be disturbing, but there is something to be said notwithstanding, we think, for the exercise of the blue pencil.' The outbreak of the 'Troubles' in Northern Ireland in 1969 thwarted another attempt.[12] It was a case of third time lucky when in 2007 the Arts Humanities Research Council (AHRC) in the UK and the Irish Research Council for the Humanities and Social Sciences (IRCHSS) in Ireland funded a collaborative project involving Trinity College Dublin and the universities of Aberdeen and Cambridge. The project aimed to conserve, digitise and transcribe the depositions, as well as making them fully available online. In October 2010, the 1641 depositions website went live, and the Irish Manuscripts Commission is in the process of publishing 12 hard copy volumes.[13]

The 1641 Depositions Project captured the popular imagination in a way that would not have been possible in the 1930s or 1960s. It made headlines around Ireland and the world with features, opinion pieces and articles appearing in the local and national press, including *The Irish Times, The Irish Independent, The Irish News, The Newsletter, The Belfast Telegraph*, as well as *The Independent, The Guardian* and *The New York Times*. RTÉ, the BBC, CBS and ABC all broadcast news items and features about the depositions. Within six months of being launched, the 1641 depositions website attracted over 40,000 registered users from across the globe. Closer to home, the Irish Department of Foreign Affairs funded a project to take the 1641 depositions into schools across Northern Ireland. Working closely with the Northern Ireland Council for Integrated Education (NICIE) and secondary school teachers throughout the province, modules aimed at fourteen-year olds have been developed for the classrooms. The magazine *History Ireland* hosted '1641 hedge schools' in Belfast, Derry, Letterkenny and Omagh, which fostered more general discussions around history and memory, identity and sectarianism.[14] None of this would have been possible when Ireland was still at war.

Easy access to the manuscripts has allowed undergraduates at Trinity and Cambridge (and no doubt elsewhere) to study them as part of their dissertations, 'special subjects' and other courses.[15] In Trinity, a new generation of masters and doctoral students work alongside teams of post-doctoral researchers on a myriad of subjects relating to the depositions.[16] The fruit of their scholarly endeavour is beginning to appear in print, but much remains unpublished.[17] Equally exciting are other associated research projects. The 'Language and Linguistic Evidence in the 1641 Depositions' was an AHRC-funded (2010–11), multidisciplinary project that aimed to develop new ways of interacting with a digitised corpus of early modern English witness testimonies. Using a suite of innovative software designed for linguistic analysis and visualisation of results, this project interrogated the depositions around a range of linguistic issues, investigating how language served various legal, political and religious agendas. The results, including some fascinating 'exhibits' and 'demos', are available online and others will appear in a variety of published outlets.[18]

Thanks in part to a close working relationship with IBM and links with the wider digital humanities community, the 1641 Depositions Project has also become a flagship technology project and attracted major European funding under the guise of CULTURA (CULTivating Understanding Through Research and Adaptivity).[19] A key challenge facing academics, curators and providers of digital cultural heritage is to investigate, increase and enhance engagement with digital humanities collections. To achieve this, a fundamental change in the way cultural artefacts, such as the 1641 depositions, are experienced and contributed to by communities is required. Thus, CULTURA will pioneer the development of next generation adaptive systems to tackle these issues. When viewed from the perspective of an historical researcher, the possibilities that technology offers are truly exciting. As emphasis shifts from the generation of digital data to how these resources can be interrogated, and as technology becomes increasingly sophisticated and user-friendly, historians – together with literary scholars, historical geographers, linguists, computer scientists and other researchers – will be able to interrogate their sources and represent their findings in ways currently unimaginable.[20]

FRESH PERSPECTIVES ON 1641

This collection of essays explores one of the key episodes in Irish history, the outbreak, course and consequence of the 1641 rebellion and particularly incidents of mass killing and extreme violence that accompanied it.[21] The contributors, many of whom draw on the 1641 depositions, adopt a variety of historical, geographic and anthropological perspectives. They situate the massacres in their early modern Irish, European and global contexts and suggest fresh ways of conceptualising how we might study both the depositions and the events they record. A number of historians – Aidan Clarke, Nicholas Canny and William Smyth – have already made very significant contributions to our knowledge and understanding of 1641.[22] Other contributors, especially non-Irish specialists, build on their own pioneering studies as well as important regional and county studies, to bring fresh perspectives and insights from related disciplines, along with ideas about where more meaningful comparisons might be drawn.[23] The 1641 massacres, for example, could be compared with the ethno-sectarian violence associated with the Khmelnytsky Uprising in Ukraine, where tens of thousands of Jews and Poles were killed, or with the Razin rebellion, when Russian soldiers murdered thousands of Cossacks.[24] Equally, as Ben Kiernan suggests, our knowledge of the 1641 rebellion has much to offer other historiographies, where native and newcomer violently clashed as they did in the Burma and Cambodian deltas in the mid-eighteenth century, a subject of Kiernan's study.[25]

By adopting a more comparative approach, historians can learn more about how best to analyse events that caused incidents of mass killing, atrocity and massacre. Ethan Shagan suggests a number of alternative conceptual perspectives.[26] Writing as an historian of early modern Britain and Europe, he wants 'to raise a series of what I hope will be provocative questions about the role of history, as opposed to memory, in considering the violent legacy of the Irish past'. His first model 'seeks to understand violence on its own terms, admitting it as a rational or at least comprehensible consequence of the perpetrator's worldview and hence looking for its causes in the minds, experiences, and cultural assumptions . . . of those who commit violent acts'.[27] His second model offers an alternative approach and sees violence as a productive space of socio-cultural interaction. The two methods, as Shagan notes, are not incompatible, but it will now be for historians of Ireland to think long and hard about whether the post-conflict history of the seventeenth century will be a project of amoral critical distance or a new ethical project.

In this volume, contributors explore what 'massacre' meant in the early modern period. Peter Wilson examines contemporary understandings, themselves often ambiguous, and suggests that scale, intent and legitimacy helped to distinguish between killing and massacre. He argues that massacre 'is defined as the ruthless and indiscriminate killing of large numbers of people. According to Wilson, 'while this implies scale, it leaves open whether a massacre results from cold-blooded premeditation, or follows from some unintended hot-blooded escalation of violence'.[28] Writing from the perspective of mid-seventeenth-century Ireland, Aidan Clarke qualifies this definition. He reminds us that the contemporary usage of the word massacre 'was not confined to mass killings'. According to Clarke, 'it also denoted a killing that was particularly shocking because it violated the proprieties of the time, in its brutality, its treachery or its transgression of the hierarchy of status'.[29] Clarke confronts the subject of a bad-tempered, centuries-long debate that only came to an inconclusive end about one hundred years ago.[30] The controversy centred around two separate but often confused questions: did the 1641 rebellion begin with a premeditated massacre of Protestant settlers, and how many Protestant settlers were killed in cold blood in the early years of the rebellion? Clarke argues that the contemporary evidence confirms the prevailing assumption that there was no premeditated massacre, but does not support the recently evolved consensus about the number of settlers killed in cold blood. Those interested in quantifying losses should, Clarke urges, do so on a county-by-county basis and adopt the 'forensic standard set some years ago by Hilary Simms in an exemplary investigation of the material for County Armagh'.[31]

Though the full details will never be known, the scale of fatalities in Ireland probably compares to the devastation caused by the Thirty Years War.[32] Peter Wilson offers a detailed study of one particularly bloody episode, the infamous sack of Magdeburg (May 1631) by forces loyal to the Holy Roman Emperor. Wilson suggests that Magdeburg's experience is both misleading and instructive. First, the drama of the siege and the scale of horror following the assault encouraged later writers to generalise from this one event. Closer inspection reveals that the deaths were largely unintended. Second, amidst the horror, contemporaries still recognised a threshold distinguishing atrocities from other acts of violence. Magdeburg attracted such attention precisely because it was so exceptional. Third, these norms constrained violence through their place in the language of political legitimacy. The boundary defining what was permissible remained contested, but the fact that accusations of atrocities had propaganda value indicates an underlying consensus on what constituted proper behaviour. Nonetheless, the rhetoric of atrocity, fuelled by developments in print media across the period, along with the war's length all contributed to the lasting impression of fearful, generalised violence which shaped interpretations of the conflict until now. The parallels with the popular memory of particular events in Ireland, such as the drownings at Portadown Bridge, are striking.[33]

The significance of propaganda, and how this shaped opinions, is explored by Hiram Morgan. The Iberian publications he examines fall naturally into three groups: pamphlets from the 'rebel' city of Barcelona all dating from 1641 and 1642; a range of material from Lisbon, the capital of the newly restored kingdom of Portugal, dating from the early and middle 1640s; and pamphlets from Castile which were, in the main, re-publications of Irish Catholic confederate material. These publications provide the opportunity to discover new factual material, not extant elsewhere, and to draw comparisons between the experiences of the Stuart and Spanish multiple monarchies during a period of rebellion and intense political crises. Given the current emphasis on the importance of fully understanding print culture, the circulation of news about the 1641 rebellion and its reception across early modern Europe are certainly topics worthy of further study.[34] The fact that these Iberian publications represented the 1641 rebellion and the accompanying atrocities in a more positive light also served to counteract damaging English language anti-Catholic propaganda emanating from the London presses.[35] According to Morgan, the Iberian printers 'saw events in Ireland not as an atrocity but a veritable triumph for human rights'.[36] Igor Pérez Tostado develops a number of these themes through his analysis of the different contemporary interpretations of 1641 rebellion in Ireland circulating in Europe. He also compares the similarities between the negative constructions of Catholic Irish identity and contemporary arguments about the cruel nature of the Spanish Empire. He concludes that the justifications, stereotypes and legitimisation tools born after 1641 have been extremely long-lived and persistent, because they have been readapted continuously to justify and explain different and evolving political conflicts.

Similarly, Erika Kuijpers and Judith Pollmann examine memories of violence in the Dutch Revolt. A series of massacres accompanied the outbreak of the revolt in the Netherlands in 1566. From the summer of 1572, Habsburg commanders tried to suppress the rebellion by besieging key cities and sacked a number by way of punishment and to set an example for others. Hundreds, sometimes thousands, of men, women and children were murdered and many others were tortured and raped. Kuijpers and Pollmann illustrate how these events have always played a key role in shaping public memories of the revolt. They show that the massacres *initially* triggered surprisingly little by way of detailed, local forms of commemoration, while it also took a long time for individual tales to find their way into the public domain. With the help of insights developed in modern memory studies, they outline a series of possible social and psychological explanations for this initial silence, before turning to the reasons why, in the course of the seventeenth century, this silence was at last broken.

Mark Greengrass adopts a very different but equally challenging approach to sectarian violence, as he engages with some of the advances in the study of 'orality'. Taking a cue from the 1641 depositions, he analyses a rather similar but smaller body of evidence – a series of testimonies rediscovered in the last decade relating to a religious riot in Cahors in south-western France in 1561. He does so, conscious throughout of the multiple difficulties in knowing how much of contemporary evidence can safely be regarded as something that had actually been 'said' and how little it can possibly reflect the context. Greengrass proposes that we need to use such documentation as a way of 'tuning in' to the orality of the civil wars, focusing on seditious preaching and its control. He suggests that a hitherto neglected part of our understanding of the French civil wars was the dilemma that the authorities faced in controlling speech-acts. There is much in his methodology that might inspire scholars of the 1641 depositions, especially given the determination of the commissioners to record the reported speech of the insurgents.

In his chapter Nicholas Canny highlights the significance of these sixteenth-century wars of religion, but argues that the appropriate context within which to investigate the 1641 rebellion is one of European expansionism. Purely European issues in the early to mid-sixteenth century became more universal over time, none more so than those associated with the emerging Atlantic world. These quickly became tainted by the Protestant/Catholic rivalries that had besmirched all politics within western and central Europe. By examining the European literature associated with colonisation and Protestant descriptions of atrocity exercised in colonial situations, Canny suggests that this literature expanded the repertoire of horror that could be drawn upon by those wishing either to boost their sales through sensationalism, or to earn greater sympathy for the travails of those who had suffered assault and torture. By developing a structural comparison between John Temple, *The Irish Rebellion*, a text published in 1646 to explain the Irish insurrection of 1641 from a Protestant perspective, and Edward Waterhouse, *A Declaration of the State of the Colony and . . . A Relation of the Barbarous Massacre*, published to record the 1622 massacre of the English colonists in Virginia by native American Indians, Canny contends that Protestant reportage on the hardships suffered by them in Ireland complied with the template used for reporting on the travails endured in colonial situations.

Karen Kupperman's chapter complements Canny's work and covers again the colonial world that Waterhouse so vividly portrayed in his *Declaration*. Kupperman argues that England's leaders believed that in planting colonies abroad they had the opportunity to create more perfect versions of their own society. These colonies would then both reflect back onto the Old World, opening the way to tackle widespread corruption and decay. In order to do this, colonial planners reflected on the forms and foundations on which local society ran at home, and found recreating these forms more difficult than they had expected. The Virginia Company sought to impose a solution through martial law. If colonists were not naturally virtuous, virtue would be enforced. Martial law might force a certain level of behaviour, but would not foster the innovation and initiative required to make a success of the venture. Nor could the kind of web of mutuality on which local society ran in England emerge within such a system. By the end of the colony's first decade, and responding to advice from the settlers themselves, the investors moved to a wholly different model. In 1619, in what came to be known as the Great Charter, the company offered the colonists land in freehold ownership, a degree of self-government, the removal of all the military men and shiploads of carefully chosen women to allow family formation.

England experienced comparable challenges in ruling Ireland, and adopted similar solutions, beginning with martial law. David Edwards analyses how a deep-seated fear of foreign intervention and native insurrection marked government policy. Rumours of invasion punctuated the early decades of the century, with full-scale invasion scares in 1613, 1615, 1624, 1625 and 1639. The government maintained an extensive network of forts and garrisons to secure the island from external threat and sought to intimidate the population through widespread recourse to martial law. Despite these heavy handed security measures, the authorities received reports of numerous small rebellions and violent disturbances around the country, especially in areas bordering on recently planted or colonised land. Partly because of an over-reliance on a limited number of (chiefly printed) sources, historians have almost entirely overlooked these lesser revolts, but the so-called 'early Stuart peace' is revealed here as something very brittle. Edwards concludes by suggesting that 'the near-constant spark and crackle of localised rebellion helped to bring Ireland to the brink of a major conflagration in October 1641'.[37]

As Edward's chapter highlights, the causes of the rebellion remain contested. The same can be said of the 1641 depositions themselves. William Smyth, a historical geographer, argues that more attention should be paid to the carto-graphic, contextual, comparative and conceptual dimensions relating to the 1641 depositions, in order to enlarge our interpretations of the rebellion. The first part of Smyth's chapter deals with methods and sources for a more comprehensive mapping of the content of the depositions, emphasising the use of mid-seventeenth century cartographic evidence such as the Down Survey. The second part examines how such a geographical analysis of the depositions helps us to understand the forces shaping the nature of the 1641 rebellion at elite levels. The depositions, however, also offer a crucial 'ground–up' view, a unique source for studying ordinary people's lives in a wartime situation. Using anthropological insights in particular, the third part of Smyth's chapter provides a wider comparative framework – both cultural and demographic – to examine the certainties and uncertainties surrounding the evidence and the subsequent construction and use made of that evidence.[38]

Smyth, drawing on anthropological observations on 'mythico-history' (or narratives generated in situations of extreme ethnic violence), also reminds us of the importance of learning more about how the depositions were collected.[39] Did the commissioners lead the deponents? To what extent was testimony shared across deponents? What was the relationship between what happened, what people said happened and how it was recorded? The process by which oral testimony became written evidence is of particular interest to John Walter. In his chapter Walter draws on David Riches's influential essay on the anthropology of violence, which highlights how the meaning of performative violence is contested in a negotiation between performer, victim and witness. Taking inspiration from the body of work associated with what has been called the new social history of politics and popular violence in early modern England, Walter offers a comparative perspective on the meaning of the pattern of violence in the Irish rebellion. He highlights the similarities and differences between the 1641 depositions and comparable bodies of English legal records.[40] Walter also questions the appropriateness of the influential model of a two-part rising with the political elite losing control in the face of peasant fury, suggesting instead a greater level of political engagement at all levels.

HISTORY AND MEMORY

On 22 October 2010, the anniversary of the outbreak of the 1641 rebellion, Dr Mary McAleese, President of Ireland, launched the 1641 website and an accompanying exhibition on 'Ireland in Turmoil' in the Long Room at the Trinity College Library.[41] She acknowledged that 'the events of 1641 have been the subject of considerable dispute and controversy . . . Facts and truth have been casualties along the way and the distillation of skewed perceptions over generations have contributed to a situation where both sides were confounding mysteries to one another.' The President concluded her perceptive remarks with the recognition that:

> We are, even after the publication of the Depositions, unlikely to agree a common version of history but we can agree that to have a common future, a shared and peaceful future, there is nothing to be gained from ransacking the past for ammunition to justify the furthering of hatred and distrust. There is however everything to be gained from interrogating the past calmly and coherently, in order to understand each other's passions more comprehensively, to make us intelligible to one another, to help us transcend those baleful forces of history so that we can make a new history of good neighbourliness understanding and partnership between all the people and traditions on this island.[42]

Building bridges and reconciliation were major themes of Mary McAleese's presidency, but the launch of the 1641 exhibition offered her an opportunity to make a powerful statement on the importance of acknowledging our shared and contested past without being bound by it.

Ian Paisley, who had previously invoked 1641 purely in a negative context, also attended the launch and responded to the President's remarks. 'Here are the tragic stories of individuals, and here too is the tragic story of our land. To learn this, I believe, is to know who we are and why we have had to witness our own troubles in what became a divided island. A nation that forgets its past commits suicide.' He continued by paraphrasing the former British Prime Minister, Tony Blair, who did so much to promote the peace process in Ireland:

> Before us in these cases is the real hand of history! . . . And tonight that hand reaches out beyond its page, beyond its century, and touches us.
> Now, the question is, what will we do?
> Let us grasp that hand and hold fast to it and introduce its work to our schools.
> If we learn the lessons of the past, we may use them to unlock a stable and promising future for everyone on this island.[43]

The fact that Ireland is now at peace has allowed our political leaders to embrace with such enthusiasm an historical project that until relatively recently polarised communities along sectarian lines. This provides us with the possibility of approaching the past differently, as Ethan Shagan points out:

> Ireland's seventeenth century may finally be passing from memory to history, presenting historians with a rare opportunity. While their relevance may wane, they can point the way towards new questions and new interpretations of seventeenth-century Ireland that transcend the legacy of imperialism and civil war and instead locate Ireland within other historical contexts . . . The violence of the past might usefully be integrated into Irish history (the way it has been integrated into French or Spanish history) without having to make reference to the present subject-positions of the descendants of that violence.[44]

The 1641 Depositions Project and this collection of essays forms part of this process, enabling new modes of interpretation in which Irish historiography can break free of the legacy of imperialism and civil war and instead relocate the histories of this island within very different contexts. The importance for the contemporary world of understanding why atrocity, massacre and ethnic cleansing occur cannot be overstated. Depositions, like the one by Lady Ann Butler, record Ireland's own experiences of mass killing and ethnic cleansing. By studying these past occurrences of atrocity and massacre and by attempting to unravel why they occurred, how the victims survived, how they remembered, how perpetrators were punished and how communities were reconciled (or not) will enable our understanding of the present to be more fully informed.

NOTES

1 Pádraig Lenihan, 'War and population', *Irish Economic and Social History*, 24 (1997), 1–21.

2 Aidan Clarke, 'The 1641 depositions', in Peter Fox (ed.), *Treasures of the Library: Trinity College Dublin* (Dublin, 1986), pp. 112–13.

3 Marsh's Library Dublin, MS Z2.1.7, Establishment of the High Court of Justice in Kilkenny, fol. 51.

4 Toby Barnard, 'The uses of 23 October 1641 and Irish Protestant celebrations', *English Historical Review*, 106 (1991), 889–920.

5 Clarke, '1641 depositions', p. 112.

6 Trinity College Dublin (TCD) MSS 809–41. The collection also contains one volume of indexes of the 1650s material and one volume of miscellaneous material.

7 TCD, 1641 Depositions Project, http://1641.tcd.ie/deposition.php?depID<?php echo 812069r093?> (accessed Tuesday 2 August 2011).

8 Ibid.

9 See pp. 262, 265 below.

10 John Gibney, 'The most controversial documents in Irish history?', *History Ireland*, 19 (2011), 18–19.

11 Toby Barnard, 'Parlour entertainment in an evening: Histories of the 1640s', in Micheál Ó Siochrú (ed.), *Kingdoms in Crisis: Ireland in the 1640s* (Dublin, 2001), pp. 20–43; Clare O'Halloran, *Golden Ages and Barbarous Nations: Antiquarian Debate and Cultural Politics in Ireland, c.1750–1800* (Cork, 2004); Guy Beiner, *Remembering the Year of the French: Irish Folk History and Social Memory* (Wisconsin, 2007).

12 We are grateful to Deidre McMahon for providing us with the relevant correspondence. See Michael Kennedy and Deidre McMahon, *Reconstructing Ireland's Past: A History of the Irish Manuscripts Commission* (Irish Manuscripts Commission, Dublin, 2009), pp. 70–3.

13 The principal investigators on the project, which began in 2007 and ended in 2011, were Professors Jane Ohlmeyer, John Morrill, Thomas Bartlett and Micheál Ó Siochrú. Professor Aidan Clarke edited the transcriptions, while the researchers were Dr Edda Frankot, Dr Annaleigh Margey and Dr Elaine Murphy. For the online depositions, see http://1641.tcd.ie.

14 www.historyireland.com/hedge/.

15 John Morrill teaches a final year undergraduate special subject in Cambridge University on 'The Irish rebellion of 1641: causes, course, consequences'. At Trinity, Jane Ohlmeyer and Micheál Ó Siochrú draw on this remarkable resource in a special subject class on 'From rebellion to restoration: war, politics and society in Confederate and Cromwellian Ireland'.

16 The 1641 depositions will be integrated into the 'Research Challenge' module of the M.Phil. in early modern history at Cambridge. Jane Ohlmeyer and Micheál Ó Siochrú offer an M.Phil. course 'War and Society in seventeenth-century Ireland', which also features the depositions.

17 Some of this recent research on society and culture in pre-war Ireland, the nature of warfare during the 1640s, print culture and cultural memory appears in Eamon Darcy, Annaleigh Margey and Elaine Murphy (eds), *The 1641 Depositions and the Irish Rebellion* (London, 2012); Inga Volmer, 'A comparative study of massacres during the wars of the three kingdoms, 1641–1653' (Ph.D. thesis, Cambridge, 2007);

Eamon Darcy, 'Pogroms, politics and print: the 1641 rebellion and contemporary print culture' (Ph.D. thesis, TCD 2009); Ciska Neyts, 'The rider on the horse: warfare during the outbreak of the 1641 rebellion in four Ulster counties' (M.Phil. thesis, Trinity College, Dublin, 2010).

18 See the 1641 Collaborative Linguistic Research and Learning Environment at http://kdeg-vm-15.cs.tcd.ie/omeka-1.2.1/about; Mark Sweetnam, 'Natural language processing and early modern dirty data: IBM *LanguageWare* and the 1641 depositions', December 15, 2011, *Linguistic and Literary Computing* 10.1093/11c/fqr050.

19 CULTURA is an EU FP7-funded, three-year (2011–2014) Specific Targeted Research Project (STReP) held in partnership with the universities of Sofia, Padua, Graz, IBM (Haifa and Dublin) and Commetric, a SME based in Sofia and London. See the project website at www.cultura-strep.eu/home.

20 Mark Greengrass and Lorna Hughes (eds), *The Virtual Representation of the Past* (London, 2008).

21 See also Brian MacCuarta, 'Religious violence against settlers in south Ulster, 1641-2', in David Edwards, Pádraig Lenihan and Clodagh Tait (eds), *Age of Atrocity: Violence in Political Conflict in Early Modern Ireland* (Dublin, 2007), pp. 154–75; John R. Young, ' "Escaping massacre": refugees in Scotland in the aftermath of the 1641 Ulster rebellion', in Edwards, Lenihan and Tait (eds), *Age of Atrocity*, pp. 219–41; Kenneth Nicholls, 'The other massacre: English killings of Irish, 1641-3', in Edwards, Lenihan and Tait (eds), *Age of Atrocity*, pp. 176–91; Mark Clinton, Linda Fibiger and Damian Shiels, 'Archaeology of massacre: the Carrickmines mass grave and the siege of March 1642', in Edwards, Lenihan and Tait (eds), *Age of Atrocity*, pp. 192–203; Joseph Cope, 'The experience of survival during the 1641 Irish rebellion', *Historical Journal*, 46 (2003), 295–316.

22 Clarke 'The 1641 depositions', pp. 111–22 and 'The commission for the despoiled subject, 1641-7', in Brian MacCuarta (ed.), *Reshaping Ireland 1550-1700: Colonization and its Consequences, Essays Presented to Nicholas Canny* (Dublin, 2011), pp. 241–60. Nicholas Canny has made extensive use of the depositions in a variety of works: *Making Ireland British, 1580-1650* (Oxford, 2001), 'The 1641 depositions as a source for the writing of social history: County Cork as a case study', in P. O'Flanagan and Cornelius Buttimer (eds), *Cork: History and Society* (Dublin, 1993), pp. 249–308 and 'Religion, politics and the Irish rising of 1641', in J. Devlin and R. Fanning (eds), *Religion and Identity* (Dublin, 1997), pp. 40–70; William Smyth, *Map-making, Landscapes and Memory: A Geography of Colonial and Early Modern Ireland c.1530-1750* (Cork, 2006).

23 See, for example, Hilary Simms, 'Violence in County Armagh, 1641', in Brian Mac Cuarta (ed.), *Ulster 1641: Aspects of the Rising* (Belfast, 1993), pp. 122–138; Aoife Duignan, 'All in confused opposition to each other: politics and war in Connacht, 1641-9' (Ph.D. thesis, University College, Dublin, 2006); Charlene McCoy, 'War and revolution: County Fermanagh and its borders, c.1640-c.1666 (PhD thesis, Trinity College Dublin, 2007); Brendan Scott, 'Reporting the 1641 rising in Cavan and Leitrim', in Brendan Scott (ed.), *Culture and Society in Early Modern Breifne/Cavan* (Dublin, 2009), pp. 200–14; Jason McHugh, 'For our owne defence: Catholic

insurrection in Wexford, 1641-2', in MacCuarta (ed.), *Reshaping Ireland 1550-1700*, pp. 214-40.

24 See chapter 2.

25 See chapter 14.

26 See chapter 2.

27 See pp. 18, 22-3 below.

28 See pp. 154-5 below.

29 See p. 38 below.

30 See chapter 3 below and Barnard, 'Parlour entertainment in an evening', pp. 20-43.

31 Simms, 'Violence in County Armagh, 1641', pp. 122-38.

32 In the most recent authoritative account of the Thirty Years War, Peter Wilson estimates that five million people lost their lives through bloodshed and disease, a number equivalent to one-fifth of the pre-war population of the Holy Roman Empire. See Peter Wilson, *The Thirty Years War: Europe's Tragedy* (Cambridge, MA., 2009), pp. 786-95.

33 Joseph Cope, *England and the 1641 Irish Rebellion* (Woodbridge, Suffolk, 2009); Jane Ohlmeyer, 'Historical contexts: Ireland', in Joad Raymond (ed.), *The Oxford History of Popular Print Culture: Cheap Print in Britain and Ireland to 1660* (Oxford, 2011), pp. 39-49; David O'Hara, *English Newsbooks and Irish Rebellion 1641-1649* (Dublin, 2006); Micheál Ó Siochrú, 'Propaganda, rumour and myth: Oliver Cromwell and the massacre at Drogheda', in Edwards, Lenihan and Tait (eds), *Age of Atrocity*, pp. 266-82; Kathleen Noonan, 'The cruell pressure of an enraged, barbarous people: Irish and English identity in seventeenth-century propaganda', *Historical Journal*, 41 (1998), 151-77; Ethan Shagan, 'Constructing discord: ideology, propaganda, and English responses to the Irish rebellion of 1641', *Journal of British Studies*, 36 (1997), 4-34.

34 The Dutch pamphlets relating to the 1641 rebellion and the Protestant war-effort in the Fagel collection at Trinity await analysis. See, for example, *Ootmoedighe Requeste, van de Raetheeren ... van Londen ... Daer by gevoecht zijn de Copien van twee bysondere Missiven uyt Yerlandt, daer in vermelt werden de Barbarische ende onmenschelijcke wreetheden, die by de Rebelle Papisten aldaer, aen de Protestanten ghepleecht werden* (Amsterdam: Theunis Jacobsz, 1642) [Humble request by the councillors of London. With addition of copies of two special missives from Ireland, wherein noted the barbaric and inhuman cruelties that have been committed by the rebel Papists there, to the Protestants] Old Library, TCD, Fag. H.3.24, no. 41; *Nieuwe ende goede tijdinge uyt Yrlant, mede-brengende eene verklaringe van den Lord Jnchequin [et al. ... vervattende de redenen von hare tegenwoordige oppositie van den stilstant van wapenen / met de bloet-doorstige Yrische Rebellen ... schrickelijcke t'samen-rottingen van Monnicken, Priesteren ende Jesuiten, om ons te verraden ...*, gedruckt by I. Wright [London] ende nu by A. Jacobsz, Anno 1644 [New and good news from Ireland, bringing a declaration of the Lord Inchequin, comprising the reasons of her present opposition to the ceasefire with the blood thirsty Irish rebels ... terrible plotting of monks, priests and Jesuits to betray us ...*, printed by I. Wright (London) and now by A Jacbosz Anno 1644] Old Library, TCD, Fag. H.3.26, no. 2; *Yrlands Bloedende Request, aen*

de Gereformeerde Kercken der vereenigde Nederlandsche Provintien: waer inne naer eene sommarische Verthooninghe van haren uyttersten noodt, een beete broods versocht wert, tot onderhoudinge van haer meer dan ellendigh leven ... (n.p., n. pub., 1643) [Ireland's bleeding request to the reformed Churches of the United Provinces of the Netherlands, in which, after a summery exposition of the utmost need, a mouthful of bread, to sustain her more than miserable life] Old Library, TCD, Fag. H.1.81, no. 4; Den Brittannischen Donderslach ... Brittan nischen Blixem ... (n.p., n.pub., 1643) [The British Thunder ... British Lightning] Old Library, TCD, Fag. H.1.81, nos. 8 and 11; Fag. H.2.63, no. 16. There was also a Dutch translation of Cranford's Teares of Ireland – Yrelandtsche Traenen: waer in levendich is affgebeelt / ende als in een Schilderie verthoont / een Lijste, vande noyt gehoorde wreedtheden / ende barbarische verraderyen der bloet-dorstighe Jesuwijten, met de Papistische factie aldaer (Colophon: Leyden: Willem Christiaens 20.12.1642) Old Library, TCD, Fag. H.3.23, no. 22. We are grateful to Tim Jackson for drawing these to our attention and to Ciska Neyts for providing the translations.

35 Jason McElligott, '1641', in Raymond (ed.), Oxford History of Popular Print Culture, pp. 599–608.

36 See p. 129 below.

37 See p. 109 below.

38 Smyth's chapter bristles with ideas for further research on family structure, settlement patterns, notions of Gaelic kingship and the role of women as victims and perpetrators of extreme violence. See also Marie-Louise Coolahan, Women, Writing and Language in Early Modern Ireland (Oxford, 2010); Naomi McAreavey, 'Paper bullets: gendering the 1641 rebellion in the writings of Lady Elizabeth Dowdall and Lettice Fitzgerald, baroness of Offaly', in Thomas Herron and Michael Potterton (eds), Ireland in the Renaissance, c.1540–1660 (Dublin, 2007), pp. 311–24; William Palmer, 'Gender, violence, and rebellion in Tudor and early Stuart Ireland', Sixteenth Century Journal, 23 (1992), 699–712.

39 Clarke, 'Commission for the despoiled subject', pp. 241–60.

40 See chapter 8 below.

41 An exhibition, entitled 'Ireland in Turmoil', which featured the depositions and related material was on display in the Long Room between October 2010 and April 2011. For a virtual tour of the exhibition, see www.tcd.ie/Library/assets/swf/Exhibitions/1641/TCD/

42 For the full text of the President's speech, see, remarks by President McAleese at the launch of the '1641 Depositions "Ireland in turmoil"' exhibition, TCD, 22 October 2010, www.president.ie/index.php?section=5&speech=878&lang=eng accessed 2 August 2011.

43 The speech of Ian Paisley (now Lord Bannside), at the launch of the '1641 Depositions "Ireland in turmoil"' exhibition, TCD, 22 October 2010.

44 See pp. 17, 32 below.

2

Early modern violence from memory to history: a historiographical essay

ETHAN H. SHAGAN

The seventeenth century is alive in Ireland in ways like few other places in the modern world. People, places and events from that distant past – the Flight of the Earls, the 1641 massacres, Oliver and Drogheda, William and the Boyne – still have meaning in popular culture, still inform public debates and still elicit strong emotional responses. This unique configuration is both a blessing and a curse to the business of professional history. On the one hand, it gives historians of the seventeenth century real relevance and an opportunity to contribute to the peace process that has so profoundly improved the lives of both British and Irish citizens on the island. On the other hand, it makes history the handmaid of memory, trapping Irish historiography within a series of problems and paradigms that might better be left behind in favour of more productive avenues of exploration.[1] Now, however, with the cessation of active hostilities in the 1990s, and with the slow easing of sectarian tensions in the early twenty-first century, there is a palpable sense that this anomalous condition may be ending. Ireland's seventeenth century may finally be passing from memory to history, presenting historians with a rare opportunity. While their relevance may wane, they can point the way towards new questions and new interpretations of seventeenth-century Ireland that transcend the legacy of imperialism and civil war and instead locate Ireland within other historical contexts. We can imagine a day when an Irish historian studying the rebellion of 1641 might no more be accused of partisanship than a French historian studying the *Fronde*.

In this brief essay, therefore, I want to think conceptually about what it might mean to write about the 1641 massacres and other instances of large-scale early modern violence in the post-sectarian climate of the twenty-first century.[2] I am not the first historian to do so; I follow self-consciously in the footsteps of Clodagh Tait, David Edwards and Pádraig Lenihan, whose important collection *Age of Atrocity* brought violence to the centre of post-sectarian Irish history and whose introduction to that collection considered with considerable theoretical acuity the ideological pitfalls of either emphasising or deemphasising violence.[3] My claim to novelty, then, is two-fold. First, I write not as an Irish historian but as an historian of early modern Britain and Europe, in hope that an oblique angle may offer some useful perspective to Irish historical studies; for indeed, as John Morrill has written, the escalating violence of early modern Ireland 'makes Irish history look much more like continental European history'.[4] Second, I want to think explicitly about the problem of violence as it moves from memory to history, as a way of suggesting that other European and Atlantic historians have been down roads that are at least superficially similar, and that their experiences might provide some useful guidance about both shortcuts and pitfalls along the way.

In particular, I want to suggest that what a post-sectarian history of violence will look like is not as obvious as it might at first appear. There are, it seems to me, two very different paths that historians might take. First, historians might choose to study violence through the intellectual and cultural systems that authorised and shaped it, with the goal of understanding its causes. Second, historians might choose to study violence as a space of socio-cultural interaction, with the goal of understanding its consequences. The first framework treats violence as fundamentally anomalous, a disjunction from ordinary existence that requires an explanation. The second framework treats violence as fundamentally normal, a mode of interpersonal contact and communication akin to other social spaces, so that violence *is* the explanation.

Now certainly, many Irish historians have already started down one or the other path, but it seems to me that, with some exceptions, they have done so without much theoretical speculation about the alternatives available and the implications of different models.[5] For while my two paths are not necessarily incompatible, and certainly historians can and should adopt both in some circumstances, nonetheless in ways that are not immediately obvious they do very different sorts of ideological work. The first renders historical violence distant, the second leaves historical violence immanent but as something far more complex and ambivalent than commemoration; the first treats violence as a destructive product, the second allows that it is also a constructive producer. Irish historians will need to think long and hard about whether they want the transition of seventeenth-century violence from memory to history to be a project of empathy, of understanding historical actors on their own terms, or whether they are comfortable with a more impassive project, understanding how violence shaped Irish history.[6] I will not propose a settled answer – after all, this is not my field – but I want to raise a series of what I hope will be provocative questions about the role of history, as opposed to memory, in considering the violent legacy of the Irish past.

I

Historians of seventeenth-century Europe are no strangers to violence. In the most recent authoritative account of the Thirty Years War, Peter Wilson estimates that the conflict killed some five million people through bloodshed and disease, a number equivalent to one-fifth of the pre-war population of the Holy Roman Empire.[7] The early modern witch hunts, centred in France and Germany and extending from the fifteenth to the eighteenth centuries, resulted in no fewer than 30,000 judicial murders and perhaps three times that number.[8] The English Civil Wars, according to Charles Carleton, killed at least 84,000 in battle and something over 100,000 from disease.[9] The Khmelnytsky Uprising in Ukraine killed tens of thousands of Jews and Poles.[10] Russian soldiers put to death tens of thousands of Cossacks in the Razin rebellion.[11] Europeans transported some 1.5 million African slaves across the Atlantic Ocean before 1700, of whom at least 20%, or 300,000, died en route in the so-called 'middle passage'.[12] This large-scale violence can be traced to several factors, including but not limited to: the injection of ideology into politics in the Reformation; the social dislocation of the 'little ice age'; the new military technologies and organisational capacities of early modern states; and the rise of Europe as a 'civilisation' with the goal of enforcing its worldviews upon subordinates both near and far.[13]

These early modern body counts, and the individual atrocities that under-lay them, are largely part of history rather than memory: they are most often the subject of professional scholarship rather than public memorial, the stuff of rational analysis rather than emotional response. I do not wish to exaggerate this distinction, either through naive positivism or through the denial of the politics of history, but nonetheless we can see how well this distinction usually applies by noticing how starkly the exceptions stand out from the norm. One such exception is the historiography of the African slave trade, where (at least in the United States) emotions run high, scholarly debates often spill out into the public sphere and those debates often invoke the modern ethical and political implications of historiographical arguments. There are also occasionally exceptions where early modern divisions still have contemporary relevance, so the historiography retains a partisan flavour. One example here is the Khmelnytsky Uprising, perhaps the closest parallel to the Irish rebellion in terms of its ethno-religious tensions. Since the divisions at the heart of the uprising have modern legacies – Ukrainians against Poles, Eastern Orthodox against Roman Catholic and everyone against the Jews – the relationship between history and memory sometimes resembles the Irish case.[14] In other cases, where the contemporary issues at stake are refracted but still recognisable, scholarship can take on a didactic tone even if it is not overtly partisan. Here one clear example is the historiography of the European witch hunts, which are often framed in terms of the history of violence against women, or around the perversion of law, issues which are easily transferable to more modern, metaphorical 'witch hunts'.

But, generally, historians do not frame early modern violence in the visceral and emotional terms of memory, since the issues at stake are too alien to modern sensibilities to render them useful, compelling or divisive. The Thirty Years' War is the prime example here. Before the 1940s, the Thirty Years' War was deeply imbedded in German memory as the crucible of the modern state: the fires of the Reformation burned themselves out in a final paroxysm of violence, clearing the path for the rise of the rational state system and its greatest offspring, a unified Germany. The horrors of National Socialism, however, rendered this narrative awkward and today the Thirty Years' War has almost entirely passed from memory to history. The confessional tensions of the war itself have long since declined; the major historical lessons – never trust a Swede! – seem unhelpful in the modern world; and the atrocities, once the stuff of German nationalist fervour, are now rarely taken as more than artefacts of past worldviews or timeless reminders of man's inhumanity to man.[15] Much the same can be said about most other early modern paroxysms of violence. Modern Britain has few Roundheads or Cavaliers to get incensed about the denial of quarter to cities surrendered in the Civil War; the two sides who committed such atrocities have long been mocked, in the immortal words of *1066 and All That*, as 'right but repugnant' and 'romantic but wrong'. In France, the inexhaustible historiographical debate over who instigated the St. Bartholomew's Day Massacre includes no *Guisards* or Valois loyalists, nor even many Huguenots who still feel the brunt of oppression strongly enough to identify with the victims; the past offers insights, but it is largely *the* past rather than *our* past.

The exception that proves the rule, so to speak, is the debate over colonial violence, particularly the mass extermination of Native Americans, in the decades after 1492. Today, while this historiography is hardly devoid of emotion, it basically looks like other subjects of historical inquiry, and (except within the rarefied world of Native American Studies) scholars are rarely accused of partisanship. But this was by no means true twenty years ago, when the furore surrounding the quincentennial of Columbus's voyage briefly returned the issue from history to memory, setting off a controversy which unfortunately coincided with the nadir of the culture wars in American intellectual life. The standard-bearer of the 'left', the popular historian and anti-imperialist activist Kirkpatrick Sale, argued in *The Conquest of Paradise* (1990) that the murder of millions of American indigenes was the logical and inevitable outcome of Europe's fundamental pathology, and that all of the horrors of the modern world resulted from Europe's metastasis. As he put it in an article in *The Nation* in October 1990, Columbus's voyage led to 'the genocide of the indigenes, the slavery of people of color, the colonization of the world, the destruction of primal environments, the eradication and abuse of species, and the impending catastrophe of ecocide for the planet Earth . . . it began the process by which the culture of Europe, aptly represented by this captain, implanted its diseased and dangerous seeds in the soils of the continents that represented the last best hope for humankind – and destroyed them'.[16] On the 'right', by contrast, the prominent cultural critic and Dartmouth professor Jeffrey Hart denounced Sale's book in the conservative magazine *National Review*: 'To those who would denigrate Columbus and the other pioneers one can apply Nietzsche's term "garbage-can philosophers", or Thomas Carlyle's term *Teufelsdreck* (devil's turd) – that is, nihilists, the sour enemies to human aspiration. To denigrate Columbus is to denigrate what is worthy in human history and in us all.'[17]

This controversy soon absorbed much of the American historical profession. In February 1992, *The History Teacher* published a 'position statement', issued by the National Council on the Social Sciences (NCSS) and endorsed by thirty other learned societies, including the American Historical Association (AHA), entitled 'The Columbian quincentenary: an educational opportunity'. This was intended as a careful and balanced set of guidelines for teachers, summarising recent scholarship in the field. Among the numbered items it asked history teachers to highlight in their classes was the fact that, 'As a result of forces emanating from 1492, Native Americans suffered catastrophic mortality rates.'[18] A year later, however, an angry 'Response' appeared in the same journal, signed by fourteen historians, most importantly the Berkeley pioneer in ethnic studies, Ronald Takaki. They accused the NCSS and AHA of warm and fuzzy multiculturalism, perpetuating myths of 'black, copper-colored and white peoples sitting down together, teaching and learning from each other . . . bringing their own special offerings to a multicultural feast'; the truth was the brutal exploitation and extermination of Native American and African peoples by 'violent and rapacious Europeans'. Moreover, they ridiculed the term 'as a result of forces' as evasive or cowardly; its vague and passive tenor and the discussion of disease that followed allowed conservatives to maintain that micro-organisms were the chief villains and that 'centuries of war and genocide . . . only reinforced the lethal role of germs'.[19] Nine months later, inevitably, a 'Reply' appeared from one of the original drafters of the NCSS statement, the Northwestern University historian Lee Anderson, who pointed out with self-righteous indignation that micro-organisms *really were* the chief villains and that war and genocide *really did* only reinforce the lethal role of germs.[20]

While the issue of violence in the Columbian exchange has not been entirely drained of this emotional energy – nor can it, given the complex role of Native Americans in the multicultural politics of the United States – a glance at a special issue of the *Journal of World History* from 2006 on 'violence in the early modern Atlantic world' shows how far we have come. In the introduction, Brian Sandberg, while critiquing the way the language of 'encounter' sometimes belittles colonial violence, self-consciously pushed past modern subject-positions to re-contextualise early modern violence. Noting that borderlands are habitually sites of ethnic violence with their own social dynamics, he asked readers to consider the 'consumption' or 'reception' of violence alongside its production. He asked readers to think about how in colonial settings, alternative cultures of violence – different sets of rules for limiting conflict and different modes of legitimation – blurred and accommodated one another, producing syncretism. He asked readers to consider how the historical effects and significance of violence are mediated by local conceptions of the body, pain and community, for 'suffering is a social experience'.[21] Another article in the same issue, by H. E. Martel, addressed the fraught issue of Native American cannibalism, attempting to transcend ancient and insoluble debates over the reality of such claims by arguing that at least one Indian people, the Tupinamba of Brazil, self-consciously encouraged the rumour of their cannibalism in order to gain the respect of their terrified European neighbours.[22] Whether or not we agree with the arguments of Sandberg, Martel and other scholars breaking new ground in this field, clearly they are asking questions that would be nearly unthinkable in a context where history was still the handmaid to memory.

Clearly, there are both ethical and political reasons why we may not want to remove the past entirely from memory to history, and Irish historians might well choose not to do so. The massive *Lieux de Mémoire* project in France was motivated precisely by the fear that the visceral connection of the French people to their past was being replaced by cold, critical contextualisation, and Bernard Bailyn argued in an important essay that the historiography of the Atlantic slave trade must be made 'constantly relevant and urgent by the living memory we have of it'.[23] One problem of alienating the past and transforming it entirely from memory to history is that we lose our ethical connection to it, running the risk of dehumanising our subjects and putting historians uncomfortably close to the subject-position of perpetrators. For now, however, I want to bracket this question – we will return to it – and assume that historians of Ireland really do want to analyze rather than memorialise early modern violence. The question is: what models are available to do so?

II

The first model seeks to understand violence on its own terms, admitting it as a rational or at least comprehensible consequence of the perpetrator's worldview, and hence looks for its causes in the minds, experiences and cultural assumptions – encompassed by the French term *mentalités*, or the German *Weltenschauung* – of those who commit violent acts. As is well known, this approach emerged from the close encounter between historians and cultural anthropology in the late 1960s and 1970s, especially the work of Natalie Davis. Davis's classic 1973 article 'The rites of violence: religious riot in sixteenth-century France', following on earlier studies of the rationality of crowd action by E. P. Thompson and George Rudé, asked, 'What then can we learn of the goals of popular religious violence? What were the crowds intending to do and why did they think they must do it?'[24] These questions immediately focused on the subjectivities of the rioters themselves, rather than (as the previous generation of historians had done) the objective social conditions that compelled them. Davis argued that French religious mobs intended not merely to promulgate the truth as they understood it, but to purge the community of 'pollution', variously defined as heresy or idolatry, but always closely associated with sexual deviance and other forms of sinfulness that would provoke the wrath of God upon the whole community. Just as importantly, Davis argued that the cultural system of the rioters shaped the performance of the violence they committed. Government authorities had failed in their duties to keep the community pure, and rioters drew upon a long tradition, developed in grain riots and other popular movements, that when authorities failed to enforce the law, the *menu peuple* might take it into their own hands; hence their riots mimicked the forms of official justice. Likewise, riots took on the ritual forms of processions and other types of worship, or of charivari and carnival, in ways that authorised and legitimated them. Davis argued, then, that violence must be understood as the structured enactment of the beliefs and cultural assumptions of violent actors, and that historical violence should thus be approached through the study of those beliefs and cultural assumptions.

Within the framework of the French Wars of Religion, the relationship between violence and *mentalités* reached its apotheosis in Denis Crouzet's massive *Les Guerriers de Dieu: La Violence au Temps des Troubles de Religion* (1990), which both adopted and transcended Davis's cultural history methodology. Not content to study only popular religious riots, Crouzet framed those riots within a larger body of violence that included government prosecution, political assassination and even what he called 'interiorised violence'. By reading essentially the entire output of French printing presses between 1525 and 1610, and attempting to collate the different themes associated with violence, he argued that the issues of pollution, deviance and ritual outlined by Davis were real but epiphenomenal to the great *mentalité* that authorised and legitimated the violence of early modern France: the 'eschatological anguish' that convinced religious enthusiasts that the end of the world was at hand, thus rendering normal constraints on human action obsolete.[25] Here, then, was an explanation both for the ferocity of violence in the French Wars of Religion and for the eventual waning of that violence as the Bourbon polity reconstituted itself in stubborn defiance of the promised *eschaton*.

Within the historiography of official, judicial violence, the most influential version of the *mentalités* framework is Brad Gregory's comparative study of martyrs and their persecutors across the spatial and theological landscape of Reformation Europe, *Salvation at Stake* (1999). Part of Gregory's analysis involved sensitive reading of what he called 'the willingness to kill', describing the execution of heretics both as part of a larger strategy to correct heterodoxy and as a reasonable application of the public responsibilities felt by early modern magistrates charged with defending orthodoxy. Violence was always the last resort. Magistrates wanted to make converts rather than martyrs, but given the firm beliefs of early modern Christians that tolerance of heretics represented a form of cruelty, allowing them to damn the souls of their followers and bring divine vengeance upon society, violence flowed inevitably from the unwillingness of religious minorities to renounce their errors. Thus, the second part of Gregory's analysis was an equally sensitive reading of what he called 'the willingness to die', showing martyrs and their persecutors locked in a dialectical relationship to one another, created by their largely shared belief system. The steadfastness of Christians when faced with potential martyrdom led persecutors to take the final step of violence against them, while this violence convinced potential martyrs that their opponents were anti-Christian and hence worth defying. In short, the violence of early modern religious persecution emerged not from any unique or perverse perspective of the persecutors but from the *mentalité* they shared with their victims, who in other contexts were sometimes persecutors themselves.[26]

Every field has its version: if the violence of the past does not make sense to us, we must determine how and why it made sense to contemporaries rather than pronouncing it irrational from an Olympian modern perspective. So, for instance, in a classic article Sabine MacCormack attributed the rise of missionary violence in Spanish colonial Peru to two factors: 'the conviction that Inca and Andean religion had been inspired by demons', and the missionaries' assumption that Indian society itself, rather than simply their idolatry, had to be eradicated to make way for their assent to Christian doctrine.[27] Lisa Silverman, in her account of judicial torture in early modern France, analyzed the emergence and collapse of the *mentalité* that authorised it: that original sin rendered voluntary statements suspect; that truth lay in the physical body rather than the fallen will; that truth could be extracted from the physical body through pain; and that pain had both spiritual and physical benefits for the victim.[28] Lyndal Roper's *Witch Craze: Terror and Fantasy in Baroque Germany* (2004) argued that witchcraft accusations, with their attendant fears about motherhood, harvests, charity and nourishment, reflected a cultural obsession with fertility. In a world where crops failed and children died inexplicably, the concern that society would fail to reproduce itself was never far from the surface, hence witchcraft accusations provided a peculiar kind of comfort, creating a narrative of containment to address both magistrates' and victims' anxieties about fertility.[29]

This is the ordinary mode in which most of the historiography of early modern violence – at least mass violence, if not quotidian violence – has been conducted since the breakthrough of the 1960s and early 1970s, which first accepted violence as 'rational' and hence requiring sensitive investigation. It is worth noting, given Irish historiography's complex debate over the significance of religion as an autonomous ideological force, that this methodology has particularly influenced the scholarly literature on *religious* violence. Religion was the quintessential *mentalité* of the early modern world, and the intense role of religion in public controversy seems particularly irrational to late moderns for whom religion remains largely confined to the private sphere of belief. This methodology has thus served as a vehicle for historians to re-inscribe belief – now described in modish terms of culture – as the motive force of history. More broadly, however, it has also offered a pathway for historians to study and appreciate the horrors of early modernity, with all their baroque ingenuity, without either implicating modern actors or enflaming modern passions.

III

An alternative approach to the history of early modern violence, however, sees violence as a productive space of socio-cultural interaction. This is analogous to, for instance, the way the history of the book imagines reading as an action that brings together writer, reader, printer, compositor, censor and other parties within a locally defined set of rules to yield new social relations and cultural forms. Or, for another example, it is comparable to the way the history of marriage takes a social relationship – defined locally by laws and conventions but also with a strong cross-cultural dimension – and spins outward from that social relationship to understand the world created by its negotiation and repetition. Here violence is, almost by definition, significant not because it is anomalous but because it is so very immanent; to paraphrase Clauswitz, it is the extension of the social by other means.

This mode of analysis can be imagined as a divergent strand that also owes its genesis to Natalie Davis; as Suzanne Desan wrote in a 1989 essay, Davis's insights might have been developed both by paying more attention to the effects of violence and by paying more attention to how social context gave violence its meanings.[30] One of the earliest significant works to push the cultural history of violence in these directions was Inga Clendinnen's 1982

Past and Present article 'Disciplining the Indians: Franciscan ideology and missionary violence in sixteenth-century Yucatán' and her subsequent full-length study *Ambivalent Conquests: Maya and Spaniard in Yucatan, 1517–1570.*[31] Clendinnen studied an extraordinary, three-month long reign of terror in 1562 by Franciscan missionaries in the colonial frontier region of the Yucatán peninsula, where some 4,500 Indians were tortured and at least 157 killed in response to the discovery that their apparent conversion to Christianity had merely been feigned. Clendinnen devoted parts of her work to understanding the *mentalités* of the perpetrators, especially the ways the missionaries imagined themselves as paternal guardians of childlike Indians and felt genuinely betrayed by their apostasy. But, more originally, Clendinnen also explored how outbursts of violence were interwoven with other sorts of social interactions in a dialectical relationship in which the Maya acted in the role of participants rather than victims. The Franciscans initially enjoyed great success as missionaries in part because they offered the Maya a space of protection from the violence of lay *conquistadores*. This space of Franciscan–Mayan interaction produced its own new cultural forms, including forms of violence, most importantly the inflexion of Mayan ritual with Christian symbolism: the Maya apparently reframed some human sacrifices as crucifixions. This cultural space of interaction then shaped the dynamics of Franciscan violence in 1562, which was so brutal precisely because the missionaries had genuinely loved the Maya and mistakenly believed the Maya loved them in return. This legacy of violence then shaped the subsequent history of religious syncretism in the Yucatán, in which Mayan Christianity was rendered simultaneously profound and ambivalent by the dynamics of power that underlay it. In Clendinnen's analysis, therefore, understanding the history of violence is not an end in itself, it is rather a means to understanding the culture that violence helps produce.

This methodology came of age with the publication of David Nirenberg's *Communities of Violence: Persecution of Minorities in the Middle Ages* (1996), a work of medieval history that has impacted profoundly on early modernists. Nirenberg argued that violence was an ordinary and well-structured element of social relations between Christians, Muslims and Jews in fourteenth-century Iberia. As such, instances of cataclysmic violence were not aberrations that might point towards the massacres and holocausts of modern Europe, but rather existed at the extreme end of a normal spectrum of 'constructive relationship between conflict and coexistence'. Violence, whether institutional or interpersonal, was as a sphere of interaction where Christians, Jews and Muslims came together, albeit with varying levels of power in different contexts, to negotiate and maintain the boundaries that enabled them to coexist. 'Violence was a central and systemic aspect of the coexistence of majority and minorities in medieval Spain, and . . . that coexistence was in part predicated

on such violence.'[32] It should be noted that Nirenberg's work owed a significant debt to the important theoretical arguments of René Girard, who argued
in his seminal work *Violence and the Sacred* that religion in part answers the
problem of human violence not by eliminating it but by making it generative
of social stability rather than instability. Structures of religion like ritual,
sacrifice and law are constitutive of culture precisely insofar as they manage
and contain the necessary social work of retribution. Religion thus yields
'violent unanimity' rather than division; it 'curtails reciprocal violence and
imposes structure on the community' even if that structure comes at the cost
of sacrificial victims.[33]

Probably the most profound work of early modern history to frame violence
this way is Benjamin Kaplan's *Divided by Faith: Religious Conflict and the
Practice of Toleration in Early Modern Europe* (2007). Kaplan's subtitle signals
his thesis: religious conflict was not the antithesis of toleration but rather produced the varied, peculiar, complex arrangements that allowed antagonists to
coexist throughout the early modern centuries. So, for instance, the technique
known in Austria as *Auslauf* or 'walking out' – in which every Sunday tens
of thousands of people left their home communities to worship across spatial
borders where such worship was legal, then returned home again the same
evening to religiously mixed communities – represented a carefully negotiated
solution to the problem of how not to kill one's neighbours or be killed by
them. But it was also, according to Kaplan, a solution intended to realise the
confessional dream of religious uniformity by eliminating heterodox worship,
and it emerged not from a desire for peace so much as from the legal dynamics
of heresy prosecution by the Emperor. Crucial to Kaplan's arguments, and
particularly apropos for Irish historians, is the fact that 'just three types of
event: processions, holiday celebrations, and funerals' triggered most incidents
of religious violence in early modern Europe. Religious violence was thus the
violence of boundary-drawing, delimiting the social body, and as such it set
the terms by which Europe's religiously mixed social bodies functioned: how
and when opposed religious communities might share churches, study at one
another's schools, sell to one another at market and intermarry.[34]

Very different sorts of historical change can be detected emanating from
the social space of violence. So, for instance, in an extraordinary work of
scholarly imagination and virtuosity, Stuart Clark used the European witch
craze as a window into the changing meanings of *vision*, the ways that the
relationship between reality and perception were understood and contested
in early modern Europe through the problem of combating an unseen foe.[35]
Andy Wood argues that popular insurrection in early modern England was
widely understood as an occasion for *speech*. The hubbub of plebian voices
proved no less significant than the violence that authorised it in challenging
a social order in which only elite men were entitled to public voices while

women and the lower classes maintained silent deference.[36] Mark Greengrass, in his study of the 'hidden transcripts' of the St. Bartholomew's Day Massacre, illuminates a social space that emerged in the massacre's aftermath in which both perpetrators and survivors had ample reason to remain silent about what they had done and witnessed, clearing the way for inaccurate meta-histories to define the event.[37] In a very different vein, Otto Ulbricht's article 'The experience of violence during the Thirty Years War: a look at the civilian victims' focuses on the social outcomes of violence that might be considered positive: increased village cooperation, including the rise of 'mutual supplica-tions, which gave the villagers a collective voice even at times when no redress could be expected'; the emergence of overt popular criticism of territorial rulers and a new discourse of 'tyranny'; and the development of an infra-structure of human rights, a 'moral campaign for the better treatment of civilians in war times'. Ulbricht argues that violence, as a social space, is more contested than it appears and often begets its antithesis.[38] In yet another vein, and significantly influenced by David Nirenberg, Thomas Brady contends that in most local contexts 'spontaneous communal violence [was] limited by the communal dynamics every social order contains': it was almost always the intrusion of state power that turned ordinary social violence into massacres (whether judicial or popular); hence violence ought to be studied as part of the greater state building project of early modernity.[39]

Important elements of this perspective have arisen in opposition to the so-called 'decline of violence' thesis, which began with the works of Johan Huizinga and especially Norbert Elias[40] in the first half of the twentieth century. Many historians of early modern quotidian violence (as opposed to large-scale or spectacular violence) continue to work within the Elias paradigm, arguing that violence on the whole was gradually tamed and became domesticated in early modern Europe as new social norms of self-restraint – the 'civilising process' – percolated through society. Notable exemplars include Julius Ruff and more recently Robert Muchembled, who makes the case in a series of smaller studies and in his massive *Une histoire de la violence* for a seven century-long pacification of masculine, and especially youthful, violence.[41] These historians of course acknowledge that warfare has hardly declined in Europe since the middle ages, and that European violence overseas remains a powerful motif in the story of modern globalisation, but they argue that this sort of rationalised, impersonal, state-sponsored violence is qualitatively different from the irra-tional violence of interpersonal relations, so successfully bridled by the rise of the centralised state and the capitalist market.

By contrast, some historians of early modern violence have self-consciously rejected the decline of violence thesis, noting how convenient and arbitrary its categorical inclusions and exclusions sometimes seem. For instance, in a withering critique Stuart Carroll noted that the thesis essentially *defines* violence as 'meaningless, irrational and senseless, the very antithesis of civilization', hence wars, executions and other forms of officially sanctioned death 'based on the justice of a cause' become by definition un-violence, the makers of civilisation.[42] Thus, in Carroll's major work *Blood and Violence in Early Modern France*, he not only argued empirically that the rise of duelling increased rather than (*pace* Elias) decreased murder rates, he also claimed that violence constituted a crucial strategy by which noblemen established their social identities. Resort to the sword differentiated the nobility, both on grounds of honour and on the more rough-and-ready grounds that their wealth and patronage made them virtually immune to legal sanction. This fed directly into the more formally delineated and 'rational' carnage of the French Wars of Religion, which in turn fed the militarisation of the French aristocracy. In this model, there can be no firm boundary between quotidian violence and spectacular violence; they are interconnected parts of the same social space.[43]

In an important review article published the same year, Alexandra Shepard drew attention to such phenomena as 'the state's growing investment in military rather than judicial brutality', and the shift from public murders of rivals to private murders of family members, to suggest the 'displacement and repackaging of violent interaction' rather than its decline. She argued that historians ought thus to stop measuring violence and instead study how 'violence calibrated relations of power', or how 'violence served to express and regulate social relations, gender identities, and the distribution of power'.[44] Moreover, historians of women point out that traditional measures of violence do not take cognisance of domestic violence, ordinarily understood as a subset of order rather than disorder, and that such orderly violence is interwoven with the broader history of violence in society. Julie Hardwick argues that in seventeenth-century France, both the level of violence considered normal and the state's willingness to commit violence in the name of justice shaped the choices husbands and wives made in their homes.[45] Likewise, in an article on the social meanings of violence in England, Susan Amussen points out that in cases of domestic violence 'discipline was the justification for punishment, and punishment was central to many other forms of violence'. The state's monopoly on legitimate violence actually depended upon it delegating that violence to many actors in society, including husbands, so the macro-history of warfare, rebellion and judicial punishment helped to shape the micro-history of domestic relations.[46]

The 'social spaces' model, therefore, tends to reframe history's great slaughters within more quotidian histories, contextualising well-known paroxysms of violence within the commonplace violence of social life, and vice versa.[47] This does not mean, however, that early modernists have opted for more expansive definitions of 'violence' that would subsume 'structural violence', 'symbolic violence' 'psychological violence', 'economic violence' or 'verbal violence' within the same category as rape or murder.[48] Some note that the line between repression and coercion is often invisible in the historical record, but most historians have balked at the consequences of treating diverse forms of social injustice or interpersonal conflict as 'violence' without some overt physical harm to the bodies of victims; to do so, as Pieter Spierenburg has written, would not only divest the term of analytical specificity, it would also tend to authorise the use of bullets in response to words.[49] What early modern historians have done, however, is recognise that even taking Spierenburg's relatively restricted definition of violence as 'intentional encroachment upon the physical integrity of the body', violence shaped the broader context of social relations even as social relations gave such violence its meanings.

IV

The two models outlined here are not incompatible. Sometimes it makes sense to apply both to the same event, seeking to understand, for instance, the belief system that authorised a massacre as well as the social relations in which that massacre was imbedded. At other times, it may be that one model works well for one event but not for others. But while historians can legitimately claim that both models are useful arrows in their analytical quiver, it is important to stress that in practice they do very different sorts of ideo-logical work.

On the one hand, the consequence of the study of *mentalités* is to alienate past violence from the present and to render it comfortably other, a world we have lost. Denis Crouzet's *Les Guerriers de Dieu*, for instance, is very specific in displacing early modern violence from the modern world: he calls his key concept, eschatological anguish, *'l'angoisse que nous avons perdue'* – the anguish we have lost.[50] His final chapter thus outlines the waning of eschatological anguish and the rise of Reason in its place, ending a century of fury and generating peace. It is, in this sense, finally a congratulatory story in which we can feel good about our own place in the world, if only in con-trast to the horrors of the past. In the conclusion of *Salvation at Stake*, Brad Gregory argues that the early modern cycle of violence he describes would only be broken when the damage it inflicted on the Christian world rendered problematic the certain knowability of God's will, and convinced at least some Europeans that the state had to be separated from the imperatives of religious orthodoxy.[51] In this sense, the alien worldview Gregory excavates is not religion *per se*, but rather the operation of states and judicial systems without well-delineated concepts of the 'civil' that could be walled-off from religion; his conclusion points towards such separation as the wellspring of modern toleration as well as the modern state.

Yet, there are problems with this model. At an ethical level, some historians may not be comfortable with the way this scholarship exculpates the present and is at least partially predicated on the civility of the modern. It is worth noting here that while every era's violence stems from its own *mentalité*, no *mentalité* seems to be immune from the capacity to produce horrific violence, so one is sometimes left wondering whether the study of violence through *mentalités* is more than an antiquarian exercise. Moreover, at a practical level, these sorts of maneuvers may come at significant cost in terms of the analytical power of the historian. That is to say, a study that limits its field to the subjective under- standings of its subjects, and which seeks to understand a given era purely on its own terms, may perhaps sacrifice some of the purpose of historiography: mediating between past and present. Brad Gregory in particular has argued that any study of early modern religious violence must produce conclusions that would be recognisable to its subjects; hence the whole toolkit of modernist and postmodernist historiography – the Freudian subconscious, Weberian sociology, Marxian materialism, the Foucauldian analysis of power – is placed out of bounds. The benefit of alienating the past is that it denaturalises the present; the risk is that it can place the past beyond our reach.

The study of violence as a space of social interaction, by contrast, does not alienate past violence since it sees that violence as in some sense productive or generative; violence gives rise to things, with the distinct possibility that those things, in the aggregate, may be modernity and indeed ourselves. The strength of this model is, first of all, that it acknowledges that most violence is intensely social: it almost always emerges out of close proximity and inter- action rather than mental abstraction, and within that history of proximity and interaction violence is both cause and effect. Second, this model is some- what better suited than the *mentalités* model at explaining change-over-time. If violence is productive, then it becomes a historical subject rather than an object, analytically rich rather than an end in itself. Third, this model desensationalises violence, suggesting that its discovery in the past need not surprise us or force us to go searching for peculiar worldviews to explain it. The weakness of this perspective, however, is how easily it can shade into amorality and indeed reckless indifference to human suffering. Imagining violence as a productive sphere of social interaction tends to efface moral differences between victims and perpetrators, to ignore the differences between violence and other sorts of dispute resolution, and even to create a historio- graphy that reproduces the dehumanising discourse of violence itself. By asking what violence produced, by looking at violence as a point of social contact comparable to the history of the book, by imagining sufferers of rape or torture as in some sense participants rather than victims, we surely miss another of the central tasks of historiography: respecting the humanity of the past and rescuing them from the enormous condescension of posterity.

Before concluding, I want to reflect for a moment on the relationship between the two frameworks discussed here and the two frameworks for early modern Irish history proposed in the 1980s in a famous historiographical debate between Steven Ellis and Brendan Bradshaw. In that debate, Ellis began by suggesting a series of alternative questions for early modern Irish history that complicated the modern division of Ireland into polarised communities; this was, for Ellis, a way of transcending presentism and offering a history that could quench rather than fuel political controversy.[52] Bradshaw responded by rejecting 'value-free history', in part because of what he called the 'credibility gap' between such revisionism and the historical memory of the Irish public. In his view, Irish history should emphasise the 'catastrophic violence' of English intervention, which he claimed Ellis had elided, precisely because Ireland needed 'a form of public history in which the historical consciousness of the community was expressed and transmitted'.[53] In his reply, then, Ellis stressed that such a memorialising project was dangerous because it necessarily adopted the subject-position of one modern community rather than another. Instead, he suggested something very much like the *mentalités* model that I have described in this essay: the desire to understand 'past societies in Ireland, their aspirations and values, in their own terms' was precisely a way to cool modern tensions.[54]

Ellis was absolutely right that studying early modern violence as the scars of extinct *mentalités* rather than as the raw materials for present memorialisation is a valuable option within a historiography that seeks to reincorporate that violence without participating in its legacy; it remains a viable alternative to Bradshaw's fusion of history with memory. The present essay has suggested, however, that Ellis's model is not the only one and that Bradshaw was not wrong to acknowledge the long shadow of historical violence. In the 2010s, unlike in the 1980s, it might be possible to emphasise the violence of Irish history in a way that neither presumes nor sidesteps modern tensions but instead treats those tensions themselves as history. The violence of the past might usefully be integrated into Irish history (the way it has been integrated into French or Spanish history) without having to make reference to the present subject-positions of the descendants of that violence.

This, therefore, is the dilemma that I put to historians of early modern Ireland and the 1641 massacres. It brings us back, finally, to the question I bracketed earlier: whether they really want to abandon emotion for cool, analytic reason. If they do not, entirely – and I suspect that some elements of memory will always remain imbedded in this scholarship, as they do in other colonial legacies like the violence of slavery and the Columbian exchange – then Ellis's question remains paramount: whose past should be remembered for whose present? But if history really can transcend memory, I have tried to suggest that another, perhaps equally difficult question remains: what sort of history? If it is history that looks back in horror and celebrates the hard-fought victories of modernity, then the first model offers a path; it if is history that sees modernity as in some sense the legacy of that horror, then the second model offers a path. The choice is theirs.

NOTES

The author would like to thank Tom Brady, Brendan Kane, Krista Kesslering, Jane Ohlmeyer, Jonathan Sheehan and Micheál Ó Siochrú for reading and commenting on earlier drafts of this essay.

1 On the relationship between memory and history in Ireland, see, for example, Ian McBride (ed.), *History and Memory in Modern Ireland* (Cambridge, 2001); and Guy Beiner, *Remembering the Year of the French: Irish Folk History and Social Memory* (Madison, Wisconsin, 2007).

2 This essay is principally concerned with large-scale violence like the 1641 massacres rather than interpersonal violence, although the issue of interpersonal violence will appear briefly below in the context of how the exceptional relates to the quotidian.

3 Clodagh Tait, David Edwards and Pádraig Lenihan, 'Early modern Ireland: a history of violence', in Clodagh Tait, David Edwards and Pádraig Lenihan (eds), *Age of Atrocity: Violence and Political Conflict in Early Modern Ireland* (Dublin, 2007) pp. 9–33.

4 John Morrill, 'Concluding reflection: confronting the violence of the Irish Reformations', in Alan Ford and John McCafferty (eds), *The Origins of Sectarianism in Early Modern Ireland* (Cambridge, 2005), p. 230.

5 For some examples of important recent work on violence in early modern Ireland, besides the many excellent essays in *Age of Atrocity*, see, for example, Micheal Ó Siochrú, *God's Executioner: Oliver Cromwell and the Conquest of Ireland* (London, 2008); Robin Clifton, 'An indiscriminate blackness? Massacre, counter-massacre, and ethnic cleansing in Ireland, 1640–1660', in Mark Levine and Penny Roberts (eds), *The Massacre in History* (New York, 1999) pp. 107–26; Patricia Palmer, 'At the sign of the head: the currency of beheading in early modern Ireland', in Stuart Carroll (ed.), *Cultures of Violence: Interpersonal Violence in Historical Perspective* (New York, 2007) pp. 129–55; Patricia Palmer, ' "An headless Ladie" and "a horses load of heads": writing the beheading', *Renaissance Quarterly*, 60 (2007), 25–57; Dianne Hall and Elizabeth Malcolm, ' "The Rebels Turkish tyranny": sexual violence in Ireland during the 1640s', *Gender and History*, 22(1) (2010), 55–74; Nicholas Canny, 'Religion, politics, and the Irish rising of 1641', in Judith Devlin and Ronan Fanning (eds), *Religion and Rebellion: Papers Read Before the 22nd Conference of Historians* (Dublin, 1997) pp. 40–70; Nicholas Canny, 'What really happened in Ireland in 1641?', in Jane Ohlmeyer (ed.), *Ireland from Independence to Occupation, 1641–1660* (Cambridge, 1995) pp. 24–42; Martyn Bennett, *The Civil Wars Experienced: Britain and Ireland, 1638–1661* (London, 2000); Hilary Simms, 'Violence in County Armagh, 1641', in Brian Mac Cuarta (ed.), *Ulster 1641: Aspects of the Rising* (Belfast, 1993) pp. 123–38; Raymond Gillespie, 'The murder of Arthur Champion and the 1641 rising in Fermanagh', *Clogher Record*, 14(3) (1993), 52–66; David Edwards,

'Ideology and experience: Spenser's *View* and martial law in Ireland', in Hiram Morgan (ed.), *Political Ideology in Ireland, 1541–1641* (Dublin, 1999) pp. 127–57.

6 On the question of empathy, see the famous debate between Steven Ellis and Brendan Bradshaw in the pages of *Irish Historical Studies*: Steven Ellis, 'Nationalist historiography and the English and Gaelic worlds in the late Middle Ages', *Irish Historical Studies*, 25 (1986), 1–18; Brendan Bradshaw, 'Nationalism and historical scholarship in modern Ireland', *Irish Historical Studies*, 26 (1989), 329–51; Steven Ellis, 'Historiographical debate: representations of the past in Ireland: whose past and whose present?', *Irish Historical Studies*, 27 (1991), 289–308. I will discuss this debate more below.

7 Peter Wilson, *The Thirty Years War: Europe's Tragedy* (Cambridge, MA, 2009), pp. 786–95.

8 For recent overviews of persecution, see, for example, Lyndal Roper, *Witch Craze: Terror and Fantasy in Baroque Germany* (New Haven, 2004); Brian Levack, *The Witch Hunt in Early Modern Europe* (3rd edn, London, 2006).

9 Charles Carlton, *Going to the Wars: The Experience of the British Civil Wars, 1638–1651* (London, 1992), chapter 9.

10 See, most recently, Serhii Plokhy, *The Cossacks and Religion in Early Modern Ukraine* (Oxford, 2001). Scholars give wildly varied casualty estimates ranging from as low as 6,000 to as high as 500,000; there seems to be not enough evidence for more precise figures. See Paul Magocsi, *A History of Ukraine* (Seattle, 1996).

11 Paul Avrich, *Russian Rebels 1600–1800* (New York, 1972).

12 David Eltis, 'The volume and structure of the transatlantic slave trade: a reassessment', *William and Mary Quarterly*, 58 (2001), 9–16.

13 For an attempt to place the seventeenth century alongside the fourteenth century and the twentieth century as periods of anomalous violence, see Joseph Canning, Hartmut Lehmann and Jay Winter (eds), *Power, Violence and Mass Death in Pre-Modern and Modern Times* (Aldershot, 2004).

14 See, for example, Zenon Kohut, 'The Khmelnytsky Uprising, the image of Jews, and the shaping of Ukrainian historical memory', *Jewish History*, 17 (2003), 141–63.

15 Credit or blame for this oberservation goes to my colleague Jonathan Sheehan.

16 Kirkpatrick Sale, 'What Columbus discovered', *The Nation* (22 October 1990).

17 Jeffrey Hart, 'Discovering Columbus', *National Review* (15 October 1990).

18 'The Columbian quincentenary: an educational opportunity', *The History Teacher*, 25(2) (February 1992), 145–51.

19 'Response to the Quincentenary Statement of the NCSS and AHA', *The History Teacher*, 26(2) (February 1993), 247–54.

20 Lee Anderson, 'A reply to the response to the Quincentenary Statement of the NCSS and the AHA', *The History Teacher*, 27(1) (November 1993), 63–72.

21 Brian Sandberg, 'Beyond encounters: religion, ethnicity, and violence in the early modern Atlantic world, 1492–1700', *Journal of World History*, 17 (2006), 1–25.

22 H. E. Martel, 'Hans Staden's captive soul: identity, imperialism, and rumors of cannibalism in sixteenth-century Brazil', *Journal of World History*, 17 (2006), 51–69.

23 Bernard Bailyn, 'Considering the slave trade: history and memory', *William and Mary Quarterly*, 58 (2001), 245–51, quote on p. 251.

24 Natalie Davis, 'The rites of violence: religious riot in sixteenth-century France', first published in *Past and Present*, 59 (1973), 51–91, reprinted in her *Society and Culture in Early Modern France: Eight Essays by Natalie Zemon Davis* (Stanford, 1975), p. 156. See also George Rudé, *The Crowd in the French Revolution* (Oxford, 1960); George Rudé, *The Crowd in History: A Study of Popular Disturbances in France and England, 1730–1848* (New York, 1964); E. P. Thompson, 'The moral economy of the English crowd in the Eighteenth Century', *Past and Present*, 50 (1971), 76–136.

25 Denis Crouzet, *Les Guerriers de Dieu: La Violence au Temps des Troubles de Religion vers 1525-vers 1610* (Seyssel, 1990).

26 Brad Gregory, *Salvation at Stake: Christian Martyrdom in Early Modern Europe* (Cambridge, MA, 1999).

27 Sabine MacCormack, ' "The Heart has its Reasons": predicaments of missionary Christianity in early colonial Peru', *Hispanic American Historical Review*, 65 (1985), 443–66, quote on p. 454.

28 Lisa Silverman, *Tortured Subjects: Pain, Truth, and the Body in Early Modern France* (Chicago, 2001).

29 Roper, *Witch Craze*.

30 Suzanne Desan, 'Crowds, community, and ritual in the work of E. P. Thompson and Natalie Davis', in Lynn Hunt (ed.), *The New Cultural History* (Berkeley, 1989) pp. 47–71.

31 Inga Clendinnen, 'Disciplining the Indians: Franciscan ideology and missionary violence in sixteenth-century Yucatán', *Past and Present*, 94 (1982), 27–48; Inga Clendinnen, *Ambivalent Conquests: Maya and Spaniard in Yucatan, 1517–1570* (Cambridge, 1987).

32 David Nirenberg, *Communities of Violence: Persecution of Minorities in the Middle Ages* (Princeton, 1996), p. 9.

33 René Girard, *Violence and the Sacred*, trans. Patrick Gregory (Baltimore, 1977), first published in French in 1972. Quotes on pp. 309 and 317.

34 Benjamin Kaplan, *Divided by Faith: Religious Conflict and the Practice of Toleration in Early Modern Europe* (2007), p. 78. This dialectical relationship between tolerance and intolerance was first explored for English culture in Alexandra Walsham, *Charitable Hatred: Tolerance and Intolerance in England, 1500–1700* (Manchester, 2006).

35 Stuart Clark, *Vanities of the Eye: Vision in Early Modern European Culture* (Oxford, 2007).

36 Andy Wood, *The 1549 Rebellions and the Making of Early Modern England* (Cambridge, 2007), especially chapter 3.

37 Mark Greengrass, 'Hidden transcripts: secret histories and personal testimonies of religious violence in the French Wars of Religion', in Mark Levine and Penny Roberts (eds), *The Massacre in History* (New York, 1999) pp. 69–88.

38 Otto Ulbricht, 'The experience of violence during the Thirty Years War: a look at the civilian victims', in Joseph Canning, Hartmut Lehmann and Jay Winter (eds), *Power, Violence and Mass Death in Pre-Modern and Modern Times* (Aldershot, 2004) pp. 97–127.

39 Thomas A. Brady, Jr., 'Limits of religious violence in early modern Europe', in Kaspar von Greyerz and Kim Siebenhüner (eds), *Religion und Gewalt: Konflikte, Tituale, Deutungen (1500–1800)* (Göttingen, 2006), quote on pp. 128–9.

40 Johan Huizinga, *The Waning of the Middle Ages*, trans. F. Hopman (London, 1924); Norbert Elias, *The Civilizing Process: Sociogenetic and Psychogenetic Investigations*, revised edn, trans Edmund Jephcott (Maldon, MA, 1994).

41 Julius Ruff, *Violence in Early Modern Europe, 1580–1800* (Cambridge, 2001); Robert Muchembled, *Une histoire de la violence: De la fin du Moyen Age à nos jours* (Paris, 2008).

42 Stuart Carroll, 'Introduction', in Stuart Carroll (ed.), *Cultures of Violence: Interpersonal Violence in Historical Perspective* (New York, 2007) pp. 1–43, quotes at pp. 2, 6, 13.

43 Stuart Carroll, *Blood and Violence in Early Modern France* (Oxford, 2006).

44 Alexandra Shepard, "Violence and civility in early modern Europe', *Historical Journal*, 49 (2006), 593–603, quotes on pp. 594–5, 602.

45 Julie Hardwick, 'Early modern perspectives on the long history of domestic violence: the case of seventeenth-century France', *Journal of Modern History*, 78 (2006), 1–36.

46 Susan Amussen, 'Punishment, discipline, and power: the social meanings of violence in early modern England', *Journal of British Studies*, 34 (1995), 1–34, quote on p. 5.

47 As the editors of the recent volume *Age of Atrocity: Violence and Political Conflict in Early Modern Ireland* noted, such 'lower-level' violence has been largely absent from Irish historiography, and its inclusion in future work might make early modern atrocities 'seem either less or more exceptional': Tait, Edwards and Lenihan, 'Early modern Ireland', p. 33.

48 Two exceptions worth noting, one for England and one for Ireland, are David Cressy, 'Different kinds of speaking: symbolic violence and secular iconoclasm in early modern England', in Muriel McClendon, Joseph Ward and Michael MacDonald (eds), *Protestant Identities: Religion, Society, and Self-Fashioning in Post-Reformation England* (Stanford, 1999) pp. 19–42; D. Hall, 'Words as weapons: speech, violence, and gender in late medieval Ireland', *Éire–Ireland*, 41 (2006), 122–41.

49 Pieter Spierenburg, 'Violence: reflections about a word', in Sophie Body-Gendrot and Pieter Spierenburg (eds), *Violence in Europe: Historical and Contemporary Perspectives* (New York, 2008). Few early modern historians have theorized these definitional issues. I suspect that this is due less to their perennial uneasiness with theory and more to the fact that bodily harm is much easier to identify in early modern archives than complex forms of violence of the sorts identified by scholars like Michel Foucault and Judith Butler.

50 Crouzet, *Guerriers de Dieu*, p. 297.

51 Gregory, *Saluation al Stake*, conclusion.

52 The debate is in Steven Ellis, 'Nationalist historiography and the English and Gaelic worlds in the late midde ages', *Irish Historical Studies*, 25(97) (May 1986), 1–18; Brendan Bradshaw, 'Nationalism and historical scholarship in modern Ireland', *Irish Historical Studies*, 26(104) (November 1989), 329–51; Steven Ellis, 'Historiographical debate: representations of the past in Ireland – whose past and whose present', *Irish Historical Studies*, 27(108) (November 1991), 289–308.

53 Bradshaw, 'Nationalism and historical scholarship', pp. 336–9, 346, 350.

54 Ellis, 'Historiographical debate', pp. 290–1, 306–8.

3

The '1641 massacres'

AIDAN CLARKE

The '1641 depositions' have attracted a good deal of attention in recent years as the richness of the information they contain about all aspects of Irish society in the period has been recognised.[1] Historically, interest in them has been very different. They have been known, or have been notorious, as the principal body of evidence of one of the most contentious episodes in Irish history, the alleged 'massacres of 1641'. Generations of scholars and propagandists passionately affirmed or indignantly denied their veracity until the early years of the last century. One of the stated aims of the major 1641 transcription and digitisation project was 'to resume the debate on the alleged massacres on a constructive and thoroughly informed basis', by making the material universally accessible.

The aim of this essay is to pre-empt the reopening of that debate by suggesting what needs to be debated and what does not. I am prompted to do so by a conviction that the suspension of the debate throughout the twentieth century has led to the emergence of a poorly informed consensus about the massacres that demands critical examination. I hope to demonstrate the validity of two propositions. The first is that the fundamental question on which the historical debate turned for two and a half centuries can be convincingly answered from the contemporary evidence and does not need to be revisited. The second is that the present state of opinion on the supplementary question – how many were killed? – relies on a selective use of the historiography, rests on no evidential base whatsoever and needs to inform itself. The fundamental question has been the truth or falsehood of the original and constantly repeated allegation that the outbreak of the rebellion had been accompanied by the premeditated slaughter in cold blood of many thousands of Protestant settlers. As the contemporary politician, the earl of Clarendon, put it, in his later role as contemporary historian, an 'incredible number' were murdered 'within the space of ten days'.[2] This was, in the language of the time, a 'general massacre'. The qualification was required because there were other kinds. To take two examples from among many: in 1642 a King's County settler reported that his neighbour, 'an honest Englishman', had been 'most cruelly murthered masecred and chopt in peecs' and Judith Walcott in County Dublin recounted how the rebels had 'murdred and massacred' her husband, who had 'at the least forty wounds on his body'.[3] One is reminded of the historian, writing in 1606, who described how Julius Ceasar had been massacred with twenty-two wounds – or, at a more elevated level, that Shakespeare wrote in *Richard III* of the 'piteous massacre' of the princes in the tower. The contemporary usage of the word 'massacre', in short, was not confined to mass killings. It also denoted a killing that was particularly shocking because it violated the proprieties of the time, in its brutality, its treachery or its transgression of the hierarchy of status.

The first allegation of a general massacre came before the event, from Owen Connolly, a Protestant gentleman in the service of a prominent member of the English Commons, the Antrim planter Sir John Clotworthy. On 22 October, after a famous evening's drinking with his foster brother, Hugh MacMahon, Connolly informed the lords justices 'that the Irish had prepared men in all parts of the kingdome to destroy all the English inhabiting there tomorrowe morning by ten of the clock, and that in all the seaports and other townes in the kingdom, all the Protestants should be killed this night'.[4] It was in these terms that the outbreak was reported by the lords justices to the lord lieutenant in England in a letter carried by Connolly himself: as a 'damnable conspiracy' which envisaged 'that all the Protestants and English throughout the whole kingdom that would not join with them should be cut off, and so those Papists should then become possessed of the government and kingdom at the same instant'.[5] Connolly's account of what had been intended, which bore some resemblance to the notorious events of St Bartholomew's Day in France almost seventy years before, closely matched English expectations of what, sooner or later, the wars of religion were likely to bring. The leaders of the commons, convinced that the rebellion in Ireland was part of an international conspiracy, unhesitatingly set about guarding against the likelihood of an associated Catholic rising in England.

Connolly's account, and the inferences drawn from it, appeared to be validated in March 1642 by the report of a clerical Commission for the Distressed Subjects.[6] Initially charged in December 1641 with recording losses suffered as a result of rebel action, the commission's brief was extended in January to ascertaining 'what number of persons have beene murdered by the rebels or perished afterwarde on the way to Dublin, or other places whither they fled or retired for refuge, either by way of defence or otherwise'.[7] Early in March, the commissioners distilled the information they had collected into a Remonstrance, which was presented as a fund-raising, relief-seeking address to the English House of Commons by the head of the commission, Dr Henry Jones, on March 16 and published before the end of the month.[8] Officially endorsed by the lords justices and Council of Ireland, recommended by the English Commons, based on the sworn testimony of eye-witnesses given in a form that was admissible in a court of law and verified by the inclusion of examples of that evidence in a lengthy appendix, the *Remonstrance* had every claim to be accepted as the authoritative account of what had taken place in Ireland. Its emphatic conclusion was that the rebellion did indeed form part of an international, papal directed conspiracy, the object of which was the 'utter extirpation of the Protestant religion and all the British professors thereof'.[9] Despite this unequivocal finding, an American historian, Walter Love, drew attention half a century ago to a hitherto unnoticed reticence in the development of the theme.[10]

The major emphasis of the eighty-three extracts from the depositions selected for publication was not on acts of violence, which were reported in only two-fifths of them, but on spoken words, which were reported in four-fifths.[11] As the commissioners explained in the text, they had it in mind to enable their readers to discover 'the minds and intents of these conspirators' and they believed that could be done most effectively by quoting what had been said. They aimed, therefore, to show what had been intended rather than to recite what had been done. They did not claim in so many words that the rebellion had begun with an indiscriminate general massacre but rather, on the basis of the evidence they had collected, that the conspirators had planned such a massacre: 'their generall profession is for a generall extirpation, even to the last and least drop of English blood'.[12] The inference that the combination of hearsay, general allegations and eye-witness descriptions of particular acts of violence in the extracts confirmed that the plan had been carried out was there to be drawn by the reader. And both contemporary and later generations of readers eagerly obliged.

Whether the implication was deliberate is open to doubt. There is reason to believe that the authors of the *Remonstrance* did not intend to imply what they refrained from saying. Four months after it appeared, Henry Jones published an account of the outbreak of the rebellion in County Cavan in which his recital of the sequence of events as he had observed them differed markedly from the received picture of a rising characterised by unrestrained and horrific violence from the outset.[13] In Cavan, though Protestants had been disarmed and property taken, professedly for safekeeping and by the authority of the county sheriff, there had been no violence before Jones left early in November to take a petition from the O'Reillys to Dublin. When he returned on 12 November, the situation had worsened: Protestants had been expropriated, stripped, assaulted and expelled. Killing came later still, most spectacularly a mass drowning in Belturbet early in 1642.

The witness statements collected by the commissioners tell much the same story. That point may be illustrated by looking at a very small sample made up of refugees from County Leitrim, all of whom came from the three south-eastern baronies. The particular significance of this area lies in the fact that the local leaders of the rebellion were involved in the original conspiracy and kept faithfully to the original plan of action. The rebellion began there on 24 October, less than two full days after the initial outbreak. Within a week, the settlers had been dispossessed and either taken refuge in strongholds or fled to Dublin, and a second phase of localised siege warfare began. There were twenty-seven deponents from this area, nine of whom reported deaths – a total of more than ninety-five in the first two years of the rebellion. Examined forensically, applying a strict standard of accepting only first hand or familial knowledge as likely to be reliable, seventeen of these deaths pass the test and the rest are excluded as hearsay.[14] Two of the seventeen sufficiently attested deaths took place in February 1642 and one early in 1643, so that only fourteen were victims of the immediate outbreak. Of these, two were hanged in mid-November as they fled through Cavan;[15] nine were children who had died of cold and hunger after being stripped and turned out 'in the cold air';[16] another allegedly died of grief in Dublin on his way back from England.[17] That leaves only two killings authenticated at first hand as having taken place at the time of the outbreak of the rebellion in Leitrim: a girl whose brains were beaten out 'against an oken tree or block' when the rebels discovered that she was the daughter of a Scotsman, and a Mr Adshed, murdered 'in the open field' after being robbed.[18] From this evidence, two conclusions seem to follow: first, that the rebellion did not commence with a general massacre in Leitrim; and, second, given that the rising in Leitrim formed part of the original plot rather than an imitative follow-up, it seems safe to say that had the plan involved a premeditated massacre there would have been more than two killings in the county.

The depositions from other counties disclose a similar sequence, with local variations, but there is no need to pursue them, as the conclusive evidence comes from the commissioners themselves, contained in an unpublished and untitled sequel to the *Remonstrance* they prepared in the summer of 1643.[19] Their aim on this occasion was to highlight the horrors of the first year of the rebellion in the hope of subverting truce negotiations that had begun in March and were to lead to a cessation of hostilities in September. Following the model of the *Remonstrance*, the text of this sequel was keyed to an appendix of 208 depositions. In the text, the commissioners held firm to their conviction that a general massacre had been intended and, indeed, still was if the opportunity should arise.[20] Their approach was defensive. They believed that in some quarters the *Remonstrance* had been received sceptically and dismissed as a 'tragicale fiction' rather than a 'true narration'.[21] They needed to counteract that criticism by explaining why the intended massacre had not taken place. Their answer focused on the failure of the essential component of the plot – the 'Grand Design' to take Dublin Castle and to distribute the arms and ammunition it contained.[22] This mishap, they argued, frightened off the southern members of the conspiracy, who decided to wait upon events before showing their hand. They only committed themselves after being reassured by the defeat of a government force at Julianstown late in November 1641. By then, Protestants were either on the alert or in refuge and the opportunity to take them by surprise had passed.[23]

With regard to Ulster, the commissioners' explanation was more complex. There too, waiting for news from Dublin played a part, as did a false expectation – 'that the onely stripping of soe many thousands, men women and children of all sorts and ages in such season of the year would have infallibly killed them'.[24] But there had been, they insisted, 'manifold most barbarous butcheries . . . instantly upon the day'.[25] Thereafter, the news from Dublin briefly brought restraint; Julianstown restored confidence and resulted in renewed violence; and in the months that followed, the rebels fell upon 'the poore, naked, unresisting and innocent among them on occasion of every defeat of their parties by the British'.[26] This was the commissioners' second self-appointed task: to show that although the planned general massacre had been thwarted, 'many thousands howsoever have perished by their lusty and unbridled rage'[27] in ways that were carefully and graphically documented in the appended extracts, four-fifths of which included acts of extreme, gratuitous violence. The commissioners' efforts came to nothing. The sequel was suppressed by the earl of Ormond and remained unnoticed for some 350 years. I believe that it conclusively answers the fundamental question: there was no 'general massacre'. But it does not answer the supplementary question: how many were killed in cold blood in the early years of the rebellion?

'Many thousands' was as close as the commissioners got to estimating the number of victims. Others proved less circumspect, and it may be appropriate to introduce my second proposition by reviewing some of the most notable of their estimates. The first to gain popular currency was reported to the commissioners by Archdeacon Robert Maxwell of Tynan in County Armagh in August 1642. Maxwell, who had a strong claim to credence as a long-term prisoner of the Ulster commander-in-chief, Sir Phelim O'Neill, reported that the rebels, 'least they should hereafter be charged with more murthers then they committed' had commanded the Catholic clergy to bring in 'a true Accompt of' the number killed: the response, in March 1642, gave the total as 154,000.[28] This estimate achieved authoritative status when it was incorporated in *A Declaration* of the English Commons on '*the rise and progress of the grand rebellion in Ireland*', published in July 1643 with orders that it should to be read out in all churches.[29] The estimate was surrounded by some confusion:

whereas most contemporary reports gave Maxwell's figure as the total for Ulster, the commons gave it as the total for all of Ireland. Early in 1650, the former secretary of the Commission for Distressed Subjects, Thomas Waring, who had been employed by the English Council to publish the depositions, issued a promotional pamphlet.[30] In spite of his close involvement in the collection of the depositions, he relied on Maxwell's figure, but qualified it by stressing that it referred to only one of four provinces and invited the reader to consider how many more killings there must have been. John Milton accepted this invitation. In 1649, in the first edition of his answer to the 'Kings Book', *Eikonoklastes*, he had followed the commons *Declaration;*[31] in the second edition in 1650, he noted that the estimate was for Ulster alone and concluded that 'the total sum of that slaughter [was] in all likelihood four times as great'.[32] The source of the confusion was an initial careless reading of the text. In his deposition, Maxwell had specifically entered a caveat: 'whither in Ulster only or the whole kingdome,' he said, 'the deponent durst not enquire'.

Careless reading is a recurrent influence in this story. The reason why Maxwell's figure had not been superseded before 1650 by what is, to this day, described as the 'estimate of 300,000 killed' given by Sir John Temple four years earlier in his history of *The Irish Rebellion*, is that Temple gave no such estimate.[33] The belief that he did so appears to be indelible, but what he actually wrote was that between the outbreak and the cessation agreement (that is, from October 1641 to September 1643) there were 'above 300,000 British and Protestants cruelly murthered in cold blood, *destroyed some other way, or expelled out of their habitations* [my italics], according to the strictest conjecture and computation of those who seemed best to understand the numbers of English planted in Ireland'.[34] The sentence encompasses the various ways the Protestants were affected by the rebellion, by death to be sure – death from starvation, cold and ill-usage as well as from violence – but also by disposses-sion, expulsion and forced flight; and it reports that the informed estimate of the Protestant population in the areas so affected amounted to 300,000. That figure was a gross over-estimate, but that is not the point. The point is that it was not a death toll.

Temple's treatment of the massacre theme derived from the commissioners' collection of depositions or, more exactly, largely from the two sets of excerpts that they had compiled in the *Remonstrance* and its sequel.[35] That collection was not the collection now known for convenience as the '1641 depositions'. Temple had access to some 1,600 depositions collected by the Dublin com-missioners: by the time the commission closed in 1647, this had increased to about 1,860. To these were later added another 1,600 depositions taken by a sub-commission in Munster in 1642–43 and close to a further 3,000 records of examinations into particular incidents and individuals conducted from mid-1652 to mid-1654. The depositions are essentially statements of losses incurred as a result of the rebellion, usually with the names of those respon-sible and often with an account of the attendant circumstances. They were lodged in the hope that they would be accepted as a basis for restitution and compensation in the future, and certificates were issued to facilitate such claims. The additional information was collected as evidence to be used in subsequent prosecutions. More than 90 per cent of the deponents reported losses; less than 20 per cent reported deaths – whether by murder, in battle, or through cold, starvation and ill-treatment. Like Temple, the deponents did not distinguish between varieties of victimhood. As Sir Audley Mervyn put it, nakedness, famine and disease 'were adjudged overflow executioners'.[36]

The examinations taken in the 1650s, by contrast, were concerned speci-fically with the collection of evidence for the prosecution of those responsible for murders and massacres. They were taken from Irish as well as English witnesses and they add richly to what we learn from the 1640s material, but they do not add significantly to the number of incidents previously reported. The proceedings were directed by high courts of justice, established for the purpose in 1652, but the conduct of the investigations was largely entrusted to locally based commissioners and subject to variation. In Wexford, for instance, while murders and massacres were not neglected, the commissioners spent much of their energy in identifying landowners who had been in arms in the first year of the rebellion and were therefore liable to the maximum penalties of the act of settlement. In the north-east, a good deal of, no doubt, politically motivated attention was paid to the killing of native Irish by Scots early in 1642, most famously on Island Magee. In general, however, it looks very much as though the commissioners of the 1650s used the records of their predeces-sors to identify the cases that seemed worthy of detailed investigation. Their decisions, in all probability, serve as a guide to what was contemporarily judged to be credible or provable in the depositions and what was not. By and large, they concentrated on individual murders, small-group killings and violations of quarter given. Apart from a couple of dozen or so well-attested cases, they made little or no attempt to pursue the familiar general allegations of mass murder in the next parish or the neighbouring county, nor did they discover any that were previously unreported, except in the area east of the Bann, from which very few deponents had reached Dublin.

Although this material was used as an administrative resource in the Cromwellian settlement, it was to be some time before it was used as a source for the history of the period. The principle contender for the succession to Maxwell's 154,000 killings and Temple's supposed 300,000 was one of 'about 40,000' off-handedly given by Clarendon in his *History of the Rebellion and Civil Wars in England*, published in 1702, long after his death.[37] Although he had abandoned this estimate in his later *The History of the Rebellion and Civil Wars in Ireland*, in favour of 'an incredible number',[38] the trenchant endorsement of his figure of 40,000 in the widely read *The History of Great Britain* by David Hume, who knew nothing whatever about the matter, gave it widespread currency for many years.[39] It was, indeed, disinterred as late as 1956 in a history of Irish Presbyterianism.[40] Hume's history was published in 1754, thirteen years after a seminal event in the historiography of the massacres: to mark the centenary of the rebellion, Bishop Stearne of Clogher, who had bought the deposition material some decades earlier, presented the collection to Trinity College Dublin, where it was bound, county by county, in thirty-one volumes, to which were added two further volumes of ancillary papers. For the first time, the depositions became available for study and the first scholar to take the opportunity to investigate them in detail was Ferdinando Warner, a Church of England cleric. After publishing an *Ecclesiastical History of Ireland before 1171* in 1763, he set about writing a *History of the Rebellion and Civil-War in Ireland*, which appeared in 1767. He had already acquired a manuscript collection of copies of depositions, authenticated by the signatures of the commissioners, and was prompted to travel to Dublin to see the originals.

He 'took a great deal of pains,' he wrote, 'and spent a great deal of time, in examining these books'. He was wholly contemptuous of what he discovered as although 'all the Examinations signed by the Commissioners are said to be upon oath, yet in infinitely the greater number of them the words "being duly sworn" have the pen drawn through them'. Moreover, he continued, 'in several of those where such words remain, many parts of the examination are crossed out'. He drew three conclusions: first, that the deletions had been intentionally invalidated; secondly, and consequently, 'that the bulk of this immense collection is parole evidence [i.e. unsworn] and upon report of common fame' and therefore 'not to be depended on'; and, thirdly, that the collection of copies in his own possession, all sworn and all verified, had been brought together precisely because they were the only ones that were fully attested. His document, he reasoned, 'is therefore as much an original as that collection'.[41] He chose to ignore the evidence provided by the unexpected discovery of numerous examinations from the 1650s, duly sworn and free of deletions, which he dismissed in half a sentence, observing only that they had been 'taken ten years later, by Justices of the Peace appointed by the Commissioners of the English Parliament'.[42] Having thus satisfied himself that the deposition books were worthless as evidence, he returned to England and confined his use of the depositions, and his calculations of fatalities, to the manuscript with which his researches had begun: 'Here then it is only that we can expect the most authentic account of the Irish Massacre.' It was, he wrote, 'the authority from which I write of this tragical event' and he set out to 'ascertain from it, as near as may be' the number 'destroyed OUT OF WAR'.[43] The conclusion he reached was that 'upon positive evidence collected in two years' only 2,109 had been murdered; on the evidence of other

Protestants, a further 1,619; and upon evidence from 'some of the rebels', 300 more: a total of 4,028. Evidence 'on the report of others' from the same collection indicated that some 8,000 had been killed by "ill-usage".[44]

His assessment of the collection brought the evidence into disrepute and the spasmodic debate on the massacres was largely sidetracked for more than a century into uninformed and ill-tempered exchanges about the credibility of the depositions. The detail is immaterial to the present purpose, but the climax was transformative. In 1878, the first two volumes of W. H. Lecky's *History of England in the Eighteenth Century* were published.[45] They contained a lengthy background chapter on Ireland in which Lecky reviewed the state of knowledge of the 1641 rebellion in measured, judicious and persuasive terms, exposed the unreliability of Temple's *Irish Rebellion*, on which the proponents of massacre chiefly depended, and concluded that there had been no plan for a general massacre, and no general massacre, but that there had been extreme violence, on both sides. The impact of this contribution rested on its manner: though it was the work of a Protestant unionist, it impressed as fair-minded, rational and, above all, non-sectarian. Widely applauded as a successful, non-partisan resolution to an unedifying quarrel, it received canonical status when endorsed some years later in the final volume of Samuel Gardiner's magisterial *History of England from the Accession of James the First to the Civil War*.[46] Though Lecky had carried out much of his research in Dublin, he had not thought it necessary to examine the depositions, for two reasons. The first was because those who held that there had been a general massacre, and particularly his principal target, J. A. Froude, had not done so.[47] The second was because he believed that the task had already been satisfactorily performed. Taking Warner at his own evaluation (and mistakenly supposing him to have been a fellow of Trinity), he concluded that his careful 'sifting of the evidence' and 'very honest, modest and painstaking' work had produced an estimate that was 'probably more correct than any of his predecessors'.[48]

Lecky's triumph in producing a treatment that, it seemed, only bigots could object to, was briefly challenged a few years later when Mary Hickson, who had examined the depositions carefully, published her findings in an introduction to a selection of the material.[49] Hickson did not subscribe to the emerging liberal consensus and she did not enhance her chances of a sympathetic reception by settling upon a probable death toll of 27,000, based not on her reading of the depositions, but on a reworking of the mingled calculations and guesswork of the seventeenth-century statistician, Sir William Petty, who had arrived at a figure of 37,000.[50] The most important of her findings, however, were not affected by the whiff of sectarianism that tainted her presentation. Her familiarity with the original material enabled her to demonstrate that Warner's conclusions were mistaken. She was able to show, first, that the deletion from the text of the words 'being duly sworn' could not have had the significance that Warner had attached to it because the formal words of validation – 'Jurat coram nobis', or 'sworn before us' – always remained; and, secondly, that the material 'struck out' was confined to detailed descriptions of property losses, for which a concise statement of the total value had been substituted. She argued that the features that had led Warner to dismiss the collection as worthless were actually directions for the abbreviation of the text, and she produced evidence that the secretary of the commission had testified to this effect in court in 1653.[51] Gardiner was impressed by these findings.[52] Lecky was unperturbed: in a brief public exchange of letters with Hickson, he dismissed the depositions on the fresh grounds that statements made by witnesses who had not been subjected to cross examination were of no evidential value and he incorporated that argument in later versions of his *History*.[53] It seems not to have occurred to him that the statements on which Warner had relied were equally open to the same criticism. Logically, he should have reconsidered his concurrence with Warner's estimates, but he did not do so and his view prevailed.

Though adherents of Temple remained unconvinced, a tacit scholarly consensus emerged in the twentieth century, best represented in 1966 in the graceful evasions of Beckett's *Making of Modern Ireland*.[54] For some time, controversy was abandoned in favour of a pragmatic acceptance that the rebellion had witnessed its share of atrocities, on both sides, the word 'massacre' disappeared from the lexicon and numbers ceased to be mentioned. In 1976, however, in the third volume of *A New History of Ireland*, Patrick Corish broke ranks and opted for the lowest estimate offered in the years of contention – figures of 'perhaps 4,000' murdered, together with 8,000 deaths from privation.[55] Since then, reticence has been replaced by confident assertion and 'about 4,000' has become the estimate of choice – most notably in Robinson's *Plantation of Ulster*,[56] Foster's *Modern Ireland*,[57] Bardon's *History of Ulster*[58] and, most recently, Sean Connolly's *Divided kingdom*.[59] In each case, starting with Corish, the authority cited is Lecky, sometimes with Gardiner added for good measure. Others have given estimates of 2,000, 3,000 and 'about 5,000', citing no authority. Only Connolly mentioned Warner, in a paraphrase of Lecky's tribute to the quality of his work. In fact, Warner's work underpins this recent assumption that we know the order of magnitude of the killings that took place in and after 1641. It is time to acknowledge its deficiencies.

Hickson revealed some of Warner's errors of judgement and observation, but she did not succeed in conveying how fundamental they were. To readers who were unfamiliar with the collection, they sounded like pedantic quibbles. In fact, Warner's scholarship was much worse than Hickson realised, and in less recondite ways. For instance, he concluded, from the material contained in the manuscript that prompted his interest, that the Commission, though appointed in December 1641, did not begin work until the following March, and had finished its business by July 1643, with the exception of one last deposition taken in October 1643.[60] He did not notice that the depositions he saw in Dublin ranged in date from 30 December 1641 to 30 September 1647. He described the collection as consisting of thirty-two books, 'besides one which contains the examinations that were taken by Archdeacon Bysse for the Province of Munster'.[61] There is no such book. The depositions taken by Bysse are spread across the ten volumes of Munster material. In the early 1650s, they had been edited for publication by the clerk of the commission, who had systematically deleted redundancies and tedious inventories of property lost. Warner clearly saw some of these as they are the only originals in the collection that match his description, but he seems not to have recognised them for what they were. The depositions taken by the Dublin commissioners had not been prepared for the printer in the same way. A set of fair copies had been used instead. Warner noticed these, and dismissed them as 'said to be taken by' the commissioners, but unsigned and 'therefore of no authority'.[62] He did not notice that each set of county copies had been certified at beginning and end by the signatures of Henry Jones (signing in his episcopal style, as bishop of Clogher) and his fellow commissioner William Aldridge. And he did not notice that the originals, more than 1,800 of them, were in the collection. Nobody who knows the deposition books will be surprised by these errors. They are bewildering: the diverse materials are jumbled together with no discernible principle of order apart from the county to which they were deemed to belong. They require more time than Warner gave them, and the blunt truth is that he was unable to make head or tail of them.

Warner gave no indication of the size or contents of the 'manuscript document' to which he resorted after his Dublin fiasco, but it is readily identifiable by the mistaken impression it conveyed of the span of the commission's work. It was the appendix attached to the sequel to the *Remonstrance*, compiled by the commissioners in the summer of 1643. It consisted of 208 depositions selected – in order to avoid overlapping with the appendix to the *Remonstrance* – from those taken between late March 1642 and July 1643, with the last-minute addition of a particularly cogent deposition taken in October 1643.[63] It is worth spelling out in detail what that means: Warner's source, the 'authority' from which he wrote, did not include any of the 700 or so depositions taken in Dublin before 25 March 1642; it did not include the 554 depositions taken between March 1642 and August 1643 that had not been selected by the commissioners; it included only one of the 278 depositions taken between August 1643 and September 1647; it did not include any of Bysse's 1,600 depositions from Munster; and it did not include any of the 2,800 or so examinations taken in the 1650s. Leaving aside that last omission (on the charitable grounds that these materials have never been part of the argument), Warner's estimate was based on 6% of the 3,500 depositions. If we were to follow the example of John Milton, by assuming the sample to be representative and applying a simple multiple, the grand total of people murdered would come to about 67,000. As it happens, we know that the sample was not representative: ironically, these depositions had been chosen to illustrate the savagery of the rebels.

It is to be hoped that when the debate is resumed it will proceed from the following two premises: that the evidence shows there was no general massacre, either in intention or in fact, but does not show that 'about 4,000' people were killed 'out of war', in Warner's phrase. It seems more than likely that the publication of the depositions will spawn fresh calculations of the death toll, and that these will tend to shape the debate. We will need to prepare our critical defences against them, in a number of ways. The first is to resolve that fresh counts should be judged by the forensic standard set some years ago by Hilary Simms in an exemplary investigation of the material for County Armagh.[64] It is tempting to agree with those who have argued (in private) that the mystery could be solved in thirty-one steps by dealing with the remaining counties in the same way. But that depends on what the mystery is. The matter is not perhaps as straightforward as Simms's work makes it appear, because we also need to keep in mind the confusion that the debate itself has created between what happened in the rebellion and the evidence of what happened. The two have become so closely associated in debate as to make it seem that if we can find out how many killings are credibly recorded in the depositions we will know how many people were killed. We will not, of course. To adapt a ridiculed, but pertinent, recent observation: we still won't know what we don't know.

The commissioners understood that. It is the reason why they did not offer a more exact estimate than 'many thousands'. Their concern was with the number who died 'through the rebels meanes' and in their sequel to the *Remonstrance* they classified murders under six headings – by the sword, by fire, by drowning, by hanging, by burying alive and 'by starving by cold'. It was the last of these, the people who had 'perished unseene', 'by the high waies and in wast places', and of whom they had 'few certain names or numbers', that made it impossible for them to attempt an estimate.[65] The perspective of the deponents was more expansive still, as can be seen if one looks in another way at the evidence of the depositions from Leitrim and the seventeen sufficiently authenticated deaths that they yield.

The allegations discarded as hearsay include the evidence of a widow who testified that only eight of the group of thirty-seven refugees with whom she had left Leitrim had reached Dublin alive, the rest '(as shee is assured) were either starved killed drowned or hanged by the rebels in the way'.[66] They also include a claim that an unknown number of refugees who fled to Sir James Craig's castle at Croghan in Cavan for safety 'there famished starved and dyed for want of meanes'.[67] And they contain a report from Ellynor Bryant that her husband and about forty others, who had been killed in the course of a sortie from the beleaguered garrison at Jamestown, had been 'cruelly murthered'.[68] The difference of perspective is clear. Forensic examination is dispassionate and reductive: the victims' view was emotional and inclusive. Though Thomas Bryant was killed in action and John Read was thought to have died of grief, they, in common with others who died of cold, hunger and ill treatment, or of starvation under siege, or who went missing, presumed dead, on the road to Dublin, were equally casualties of the rebellion. The victims did not draw distinctions and confine victimhood to civilians who were killed in cold blood. Their alternative truth was that more than ninety-five people, who would otherwise be alive, were dead 'by meanes of the rebellion'. The final thing we need to keep in mind is that the historiographical concentration on massacre had more to do with national and religious stereotyping than with history. In reality, the significant number is not the number who were killed in cold blood, but the number who died, by whatever means. The fact that this number is unknowable is unfortunate, but it is the truth we must learn to work with.

NOTES

1 The depositions are housed in the Library, Trinity College Dublin (TCD) MSS 809–41. Manuscript references are to this collection which is described in Aidan Clarke, 'The 1641 depositions', in P. Fox (ed.), *Treasures of the Library, Trinity College Dublin* (Dublin, 1984), pp. 111–22

2 Edward Hyde, earl of Clarendon, *The History of the Rebellion and Civil Wars in Ireland* (London, 1721), p. 12.

3 TCD MS 814, fol. 178v (Henrie Aylyffe); MS 810, fol. 184r (Judith Walcott).

4 TCD MS 809, fol. 13v.

5 *Report on the Manuscripts of the Duke of Ormonde, new series* (Ormonde MSS) (HMC, 8 vols, London, 1902–20), vol. ii, p. 1.

6 For the Commission, see Aidan Clarke, 'The commission for the despoiled subject, 1641–c.1647', in Brian Mac Cuarta (ed.), *Reshaping Ireland, 1550–1700: Colonization and Its Consequences* (Dublin, 2011), pp. 241–60.

7 TCD, MS 815, fols 4–4v.

8 Henry Jones, *A Remonstrance of Divers Remarkable Passages Concerning the Church and Kingdome of Ireland* (London, 1642).

9 Jones, *Remonstrance*, p. 1.

10 W. D. Love, 'Civil war in Ireland: appearances in three centuries of historical writing', *The Emory University Quarterly*, 22 (1966), 57–72.

11 As Joseph Cope has shown, the proportion of both themes in the collection as it stood when the extracts were chosen was of the order of 22–23%. Joseph Cope, 'Dr Henry Jones and the plight of Irish Protestants', *Historical Research*, 74 (2001), 279, Table I.

12 Jones, *Remonstrance*, p. 6.

13 Henry Jones, *The Beginning and Proceedings of the Rebellion in the County of Cavan in the Province of Ulster, from the 23 of October 1641 until the 25 of June 1642* (London, 1642). It was printed for Godfrey Emerson, who had also been responsible for the *Remonstrance*.

14 TCD MS 831, fols 17r–52v.

15 TCD MS 831, fols 30r–30v (Ann Dudd).

16 TCD MS 831, fol. 32v (Elizabeth Kiddier); MS 831, fol. 39r (Ann Read).

17 'comeing out of England to Dublin & hearing of the Rebellion & being told that this deponent & her children were robbed stript and dead in a ditch: Hee being overcomen with greef & beleeving the same to be true fell into sicknes whereof he soon after died'. TCD MS 831, fol. 39v (Ann Read).

18 TCD MS 831, fol. 43r (Susanna Stephenson); MS 831, fol. 33r (Helenor Adshed).

19 British Library, London Harleian (Harl.) MS 5999. For a discussion of the substance of this 'Discourse', see Aidan Clarke, 'The 1641 rebellion and anti-popery in Ireland', in Brian MacCuarta (ed.), *Ulster 1641* (Belfast, 1997), pp. 151–7.

20 October 22/3 was described as the day 'selected for our general massacre'. Harl. MS, 5999, fol. 17v.

21 Harl. MS 5999, fol. 1.

22 Harl. MS 5999, fol. 27v.

23 Harl. MS 5999, fols 26v–27r.

24 Harl. MS 5999, fol. 27v

25 Harl. MS 5999, fol. 27v

26 Harl. MS 5999, fols 26r–27r.

27 Harl. MS 5999, fol. 27v.

28 TCD MS 809, fol. 8v (Robert Maxwell).

29 *A Declaration of the Commons Assembled in Parliament; Concerning the Rise and Progress of The Grand Rebellion in Ireland* (London, 1643), pp. 9–10. Maxwell's figure had been conveyed to the King, on 16 March 1643, as part of an argument against the initiation of negotiations with the rebels, see *Ormond MSS*, p. 248.

30 Thomas Waring, *A Brief Narration of the Plotting, Beginning and Carrying on of that Execrable Rebellion and Butcherie in Ireland* (London, 1649/50).

31 John Milton, *Eikonoklastes* (London, 1649), p. 115.

32 John Milton, *Eikonoklastes* (London, 1650), p. 112.

33 Raymond Gillespie, 'Temple's fate: reading *The Irish Rebellion* in late seventeenth-century Ireland', in Ciaran Brady and Jane Ohlmeyer (eds), *British Interventions in Early Modern Ireland* (Cambridge, 2005), p. 325.

34 Sir John Temple, *The Irish Rebellion* (London, 1679), pp. 10–11.

35 Clarke, 'The commission for the despoiled subject, 1641–c.1647' p. 255.

36 Sir Audley Mervyn, *An Exact Relation of All Such Occurences as Have Hapned in the Severall Counties of Donegall, London-derry, Tyrone, and Fermanagh* (London, 1642), p. 5.

37 Edward Hyde, earl of Clarendon, *The History of the Rebellion and Civil Wars in England* (6 vols, Oxford, 1888), vol. i, p. 397.

38 Clarendon, *The History of the Rebellion and Civil Wars in Ireland*, p. 12.

39 David Hume, *The History of Great Britain* (2 vols, Edinburgh and London, 1754–7), vol. i, p. 300; David Berman, "David Hume on the 1641 rebellion in Ireland', *Studies*, 65 (1976), 101–12.

40 J. M. Barkley, *A Short History of the Presbyterian Church in Ireland* (Belfast, 1959), p. 10.

41 Ferdinando Warner, *History of the Rebellion and Civil War in Ireland* (London, 1767), p. 295. A two-volume edition was published in Dublin in the following year.

42 Ibid., p. 295.

43 Ibid., p. 296.

44 Ibid., p. 297.

45 W. E. H. Lecky, *History of England in the Eighteenth Century* (2nd edn, London, 1879).

46 Samuel Gardiner, *History of England from the Accession of James the First to the Civil War* (2nd edn, London, 1883–4), vol. i, pp. 68–9.

47 On Lecky and Froude, see Donal McCartney, *W. E. H. Lecky, Historian and Politician, 1838–1903* (Dublin, 1994), chapter 4.

48 Lecky, *History of England*, vol ii, pp. 152–3.

49 Mary Hickson, *Ireland in the Seventeenth Century, or the Irish Massacres of 1641–2, their Causes and Results* (2 vols, London, 1884).

50 Ibid., vol. i. p. 163. Sir William Petty, *The Political anatomy of Ireland* (London, 1691), pp. 17–18.

51 Hickson, *Ireland in the Seventeenth Century*, vol. i, pp. 128–32.

52 *Academy*, new series, vol. 26, no. 638 (26 July 1884), p. 53.

53 *Academy*, new series, vol. 26, nos 640, 642, 644, 645, 647, pp. 95, 121–2, 153–4, 169, 202.

54 J. C. Beckett, *The Making of Modern Ireland* (London, 1966).

55 P. J. Corish, 'The rising of 1641 and the Catholic confederacy, 1641–5', in T. W. Moody, F. X. Martin and F. J. Byrne (eds), *A New History of Ireland, Vol. 3: Early Modern Ireland 1534–1691* (Oxford, 1978), pp. 289–316, at 291–2.

56 P. S. Robinson, *The Plantation of Ulster: British Settlement in an Irish Landscape, 1600–1670* (Dublin, 1984), p. 191.

57 R. F. Foster, *Modern Ireland 1600–1972* (London, 1988), p. 85.

58 Jonathan Bardon, *A History of Ulster* (Belfast, 1992), p. 138.

59 S. J. Connolly, *Divided Kingdom: Ireland, 1630–1800* (Oxford, 2008), p. 46.

60 Warner, *Rebellion and Civil-War*, p. 159.

61 Ibid., p. 294.

62 Ibid., p. 295.

63 Harl. MS 5999.

64 Hilary Simms, 'Violence in County Armagh, 1641', in Brian Mac Cuarta (ed.), *Ulster 1641: Aspects of the Rising* (Belfast, 1993), pp. 122–38.

65 Harl. MS 5999, fols 29r–29v.

66 TCD MS 831, fol. 30r (Ann Dudd).

67 TCD MS 831, fol. 19r (Elizabeth Vawse).

68 TCD MS 831, fol. 51r (Ellynor Bryant); fols 49v–50v (James Stevenson).

4

1641 in a colonial context

NICHOLAS CANNY

When, for the purposes of this chapter, I was commissioned to consider the Irish Insurrection of 1641 in a colonial context it brought to mind D. B. Quinn's excellent but now seldom-cited 1966 book, *The Elizabethans and the Irish*, and particularly its ninth chapter 'Ireland and America intertwined'.[1] This chapter was devoted principally to two issues. The first focused on how negative depictions of Native Americans constructed by Elizabethan adventurers were sometimes evocative of, or even influenced by, what English adventurers had to say of the social and political mores of the populations of Ireland, especially the Gaelic Irish. It also considered the reverse of this: how English adventurers in Ireland sometimes likened what they described as the 'manners' of the Gaelic Irish to social practices they associated with the native population of America. Quinn was keenly conscious of the preposterous nature of Elizabethan claims that the Gaelic Irish and Native Americas were kindred peoples. He had no doubt, however, that some Elizabethan authors, and their readers in England, were convinced that the Gaelic Irish and Amerindian peoples operated at a similarly low level of cultural attainment, which corresponded with that of the ancient inhabitants of Britain before they had been brought to a civil condition through a process of conquest.[2] This implied, of course, that the English had a moral obligation to bring the native Irish and the native Americans to civility through a process of conquest in the same way that the ancient Romans had rescued their own ancestors from barbarism. The second problem posed, but not resolved, by Quinn considered whether the rhetorical representation of people in a negative or dismissive fashion made it easier for some English adventurers to inflict cruel or extra-legal actions (including massacre) upon elements of the Gaelic Irish and Native American populations.

Quinn's work on Ireland, however, has fallen out of favour with many recent historians, and particularly with advocates of the New British History who take a special interest in the early modern period. Rather than concede that Ireland's historical experience during the sixteenth and seventeenth centuries was significantly different from that of Britain in matters other than confessional choice, the New British historians concentrate on what Ireland and Britain shared in common. Consequently, they tend to dismiss English negative portrayal of Irish people as inconsequential rhetoric, and to disregard evidence that the English crown government did not always intend to absorb all elements of the population of Ireland into a single British polity. While few practitioners of New British History take cognizance of the very extensive secondary literature on English (and also Scottish) efforts to create British-like communities on the far side of the Atlantic, they also discount the evidence that English officials in Ireland resorted to legal and military stratagems that would not have been considered appropriate for England and Wales; whatever of Scotland.[3] This chapter will attempt to extend the Quinn discourse into the seventeenth century, and in the course of doing so reopen the debate over the context English people of the sixteenth and the seventeenth centuries considered appropriate for discussing the condition of Ireland.

There are continued references by seventeenth-century English people to the supposed cultural shortcomings of Irish and Native American populations, cited with the purpose of debasing both peoples. In the case of Ireland, however, English invective against the different segments of the country's population tapered off after the first decade of the seventeenth century, when conditions became more orderly throughout the country. Moreover, disparaging comments became increasingly couched in the rich anti-Catholic rhetoric commonplace in England, rather than the cultural terms favoured in Elizabethan discourse on Ireland.[4] Consequently, when studied together over the full course of the seventeenth century, the differences between England's engagement with societies in Ireland and North America are more striking than the similarities. Also, as the seventeenth century proceeded, the promoters of plantations in the two locations competed with each other to attract desirable Protestant settlers from Britain or further afield.[5] The fact, however, that Ireland was subjected to repeated phases of plantation during the early modern centuries indicates that it was treated differently from the other domestic jurisdictions of the British monarchy. Indeed, many in Britain considered Ireland to be a place where colonies might be established even when the jurisdiction as a whole was being described as a kingdom.

Evidence of parallels between England's engagement with Ireland and North America can be found in violent actions against Native American peoples during the early decades of the seventeenth century. The massacre of the population of an entire village of Pequot Indians by English colonists in 1637, for example, bore some resemblance to mass killings enacted by English soldiers

on Rathlin Island in 1575 and at Mullaghmast in 1578. However plausible it
might be to liken these events, it is impossible to point to any direct causal
connections, given that those responsible for the Pequot massacre were hard-
ened soldiers who had fought with the Elizabethan army in the Low Countries,
rather than veterans of the Irish war during the final years of Elizabeth's
reign.[6] Colonial parallels for what happened in Ireland in 1641 (or for particular episodes within what was a very complex disturbance) prove equally
difficult to find. Essentially, the Irish insurrection of 1641 represented an
assault by the Catholic Irish upon the English and Scots who had settled in
their midst. The search for an American counterpart to this major Irish
conflagration, therefore, must be confined to episodes where Native Americans
engaged in what the English described as a surprise attack upon 'defenceless'
victims; of which there are many examples.[7]

Among the English-language texts devoted to a discussion of what happened in Ireland in 1641, many of those composed *after the event* portrayed
an unjustified attack upon innocent settlers. Plentiful evidence within these
texts suggests that English authors again drew upon the vocabulary of cultural
disparagement rampant in Elizabethan writing on Ireland. On the other hand,
those, whether Irish or English, who wrote of the condition of Ireland in the
decades *previous to 1641*, usually represented Ireland as a kingdom, and rejected
the colonial template as inappropriate for sustained discussion. Nonetheless,
some English officials who then expounded on Ireland still made some use
of the culturally abusive language of the Elizabethans, mingled now with the
florid vocabulary of anti-Catholicism, whenever they sought to justify the
expropriation of the property of surviving Irish landowners. Lord Deputy
Thomas Wentworth certainly believed that his allegations of the cultural and
religious deficiencies of the Irish justified him in depriving them of much of
their property and denying them rights and liberties which people in England
took for granted. Wentworth also reverted to the narrow English view, widely
held in Elizabeth's reign, that the Scots (whether Catholic or Protestant,
Highland or Lowland) had no business in Ireland, and could be treated with
contempt. More controversial in the eyes of contemporaries was his further
contention that English-born Protestants, resident in Ireland for less than a
generation, had become corrupt within a colonial environment where he
contended English ethical norms did not apply.[8]

Nonetheless, participants in political debate during the first half of the
seventeenth century, including Wentworth, generally chose a more measured
vocabulary than their sixteenth-century predecessors when discussing Irish
affairs. This is explained in part by the fact that the crown government now
dealt with a more compliant population, which included substantial communities of English and Scottish Protestant settlers. These newcomers, for
the most part, displaced those most vehemently opposed to English rule in

Ireland, who had either been killed in wartime or fled the country to take refuge in Catholic Europe.[9] The generally peaceful condition of Ireland from 1603 to 1641 encouraged many to see the country as one of the three composite monarchies ruled over by the British crown. Many Catholic exiles, and those in Ireland who identified with them, also took to describing Ireland as a kingdom, albeit a kingdom that might be offered to a Catholic monarch from the continent.[10] Those exiles who sought a more radical solution for the future governance of Ireland similarly looked to European rather than colonial models. These contemplated a Republic that would make allowance for provincial (and presumably ethnic) particularities, which, for them, would be a Catholic counterpart to the Protestant Republic in the United Provinces.[11]

Spanish intervention in the Nine Years' War, 1594–1603 is another factor that accounts for the normalisation, or Europeanisation, of the vocabulary employed to discuss the condition of Ireland. Before this, English commentators depicted most conflict in Ireland either as unwarranted rebellions against a legitimate monarch fought by renegades who adopted cowardly guerrilla tactics and refused to confront the crown army in the open field, or as wasteful internecine warfare that produced mindless destruction of property and the impoverishment of the most vulnerable in Irish society.[12] Once Spain became formally involved, participants on both sides took to describing the war, especially when discussed retrospectively, as part of a wider European Catholic/Protestant conflict.[13] Defeat for the Catholic interest meant the loss of property and political power for the Catholic population of Ireland, as would have happened to the defeated side in any such European conflict. Moreover, the advocates of the Catholic interest, and most particularly those who went into exile in the aftermath of defeat, represented themselves to the Spanish authorities as people who had suffered harsh penalties for their attachment to their faith and to the Spanish crown, rather than as victims of a colonial conflict. They believed that they could look forward to a recovery of what they had lost only in the event of a further outbreak of hostilities between England and Spain.[14]

On the other side, while English and Scottish Protestants in Ireland (or those who spoke on their behalf) still represented themselves as being engaged upon a civilising and missionary endeavour, they seldom pronounced their mission in colonial terms, except when advocating plantation as the prime instrument for Anglicising and Protestantising the country. They also took to describing the Nine Years War as a European conflict, in which English forces, aided by Irish allies, confronted an invasion force supplied by the Spanish monarch and supported by those in Ireland opposed to the English crown. Moreover, the rejection by some Irish of the crown's authority was increasingly attributed to the persuasions of Irish Catholic bishops, inspired by the Papacy, rather than as the product of innate barbaric opposition to civility.[15]

After attaining victory in the Nine Years War and implementing a sequence of plantations, most notably in the Province of Ulster, British Protestants in seventeenth-century Ireland portrayed themselves as a dominant minority, whose pre-eminence over feeble demilitarised opponents would be threatened only in the event of the discontented elements within the country receiving military assistance from Spain, or more specifically from Irish regiments in the army of Spain. Protestant clergy in Ireland proved less sanguine, but even their jeremiads were couched in terms that would have been familiar to Protestants throughout Europe. In these they predicted that if true believers in either Britain or Ireland strayed from the path of righteousness, God would permit evil to befall them, at least for an interlude, as a trial of their faith, while keeping a watchful eye on the fate of Protestant communities in Bohemia, the Palatinate and elsewhere on Continental Europe.[16] Speaking in these apocalyptic terms, the clergy readily recalled the martyrologies of those who had died for true religion in these and other European conflicts, particularly in Marian England and during the course of the Wars of Religion in France. This mode of thinking explains why, when the doomsday situation did materialise in the shape of the Irish Catholic uprising of 1641, some clergy immediately devoted themselves to compiling witness statements from among the Protestant survivors, which would among other things supply material for an Irish Protestant martyrology analogous to Foxe's Book of Martyrs.[17]

Taking their lead from contemporary explanations, historians of the twenty-first century (including the present author) have interpreted the outbreak of the 1641 insurrection in Ireland either in a Three Kingdom's context or as part of a broader Catholic/Protestant conflict that culminated in the Thirty Years War.[18] The colonial context, however, so frequently invoked in the discourses of the sixteenth century, was never entirely forgotten by English contemporaries. In the months and years after the 1641 insurrection it re-emerged more plainly in the writings of those Protestants who sought to explain why the Irish Catholic population rose in arms to slay their unsuspecting Protestant neighbours. They began by locating events within a European context contending that the Pope with his priestly conspirators had used the Catholic landowners to effect the destruction of all the Protestants in Ireland. For some, this assault presaged the first step towards reversing the success of the Protestant Reformation in England and Scotland as well. As they proceeded, however, several authors attributed the sheer brutality and perverse destruction, which they described in detail, to the innate barbarism of the Irish. This subsequently justified wreaking total revenge upon the perpetrators, as England's rulers had long been responsible for eliminating barbarism from Ireland.

Most commentators, including the continental authors Gerard and Arnold Boate, who drew their information from Irish Protestant refugees in London as well as from personal observation, cited the twelfth-century commentaries of Giraldus Cambrensis to support their claims concerning the innate barbarism of the Irish. The events of 1641 confirmed for the Boate brothers what they had read of the Irish in Cambrensis and in the works of other medieval detractors, when 'those barbarians, the naturall inhabitants of Ireland' not only 'murdered or expelled their English neighbours (upon whom with an unheard-of and treacherous cruelty they fell in the midst of a deep peace without any the least provocation)' but they also:

> endeavoured quite to extinguish the memory of them, and of all the civility and good things by them [the English] introduced amongst that wild nation; and consequently in most places they [the Irish] did not only demolish the houses built by the English, the gardens and enclosures made by them, the orchards and hedges by them planted, but destroyed whole droves and flocks of English Cows and Sheep, so as they were not able with all their insatiable gluttony to devour the tenth part, but left the rest lie stinking and rotting in the fields. [19]

The Boate brothers and other Protestant commentators attributed the character of the Irish assault upon an unsuspecting settler population to a cultural recidivism innate to all barbarians. Here they were influenced by medieval and Elizabethan authors who had expounded on the 'degeneration' of successive waves of civil settlers introduced to Ireland through the centuries. Through their access to an altogether more fertile repertoire of atrocity narratives (actual or exaggerated) than had been available to Elizabethan authors, they described in more graphic terms than their predecessors how an apparently civil people could revert to barbaric practice. For example, in the late sixteenth-century when the poet Edmund Spenser strove to evoke revulsion against barbaric practice, his depiction of ghoulish behaviour came from classical, mythological or entirely fictional incidents, more than from reference to contemporary incidents in Ireland or the Netherlands, which he only occasionally alluded to, and then in veiled allegory. [20] Protestant authors of the mid-seventeenth century, however, who wished to depict any particular people as barbaric had less need to look to classical literature for suitable illustrations of inhumane actions because they could presume that their audiences would be familiar with an extraordinary range of the tortures and cruel rituals that humans inflicted on each other. Woodcuts and copper engravings regularly enhanced texts devoted particularly to portraying the tyranny inflicted by Catholics upon true believers. Representations of Spanish cruelty in the Low Countries were often augmented by reference to the treatment meted out by the conquistadores to the native populations of the Americas. Those who wished to render more compelling depictions of Spanish tyranny extended their purview to the colonies and took to citing the moralising criticism of the missionary priest Fra Bartolomé de Las Casas. Las Casas complained that Spanish colonists in the Americas excessively exploited the native population to advance their own enrichment, neglecting their missionary responsibilities in the process. Protestant anti-Spanish literature took the complaints of Las Casas out of context, while Las Casas himself became almost a Protestant divine by adoption.

Reference to America, and the alleged Spanish tyrannising there, opened the way to representations of the cruelties, cannibalism and sexual aberrations supposedly practiced by Native American peoples within their own communities. The general atrocity literature absorbed these accounts, which were often conflated by publishers, encyclopaedically as in Theodore de Bry's *America*, published from Frankfurt and quickly reprinted and translated into the principal northern European languages during the early years of the seventeenth century. In addition to the wealth of information, De Bry's *America* also served as a powerful Protestant polemic that enriched the imagination of Protestants whenever they contemplated victim experience, by effecting a visual cross-fertilisation of the cruelties practiced in various parts of the world. These sometimes made reference to the ungodly barbarism of Native American populations, but they devoted particular attention to the tyranny of Catholics, whenever they had the opportunity to laud it over others, whether Native Americans or upholders of the true religion.[21]

The fertility of Protestant imagination in conjuring up images of atrocity helps explains the readiness with which Protestants survivors from the 1641 insurrection in Ireland came forward with lurid horror stories, which they swore had been narrated to them by credible third party witnesses. Many of the stories from the depositions were further recorded in the multitude of pamphlet narrations of these same events, published in the immediate aftermath of the insurrection, and thus came to be accepted as truth by a wide British Protestant audience. Modern scholars frequently dismiss these accounts as nothing more than propaganda reliant entirely on hearsay evidence. Events such as spectres appearing at the sites of atrocity both before and after the episodes being described; pregnant women being hanged and delivered of dead infants while on the gallows; babies being torn from the wombs of women; foetuses being fed to dogs; the heads of babies being shattered on rocks; and human fat being rendered into candles, may never have occurred, but these would have seemed very real to those who heard and read of them, not least because of their familiarity with conflated atrocity narratives within Europe and beyond.[22] These narrations did much to convince a wider public that the Irish who perpetrated these atrocities were not only bloody papists but also outlandish barbarians, living beyond the realm of civil as well as of Christian community.

The narrators and publishers of such alleged atrocities not only reverted to the Elizabethan practice of levelling charges of cultural depravity against the Irish, which they sustained by reference to barbaric practice, they also pointedly chose modes of presentation which readers would have associated with stories of attacks perpetrated by Native Americans upon English settlers. In fact, the structure of the most potent Protestant text that accounted for, and described, the Irish Catholic insurrection of 1641 was almost identical to the best-known narration of a widely publicised English colonial reverse; the so-called Virginia massacre of 1622. The two texts are Sir John Temple, *The Irish Rebellion: or, an History of the Attempts of the Irish Papists to extirpate the Protestants in the Kingdom of Ireland; together with the Barbarous Cruelties and Bloody Massacres which ensued thereupon*, published in London in 1646, and Edward Waterhouse, *A Declaration of the State of the Colony and Affairs in Virginia with A Relation of the Barbarous Massacre in the time of Peace and League*, published in London in 1622.[23]

English officials in Ireland during the 1640s attributed the planning of what they asserted was an intended massacre of all Protestants in Ireland to the Pope and his priestly agents in Ireland. The views of Sir John Temple, Master of the Rolls in the Dublin administration, accorded with this interpretation.[24] His book, *The Irish Rebellion*, seemed very European in its focus. He likened the task of explaining and describing the events of 1641 in Ireland to that undertaken, but never completed, by Monsieur du Plessis, a minister of state to King Henry IV of France, 'to write a History of those times wherein he lived', which for du Plessis involved the Wars of Religion in France, including the notorious St Bartholomew's Day Massacre of 1572.[25] As with du Plessis in the case of France, Temple wished posterity to know 'of the first beginnings and fatal progress of this rebellion, together with the horrid cruelties most unmercifully exercised by the *Irish Rebels*, upon the *British* and *Protestants* within this Kingdom of *Ireland*'.[26]

Temple traced the origins of the Irish who, despite the efforts of missionaries from Britain during medieval times to effect 'the conversion of a barbarous people', retained their 'depraved and barbarous manners' until 1172, when King Henry II of England undertook 'to conquer Ireland and reduce those beastly men unto the way of truth'.[27] There, according to Temple, King Henry found:

> a beastly people indeed; for the inhabitants were generally devoid of all manner of civility, governed by no settled laws, living like beasts, biting and devouring one another, without all rules, customs, or reasonable constitutions, either for regulation of property, or against open force and violence; most notorious murthers, rapes, robberies, and all other acts of inhumanity and barbarism, raging without control, or due course of punishment.[28]

This condition of the people, averred Temple, left King Henry with no option but to seize 'by the sword . . . all the lands of the whole kingdom'. This action was further justified, claimed Temple, because:

the land itself he found it good, and flourishing with many excellent commodities, plentiful in all kinds of provisions, the soil rich and fertile, the air
sweet and temperate, the havens very safe and commodious, several towns and
little villages scattered up and down in the several parts of the country; but the
buildings so poor and contemptible, as, when the King arrived at Dublin, their
chief city, and finding there neither place for receipt or entertainment, he set
up a long house made of smooth wattles, after the manner of the country, and
therein kept his Christmas. [29]

Temple deployed the juxtaposition between a barbarous people and a
fruitful land throughout his narration to explain how, over the centuries,
several English monarchs had introduced civil institutions and civil colonies
to Ireland. They repeatedly found, however, that whenever the settlers extended
the hand of friendship the Irish took advantage of the situation to attack
them, so that 'Ireland hath long remained a true *Aceldama*, a Field of Blood,
an unsatiated sepulchre of the English nation'.[30] According to Temple, many
believed that the comprehensive military victory attained by the army of
Queen Elizabeth, and by the subsequent sequence of plantations had brought
this cycle of violence to and end. The Protestant newcomers

> who with great cost and much industry, planted themselves so firmly, as they
> became a great security to the country, and were a most especial means to
> introduce civility in those parts: so as now the whole Kingdom began exceed-
> ingly to flourish in costly buildings and all manner of improvements; the
> people to multiply and increase, and the very Irish seemed to be much satisfied
> with the benefits of that peaceable government, and general tranquillity, which
> they so happily enjoyed. [31]

Moreover, during the reign of King Charles I, Irish Catholics had been ruled
over by a government that was most 'sweet tempered, and carried on with
great lenity and moderation'.[32] The authorities had even allowed Catholics
to enjoy 'the private exercise of all their religious rites and ceremonies . . .
without any manner of disturbance'.[33] Indeed, claimed Temple, the condition
of the country was so placid that:

> the ancient animosities and hatred which the Irish had ever observed to bear
> unto the English nation, they seemed now to be quite deposited and buried in
> a firm Conglutination of their affections, and national Obligation passed between
> them. The two nations had now lived together 40 years in peace, with great
> security and comfort, which had in a manner consolidated them into one body,
> knit and compacted together with all those bonds and ligatures of friendship,
> alliance and consanguinity, as might make up a constant and perpetual Union
> betwixt them. Their intermarriages were frequent, gossipred, fostering, relations
> of much dearness among the Irish, together with all others of tenancy, neigh-
> bourhood, and service, interchangeably passed among them; nay, they had
> made as it were a kind of mutual transmigration into each others manners,

many English being strangely degenerated into Irish affections and customs, and many Irish, especially of the better sort, having taken up the English language, apparel, and decent manner of living in their private houses. [34]

As he contemplated the sudden cancellation of such marks of reciprocal respect once the Irish resorted to rebellion on 23 October 1641, Temple was convinced that the apparent contentment of the Irish Catholics had been cynically simulated. They had been plotting, he now proclaimed, to insinuate themselves into the homes and communities, as well as into the affections, of the settlers so they would have the opportunity to 'seize most treacherously' the fortified positions held by the English, and to surprise, rob and murder all British Protestants in Ireland. According to Temple, this stratagem proved so successful that the 'English were . . . easily over-run . . . and so suddenly swallowed up before they could make any manner of resistance in the very beginnings of the rebellion'.[35] During the course of this onslaught, claimed Temple:

> their servants were killed as they were ploughing in the fields, husbands cut to pieces in the presence of their wives, their children's brains dashed out before their faces; others had all their goods and cattle seized and carried away; their houses burnt, their habitations laid waste and all as it were at an instant, before they could suspect the Irish for their enemies, or any ways imagine that they had it in their hearts, or in their power, to offer so great violence, or do such mischief unto them. [36]

Temple cited the prevailing tranquillity in the months prior to the insurrection, the suddenness of the insurrection itself, its universality, and the common form that the assault upon the English assumed in all parts of the country, as proof that the insurrection had been long in preparation. The intelligence provided to the government in Dublin by Owen O'Connolly on the night of 22 October 1641, of the plans by a significant number of Irish Catholic noblemen and their followers to seize Dublin Castle, gave concrete form to Temple's circumstantial evidence. Temple described O'Connolly as 'a gentleman of a mere Irish family, but one that had long lived among the English, and had been trained up in the true Protestant religion'. His information, which officials initially considered implausible, ultimately led to a series of arrests which, according to Temple, saved the Castle from being taken and the Protestants in Dublin from being butchered.[37] Finally, the examinations, 'taken upon oath' from the Protestant survivors of the insurrection, provided for Temple the ultimate proof that the rebels intended a comprehensive massacre of settlers. From these witness statements, he averred:

> it may easily be conjectured how fatally the first Plot took, how furiously the rebels, throughout all parts of the kingdom, proceeded in their bloody executions, and what were the courses they took to bring about so suddenly the universal destruction of all the British and Protestants there planted. [38]

Temple, in common with his colleagues in the Dublin government, attributed the ultimate responsibility for the insurrection to priests, who had:

> charmed the Irish, and laid such bloody impressions upon them, as it was held, according to the Maxims they had received, a mortal sin to give any relief or protection to the English. All bonds and ties of faith and friendship were now broken; the Irish landlords made a prey of their English tenants; the Irish tenants and servants a sacrifice of their English landlords and masters; one neighbour cruelly murdered by another; the very Irish children in the very beginning fell to strip and kill English children; all other relations were quite cancelled and laid aside, and it was now esteemed a meritorious act in any of them that could, by any means or ways whatsoever, bring an Englishman to the slaughter.[39]

According to Temple, the Irish had been easily gulled by their priests to act as they did because they remained every bit as barbaric as their ancestors who King Henry II had encountered. Temple contended, however, that the Irish in 1641 operated more viciously and effectively than their twelfth-century progenitors because they:[40]

> living promiscuously among the British in all parts, [and] having from their Priests received the watch-word both for time and place, rose up, as it were actuated by one and the same spirit, in all places . . . at one and the same time; and so in a moment fell upon them, murdering some, stripping only or expelling others out of their habitations.

Temple concluded from this most recent manifestation of barbarous treachery by Irish people that no further effort should be made to bring them to civility. Rather, he pronounced, the English were now liberated from all previous constraints and free to have:[41]

> such a wall of separation set up betwixt the Irish and British as it shall not be in their [the Irish] power to rise up (as now and in all former ages they have done) to destroy and root them [the British] out in a moment.

The solution of permanent separation offered by Temple was clearly a colonial one, based on the contention that the Irish were not amenable to civil any more than religious reform. Thus, notwithstanding his acknowledgement of the service rendered by Owen O'Connolly who had proven himself a true convert, Temple decreed, as emphatically as any Elizabethan author had ever done, that the Irish as barbarians should never henceforth be considered the cultural or legal equals of English people. Temple justified his recommendation by reference to Irish and European precedent, and, like his Elizabethan counterparts, he drew heavily upon the anti-Irish invective of Giraldus Cambrensis. Unlike the Elizabethan authors, however, Temple made no reference to England's civilising role in North America to illuminate his views on Ireland. Neither he, nor his readers, would have considered this necessary because in the intervening half century several literatures of atrocity had been conflated into one, which represented all barbarians – whether from Europe or America; from past centuries or from the present – as similarly bent on the destruction of civil people and the symbols of an ordered life.

The extent to which Temple's *The Irish Rebellion* can be taken as a prime example of atrocity literature conceived in the colonial mode becomes clear when it is considered together with *A Declaration of the State of the Colony and Affairs in Virginia* by Edward Waterhouse, whose possible relative of the same name and of equally forceful opinions had served in Elizabethan Ireland.[42] The Waterhouse text described the so-called massacre of 347 English settlers by 'Native Infidels' in the colony of Virginia on 22 March 1622, and prescribed for the future security of that colony.[43] Faithful to the colonial atrocity genre, Waterhouse not only explained why it had been possible for despised enemies to enact the particular atrocity, he also advocated revenge and a fresh beginning. This latter would occur only with the arrival of new settlers to replace those who had been slaughtered. They would be placed in a secure environment which no enemy might penetrate. Each text, therefore, served as a *vade mecum* for those planters, settlers, clergy, artisans, merchants and wives considered necessary to advance the wealth and security of the specific colonial site under discussion. In order to be plausible, this reportage had to be based on 'eye-witness' accounts or on letters from credible sources. Thus, whereas Temple cited letters from contemporaries who had been in Ireland when the insurrection occurred, as well as depositions from survivors, the 'truth' in the Waterhouse text was 'drawn from the relation of some of those that were beholders of that tragedy, and who hardly escaped from tasting of the same cup, as also from the letters . . . by the Governor and other gentlemen of quality'.[44]

Given their longer-term purpose, colonial discourses always waxed lyrical on the plentifulness of the natural resources associated with a site for possible future settlement. Temple spoke eloquently of the paradisiac environment that had greeted King Henry II in Ireland, while Edward Waterhouse described Virginia as a:

> spacious and fruitful country . . . naturally rich, exceedingly well watered, very temperate, and healthful to the inhabitants, abounding with as many natural blessings, and replenished with as goodly woods, and those full of deer and sundry other beasts for man's sustenance; and the seas and rivers thereof (many therein being exceeding fair and navigable) as full of excellent fish of diverse sorts, and both water & land yielding as great variety of fowl, as any country in the world is known to afford.[45]

As Temple did when describing Ireland a quarter of a century later, Waterhouse, attributed the backwardness of Virginia to the indigenous inhabitants: 'whose barbarous savageness needs more cultivation than the ground itself, being more overspread with incivility and treachery, than that [the ground] with briars'.[46]

Notwithstanding the untamed character of the natives of Virginia, the English who encountered them, claimed Waterhouse, found them seemingly docile to the point where the newcomers dedicated themselves to reforming civil and spiritual conditions with their:

> houses generally set open to the savages, who were always friendly entertained at the tables of the English, and commonly lodged in their bed chambers . . . their familiarity with the natives, seeming to open a fair gate for their conversion to Christianity.[47]

Because the English in Virginia proceeded gently with the natives, it proved possible to negotiate:

> a peace (as all men thought) sure and inviolable, not only because it was solemnly ratified and sworn, and at the request of the native king stamped in brass and fixed to one of his oaks of note, but as being advantageous to both parts; to the savages as the weaker, under which they were safely sheltered and defended; to us, as being the easiest way then thought to pursue and advance our projects of buildings, plantings, and effecting their conversion by peaceful and fair means.[48]

This 'conceit of firm peace and amity', which subsequent events proved to be but 'treacherous dissimulation of that people who then had contrived our destruction', convinced the English in Virginia to abandon their usual defensive precautions.[49] In the lead up, therefore, to the day of the planned massacre, 'there was seldom if never a sword worn, and a piece seldomer except for a deer or fowl'. This gullibility of the English, rather than the potency of the natives, explained how the English became victims of 'the devilish murder that ensued'.[50]

In this instance, Waterhouse described, as Temple did of 1641, how the natives established 'a general combination [and] in one day plotted to subvert their whole colony, and at one instant of time' to murder all settlers dispersed in 'several plantations' on either side of the Chesapeake waterway.[51] The stratagem of the natives involved going 'unarmed . . . without bows and arrows, or other weapons' into the houses of the English on the evening of the 21 March 1622 and also 'on the Friday morning (the fatal day) the 22 March', bringing with them:

> deer, turkeys, fish, furs, and other provisions to sell and truck with us for glass, beads and other trifles; yea in some places sat down at breakfast with our people at their tables, whom immediately with their own tools and weapons, either laid down or standing in their houses, they basely and barbarously

murdered, not sparing either age or sex, man, woman or child; so sudden in their cruel execution, that few or none discerned the weapon or blow that brought them to destruction.[52]

In Virginia on 'that fatal Friday morning' a total of 'three hundred forty seven men, women and children':

> fell under the bloody and barbarous hands of that perfidious and inhumane people, contrary to all laws of God and men, of Nature and Nations . . . most by their own weapons, and not being content with taking life alone, they fell after again upon the dead, making as well as they could, a fresh murder, defacing, dragging, and mangling the dead carcasses into many pieces, and carrying some parts away in derision, with base and brutish triumphs.[53]

Waterhouse reported that those killed in Virginia constituted but a fraction of the total settler population – 'about eleven part of twelve still remaining'. The majority had been saved from the intended 'universal slaughter' only 'by the means of some of themselves converted to Christianity'. These native converts, as would be the case with Owen O'Connolly in 1641, become God's 'instruments' to save the lives of those 'whose souls they had formerly saved'.[54] Unlike the reports of 1641, where the name of Owen O'Connolly became celebrated as the *converso* whose intervention saved Dublin's Protestants from slaughter, the Christianised Indians were identified only by the names of their masters who had effected their conversions. It became possible, therefore, to depict all as a 'false hearted people, that know not God nor faith'.[55] As John Temple would do with *The Irish Rebellion*, Waterhouse concluded his text on a triumphant note, pronouncing that the English whose hands had previously been:

> tied with gentleness and fair usage [were] now set at liberty by the treacherous violence of the savages . . . so that [the English] who hitherto [had] had possession of no more ground than their waste, and our purchase at a valuable consideration . . . may now by right of war and law of nations, invade the country, and destroy them who sought to destroy us; whereby we shall enjoy their cultivated places, turning the laborious mattock into the victorious sword (wherein there is more both ease, benefit and glory) and possessing the fruits of other labours.[56]

Waterhouse carefully identified by name and location of all the English who had been killed, because each was now 'a glorious martyr' and also, in a manner similar to the 1641 depositions, to ensure 'that their lawful heirs, by this notice given, may take order for the inheriting of their lands and estates in Virginia'.[57]

The texts by Edward Waterhouse and John Temple were not only read extensively by the English audience to which they were initially addressed but proved potent in reminding settlers of succeeding generations in Virginia and Ireland that they should be constantly on their guard against native assault. This, in itself, establishes them as colonial texts, but when they are considered together similarities also emerge between the two publications under the headings of themes, tropes and format. This is not to suggest that Temple plagiarised Waterhouse or was even familiar with his account of the 1622 massacre. The similarities can more probably be attributed to the fact that each belongs to a textual genre of colonial discourse, fashioned to explain, describe and take lessons from assaults launched by those represented as barbaric peoples upon civil settler communities. The formulaic reports suggest that the details had been chosen selectively (if not fabricated) in order to justify the dramatic remedial action being recommended. Each of the two authors would have recognised that the course outlined as a guide for future policy deviated from what would have been considered acceptable by British, or indeed Christian, norms. An appreciation of this reality explains why each chose for his discourse a genre specifically designed to 'exoticise' and dehumanise their adversaries. This, in turn, enabled them to account for the collapse of the relationship between the English/British settler communities and those native peoples for whose governance they had assumed responsibility. The newcomers resorted to sententious outpourings in preference to engaging upon a critical analysis of their own dealings with the populations they depicted as their cultural inferiors. They concluded that people, who by their actions and way of life had proven themselves to be uncivil, could be denied those entitlements to property, political authority or even to life itself, previously conceded to them by the English. In each instance, a case was made to justify further acts of expropriation and colonisation, leading to a consolidation of English power and the advance of civility into previously barbaric places.

This brings us back to the question with which this chapter opened – whether it is appropriate to locate developments in seventeenth-century Ireland within a colonial context? The evidence suggests that the answer is less straightforward than the question. The Catholic population of Ireland, and particularly those of Gaelic ancestry, always resented being likened to barbarians or American Indians. As the seventeenth century progressed, they began to place greater emphasis than their sixteenth-century forbears on an entitlement to be considered a European nation. English observers proved more willing than their Elizabethan predecessors to acknowledge Ireland as a kingdom, with the potential to become a constitutional equal to the kingdoms of England and Scotland, where the inhabitants might enjoy the same rights under the law as did English subjects of the same crown. Despite such benevolent expressions, some officers of the crown in Ireland continuously challenged the titles of Irish landowners. Moreover, some publicists constantly harkened back to the arguments of the Elizabethans that the Irish could not be trusted with the ownership of property and with political power either, because they were Catholic, or uncivil, or both. As a result, the position of Irish subjects under the English crown was altogether less secure than that of their English or Scottish counterparts within their respective kingdoms. Any ambivalence towards the Catholic community in Ireland in normal times gave way at moments of crisis to the certainty that they had no entitlement to be considered civil people, much less subjects of the British monarchy.

Sir John Temple is a prime example of an official who lost no time in locating the Irish insurrection in a colonial context, and in formulating the argument that the insurrection provided an opportunity to the English to enter upon a fresh phase of colonisation. Unlike the Elizabethan authors, however, who penned texts to the same purpose, Temple drew no parallels between England's engagement with Irish Catholics and simultaneous English engagements with the indigenous population of North America. Temple did not see the need to make such connections, as Irish Catholics were clearly barbarians, and had repeatedly demonstrated their unwillingness to be absorbed into civil society. Temple's negative recommendations clearly went beyond being mere rhetoric. As a senior government official he could directly influence policy, but more importantly his idea to place a permanent wall of separation between Catholic and Protestant people in Ireland clearly inspired some of the more draconian measures considered by Cromwellian officials just a few years later.[58]

Historians, therefore, have no choice but to follow the example set by David B. Quinn in 1966 and keep an open mind to considering developments in early modern Ireland in a colonial context, if for no other reason than that English actors of the time sometimes did so. This enabled them to justify the employment of extreme measures in Ireland that involved the curtailment of fundamental rights, which would have been considered reprehensible if recommended for application within England. Historians who disregard discontinuities in practice between what happened in Britain and Ireland, and ignore extreme assertions, such as those made by Sir John Temple in *The Irish Rebellion*, have little prospect of understanding the totality of the relationship between Britain and Ireland during the early modern centuries.

NOTES

1 D. B. Quinn, *The Elizabethans and the Irish* (Ithaca, 1966), pp. 106–22; see also Quinn, *Ireland and America: Their Early Associations, 1500–1640* (Liverpool University Press, 1991); Quinn was writing in the tradition of Margaret T. Hodgen, *Early Anthropology in the Sixteenth and Seventeenth Centuries* (Philadelphia, 1964), which is also a book now seldom cited.

2 This suggestion was promoted pictorially in the drawings of John White where his depiction of the inhabitants of Roanoke island were juxtaposed with those of

Ancient Picts and of a Tartar or Uzbek man; see Paul Hulton, *America 1585: The Complete Drawings of John White* (Chapel Hill and London, 1984).

3 For two very different examples of challenge to the Atlantic approach, see Hiram Morgan's review of Nicholas Canny, *Kingdom and Colony: Ireland in the Atlantic World, 1560–1800* (Baltimore, 1988), *International History Review*, 13 (1991), 801–6 and Rory Rapple, 'Writing about violence in the Tudor kingdoms', *Historical Journal*, 54 (2011), 829–54. For a convenient introduction to the debates concerning the New British History, see Alexander Grant and Keith Stringer, *Uniting the Kingdom? The Making of British History* (London, 1995); and for an example of the New British History in Irish livery, see Steven Ellis and Sarah Barber (eds), *Conquest and Union: Fashioning a British State, 1485–1625* (London, 1995). For an example of a multi-authored collection on early modern Ireland that deliberately concentrates on Irish commonality with Britain and continuity over time, see Ciaran Brady and Jane Ohlmeyer (eds), *British Interventions in Early Modern Ireland* (Cambridge, 2005); see also a review of that volume by Nicholas Canny, in *English Historical Review*, 121 (2006), 840–2. For a volume that, while not conceived in the Atlantic mode, exposes a fault line in the New British History paradigm, see David Edwards, Pádraig Lenihan and Clodagh Tait (eds), *Age of Atrocity: Violence and Political Conflict in Early Modern Ireland* (Dublin, 2007), which is that discussed by Rory Rapple in the publication cited above.

4 Alan Ford, *The Protestant Reformation in Ireland, 1590–1641* (Frankfurt am Main, 1985).

5 The extent to which the British experience of populating Ireland countered their efforts to draw settlers to America is discussed in Nicholas Canny, 'The origins of Empire: an introduction', in Nicholas Canny (ed.), *The Origins of Empire, vol. I: The Oxford History of the British Empire* (Oxford, 1998), pp. 1–33; for an example of some seventeenth-century continuity of practice between Ireland and America, see Annaleigh Margey, 'Representing Colonial landscapes: early English maps on Ulster and Virginia, 1580–1612', in Brian Mac Cuarta, S. J. (ed.), *Reshaping Ireland, 1550–1700: Colonization and its Consequences – Essays Presented to Nicholas Canny* (Dublin, 2011), pp. 61–81.

6 On Rathlin Island, see Nicholas Canny, *The Elizabethan Conquest of Ireland: A Pattern Established, 1565–76* (Hassocks, 1976), p. 90; on Mullaghmast, Vincent Carey, 'John Derricke's image of Ireland, Sir Henry Sidney and the massacre at Mullaghmast, 1578', *Irish Historical Studies*, 31 (1999), 305–27; Ronald Dale Karr, '"Why should you be so furious": the violence of the Pequot War', *The Journal of American History*, 85 (1998), 876–909; many English soldiers who fought in Ireland during the Nine Years War, 1594–1603, were, of course, veterans from conflict in both the Netherlands and Brittany.

7 Jill Lapore, *The Name of War: King Philip's War and the Origins of American Identity* (New York, 1998), Lapore discusses the 'slippery' nature of words used to describe atrocity by which she means that when actions described by the English as atrocity are considered from a 'native' perspective they can be described as retaliatory actions exerted by an unjustly dispossessed people upon vainglorious colonists; this conflict of opinion has been present in discussions during every century concerning the Irish insurrection/rebellion of 1641.

8 Nicholas Canny, *Making Ireland British, 1580–1650* (Oxford, 2001), pp. 279–85.
9 Gráinne Henry, *The Irish Military Community in Spanish Flanders, 1586–1621* (Dublin, 1992).
10 Bernadette Cunningham, *The Annals of the Four Masters: Irish History, Kingship and Society in the Early Seventeenth Century* (Dublin, 2010); Breandán Ó Buachalla, *The Crown of Ireland* (Research Papers in Irish Studies, 3, Galway, 2006).
11 Tomás Ó Fiach, 'Republicanism and separatism in the seventeenth century', *Léachtaí Cholm Cille*, 2 (1971), 74–87; more generally Hiram Morgan (ed.), *Political Ideology in Ireland, 1541–1641* (Dublin, 1999); Jane H. Ohlmeyer (ed.), *Political Thought in Seventeenth Century Ireland: Kingdom or Colony* (Cambridge, 2000); it is significant that the model of government chosen by the Catholic Confederation during the 1640s and 1650s was structured on provincial lines.
12 Canny, *The Elizabethan Conquest.*
13 Óscar Recio Morales, *Ireland and the Spanish Empire, 1600–1825* (Dublin, 2010); Hiram Morgan (ed.), *The Battle of Kinsale* (Bray, 2004).
14 Morales, *Ireland and the Spanish Empire*; Igor Perez Tostado, *Irish Influence at the Court of Spain in the Seventeenth Century* (Dublin, 2008); Benjamin Hazard, *Faith and Patronage: The Political Career of Flaithrí Ó Maolchonaire, c.1560–1629* (Dublin, 2009).
15 Canny, *Making Ireland British*, pp. 165–76.
16 Ford, *The Protestant Reformation.*
17 On the many purposes behind the collection of the depositions see Aidan Clarke, 'The Commission for the Despoiled Subjects, 1641–7', in Mac Cuarta (ed.), *Reshaping Ireland, 1550–1700*, pp. 241–60.
18 Raymond Gillespie, 'The end of an era: Ulster and the outbreak of the 1641 rising', in Ciaran Brady and Raymond Gillespie (eds), *Natives and Newcomers: The Making of Irish Colonial Society* (Dublin, 1986), pp. 191–213; Michael Perceval Maxwell, *The Outbreak of the Irish Rebellion of 1641* (Dublin, 1994); Canny, *Making Ireland British*, pp. 461–550.
19 Gerard Boate, *Ireland's Naturall History* (London, 1652), reprinted in *A Collection of Tracts and Treatises Illustrative of the Natural History, Antiquities . . . of Ireland* (Dublin, 1860), pp. 1–148, at p. 77.
20 Canny, *Making Ireland British*, pp. 1–58.
21 Jean Frédéric Schaub, 'Violence in the Atlantic: sixteenth and seventeenth centuries', in Nicholas Canny and Philip Morgan (eds), *The Oxford Handbook of the Atlantic World, 1450–1850* (Oxford, 2011), pp. 113–29.
22 The 1641 depositions can be accessed online at http://1641.tcd.ie.
23 John Temple, *The Irish Rebellion: or, an History of the Attempts of the Irish Papists to extirpate the Protestants in the Kingdom of Ireland; together with the Barbarous Cruelties and Bloody Massacres which ensued thereupon* (1646); the page references are from the London edition published in 1746; Edward Waterhouse, *A Declaration of the State of the Colonie and affairs of Virginia: With a relation of the Barbarous Massacre in the time of peace and league, treacherously executed upon the English by the native infidels* (London, 1622).
24 Aidan Clarke, 'Temple, Sir John (1600–77)', in James McGuire and James Quinn (eds), *Dictionary of Irish Biography* (9 vols, Cambridge, 2009), vol. ix, pp. 293–6.

25 Temple, *The Irish Rebellion*, preface, p. v.
26 Ibid., p. vii.
27 Ibid., pp. 6–7.
28 Ibid., pp. 7–8.
29 Ibid., pp. 5–6.
30 Ibid., p. 13.
31 Ibid., pp. 20–1.
32 Ibid., p. 23.
33 Ibid., p. 24.
34 Ibid., p. 25.
35 Ibid., pp. 60, 68.
36 Ibid., pp. 61–2.
37 Ibid., p. 30.
38 Ibid., pp. 215–16.
39 Ibid., p. 61.
40 Ibid.
41 Temple, *The Irish Rebellion,* preface, p. viii.
42 Terry Clavin, 'Waterhouse (Waterhous), Sir Edward (1535–91)', in McGuire and Quinn (eds), *Dictionary of Irish Biography*, ix, 807–8.
43 Waterhouse, *Declaration*, title page.
44 Waterhouse, *Declaration*, sig. A3v.
45 Ibid., sig. B2.
46 Ibid., sig. C2.
47 Ibid., sig. C2v–C3.
48 Ibid., sig. C2v.
49 Ibid., sig. C3.
50 Ibid., sig. C3.
51 Ibid., sig. Dv.
52 Ibid., sig. C3, C3v.
53 Ibid., sig. C3v.
54 Ibid., sig. Dv.
55 Ibid., sig. A3v.
56 Ibid., sig. D3v–D4.
57 Ibid., sig. D and sig. F2. This enumeration of names was prepared by Henry Briggs.
58 John Cunningham, 'Oliver Cromwell and the Cromwellian Settlement of Ireland', *Historical Journal*, 53 (2010), 919–37.

5

Towards a cultural geography
of the 1641 rising/rebellion

WILLIAM J. SMYTH

It is now agreed that the '1641 depositions' comprise a conflation of documents, containing confusing and often contradictory statements of evidence. Even more problematical, these depositions have generated passionate controversies down the centuries and still constitute contested terrain.[1] This chapter seeks to illustrate the role that cartography and geography can play in understanding and contextualising the 1641 rising/rebellion. In addition, the insights and advantages to be gained from bringing a broad-based comparative perspective to bear on the subject will be explored, which in turn will allow for a reconceptualising of the rising/rebellion. From the outset, the difficulty of writing about this topic needs to be noted.[2] Memories of the horrors of 1641 and its aftermath persist to the present – so many innocent lives lost, so many human tragedies piled up across the Irish landscape. Moreover, there is always the danger of bringing too much order to bear on what was a chaotic, highly complex and often paranoid world. To reduce the complexities, the chapter will adopt a ground–up view of the rising/rebellion, based on the evidence of the depositions. Geographic techniques and concepts as well as some anthropological theory will be used to explore the tumultuous, frenetic and often violent activities of the less powerful people. Since the powerless rarely find a place on the public stage, the 1641 depositions provide a unique source for studying the lives and fears of ordinary people in a time of great upheaval. Such people have much to say when they finally get the opportunity.[3]

I

Geographers' first question relates to the 'whereness' of things. Geographers try to situate habitations, events and people as precisely as possible in space. They are better able to do this when dealing with comprehensive sources such as the 1641 depositions, which contain data for all the counties and baronies of Ireland. A series of tables created a kind of cartographic synthesis of the distribution of activities reported in the depositions. These include the record of robberies and material losses, murders/killings of settlers, rare entries on the murders/killings of the Gaelic Irish, the reporting of 'rebel' talk, the desecration of church properties, the intimidation of Protestant settlers to go to Mass, as well as accounts of stripping and other acts of cruelty, burning and pillaging. This anchor map also includes the distribution of Protestant/ planter land as returned in Petty's Down Survey maps of the 1650s.

There are three outstanding regions of devastation and settler disruption and displacement. The core of the Munster province – with foci around the cities of Cork, Limerick and Waterford – reveals a major region of disturbances stretching from south and mid Clare through most of Limerick county, north and mid Cork and also including south Tipperary and much of Waterford. The evidence suggests less unrest in north Clare and north Tipperary as well as a more extensive zone in south-west Munster, all areas characterised by a very small settler population to begin with.

A second, large and strikingly compact zone of settler dislocation comprises much of mid-Leinster, stretching from Dublin westwards through Kildare to King's county (Offaly) and Queen's (Laois) and also including the northern edges of Kilkenny, Carlow, Wexford and all of Wicklow. The extent of pre-1641 settler penetration into the non-plantation zones of Leinster has probably been underestimated in the literature. On the other hand, the evidence suggests that much of south and mid Wexford, Kilkenny, Louth, Meath and Westmeath were less affected by either settler colonisation or disturbances.

The third zone of major dislocation lies in Ulster, with the distribution of losses, expulsions and murders concentrated in a number of core locations – from north Antrim and north-east Londonderry along the Bann, including the countryside of both Antrim and Tyrone flanking Lough Neagh and linking the English settlement of the Lagan valley on into Armagh, mid Monaghan and Cavan with strong extensions into the Connacht/Leinster borderlands. In Connacht, disturbances occur in outlying pockets in central Roscommon and Mayo. A small epicentre of disturbances also includes Galway city and extends northwards, but the greater part of Connacht – without any significant settler presence – remains clear of depositions. On the other hand, for significant areas in Down, mid Antrim and the greater north-west Ulster region, including much of counties Donegal, Londonderry and Tyrone, the available evidence available suggests early settler organisation and resistance and less devastation as a result (Fig. 1).

The elucidation of distributions only marks the beginning of the geographer's quest, who still needs to explore how and why these patterns arose in the first place. This brings in the second theme – contextualising the 1641 rising/

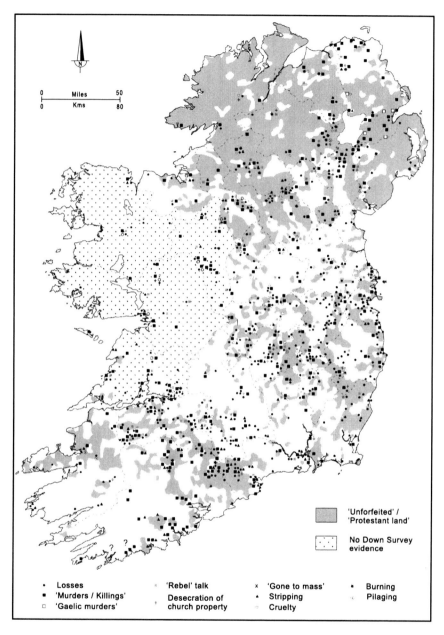

N

| 0 | Miles | 50 |
| 0 | Kms | 80 |

'Unforfeited' /
'Protestant land'

No Down Survey
evidence

•	Losses	″	'Rebel' talk	x	'Gone to mass'	•	Burning
■	'Murders / Killings'		Desecration of	▲	Stripping	··	Pilaging
▫	'Gaelic murders'	+	church property	◦	Cruelty		

Figure 1 Distribution of a range of atrocities and events,
as reported in the 1641 depositions

rebellion in a situation of much uncertainty or, to put it another way, at a time when people of all traditions sought answers in a sea of uncertainties.

II

The mid seventeenth century was a time of very different and fractured perspectives, with significant variations in levels of knowledge and narratives across the island. The depositions highlight such uneven patterns of understanding as rumours and counter-rumours reverberated from parish to parish, county to county and province to province. The depositions are profoundly important to our understanding of the experiences and fears of the often-uprooted Protestant English settlers. They also provide unique insights into the behaviours of the Catholic Irish at a number of class levels. From the depositions (and later Cromwellian examinations), one can document elite Catholic Irish fears, uncertainties and anger about property loss, religious discrimination and the continued erosion of Irish and particularly Old English administrative and judicial functions, which fuelled the 1641 rising/rebellion. There was also a growing recognition of the challenges and threats to Catholic Irish identities, given the powers exercised by the English state and its representatives in Ireland.[4]

The depositions, however, provide far more evidence on the second tier in the rising/rebellion – that of the popular level – although some of the lesser gentry, stronger farmers and clergy clearly formed structural and geographical bridges to elite levels of discourse and action. For the farmers, artisans and smallholders, this was a land-war – a war about restoring rights to ancestral lands, about the right to lease land and to have access to adequate resources and livelihoods. They fought against further displacement, marginalisation and impoverishment, against increased rental dues, tithes and often forced labour services. The destruction of protestant settler properties – the burning of settler mansions and farmhouses, the digging up of gardens, the razing of enclosures and the killing of English sheep and cattle – points to a deep symbolic motive, namely the wiping out of the cultural capital of the coloniser. It also represented a violent reaction by the Catholic Irish to the great numbers and impact of new immigrant communities being established in what they saw as *their* parishes and countryside – a process of reaction underestimated in the existing literature.

Estimates of the size of the settler population in Ireland in 1641 vary widely, but the greatest settler impact was clearly in Ulster. Philip Robinson has mapped in detail the geographic expansion of Scottish and English settlement throughout the first few decades of the seventeenth century. Apart from the older planted regions of mid and south Antrim and North Down, key areas of plantation settlement included North Armagh, East Tyrone and the Clogher valley, the Foyle basin centred on Derry and Strabane, in addition to Cavan, the Erne basin and the northern lands of County Londonderry.[5] As early as 1619, Pynnar's survey gives a total of 8,000 men of British descent ready for defence, which already suggests a total population of 30,000–40,000.[6] In 1630, the muster figures for the six plantation counties was c.6,600 and Robinson estimates a further 5,500 for the remaining Ulster counties of Down, Antrim and Monaghan.[7] That alone would suggest a total population of 55,000, assuming males aged between fifteen and sixty constituted c.22% of the total population. However, given the likely population underestimation and/or exclusion of some urban areas, the overall number of households in 1630 was more likely to be c.15,000. The probable settler population in Ulster in 1630, therefore, based on an average household size of 4.8, totalled c.72,000, and this before a second major immigrant influx in the 1630s. A 1635 reference by Sir William Brereton to the Scottish port town of Irvine (Ayrshire) suggests that 10,000 migrants for Ulster had passed through the port in the previous two years.[8] In 1639, Wentworth, while overemphasising that Scottish 'threat', nevertheless argued that 'the Scottish nation' in Ireland comprised 100,000 people.

Apart from Cullen's work, other assessments of Ulster's seventeenth-century population appear to underestimate the youthful, dynamic character of this Scottish society.[9] The depositions suggest an average of four children per young settler couple, illustrating the capacity for rapid expansion. It should be noted that William Petty estimated the ratio of settler to Irish in 1641 as 2:11.[10] If one assumes this ratio for 1641, a total population of Ireland of c.1.8m would yield a settler population of c.324,000. Even with an overall population as low as 1.5m in 1641, one is still dealing with a likely population of c.270,000 immigrants or those of immigrant descent. Within the provinces, Ulster probably contained c.42% of the total settler population, Leinster c.31%, Munster c.21% and Connacht as little as c.7%. Estimates, therefore, which place the Ulster population in 1641 as low as 30,000–50,000, need to be radically revised upwards.[11] The figure for Ulster looks more like c.130,000 people of English or Scottish descent. The popular rising/rebellion reflected the deep resentment of the long-settled Irish to the scale of these population 'intrusions', with a fear in some key regions of being totally overwhelmed by the newcomers. As with other revolts, however, the participation of individuals and families of mixed parentage/heritage on both sides of the conflict complicated matters. Ireland was a complex and often perplexing place in the 1640s.[12]

III

The beginning of the popular rising/rebellion involved the pillaging and expulsion of the settlers. The typical attack involved 'an armed group of Irish descending upon a Protestant settler family and demanding, at knife point, that they forsake their house and farm and surrender their moveable goods. Killings usually occurred only when Protestants resisted.'[13] The escalation of violence, however, into a number of grievous atrocities followed on from a series of 'rebel' defeats at Augher, Lisnagarvey and later on at Ardee. The spiral of 'ethnic' violence unleashed by the Irish after October 1641 (see Fig. 2) left a number of localities in Ireland littered with often mutilated dead bodies. English/Protestant settlers were killed/murdered in their homes, in the fields, in streets, on bridges, in woods, as prisoners, as well as in convoys trying to get to safe places.[14] Elsewhere, refugee men, women and children were hanged, drowned, starved or otherwise so badly used by stripping and expulsions as to result in their death. Some died of exposure to the winter cold, others of hunger, thirst and exhaustion.

The island-wide geography of the killings/murders as reported in the 1641 depositions is yet quite specific. Close on 85% of Irish baronies recorded a settler presence, yet four out of every ten of these baronies do not report any murders/killings (see Fig. 2). In Connacht and Leinster, six out of every ten baronies do not record any such atrocity or massacre, but the opposite is the case for Munster and Ulster, where almost two-thirds of the respective baronies record murders and killings. The overall distribution of atrocities, therefore, is concentrated in three regions: in south-west Ulster and adjacent parts of Leitrim, Meath and Longford; in a midland zone stretching from Kildare into parts of Queen's (Laois) and King's (Offaly) counties and on to the borders of Tipperary and Kilkenny; and in the Munster plantation zone stretching from Limerick across to North Cork and West Waterford.

Within these three zones, atrocities-cum-massacres peaked in a number of particular locations. In Ulster, the large number of at least 500 killings/murders in mid Armagh and even more emphatically those in the middle Erne basin are located in an exposed salient or island of English/Protestant settlement in a dominant Irish area.[15] This may also be true of isolated cluster of killings/murders, such as in the south-west of the King's county centred on Birr. Correlating the overall ratio of killings/murders with the size of *both* the settler and Irish population strongly suggests that killings were far less likely in baronies with a settler majority or numbers equal to the Irish. The most threatening ratio appears to have been where the settlers were well represented but outnumbered by two or three-to-one. Overall, these ratios reveal the highest levels of resentment between Irish and settler in north-east Ulster, followed by the other counties in Ulster. The adjacent borderlands of Connacht and Leinster, extending over the rest of east Leinster and South Munster, reveal moderate to high levels of resentment. West Munster and Connacht with an extension into Meath in Leinster reveal the apparently lowest levels of resentment. Read in reverse order, the greater the size of the

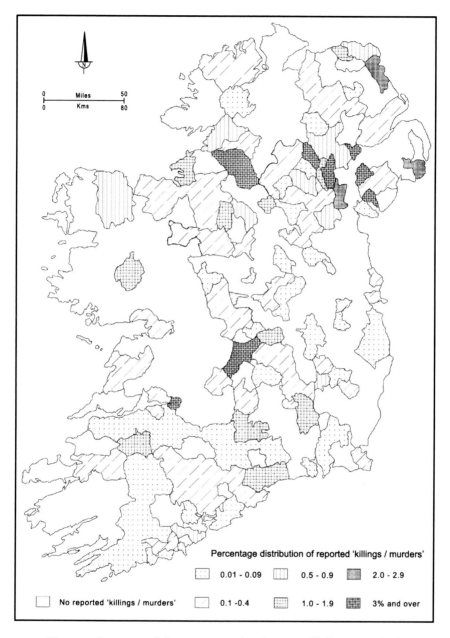

Figure 2 Summary of the percentage distribution of 'killings/murders' per barony, as reported in the 1641 depositions

settler community, the more likely the greater the local Irish resentment, but not necessarily the capacity to attack or expel such a community.

A recurring and powerful element in the many atrocity stories is that of the pregnant mother, whose body was ripped open 'till the child fell to the ground'.[16] This obsession with the hanging or stabbing of a woman with child is a central motif and symbolises, amongst other things, the drive by the Irish to eliminate a future for the settler population. The greatest number of such murders occurred in south Ulster and along the adjacent Connacht/Leinster borders, an area where the local population deeply resented the intrusion of young, fertile settler families into new territories. An analysis of the depositions suggests that adult females contributed at least a fourth of the enumerated adult settler population in this core area, with female populations as high as 32%, 29% and 28% in Donegal, Armagh and Fermanagh respectively. The proportion of children reported in the depositions as a percentage of the adult settler population is greatest in counties Armagh (35%) and Leitrim (32%).

Recurrent motifs in the depositions include the persistent mangling of bodies, including the cutting off and mocking of the genitals of some male victims. Martha Piggott reports on the death of her husband Captain John Piggott:

> Butchered and murdered this examt's husband and her said son before her face, herself and her two grandchildren standing naked in the room as spectators of that inhuman massacre and the rebels not contented with sundry mortal wounds in his body given by them but also (modesty would blush to relate it) this examt's husband lying dead and breathless upon the ground some of these cruel executions slitted and scarred his private parts in many places.[17]

Reports suggest that children from Armagh also engaged in this kind of mutilation: 'beating dead men's bodies about their privy members until they had beaten or thrashed them off and then returning with great joy to their parents.'[18] Sexual mockery and humiliation is central to a reported Sligo city killing where the assailants 'laid and placed some of the dead bodies of the naked murdered men upon the naked bodies of the women in a most immodest posture', as if engaged in intercourse.[19] This ritual attention to the symbols of fertility amongst settler men and women emphasises Irish awareness of the dynamic and rapidly expanding nature of the settler population. It emphasises their desire to cut off that energy and deny a future to the settler population. Another dominant image from almost all counties is the stripping of settlers and their expulsion from homes and farms, to be exposed to the rigours of winter snow and frost. Although some of the early strippings related more to robberies of clothes, and monies concealed on the persons, the dominant image is of a further degrading and humiliation of the victims in a ritualized way, especially when such strippings took place as refugees fled in convoy to try to reach safe havens.

One of the most emphatic and regular motifs that emerges from a reading of the 'depositions' is the centrality of Mass-going, which had become a central symbol of *political* identity for the Catholic Irish. With the explosion of violence that followed on from the rising/rebellion, the depositions from practically every county report on the enormous intimidation that prevailed in local communities to force Protestants to attend Mass and thus deny their own Protestant/English heritage. Indeed, it could be argued that the Catholic Irish were reciprocating in kind the pressures placed on them in earlier decades to conform to the Protestant norm. Parallel to the pressures on the Protestant community 'to turn to Mass' was the treatment meted out to Protestant churches and in particular to the bible, seen as the supreme symbol of the Protestant faith. The Catholic Irish population remembered their fathers and mothers recalling the impact of the English Reformation laws and edicts on the parish churches – the stripping of the altars, the breaking of the altar-rails, the burning of images, shrines and relics, and the destruction of abbeys and friaries. Likewise they had seen what they regularly described in the depositions as the new 'heretic' religion established, which in its turn abhorred 'graven images' and made central the reading and knowing of the book. Tearing up the bibles, therefore, meant tearing up and attacking the source of the Protestants' beliefs, their power and their certainties.[20]

Attacks on Protestant settler churches, ministers and the desecration of church property (including the burning of altars and pews) occurred in all four provinces, but particularly in mid and south Ulster, midland and south Leinster and parts of Munster. Some of the more horrific episodes are associated with the burning and killing of Protestant settler populations in or near churches, where they had sought physical and spiritual refuge. At Fethard-on-Sea 'they [the rebels] cut the pulpit cloth and the Minister's books in pieces and strewed them about the churchyard and caused the pyper to play whilst they danced and trampled them under their feet and called the Minister dog and stripped him of his clothes'.[21] A disproportionate number of ministers of the church were murdered, while many suffered significant material losses, including eviction from their residences. The Irish resented these ministers not only because of their ethno-religious and tithe-benefiting functions, but also because of the involvement of some in money-lending activities.

The depth of the ethno-religious divide is nowhere better revealed than in the treatment of parish graveyards, where we encounter deep feelings about ancestral burial grounds. In a number of locations scattered throughout the island – from Fermanagh in the north, through Kildare town and county, King's County and on into counties Limerick and Wexford – priests and friars instructed their parishioners to dig up the bones of the 'heretic' Protestant dead and remove them from the sacred precincts. This proved a source of great distress for Protestant families, who witnessed the bones of their fathers, mothers or uncles and aunts treated so disrespectfully – sometimes burned, sometimes thrown to the dogs or dumped in the roadside or in rivers and hedges. In this age of puritanism, extremism, fanaticism and 'cultural purification', one group is 'pure' and is involved in rituals of sanctification and purification, while the 'other' is seen as polluting the sacred ground.

In the 1641 popular rebellion, ethnic insults flew fast and thick: the 'English heretics' were 'God's enemies'; and such 'Protestants served the Devil'. As the fury of the rebellion grew, the depositions detail a progressive denial of the humanity of the settler people – a direct inversion of long-held English attitudes towards the Irish. The depositions reveal a hugely hostile reaction to the incursions of the English newcomers. The local Irish see themselves as the ancient occupants of the land and the English 'as a race of foreigners'. On one sharp frontier in the Queen's county, the Irish allegedly stated that 'the English should never come in amongst them and they would make use of them for so longe as it lasted and would keep the upper hand for as long as they could'.[22] This long-term deepening of hostilities between the 'Irish' and 'the English' was characterised by mutually conflicting and competing constructions of their ethno-religious categories.

But this drive for 'ethnic purification', to expel 'the alien' faltered, especially in the strong Scottish quarters of the north-west, where the rapid mobilisation of the Laggan's forces consolidated settler control of Donegal, east Londonderry and west Tyrone, and in the north-east, where, after a series of bruising and brutal engagements, the line of rebel advance faltered at Lisnegarvie/Lurgan. The arrival of the Scottish Covenanter Army under General Monroe in the spring of 1642 further strengthened the position of the settlers in Ulster. Henceforth, and often with the severest techniques, the Scottish forces helped not only to recapture territory but also to clear spaces for further Presbyterian Scottish colonisation. Robert Armstrong provides superb insights as to how Protestant Ireland had become reliant on the state just as 'the state was becoming even more reliant on it'.[23] In Ulster especially, Protestant society had become a society under arms. Armstrong also documents the local and regional power of the Protestant planter militias throughout the country. Most significantly, the Irish drive to oust the 'alien' intruder faltered in the Pale region, where the government forces reassumed military control, and in the Cork 'enclave', where Lord Inchiquin consolidated Protestant planter defences in a triangular area around Cork, Kinsale and Bandon. Dublin and Cork would subsequently provide vital bastions and springboards for the Cromwellian reconquest.

IV

The 1641 depositions provide ideologically specific and often powerful narratives that emphasise one view of the state of the world, however valid and genuine that view may appear to the participants and deponents. There are large narrative and geographical gaps and biases in these stories, all of them in the English language. Apart from O'Mealláin's diary very little survives in the Irish language, the main language of over three-quarters of the population.[24] But much greater difficulties with the depositions arise from the use made of them from the beginning of the war. English Parliamentary propaganda quickly and deliberately turned the story of the murder of Protestant settlers killed and murdered into a *general* massacre myth. In mapping the depositions, geographic analysis of the data suggests a figure of about 4,200 murders and killings. But all of this analysis is a little futile. As Aidan Clarke has observed, we shall never know the full story of all those who died, 'by whatever means'.[25] Far more than 4,000 of the Protestant settler community died violently at this time, but the numbers involved fell far short of the mid-seventeenth-century propagandist figures. Indeed, William Petty's estimates of overall war losses and in particular his estimate at 37,000 settler deaths should be taken more seriously.[26]

In the final analysis, the critical point is not the reliability of the stories at the time but rather what the Protestant settlers believed to be true. So often in the depositions, the deponents report 'as she really believed', 'it is said', 'as I have heard'. High levels of fear, hysteria and paranoia characterised most Protestant communities at the height of the terror. John Temple observed how a frightened and distraught settler community feared 'a general extirpation of all the English, root and branch, so as not to leave their name or posterity throughout the whole kingdom'.[27] Many of the deponents gave their evidence at a time of great pain and trauma, seeking to interpret events in a situation of great uncertainty. Rumour, propaganda and the publication of tracts and pamphlets proved powerful weapons in the war to claim the high ground of certainty, correctness and morality. The evidence in the depositions (and the much later examinations) had been narrated, written and collected in different contexts and conditions and under different rules and procedures. Not surprisingly, therefore, interesting regional variations exist in reports about murders and killings. Exploring the ratio of murders and killings reported to the number of deponents actually reporting the murders can help establish levels of hearsay and possible exaggeration. For the country as a whole, the average number of murders reported by a single deponent is eight or nine murders. The most northern counties of Ulster, the eastern counties of Leinster and the south Munster counties all report ratios around the island-wide average. In contrast, counties Down and Fermanagh, with one deponent to twenty-four murders, act as the core of a region including counties Tyrone, Leitrim and Mayo, with figures well above the norm. King's county (Offaly) reveals an exceptionally high ratio of forty-four murders per single deponent. County Limerick is the only southern county returning a figure above the norm with a ratio of 1:13/14.

Figure 3 Geographical expansion of urban foundations from the medieval period with particular reference to the late sixteenth and the first half of seventeenth century Ireland

Not surprisingly, an architecture of silence surrounds the many reprisals and revenge killings carried out against the Catholic Irish population. The 1641 depositions involve the presentation of the evidence of losses of the English and Scottish settlers, of how they suffered in the early months and years of the war. Through repetition, commemoration and the reproduction of key 'memory' texts like those published by Temple, these stories of atrocities calcified into an accepted record of the horrific events and the suffering endured by the Protestant settler community. No such Catholic Irish depositions exist to tell their side of the story. Atrocities occurred on both sides of the frontier, particularly after the first months of the rising/rebellion, and particularly in Ulster as the settler militias regained the upper hand. The Cromwellian examinations for County Antrim provide some glimpses of these reprisals, but overall, the depositions reveal little of the traumas suffered by Catholic Irish communities.

Coote's early expedition into Wicklow and south County Dublin, characterised by killings and village burnings, St Leger's early and brutal campaign in mid-Munster and Sir Frederick Hamilton's vicious campaign on the borders of County Sligo confirm the thesis that paranoia is a universal feature amongst ruling elites who inflict atrocities. Large-scale killings occurred across Ulster, and in June 1642 an edict of the Dublin Lord Justices noted that 'we have hitherto proceeded with fire and sword, the soldiers not sparing the women and sometimes not the children'.[28] In mid-Ulster from 1642, reprisals by the settler Laggan army resulted in a large-scale exodus of 30,000–50,000 Ulster Irish refugees, who fled southwards into Connacht and North Leinster.[29] Some may have reached even as far south as the Iveragh Peninsula. These fleeting glimpses suggest what happened the often outnumbered Irish 'who lived in fear'. The rest is silence.

Kenneth Nicholls argues that much more precise information on atrocities committed against the Irish can be found in pamphlet literature after February 1642.[30] By then, as Robin Clifton notes, 'a spiralling war of rebellion, resistance and revenge had engulfed Ireland'.[31] From the time when English/Scottish Protestant militias and soldiers seized the initiative against the Irish, a new generation of pamphlets appeared, reporting on the activities of the forces in Ireland. These frequently involved candid accounts of atrocities against the Irish. Nicholls contends that an exhaustive trawl of the pamphlet literature and of similar narratives in manuscript would produce a significant amount of relevant credible material. He has already teased out the sequence of events showing the indiscriminate and bloody repression by government forces in Leinster in response to the killing of settlers in Ulster, which led in turn to reprisals perpetuated against local Protestant settler populations.[32] These tat-for-tat killings became a feature of bitter local skirmishes. In such a climate of terror and reprisals, it is often the telling of the violence, its narration, which in turn produces more violence.

V

The 1641 depositions and later commentaries constructed a collective memory of the awful events of the war, which accepted as real the experiences of the Protestant settlers. In interpreting these situations and descriptions, the work of anthropologists who have assessed the origin, forms and behaviours surrounding ethnic hatreds, as well as their expression in horrific bodily violence and contemporary narratives, is especially helpful. The repetitive, apparently formulaic, rendering of many of the stories in the depositions, with their use of similar motifs and images, initially raises question about their validity and reliability. Surviving families, neighbours and friends, however, often shared these stories before they finally reached the written form. They debated these events and distilled them with biblical allusions to betrayal and the persecution of a wandering, chosen people. The stories that emerged often took on the character of a morality play, creating a collective history of a particular kind, which according to the anthropologist Lissa Malkki is 'not only a description or evaluation of the past but a subversive reading and interpretation of that history in fundamental moral terms'.[33] As Canny notes, the wider victim/atrocity literature so characteristic of this violent era in European history may also have influenced such renderings and stories.[34] What emerges is 'neither history nor myth but a combination' of both – what Malkki calls a mythico-history, generated in situations of extreme ethnic violence.[35] Such a narrative continuously drives the sharpest boundaries between 'us and them'; 'the godly and the wicked'.

This comparative anthropological literature suggests that the violence itself is deeply ritualised.[36] When an oppressed ethnic group rises against a hated oppressor, similar forms of violence are found in widely separate cultural contexts. Numerous cross-cultural strands of subaltern violence identify the conditions under which the oppressed revolt. The subaltern or colonised peoples are materially underprivileged, and subject to explicit measures of political and economic discrimination.[37] Such peoples are also likely to be 'victims of symbolic forms of discrimination and violence in the form of hate propaganda and pervasive cultural stereotyping'.[38] There is also a 'concerted and considered effort by the colonisers to destroy the religious and cultural fabric of the native society'. While members of the educated elite typically lead subaltern revolts, giving voice to the underlying political ideology, the demonstrably underprivileged masses, mobilised, in part by such an ideology, participate in the most violent activities and atrocities.

A comparison of the Irish situation in 1641 with Indian uprisings against Spanish rule in Latin America is particularly revealing. In Peru/Upper Peru (present day Bolivia), 100,000 people apparently perished in a revolt which began in September 1780 and lasted close on two years.[39] The systematic

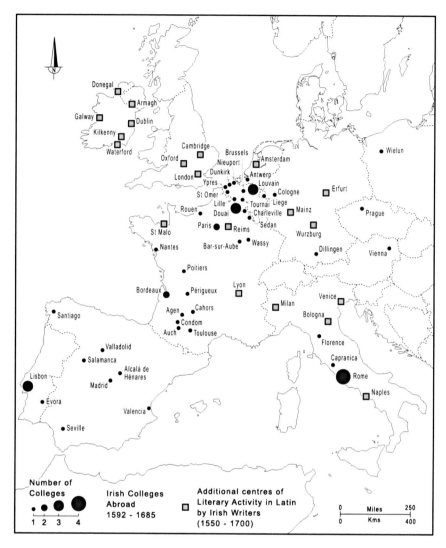

Figure 4 Distribution of Irish colleges on the continent and Irish writing in Latin in Europe as a whole (c.1550–1700)

slaughter of non-Indians throughout this territory created a legacy that would haunt the land for years. 'Long exploited, the Indians had been subjected to mounting economic pressures', and estranged by the power (and demands) of the Catholic Church.[40] 'Widespread resentment over forced labour, the imposition of unprecedented taxes on Indian staples [and] an absence of viable judicial recourse', created an atmosphere pregnant with prophecies predicting the return of Indian self-rule.[41] Many of the Spanish and their creole/mestizo allies found no refuge in their barricaded churches. The Spanish governor and one-third (c.10,000) of the population of the capital La Paz perished when Indian 'rebels' besieged the city. As in Ireland, the popular revolt and the actions of local leaders went well beyond the limits specified by their commanders. Similarly, the fundamental objective of the Indians was the expulsion of the Spaniards and their allies, including the Hispanicised Indians.

The symbolic dimensions and expressions of subaltern violence emerge as a recurring theme in this and other Latin American revolts. While the insurgents left little in the written record, their actions 'spoke loudly and clearly'.[42] They sought to kill or expel their enemies, identified not only on the basis of race and ethnicity but also on the basis of occupation, primary language and religious affiliation, as well as 'mundane habits such as the style of dress and food they ate'.[43] These identifications in turn revealed the central and contrasting motifs of the Indian culture. The insurgents demanded that all the people use Indian dress, language and other dietary customs. As in Ireland, the revolt did not stop at the drive to expel the Spanish and their allies – the rebels also sought to erase all aspects of Spanish culture and its symbols and so 'extinguish the cattle and seeds of Spain.'[44] The Indians fought for 'the rebirth of native ways, to reclaim native culture, governance, religion and lands'.[45]

In many respects, the actions of those 'rebels' represented a mirror-image of the prior genocidal attacks by the Spaniards on the Indian communities, their imposition of Catholicism by forced conversion and the deliberate and systematic campaign against Indian shrines, artefacts and religious rites. Spanish rule had seen the torture and death of Indian leaders and various forms of land seizure, along with the imposition of forced labour, which deprived many Indians of their livelihood and sometimes their lives. The Indian insurgents sought to get rid of Spanish rulers at all levels so that 'they would be slaves no more'.[46] Another inversion involved forcing Spanish and Hispanicised Indian women to carry out the most menial tasks, while attacks on Spanish religious sites and symbols reveal not only objectives but causes – acts not only involving material destruction but also 'symbolic of prior oppression'.[47] Sexual mockery and humiliation also featured in the Indian revolts. In one instance, the Indian insurgents executed 400 men, women and children, leaving 'some on top of others and many in shameless positions'.[48] The stripping of victims, a common mode of humiliation, 'also served to highlight the inversion of traditional power and social relations'.[49]

The literature on subaltern violence and insurgency, therefore, contains numerous examples of the 'great significance attached to symbolic and ritualistic forms of rebellion'.[50] Everywhere the uprisings are seen as acts of justice and cleansing, revealing a prophetic redemptive dimension – a looking back to a golden age of freedom and a dream of the utopian and the intangible.[51]

However, it seems to me that the most profound insight from this literature relates to issues of humiliation and inferiority. Evelin G. Lindner contends that humiliation – 'the enforced lowering of a person or group, a process of subjugation that damages or strips away their pride, honour and dignity' – is not just about power.[52] Rather she sees it as prompting the perpetrators to seek revenge for past humiliations, perceived or otherwise. She further argues that it may also represent 'an effort to cleanse fears of future subjugation or to purge feelings of *admiration* for the victims'.[53] This latter point is very significant. This notion of humiliation also carries the need to rid oneself of admiration for the culture and life of the conqueror – the original humiliating force. For Lindner, humiliation is 'the nuclear bomb of the emotions', leading to the explosive action often described in the 1641 depositions as 'the fury of the rebels'.[54] The popular rising/rebellion, therefore, was more about the humiliation of one's enemies than about killing them. As Lindner points out, however, the people responsible for this kind of ethnic violence rarely if ever achieve their goals.[55] They end up in a worse situation than before, as happened to the insurgent Irish both during and after the Cromwellian conquest.

VI

Much has been written on the complex nature of the conflict in and after 1641. In the light of the above analysis, the interconnections between the following key structural forces might be added for consideration – the importance of early modernity and the consequences of colonialism for Ireland; the role of the Irish language intelligentsia and the Irish diaspora in creating a new national consciousness; the revitalisation of a range of cultural techniques to sustain and further the rising/rebellion; and the significance of the profound identification of Irish landowning kin-groups with their home territories.

The establishment of 200 new towns (70% of the total) between 1603 and 1641 is just one example of the impact of 'early modernity' on Ireland. The early modern era constituted a significant watershed in Ireland's dealings with England, which reached back to medieval times. A new knowledge/power equation intruded massively on Ireland, bringing new ways of seeing, representing and acting on the world.[56] Mapping, surveying and emerging military technologies led this movement. English imperial ideology, characterised by a discourse of cultural supremacy, 'improvement' and reform, 'othered' the Irish. A new regime of truth prevailed. New spatial/geographical practices created a privileged outside view of Ireland and attempted to turn Irish space into another England. Accounting, measurement, efficiency, profit accumulation and security were central motifs for the nationalising literate English elite, with the printing press playing a key innovative role.[57]

The speed, intensity and uneven geographical spread of this new ethos shook the Irish economic and social order to its foundations. The depositions highlight the occupational sophistication and diversity of the New English (and Scottish) culture in Ireland. New spaces of innovation emerge, including these new market towns, mansions, gardens, enclosures, mines and industries, which contrasted strongly with the more self-sufficient worlds of Gaelic and Gaelicised Ireland. A whole new series of economic and labour practices disrupted old rhythms, and left many Irish lords and clans behind. In addition to the enormous economic shock, the cultural shock also carried with it feelings of envy, admiration, humiliation, confusion.

This notion of modernity involved 'violent, coercive and insidious cultural practices' against so-called traditional societies, including Ireland.[58] 'Colonialism' was the other side of the coin of 'early modernity'. The second half of the sixteenth century witnessed the bloody conquest of Ireland, achieved through a violence that was not only physical and continued long after the so-called 'pacification' of the land. For the peoples of Ireland, 'reformation', 'Anglicisation' and 'evangelisation' resulted in the imposition of legal, religious and other penalties for refusing to conform. The violence, therefore, was structural, systematic and symbolic. This constituted a physical assault on Irish experiences, in which, as Franz Fanon famously observed, the coloniser/soldier/planter 'with the clear conscience of the upholder of order . . . is the bringer of violence into the home and mind of the colonised'.[59] So in the early 1640s, we get the 'interwoven and interconnected anguish of two communities that colonialism was setting apart', with the 1641 depositions not only acting as a record but also as a weapon in the war over territory and community.[60]

A major counter-cultural movement had previously emerged within Ireland and more especially overseas, where the Irish from different provinces and backgrounds mixed in the religious, military and mercantile worlds of European cities. These exiled communities framed a new national consciousness, led by the Louvain annalists and people like Geoffrey Keating, author of the influential *Foras Feasa ar Éirinn*.[61] A new conception of the Irish – *na hÉireannaigh* – transcended the old divides between the Gaelic Irish and the Old English, and spoke in a sharper, more modern Irish language idiom.[62] The emerging literature also clashed with the hegemonic-trending discourses of people like Edmund Spenser, Fynes Moryson and Sir John Davies. A narrative which stressed self-belief and self-knowledge sought to counter the humiliation and shame that accompanied colonial domination. This counter-cultural movement, already stiffened by Counter-Reformation Catholicism, developed strongly in the 1630s, and played a significant part in the 1641 rising/rebellion.

The 1640s rising/rebellion also witnessed a revitalisation of a range of cultural techniques to assist the war effort. These included the re-emergence of clan/lordship structures, the restoration of naming patterns and prophetic codes, and the reinvigoration and expansion of women's roles. The depositions provide a very clear picture of the revitalisation of clan and lineage structures from the MacMurrragh Kavanaghs, O'Byrnes and O'Tooles in the south-east to the MacMahons, Maguires, O'Cahans, O'Neills and MacDonnells in the north. A picture emerges from the pages of the depositions of overlapping and interwoven kinship networks, which link up the so-called 'septs' of the south-east, south-west and west with those of the midlands and the north. These clan groups-cum-lordships no longer raid one another but rather unite in opposition to 'the strangers'. For example, four clan groups – the O'Molloys, Coughlans, O'Carrolls and O'Kennedys – attack the planter garrison at Birr.[63] Linked to this revival is the renewal of Old Irish concepts of kingship. The depositions contain regular references to the restoration of, for example, the O'Reillys as Kings of Cavan, the O'Rourkes Kings of Leitrim, while references to national and provincial kings also appear.[64] The Kavanaghs mock the settler families of Carlow town with threats of the restoration of the Kings of Leinster, while on numerous occasions the O'Neills – whether in the person of Sir Phelim or Eoghan Rua – are allegedly to be made Kings of Ireland.[65]

There is also a drive to restore Irish language place names, stressing the powerful link between names and identities. The most striking example is from the County Cavan depositions where the Irish state that the town of Virginia, named after Queen Elizabeth, 'shall be called Aughanure again'.[66] *Ach an iubhair* – 'the field of the yew tree' – is seen as restorative and so reclaims part of Irish culture and identity. Likewise, an emphasis is placed on the restoration of Irish forms of personal and family names, recognising that these names are the boundary markers of the body and the signifiers of the person and the groups. This renewal applied not only to forms of address but also to forms of dress. Reversing English codes of dress style, the insurgents insisted on Irish forms of dress and habits, imposing penalties against those 'who spake English'.[67] They also hoped that after capturing Dublin, which they never succeeded in doing, all records and monuments of English government would be destroyed.

So in this world of great uncertainty and high levels of alienation, the Catholic Irish attempted to make things more certain, more stable, more authentic, more familiar. They used their own arsenal of cultural techniques, as well as appropriate English modes of administration from the civil parish to the county to achieve their goals. Likewise, they invoked all forms of Catholic and quasi-Christian rituals to protect their soldiers in battle. Prophecy also played a role, with millenarian hopes of the restoration of an Irish government alongside the resurrection of Colmcille's prophecy that the Irish would not be conquered in another thousand years. The depositions also unearth the use of the mythic image and power of the *cailleach* – the helpful Goddess – to assist in local battles.[68]

The participation of Irish women in this uprising, as evidenced in other subaltern movements, is unprecedented.[69] The depositions are full of references to the women being 'more forward than the men', or 'more fierce and cruel than the men'. Women wield weapons, especially knives (skeins = Irish *scian*), serve in armies and provide leadership roles in advocating war and executions.[70] Women often constitute the juries where settlers are put on trial, willingly taking on the role of jury fore(wo)man. They act as gaolers, lookouts and guides, as well as spies and 'intelligencers', and often act as huxters/traders in disposing of stolen goods. As in other uprisings, women often get involved in inverting the social order, wearing and dancing in the finery of the former 'lady of the manor'. Indeed the evidence for Ireland and elsewhere would suggest that these kinds of uprisings provided openings for a new range of women's activities, achievements and aggrandisements. In this kind of extraordinary world, women could recreate themselves.[71]

Finally and probably again underestimated in the literature is the profound identification of Irish families and extended kin with their home territories and ancestral lands. In 1641, 10,000–12,000 Catholic Irish landowners still held estates of over 100 acres, with another 4,000 smallholders. A significant landowner averaged about twenty retainers, while thousands of former landowners had since sunk down into the tenant or artisan classes; more again were involved in soldiering. This suggests a potential reservoir of at least a quarter of a million men in Ireland, ready either to fight or to at least provide some backup support for the war. Like other colonised peoples, the Irish felt that strangers/foreigners/heretics now occupied their own territories and lands. This feeling is best exemplified by the evidence of the 1641 depositions, where new estate owners in their castle-mansions were almost invariably besieged by local Irish families and kin-groups, who regarded themselves as the *real* owners of these lands. And the Catholic clergy took a similar view of church buildings, ecclesiastical territories and incomes.[72]

VII

Most commentators are agreed that the period 1641–54, especially the final Cromwellian phase from 1649 to 1654, created what can only be described as a demographic disaster in Ireland. If the overall level of mortality after 1649 is of the order of 20–25% and, given the effects of earlier murders, sieges, battles, skirmishes, reprisals, famines, out-migrations and later transhipments, the likely scale of overall population decline may come closer to one-third of the population. Clifton suggests a massive decline of 400,000 people or 19% of the imputed 2.1m population in 1641.[73] Petty's population loss estimate of over 600,000 may equally be valid, and the loss may be out of a total 1641 population of 1.8 million rather than 2.1 million. Protestant settler population losses due to deaths and out-migrations may well total c.100,000 with Catholic Irish losses at least four, perhaps even five, times greater.[74] Whatever the estimates, Ireland's death toll 'is comparable to the devastation suffered during the Second World War by countries such as the Soviet Union, Poland and Yugoslavia'.[75]

After these wars, the rift between the Catholic Irish and the Protestant settler communities deepened and solidified. The intersection of material interests and power, reinforced by a colonial culture which linked that power to religious difference and national ideology, resulted in even greater control and domination being exercised by Protestant Ireland, and even greater marginalisation and alienation of Catholic Irish communities. But some things had changed. The Protestant settler communities no longer needed to see themselves simply as extensions of Britain, of Scotland or of England. Their mythico-history articulated a basic understanding of what it meant to be a separate people and operated as a kind of charter for their whole cultural life on the island. In a word, we see the emergence of the 'Protestant Irish', more deeply rooted than before but remaining anxious, alert, aggressive and even sometimes belligerent. Equally, the slow-burning fabrication of a Catholic Irish identity had been finally hammered out in the furnace of the Confederate wars and the Cromwellian conquest. They too would create their own mythico-history; they would be anxious and alert but needed to adopt the weapons of the weak – subtlety, verbal agility and the development of secret ways of doing and saying things. The colonial state's instruments of surveillance would run up against sophisticated cultural techniques for ensuring invisibility and impenetrability. The Catholic Irish in turn discreetly kept a watch on the rulers from the other side of the frontier.

NOTES

1 Aidan Clarke, 'The 1641 depositions', in Peter Fox (ed.), *Treasures of the Library of Trinity College Dublin* (Dublin, 1986), pp. 111–22.

2 W. J. Smyth, *Map-Making, Landscapes and Memory: A Geography of Colonial and Early Modern Ireland c.1530–1750* (Cork, 2006), pp. 103–65.

3 See J. C. Scott, *Domination and the Arts of Resistance* (New Haven and London, 1990).

4 See Smyth, *Map-Making*, pp. 107–9; Nicholas Canny, *Making Ireland British 1580–1650* (Oxford, 2001); M. Perceval-Maxwell, *The Outbreak of the Irish Rebellion* (Dublin, 1994).

5 P. S. Robinson, *The Plantation of Ulster: British Settlement in an Irish Landscape 1600–1670* (Dublin, 1984), pp. 93–101.

6 Ibid., pp. 92–8.

7 Ibid., pp. 99–110, and Appendix 10, pp. 212–24.

8 Quoted in J. Harrison, *The Scot in Ulster* (Edinburgh, 1988), pp. 55–6.

9 L. M. Cullen, 'Population trends in seventeenth-century Ireland', *Economic and Social Review*, 6 (1975), 149–65, especially pp. 152–4, 161.

10 Sir William Petty, *The Political Anatomy of Ireland*, ed. John O'Donovan (London, 1691; reprinted Shannon, 1970), p. 18.

11 See Connolly, *Contested Island: Ireland 1460–1630* (Oxford, 2007), p. 302, where he states 'by 1641 the British population of Ulster stood at 40,000 or more'; Nicholas Canny, *Kingdom and Colony: Ireland in the Atlantic World, 1560–1800* (Baltimore, 1988), p. 96. It is interesting that W. E. H. Lecky, *A History of Ireland in the Eighteenth Century* (London, 1912), p. 79 puts the number of settlers in Ulster in 1640 at 120,000.

12 In the remainder of the text, to reduce the complexity of naming of groups in 1641, I use the term the Irish (*na hÉireannaigh*) for both the Gaelic Irish and the Old English and all others who identified with the Catholic Irish in the wars; I use the term 'English' (*na Sasanaigh*) for the New English settler community and any of the above who identify with both the English polity and Protestant tradition. Within the British context, I identify the Scottish settler group wherever that distinction seems necessary.

13 Canny, *Making Ireland British*, p. 474.

14 Robin Clifton, 'An indiscriminate blackness: massacre, counter-massacre and ethnic cleansing in Ireland, 1640–1660', in Mark Leven and Penny Roberts (eds), *The Massacre in History* (New York and Oxford, 2002), pp. 107–26.

15 Hilary Simms, 'Violence in County Armagh, 1641', in Brian MacCuarta (ed.), *Ulster 1641: Aspects of the Rising* (Belfast, 1993), pp. 122–38.

16 Elizabeth Martin, for example, reports such horrific violence in Cullen, Country Tipperary. Deposition of Elizabeth Martin, TCD MS 829, fol. 330.

17 Smyth, *Map-Making*, p. 134.

18 Sir John Temple, *The History of the General Rebellion in Ireland* (London, 1646), pp. 116, 130. This kind of statement is repeated on numerous occasions by Temple.

19 Ibid., p. 184.

20 Smyth, *Map-Making*, p. 130. See, by way of contrast Eamon Duffy, *The Stripping of the Altars: Traditional Religion in England 1400–1580* (New Haven and London, 1992) on the assaults made on the material culture of the Catholic church in Tudor England.

21 Deposition of Henry Palmer, 12 January 1642, TCD MS 818, fo. 88r.

22 Ibid. What seems to be intended at the height of the fury of the early popular rising/rebellion is an act of purification and clarification: 'Ireland for the Irish, England for the English and Scotland for the Scottish'.

23 Robert Armstrong, *Protestant War: The 'British' of Ireland and the Wars of the Three Kingdoms* (Manchester: 2005), pp. 36–8.

24 Charles Dillon (ed.), '*Cín Lae Uí Mheallaín*: Friar O Meallan Journal', in Charles Dillon and H. A. Jefferies (eds), *Tyrone: History and Society* (Dublin, 2000), pp. 327–402.

25 Clarke, 'The "1641 Massacres"', this volume, p. 49.

26 Smyth, *Map-Making*, pp. 160–1.

27 Temple, *The Irish Rebellion*, p. 116.

28 Quoted by Pádraig Lenihan, *Confederate Catholics at War 1641-49* (Cork, 2001), p. 62.

29 Ibid., p. 89.

30 Kenneth Nicholls, 'The other massacre: English killings of Irish, 1641-3', in David Edwards, Pádraig Lenihan and Clodagh Tait (eds), *Age of Atrocity: Violence and Political Conflict in Early Modern Ireland* (Dublin, 2007), pp. 176-91.

31 Clifton, 'An indiscriminate blackness', pp. 113-14.

32 Nicholls, 'The other massacre', pp. 182-8.

33 L. H. Malkki, *Purity and Exile: Violence, Memory and National Cosmology among Hutu Refugees in Tanzania* (Chicago, 1994), pp. 103-4. For a further exploration of this theme, see chapter 2 'The mythico-history', pp. 52-104, and chapter 3 'The use of history in the refugee camp', pp. 105-52.

34 See chapter 4.

35 Malkki, *Violence, Memory and National Cosmology*, pp. 105-52.

36 N. A. Robins and Adam Jones, *Genocides by the Oppressed: Subaltern Genocides in Theory and Practice* (Indianapolis, 2009). See especially introduction, pp. 1-24, and chapters 1 and 2. Thanks to Professor Ben Kiernan for drawing my attention to this reference. See also N. Z. Davis, 'The Rites of violence' in eadem, *Society and Culture in Early Modern France: Eight Essays* (London, 1975), pp. 152-60.

37 Adam Jones and N. A. Robins, 'Introduction: subaltern genocide in theory and practice', in *Genocides by the Oppressed*, pp. 1-24, at pp. 10-11.

38 Ibid., p. 11.

39 Ibid., pp. 12-13.

40 Ibid., p. 1. See also Davis, 'Rites of violence', pp. 156-7.

41 Jones and Robins, 'Introduction: subaltern genocide', p. 1.

42 N. A. Robins, 'Symbolism and subalternity: the 1680 Pueblo revolt of New Mexico and the 1780-82 Andean Great rebellion', in Robins and Jones (eds), *Genocides by the Oppressed*, pp. 25-46, at p. 26.

43 Jones and Robins, 'Introduction: subaltern genocide', p. 13.

44 Ibid.

45 Robins, 'Symbolism and subalternity', p. 29.

46 Ibid., p. 25.

47 Ibid., pp. 33-4.

48 Ibid., pp. 30-5.

49 Ibid., p. 33.

50 James Wilson, *The Earth Shall Weep: A History of Native America* (New York, 1996), p. 156. See also Davis, 'Rites of violence' in relation to issues of pollution and the desecration of corpses, pp. 156-8.

51 Ibid., p. 52; E. R. Wolf, *Peasant Wars in the Twentieth Century* (New York, 1973), p. 295. See also Ben Kiernan, *Blood and Soil: A World History of Genocides and Extermination from Sparta to Darfur* (New Haven, 2006), chapter 1.

52 E. G. Lindner, 'Genocides, humiliation and inferiority: an interdisciplinary perspective', in Robins and Jones (eds), *Genocides of the Oppressed*, pp. 138-58.

53 Ibid., pp. 150-1.

54 Ibid., p. 139.

55 Ibid.
56 Smyth, *Map-Making*, pp. 14–17, 345–418.
57 Ibid., pp. 345–418.
58 C. Nash, 'Historical geographies of modernity', in B. Graham and C. Nash, *Modern Historical Geographies* (Harlow, 2007), pp. 13–17.
59 Franz Fanon, *The Wretched of the Earth*, trans C. Farrington (New York, 1963), pp. 34–8. See also Smyth, *Map-Making*, pp. 1–18.
60 Daniel Clayton, 'Colonising cartographies', *Journal of Historical Geography*, 34 (2008), p. 161.
61 J. O'Donovan (ed.), *Annála Rioghachta Éireann: Annals of the Kingdom of Ireland by the Four Masters from the Earliest Times to the year 1616* (7 vols, Dublin, 1998); S. Céitinn (G. Keating), *Foras Feasa ar Éirinn: The History of Ireland*, ed. P. S. Dineen (Dublin, 1914); see also Bernadette Cunningham, *The World of Geoffrey Keating: History, Myth and Religion* (Dublin, 2000).
62 See, for example, Cecily O'Rahilly, *Five Seventeenth Century Political Poems* (Dublin, 1977).
63 Smyth, *Map-Making*, p. 145.
64 TCD MS 830, fol. 174(v); TCD MS 836, fol. 85r. Joseph Cope in his 'Dr. Henry Jones and the plight of Irish Protestants, 1642', *Institute of Historical Research*, 74 (2001), 370–91, at p. 379 notes 'rebel' statements from the great majority of counties studied.
65 Elizabeth Fitzpatrick, *Royal Inauguration in Gaelic Ireland c.1100–1600: A Cultural Landscape Study* (Woodbridge: 2004), pp. 213–34, and especially p. 223.
66 TCD MS, fol. 149(v).
67 See, for example, Brendán Ó Buachalla, *Aisling Ghéar: na Stiobhartaigh agus an tAos Léinn* (Dublin, 1996), chapter 3.
68 TCD MS 814, fol. 164(v).
69 Jones and Robins, 'Introduction: subaltern genocide', p. 8.
70 Smyth, *Map-Making*, pp. 129–30; TCD MS 814, fol. 63(v).
71 Robins, 'Symbolism and subalternity', pp. 34–6; Adam Jones, 'On the genocidal aspect of certain subaltern uprisings', in Robins and Jones (eds), *Genocides of the Oppressed*, pp. 47–58, at pp. 51–3; Robins, '"When the rabbit's got the gun": subaltern genocide and the genocidal continuum', in Robins and Jones (eds), *Genocides of the Oppressed*, pp. 185–208, at pp. 188–9.
72 Smyth, *Map Making*, pp. 103–65.
73 Clifton, 'An indiscriminate blackness', p. 108.
74 Smyth, *Map-Making*, pp. 158–63.
75 Clifton, 'An indiscriminate blackness', p. 108.

❦

6

Out of the blue?
Provincial unrest in Ireland before 1641

DAVID EDWARDS

The origins of the Irish Catholic rebellion of 1641 are contentious, though not nearly as contentious as the scale of the alleged massacre of Protestant settlers which ensued.[1] Much of the heat of the debate is due in no small part to the fact that the various explanations offered for the causes of the rising tend to separate around the notion of 'inevitability' and its underlying dialectic of short-term and long-term causes. While the 'inevitability' of 1641 has attracted as many doubters as adherents, the same is true of its equally troublesome counterpart, 'avoidability'. The puzzle of whether or not the rising could have been avoided has focussed chiefly on two things: the growing political influence of the English royal government in Ireland in the early seventeenth century as it forged ahead with the colonisation and Protestantisation of the country, and the extent to which Parliament and the courts in Dublin enabled the crown to push through many of its policies by constitutional means, containing opposition, and even manufacturing a degree of consent among elements of the regional elites. As the debate has evolved, increasing attention has been paid to the political changes of the 1630s and the personal authority exercised over the country by Charles I's absolutist viceroy, Thomas Wentworth, earl of Strafford.[2] If Wentworth had escaped impeachment, might royal authority in Ireland have survived, and the subsequent Irish revolt been averted? Indeed, might royal power actually have strengthened in Ireland, as Wentworth pushed his policies through to completion?

Recent scholarship has begun to explore these and other related questions about the lead-up to the rebellion, and to draw upon a wider array of primary sources in the search for answers.[3] Even so, despite these advances, much remains to be resolved. Studies of political developments in early seventeenth-century Ireland have failed to address satisfactorily several key areas of inquiry that directly concern the origins of 1641. Too little is known, for instance, of the struggle for survival of the tens of thousands of native Irish dispossessed by the plantations – a veritable chasm in the historiography. Similarly, the recalibration of power relationships between the nobles, gentry and local communities in the provinces in the face of growing English and Scottish settler influence is a barely acknowledged, let alone investigated, subject. While the following essay will touch only elliptically on these areas, it hopefully will help to plug another significant gap – namely the extent of native resistance to the government and the new colonists in the generation before the rebellion.

Irish historians sometimes refer to the period 1603–41 as the 'Early Stuart Peace'. But just how peaceful was it? While the crown did not face another rising of major significance for more than thirty years after the defeat of O'Doherty's revolt in 1608, did growing English colonisation proceed unchallenged in the localities during the period? What about lesser rebellions and local disturbances? How serious a threat did they pose to the crown's regional authority, and to the colonists? By answering questions like these, historians can begin to safely grapple with the broader issues of 'inevitability' or 'avoidability' – that is, with the extent to which conditions in the country prior to Wentworth's fall were either 'revolutionary' or, as one authority has confidently asserted, 'unrevolutionary'.[4]

But before examining the surviving evidence for native unrest and episodes of resistance around the country, some consideration should be given to the government's capacity to quell disturbances, through the army and other policing agencies. The recent welcome upsurge of studies about Early Stuart Ireland contains surprisingly little information about this.[5] There are reasons for the oversight. In Ireland, the advent of the Stuart monarchy coincided with the end of a major conflict, the Nine Years War (1594–1603). Following the Treaty of Mellifont of March 1603 that formally ended hostilities, the new King, James VI & I, immediately authorised a dramatic reduction of the crown forces in the country. Relying on his fellow Scotsman Sir James Fullerton to oversee the decommissioning process, in barely three years the English army 'on the establishment' in Ireland fell from its end-of-war level of circa 17,500 men to barely 2,000 men by the beginning of 1606 – a spectacular drop by any standard.[6] But therein lurks a problem. Awareness of the scale of the army's reduction has encouraged some seventeenth-century experts to disregard the military, and treat it as a diminishing element in Irish public life throughout the Early Stuart era. This is unwise, as a permanent force of 2,000 or thereabouts was far from negligible. During the second half of the sixteenth century, except in times of absolute emergency, the standard army employed in the country by King James's predecessor Elizabeth I had averaged about 2,250 men each year. This force had proven sufficient to facilitate a policy of piecemeal conquest, and enabled the crown to undertake military operations practically anywhere at any time of year.[7] Moreover, considering the collapse of the autonomous Irish lordships during the first few years of King James's reign, and the stamping out of the native lords' ability to maintain private armies, the retention of a crown force of 2,000–3,000 men seems actually rather high.[8]

A re-evaluation of the state of the country is also necessitated by the evidence concerning the Early Stuart government's reliance on martial law. Under the Tudors, the expansion of common law and the English court system had been a frequent aspiration, but they made only limited and uneven progress. With the commencement of Stuart rule, this had changed. By the time of the Ulster Plantation (1610), regular sittings of county courts took place in every shire on the island, overseen by the crown judges on circuit.[9] Yet, in spite of this improvement, the Early Stuart government continued to make extensive use of martial law and the wide-ranging powers of summary execution of 'offenders', 'malefactors' and 'wrongdoers' that it made possible. Because martial law is only occasionally recorded in the state papers of the period (and the work of the judges is quite well referenced), most historians of early seventeenth-century Irish government have over-emphasised the supposed transition from the harsh methods of the Tudors to the 'normalising' methods of the Stuarts. The explosion and fire at the Dublin Public Record Office in 1922 destroyed nearly all the original commissions of martial law granted by the Stuart government. Extant in-house lists, however, made in the nineteenth century by Record Office staff, provide details of many of the commissions issued.[10]

Until 1605, the number of martial law commissioners remained at a peak wartime level, after which any scaling back involved a re-organisation more than a real reduction. For the remainder of King James's reign, martial law was maintained more formally than before, usually attached to important military and local government offices. Yet as in Elizabethan times, the viceroy enjoyed the prerogative right to issue new commissions, as and when he thought fit. Significantly, both Sir Arthur Chichester (viceroy 1605–16) and his successor Sir Oliver St John, Viscount Grandison (1616–22), exercised this power enthusiastically, while other important officials, such as the lords president, the marshal of the army and the provincial provosts marshal continued to enjoy the right to issue martial law commissions at a local level. Consequently, for many ordinary Irish subjects of the crown the possibility of being hanged without trial, or other arbitrary punishments, by the army or other military agents remained a daily reality, just as it had under the Tudors – except more so, as the power of the government now obtruded into every district.

But why, in peacetime, was there such widespread recourse to oppression? The dominance of government by the military interest provides one explanation. Besides the viceroyalty, held by ex-soldiers from 1603 to 1622, veterans of the Elizabethan wars also controlled the two provincial lord presidencies in Munster and Connacht during these years.[11] The inner ring of the Jacobean and early Caroline Irish Privy Council likewise consisted mainly of military figures, predisposed to strong methods of control.[12] But the fear of external attack by the monarchy's continental enemies and the encouragement that this might give to disaffected elements within the country also played a part. Ever since the end of the Nine Years War in 1603, many thousands of Irish soldiers had moved to Europe, and continued to do so.[13] The prospect of their return with continental reinforcements and of widespread rebellion haunted the Stuart government. It helped to insure that military men and military considerations remained influential in Dublin Castle.

I

Three primary sources spanning the period from the Ulster plantation to the 1641 rising, each approximately a dozen years apart, shed some light on the nature of the government's concerns. The first source is a private letter sent from Dublin by the Solicitor General of Ireland, Sir Robert Jacob, to his patron in England the earl of Northampton in November 1613. No admirer of the military clique that surrounded Chichester, Jacob was convinced that the government had failed to make Ireland safer for English and Protestant rule. 'Conspiracies', he claimed, abounded, organised around (un-named) 'former rebels' whose contacts and movements at home and abroad had not been properly investigated. Instead of pursuing these subversive elements, Jacob alleged that the Chichester regime had only made the situation worse through crude over-reliance on blanket coercion. He reserved his sharpest criticism for the 'extreme oppressions and extortions' that the army perpetrated daily on the people. Such provocative antics, he noted, 'hath ever been the ruin of this commonwealth'.[14]

The second document is an anonymous 'Abstract' of the state of Ireland from late 1625, months after the death of James VI & I and the accession of King Charles. Compiled by a single official with access to confidential government information, it brings together the contents of various reports from different parts of the country.[15] The unifying theme of the 'Abstract' is English security. In the final years of James's reign, the crown attempted to negotiate a royal marriage with Habsburg Spain, partly to increase English/'British' diplomatic influence in Catholic Europe, but also to secure a rich Spanish dowry to offset the gaping deficit in English crown finances. The negotiations collapsed and led to the outbreak of war with Spain in 1624.[16] At once Ireland became the focus of heightened concern that the recent relaxation of anti-Catholic measures in the country to facilitate Spanish demands would give confidence to the native lords and their followers. Moreover, the prospect of outside help might soon lead the Irish to act against the crown.

The compiler of the 1625 'Abstract' feared the worst, representing the country as drawing close to the brink of a major rebellion. According to the document, widespread and growing discontent existed almost everywhere, due to land forfeitures and colonisation, the renewed threat of religious persecution and the destabilising agitation of continentally trained Catholic clergy. The lack of major leaders among the Catholic Irish, particularly in Ulster, the area perceived as the most likely source of trouble, provided the one positive note in the report. Rebel elements were reckoned to be lying low, awaiting the foreign help which might bring the earls of Tyrone, Tyrconnell and other exiled lords and chieftains home as part of a foreign invasion. The report recommended that measures be adopted to prevent this prospect, giving lengthy consideration to prevailing conditions in all four provinces. In Ulster, the plantation would make little difference to crown security: the province was still too thinly populated by colonists, while resident native lords such as the earl of Antrim, Sir Connor Maguire and the chief of the MacMahons were seen as untrustworthy. Munster, apparently, did not pose such a risk, although the port towns remained in the hands of powerful Catholic merchants in regular commercial contact with Spain, Flanders and France. The report identified the western and eastern provinces as the greatest sources of immediate danger, with poor coastal defences and rebellious natives in Mayo, Wicklow and Wexford.[17]

The third item, a letter written on 30 May 1639 by Viceroy Thomas Wentworth in Dublin to Sir Henry Vane in London, is perhaps the most curious. Written in response to the crisis in Scotland, the letter opens with a characteristically confident assertion that the Scottish Covenanters posed little real threat to English rule in Ireland, but then proceeds to give an unusually frank assessment of the brittle state of the country. Historians have cited this letter as evidence of Wentworth's wariness of the Scottish settler population in Ulster, but less attention has been paid to the comments he made about conditions in the rest of the country. He recognised Connacht as highly unsettled, reeling under the threat of his hugely ambitious plantation scheme: 'He that loseth least is to have a full fourth of all his lands taken for the King.' Munster too, he admitted, contained many aggrieved landowners, uncertain of their titles. In Ulster, apart from the Scots, sizeable numbers of native outlaws and bandits in Donegal confronted the government. Gaelic Leinster, however, posed the biggest threat. Wentworth informed Vane that a rebellion of 'beggarly desperate natives' had been underway since late 1638, in an area encompassing five counties – Laois, Offaly, Carlow, Wicklow and Wexford. Though certain he would eventually prevail, Wentworth nonetheless stated that the army of 3,000 men (1,000 horse and 2,000 foot) would be insufficient for all the required military operations.[18] Wentworth never got his reinforcements, but that is not the point. Had he obtained them, the garrison in Ireland would have been restored to the levels pertaining in periods of high emergency during the reign of Elizabeth I. Wentworth may have disparaged the rebels of Ulster and Leinster as beggars, but he clearly feared their capacity to incite a more widespread show of resistance. His government's authority, not yet at breaking point, was definitely under strain.

II

Of course, three items covering thirty years is hardly a sound basis for remodelling the political state of Early Stuart Ireland. While the content of each document is striking, emphasising developments generally at odds with the more tranquil picture often favoured by scholars of the period, the underlying volatility they describe should not be accepted (or prevailing orthodoxies revised) without adequate corroboration. The ensuing pages will attempt to determine the accuracy of each of the three documents by identifying the extent to which the disturbances and other dangers they high-lighted are supported by other sources.

Taking Sir Robert Jacob's report of 1613 as an indicator of the Irish security situation during the early stages of the Ulster plantation, the emphasis he placed on the prospect of a new conspiracy led by 'former rebels' mirrored the concerns of English officialdom at the time. Like other senior servitors, memories of the Nine Years War and its unsatisfactory outcome haunted Jacob. Though not stated, his letter to Northampton coincided with fresh rumours of the imminent return to Ireland of the exiled rebel leader, Hugh O'Neill, earl of Tyrone.[19] The earl's movements invariably induced a degree of consternation, in part because of his perceived status as an Irish national leader – as a prospective 'King of Ireland', no less, according to the Mayor of Plymouth.[20] Moreover, several of the earl's former confederates had managed to survive military defeat and remain in Ireland. Jacob's fellow officials expected that Tyrone's return would reactivate these old alliances and trigger a new rebellion. Yet, as Jacob's letter shows, other factors also influenced government fears of fresh trouble elsewhere in the country. While Sir Robert failed to provide specific geographical detail, other officials identified quite precisely several parts of the country that seemed unstable. Indeed, careful perusal of government papers of the period reveals large areas acknowledged by the authorities as only very loosely under crown control.

Ulster caused particular anxiety. Although the plantation area was enclosed by a ring of forts that stretched in an arc from Ballyshannon on the Atlantic coast to Newry and the north Irish Sea, considerable unrest persisted across the province. A sense of the prevailing local conditions is revealed by the grant of a royal pardon in 1611 to five of the principal garrison commanders active in Tyrone, Armagh and the surrounding region. Issued on the instructions of Viceroy Chichester, the pardon protected the officers from prosecution for killings by martial law, carried out 'in the furtherance of His Majesty's service' since the beginning of the Plantation – killings which went far beyond the extensive powers of summary execution they already possessed.[21] Over the following few years, the government continued to indulge similar excesses by the garrison which 'in strictness of law . . . may be questioned', because in many areas the settlers arriving from England, Wales and Lowland Scotland remained vulnerable to roving bands of native rebels and bandits.[22] According to surviving evidence for the County Londonderry lands of the Company of Ironmongers, sightings of rebels hiding in nearby woods frequently inter-rupted building work on the company's estate during 1614 and 1615. The estate of the Mercers' Company fared worse: in August 1615, the company agent was 'set on by the rebels within four miles of his house and shot through the breeches', while at Christmastime a band of nine Irish kerne stabbed three English tenants to death, leaving a fourth badly wounded.[23] A sectarian element is evident in the murder of a recently arrived Protestant minister, stabbed forty-four times by his assailants, while a lay settler was slain defending another minister.[24] In order to prevent the ongoing troubles among the MacDonnells in Antrim and the Western Isles acting as a spark for more general commotion across the north, a government force sailed to Islay to lay siege to Dunyveg Castle late in 1614.[25]

Although Chichester made political capital of an ensuing conspiracy among the O'Neills and O'Cahans, exaggerating its threat to prorogue the Irish Parlia-ment in late spring 1615,[26] this action was exceptional. More usually, he and his successor Sir Oliver St John tried to play down the danger posed by native resistance in Ulster, in order to appear fully in control of the plantation project. Hence their claims that the raids and killings were carried out by just 'a few outlaws', 'six or seven score', who would soon 'be scattered without any great labour'.[27] Their reassurances masked a very different situation. In 1619, St John tacitly admitted that he was unable to keep a lid on the ongoing troubles in Ulster when he apologised to the Privy Council for not reporting sooner that 'sundry disorderly persons [had] gone into rebellion' in 'the farthest parts of the County of Tyrone', and in Londonderry likewise. In a subsequent letter, he admitted that 'within these three years' – that is, since 1616 – no less than 300 rebels had been killed by government forces in the north. 'When one sort is cut off, others arise in their places', he cried, and when 'they are sought for to be punished for disorders . . . they go to the woods to maintain themselves by the spoil'.[28]

And yet Ulster did not always constitute the chief concern of the Jacobean authorities. Echoing Sir Robert Jacob, conditions across the south troubled other senior personnel. The Boyle Papers record several instances of violence and unrest in the province of Munster during these years. Consider, for example, County Waterford, a part of the country usually ignored in the historiography: in 1613, Richard Boyle took action against a group of native outlaws targeting his lands; in 1617, his English tenants reported an attack at Dungarvan; in 1619, the county court condemned one of the Powers of Curraghmore for treason for his involvement in a conspiracy with several other unnamed people; early in 1620, the Lord President, the earl of Thomond, deemed it advisable to have troops from the garrison in Waterford City quartered on outlying parts of the shire to maintain order; while a few months later the sheriff of the county doubted his ability to keep control at the county jail, teeming with prisoners rounded up over previous months, unless the President responded to his plea to bring the troops back into the city from the countryside.[29]

But a region much closer to Dublin called 'Low Leinster', encompassing the three counties of Wicklow, Carlow and Wexford, caused the greatest concern to crown officials. Since Tudor times, the government had struggled to curb the capacity for sustained resistance of the Gaelic (and gaelicised) lineages inhabiting the mountainous and heavily wooded terrain of the area. By the time Sir Robert Jacob wrote to Northampton in 1613, the government had commenced a fresh initiative to break the back of Gaelic power in Low Leinster, primarily through the introduction of a plantation in north Wexford. As in Ulster, however, things did not exactly go to plan, despite the best endeavours of the army in expelling uncooperative natives from their former lands in 1613 and the arrival of 700 soldiers from Wales to crush opposition in 1615.[30] By 1619, attacks on settlers by small bands of horsemen and kerne had become common, and the ongoing crackdown only brought limited results. In November that year, the government announced preparations to send large numbers of soldiers from Dublin into the Wexford borders to make 'a main prosecution' – that is, a full military campaign – against the rebels.[31] Space does not permit a detailed discussion of these operations, which dragged on for a year or more; suffice it to say that the events there, combined with the simultaneous rebellion in Ulster and the growing disturbances in Munster, paint a rather different picture of the political situation in Ireland in the late Jacobean era to one of prevailing peace.

Historians have correctly identified the partial reorientation and relaxation of royal policy in Ireland in 1622–23 as an important development, which seemed to promise Irish Catholic lords and political leaders much greater influence in the years to come. The lack of attention, however, paid to the military and security measures employed by the crown immediately beforehand has caused some scholars to minimise the very serious tensions affecting the country, beneath the level of the Catholic leadership, especially in those areas affected by plantation. Looking ahead, the key question is, did the increasing dialogue between Irish Catholic leaders and the crown that characterised the high politics of the later 1620s produce any discernible improvement in the security situation?

III

The second of our key documents, the anonymous 1625 report on the state of the country, would suggest not. The dialogue between the Irish leadership and the government took place as the fear of rebellion actually intensified, stoked up by parallel concerns of a French or Spanish invasion. Indeed, the negotiations known as 'the Graces', in which the crown offered loyalist Catholics a range of concessions in return for higher taxes, were greatly complicated not just by native demands for religious toleration and better land security, but also by mounting outrage around the country provoked by the behaviour of the army and martial law officials charged with quelling the threat of insurrection.[32] Had the prospect of revolt and invasion not seemed so urgent, this problem might not have materialised.

As ever, Ulster loomed largest in government security assessments, especially the weak coastal defences of western Ulster.[33] In 1627, the landing of pirates at Killybegs in Country Donegal provoked panic far beyond the magnitude of the incident. But, as expressed in the 1625 report, the crown continued to be concerned by other parts of the country, albeit now with a far greater emphasis on Connacht and south-west Munster. In June 1625, an alleged conspiracy involving disgruntled native landowners, soldiers serving abroad, and secret clerical emissaries across Mayo, Leitrim and Longford led to the imprisonment of Sir Theobald Burke and Myles Burke in Dublin Castle. The fact that the government issued special commissions of martial law for the whole of Connacht suggests that they expected a major disturbance.[34] In Munster, the earl of Cork received intelligence in 1626 to expect an invasion around Michaelmas of up to 17,000 Spanish and Irish troops.[35] Nothing came of these rumours, but the authorities took them very seriously.

In July 1624, the army had been increased to 4,000 men, with the government subsequently under pressure to raise this to 6,000.[36] In Ulster, local Protestant landowners received commissions as governors of their districts 'as well for . . . the defence and safety' of the British colonists, as 'for the punishment and reformation of enormous (sic) and evil disposed persons'. An increased army presence was designed to prevent the natives of coastal counties provoking a war at any opportunity.[37] Munster witnessed some of the most draconian measures. Following royal instructions to the lord president to raise an emergency auxiliary force for use 'against rebels or otherwise . . . as occasion shall require', the inhabitants of the southern ports found themselves quartered with these troops for months on end, despite growing resentment and petitions by merchants predicting the ruin of the local economy.[38] In Leinster, local evidence from Kilkenny city – long a centre of Catholic loyalism – describes a tense situation in 1627–28 as the urban population attacked members of the new garrison quartered there, who went on the rampage in retaliation.[39] More serious still was the Wexford Plantation. In 1628, the main government officer in Wexford, Lawrence, Lord Esmond, had to intensify his military policing of the colonists' lands following reports of up to 600 natives, 'well armed', assembling in the woodlands near Gorey.[40] The political effect of these deployments was considerable, as it directly contradicted the crown's guarantees of army reform, given to the Catholic leadership during the negotiation of 'the Graces'.[41]

Revealingly, a number of conspiracies were discovered as military policing intensified. In August 1625, the governor of Enniskillen, and a senior martial law officer, Sir William Cole, obtained information about the intentions of the MacGoverns of Cavan and the Maguires of Fermanagh to amass a large store of weapons in anticipation of a Spanish landing. In an entry in his diary, Sir James Ware adds that the plotters intended to commence their revolt by surprising the garrison at Enniskillen Castle. The subsequent investigation identified four ringleaders and brought them to trial before a jury comprised exclusively of Englishmen. Sentenced to death, they had to be taken away to Dublin for fear of a riot; even then, they required an armed escort to prevent a rescue attempt by sympathisers.[42]

Trouble spread across the province. In April 1627, with Spanish invasion plans advancing in Madrid, reports appeared of 'a new and dangerous rebellion' in Counties Antrim, Down and parts of north-western Armagh. In Carrickfergus Castle, Sir Edward Chichester (son of the former viceroy) despatched a company of soldiers to suppress the Gaelic septs living nearby, following a series of outrages and robberies. Disturbances, including 'murders and other mischiefs', occurred around the same time in Cavan, Monaghan and Longford. As well as issuing new martial law commissions to officials in the province, the viceroy, Lord Falkland, empowered one of his most experienced counter-insurgency experts, Sir Charles Coote, to vacate temporarily his post as Provost Marshal and Vice-President of Connacht to help impose order across Ulster. A new provost marshal, Sir William Windsor, joined him before long. Basing himself in County Armagh to deal with dissidents in the centre of the province, Coote left Windsor to scour further afield, to the east. In the course of his operations, Windsor encountered several armed groups. By his own account, in July 1627 he killed 'upwards of threescore [60] rebels' in the field, 'besides others' – unarmed peasants and the like, the sort of collateral damage typical of English counter-insurgency tactics in Ireland since the middle of the previous century. Thereafter the level of native resistance declined in the north, but only partly because of the efficacy of the English military crackdown: in June 1629, Moses Hill, the principal military policeman in Ulster, complained that the local magistrates had not executed enough of those offenders he had captured, so that large numbers of 'woodkerne' remained alive, and those in Tyrone 'were almost ready to go into rebellion'.[43] In the event, Irish awareness of Philip IV's decision to abort the proposed Spanish invasion prevented a major outbreak of violence.

The authorities did not doubt that the unrest had been religious as well as political. In addition to a rumour that the third earl of Tyrone, Sean O'Neill (Hugh O'Neill's son), had obtained a golden crown directly from the Pope in Rome, more accurate intelligence identified the Catholic Bishop of Raphoe, Owen O'Cullinane, as a prime mover of the proposed invasion from his exiled base in Madrid. This resulted in extra surveillance on Catholic clergy everywhere, including one 'Father O'Dempsey' in Queen's County, and Luke Archer in Kilkenny, 'a pardoned survivor of the last rebellion [i.e., 1603]'.[44] Ware's diary records that in 1627 a priest named Patrick O'Mulvaney appeared in Dublin accusing many of treason. The government had encountered him before, when he apparently converted to Protestantism only to subsequently revert to Rome. Suspecting him of being a double-agent intent on placing loyal Catholics in doubt while hatching a real plot behind their backs, the authorities put him to the rack in Dublin Castle. Falkland's officers also swooped on another clergyman, the 'abbot of Ashcoe', but he allegedly hanged himself rather than submit to torture.[45] A year later, O'Mulvaney's claims and denials still troubled the government. Under torture, he implicated the Catholic Bishop of Down in the Ulster invasion plan. Following his arrest, the bishop died a prisoner in Dublin Castle on 23 November 1628 and was buried in secret four days later, in St Werburgh's churchyard, at 4 o'clock in the morning.[46]

IV

Although no rebellion of real size materialised during the 1610s and 1620s, reports of violent disturbances throughout the country appeared on a regular basis. In July 1633, at the very time that the new lord deputy, Thomas Wentworth landed in Dublin harbour, an anonymous memorandum entitled 'Concerning Ireland', written to represent the opinion of the most experienced officials in the country, argued that the army had to be maintained at a high level as a matter of necessity. Without it, the report said, the Protestant settlers, and each of the plantations, would be in grave danger, a view overlooked in the historiography of Wentworth's Ireland.[47]

Similarly, almost nothing has been said of the fact that after barely a year in office, Wentworth faced a serious rebel threat in central and southern Ulster, as well as in north Leinster, which seems to have experienced little unrest before this time.[48] A volume of extracts taken from Wentworth's 'Irish Docquet Book' in the late seventeenth or early eighteenth century, copied from the original manuscript which has since been lost, records details of the conspiracy.[49] The initial notice of the rebel plot is dated 26 March 1634, when Robert Blayney, son of the English military governor of Monaghan, Edward, Lord Blayney, received full martial law authority to prosecute rebels in Monaghan, Cavan, Tyrone, Fermanagh, Armagh and Louth.[50] The authorities arrested the apparent leader of the revolt, one Ross Boy McBrian Sariagh MacMahon, 'a notorious rebel and malefactor'.[51] On 10 May 1634, Robert Blayney's authority was extended by a further three months, as Ross Boy's followers and confederates remained out in arms.[52]

The revolt dragged on because MacMahon was not its only leader. Wentworth's docquet book also identifies Philip McShane O'Reilly, captured in Cavan early in the rebellion, as a prominent figure, along with Mulmory McPhilip O'Reilly of Tullygarvey.[53] As with previous risings and disturbances, the revolt failed to develop into a major outbreak, primarily due to the arrest of its leaders.[54] Even so, the rebellion was clearly significant, and Wentworth authorised measures to dissuade the local Gaelic lineages from attempting any other surprises. Ross Boy MacMahon was publicly hanged like a common thief 'by means of Mr Blayney', an insult to his status as a lesser Gaelic lord. His confederates probably met a similar fate. Mulmory O'Reilly died in 1635, while Philip McShane O'Reilly simply disappears from the records after his capture in 1634.[55] Subsequently, the government moved to bolster security in the region, despatching additional troops to augment the garrisons, and organising new musters for the English settlers, to improve their use of weapons.[56] Nevertheless, the borderlands of south-east Ulster and north Leinster remained volatile. In late July 1635, more than a year after the MacMahon–O'Reilly conspiracy, the King wrote to Wentworth on behalf of a settler in County Monaghan, whose land had recently been forcefully seized from him by a sept of the MacMahons.[57]

In his letter to Sir Henry Vane in 1639, Wentworth does not mention the MacMahons or O'Reillys, as by then Scottish settlers, rather than the native Irish, seemed to pose the greatest threat to the state. Nonetheless, serious disturbances reported from Donegal since 1636 only now received a mention.[58] Just as he claimed the Donegal attacks were a recent (and so, by implication, less serious) development, he likewise downplayed the longevity of the troubles throughout Gaelic Leinster, which also had been going on continuously for several years.[59] In May 1635, Lord Esmond brought a detachment of royal troops to New Ross in Wexford in pursuit of Simon Prendergast, 'the chief of the rogues who are in rebellion'. Esmond feared that the O'Brennans in north County Kilkenny might combine with Prendergast's force, and with other renegades said to be lurking about Mount Leinster.[60] Significantly, his efforts to secure the borders of the Wexford Plantation failed. In 1636, Prendergast's rebels attacked an English settler, Thomas Danvers, mutilating his face with a cut 'five inches long', as a means of intimidation, presumably to obtain protection payments.[61] In 1637, rebel bands were still reported as lurking around the fringes of the Wexford plantation, 'the English in those parts being altogether suppressed'.[62] During the winter of 1637–8, rebel attacks caused growing concern, as their ability to elude capture exposed the inadequacy of Wentworth's crown forces, and encouraged unrest elsewhere. The concern proved justified. By early 1638, having lain dormant for a period, rebels in neighbouring Country Wicklow once again began raiding and intimidating the settlers there.[63]

The Midlands plantations experienced similar unrest. The Davells Papers in the Carte collection in the Bodleian Library contain several items recording the activities of members of the native O'Doran and O'Lawlor families (two of the 'seven septs' of Laois) during the mid-1630s, as the planter Thomas Davells strove to drive them off the land. In presenting their legal defence, spokesmen for the two native families attempted to clear themselves of any association with a large band of local rebels in the area who were 'burning houses' of English settlers. Several of the rebels had been apprehended by the local garrison, convicted at the county assizes and executed. Unfortunately, the document describing this rebel activity is not dated, but it belongs to a clutch of papers that record developments in Laois between 1634 and 1637.[64] When added to Wentworth's letter to Vane of 1639, something notable is discovered: the executions failed to quell the unrest. In the winter of 1638–9, rebels burned down the houses of more Englishmen in Laois and Offaly.[65]

West of the Shannon, Wentworth readily admitted that the perilous situation there was due entirely to the scale of his proposed plantation of the province. In August 1638, Sir Francis Willoughby, the lieutenant-governor, brought his company to Loughrea to deal with an assembly of County Galway landowners who had gathered there to protest (peacefully) against the terms of the plantation. Willoughby's show of force inflamed the situation, with several landowners committed to prison, including some of the Burkes, the chief men of the country. Troops occupied outlying Burke lands, but similar actions on the Thomond side of Limerick city did not involve government troops for fear of the reaction.[66] The requirement that the commander of the royal forces already stationed in Limerick should attempt to disguise his forces' withdrawal as due to some other factor, lest their departure 'might [itself] stir a buzz in the people's minds', is perhaps the best indication of how nervous the authorities had become by 1639.[67] Clearly, Wentworth's letter to Vane of May 1639 concealed as much as it revealed.

During his time as viceroy, Wentworth rarely discussed regional unrest in his official correspondence or in his declarations of service, intent on maintaining the impression that everything remained under control. In 1639, by force of circumstances, as the crisis escalated across the three Stuart kingdoms, the facade slipped. He knew a Scottish Covenanter army invading Ulster would have attracted the support of disaffected elements from several areas of the country – not only the Scottish settlers in Ulster, the group invariably identified as his chief security worry, but also from angry Gaelic-Irish and Anglo-Irish in parts of Ulster, Leinster, the Midlands and Connacht. For all of his customary swagger, the Scottish invasion scare laid bare the reality that like any of his predecessors Wentworth only retained a tentative hold on the security of Ireland.

A major increase in the royal garrison, to the levels desired by Wentworth, might have finally broken the pattern of persistent local rebellion that had confronted the Dublin government for over a generation. But, of course, this did not prove possible. Charles I had no intention of sending reinforcements to Ireland; on the contrary, just days after writing to Vane, Wentworth learned that the King expected a horse troop to be 'fetched over' from the Irish garrison to strengthen the crown forces facing the Scots in the north of England.[68] The King gave Wentworth nothing more than a free hand to deal with dissent and unrest as he wished. As is well known, Wentworth subjected the Ulster Scots to special measures in the summer of 1639, surrounding their lands with crown troops and forcing them to take the 'Black Oath'. Less well known is the fact that Wentworth's soldiers targeted more than the Ulster Scots.

Beginning in November 1638, the lord deputy initiated a shake-up of the senior security personnel in the provinces to insure that those charged with the imposition of martial law and other 'emergency' measures were loyal to him, prepared to do whatever it took to quell disturbances and crush native rebellion. Accordingly, Sir Charles Coote remained in place as Provost Marshal of Connacht, but in Munster, the deputy's brother, Sir George Wentworth, replaced Sir Thomas Wenman and in Ulster he appointed a protégé, Sir Arthur Loftus, as the new provost marshal.[69] Wentworth further modified the hierarchy in the summer of 1640, appointing William Peisley, another close supporter, as provost marshal of Munster in order to facilitate Sir George Wentworth's transfer to the same post in Leinster.[70] These appointments soon proved calamitous. Although government troops killed 'divers rebels', especially in Gaelic parts of Ulster, their activities provoked widespread resentment across the country, and helped to unite opposition against the viceroy in the fateful second session of the 1640 Irish Parliament. Indeed, allegations of their misconduct featured strongly in the 'Remonstrance' prepared against him by the Irish House of Commons early in November – the same Remonstrance that shortly afterwards formed the basis of his impeachment by the English Parliament and, ultimately, his execution for treason in May 1641.[71]

And so the near-constant spark and crackle of localised rebellion helped to bring Ireland to the brink of a major conflagration in October 1641. Wentworth's primary strategy involved keeping settlers and natives (Protestants and Catholics) apart, playing one group off against the other. His authorisation, however, of severe measures against rebel areas proved hugely counter-productive: he succeeded on the one hand in revealing the full extent of the unrest and, on the other, drove settlers and natives together to form a common defence in Parliament against his indiscriminate military tyranny. The two groups would separate again, once Wentworth's fate was sealed, but the security situation did not improve with his departure. In fact, it deteriorated. In addition to a proliferation of plotting among Catholic leaders during the summer of 1641, fed by fear of government repression, fresh outbreaks of unrest occurred across several parts of the country, which revealed the government as suddenly weak. For instance, in the early months of 1641 disturbances broke out in Munster. The details are obscure but as might be expected the lord president, Sir William St Leger, oversaw a ruthless crackdown, targeting peaceful subjects alongside those in arms. On this occasion, however, St Leger felt dangerously exposed, fearing that he might suffer the same fate as Wentworth. He sought a royal pardon for his excesses, and for several months after Wentworth's execution, he took no further action.[72]

In Connacht, the government appeared similarly paralysed when a senior Gaelic lord, Teige O'Connor Sligo, raised a force 'of about two hundred men' and took possession of the lands of Wentworth's ardent supporter, Sir George Radcliffe, expelling his tenants at sword-point. Despite orders from London demanding action, O'Connor remained in possession for months until the outbreak of the rebellion in October, as officials seem to have feared the consequences of moving against him.[73] Paralysis also characterised crown personnel in southern Leinster when, late in the summer, the movements of the O'Byrnes in Wicklow and Catholic priests in north County Kilkenny unnerved the settler population.[74]

Clearly, future studies of the 1641 rebellion and its origins will have to pay more attention to all this provincial turmoil, focusing on the identity of local rebels and marginalised groups, those Wentworth tried to dismiss as 'beggarly desperate natives'. Behind such bluster, successive viceroys struggled in vain to stop the 'desperate' from destabilising the plantations and undermining government authority. Moreover, there is no doubting the direct links between at least some of these localised rebellions and the general conflagration of October 1641. As one of the senior military leaders of the 1641 rising, Colonel Richard Plunkett, stated at Newry a few weeks into the revolt, he and his colleagues had been 'for seventeen years past aplotting' – that is, since the

Spanish invasion scare of 1624, when unrest and lesser rebellions affected large parts of the country.[75]

NOTES

1 For an introduction to the contentious historiography of the rising, see Walter Love, 'Civil war in Ireland: appearances in three centuries of historical writing', *Emory University Quarterly*, 22 (1966), 57–72; Toby Barnard, '1641: a bibliographical essay', in Brian Mac Cuarta (ed.), *Ulster 1641: Aspects of the Rising* (Belfast, 1993), pp. 173–86, and Barnard, '"Parlour entertainment in an evening"? Histories of the 1640s', in Micheál Ó Siochrú (ed.), *Kingdoms in Crisis: Ireland in the 1640s* (Dublin, 2001), pp. 20–43. See also Brendan Bradshaw, 'The invention of the Irish: was the Ulster rising really a bolt from the blue?', *Times Literary Supplement* (14 October 1994), pp. 8–10, and Brian Walker, '1641, 1689, 1690 and all that: the Unionist sense of history', *The Irish Review*, 12 (1992), 56–64.

2 The best assessments of Wentworth's government remain Hugh Kearney, *Strafford in Ireland, 1633–41: A Study in Absolutism* (Manchester, 1959); Aidan Clarke, 'The government of Wentworth, 1632–40', and Clarke, 'The breakdown of authority, 1640–1', both in T. W. Moody, F. X. Martin and F. J. Byrne (eds), *A New History of Ireland, vol. 3: Early Modern Ireland, 1534–1691* (Oxford, 1976), pp. 243–69, 270–88.

3 Michael Perceval-Maxwell, *The Outbreak of the Irish Rebellion of 1641* (Montreal, 1994). Jane Ohlmeyer, 'Strafford, the "Londonderry business", and the "New British History"', in J. F. Merritt (ed.), *The Political World of Thomas Wentworth, Earl of Strafford 1621–1641* (Cambridge, 1996), pp. 209–29. This focuses chiefly on the court influence of the earls of Clanricarde and Antrim. For the Mountgarret Butlers and their links to the powerful earl of Arundel, see David Edwards, *The Ormond Lordship in County Kilkenny, 1515–1642: The Rise and Fall of Butler Feudal Power* (Dublin, 2003), pp. 297–307. Nicholas Canny, *Making Ireland British, 1580–1640* (Oxford, 2001), pp. 275–401; Canny, 'The attempted Anglicisation of Ireland in the seventeenth century: an exemplar of "British History"', in Merritt (ed.), *The Political World*, pp. 157–86.

4 Jon Crawford, *A Star Chamber Court in Ireland: The Court of Castle Chamber, 1571–1641* (Dublin, 2005), pp. 11–13, where it is also asserted (p. 13) that 'Decades after the Tyrone Rebellion, Ireland remained tranquil, if unsettled' (*sic*).

5 The exception is Joseph McLaughlin, 'The making of the Irish Leviathan: state-building in Ireland during the reign of James VI & I' (Ph.D. dissertation, NUI Galway 1999). David Edwards, 'The plight of the Earls: Tyrone and Tyrconnell's "Grievances" and crown coercion in Ulster, 1603–7', in Mary Ann Lyons and Thomas O'Connor (eds), *The Ulster Earls and Baroque Europe* (Dublin, 2010), pp. 53–76. Aidan Clarke, 'The army and politics in Ireland, 1625–30', *Studia Hibernica*, 4 (1964), 28–53. Additionally, Victor Treadwell, *Buckingham and Ireland, 1616–1628: A Study in Anglo-Irish Politics* (Dublin, 1998), contains important insights into the role of political patronage in obtaining military office and profits during the 1610s and 1620s.

6 McLaughlin, 'The making of the Irish Leviathan', chapter 10; David Edwards, 'Securing the Jacobean succession: the secret career of James Fullerton of Trinity College, Dublin', in Seán Duffy (ed.), *The World of the Galloglass: Kings, Warlords and Warriors in Ireland and Scotland, 1200–1600* (Dublin, 2005), pp. 188–219.

7 David Edwards, 'The escalation of violence in sixteenth-century Ireland', in David Edwards, Pádraig Lenihan and Clodagh Tait (eds), *Age of Atrocity: Violence and Political Conflict in Early Modern Ireland* (Dublin, 2007), pp. 66–7.

8 The reduction and partial disarming of the lordships requires detailed work; for a particularly rough outline, see David Edwards, 'Legacy of defeat: the reduction of Gaelic Ireland after Kinsale', in Hiram Morgan (ed.), *The Battle of Kinsale* (Bray, 2004), pp. 292–6.

9 John McCavitt, '"Good planets in their several spheares": the establishment of the assize courts in early seventeenth-century Ireland', *Irish Jurist*, 24 (1989), 248–78.

10 National Archives of Ireland (NAI), RC 17/4, Index to Fiants, James I, pp. 89–94; ibid., Chancery Rolls Office: Catalogue of Fiants, II, James I. These can be augmented by evidence in the Patent Rolls, Sir John Davies's warrant books and various other sources too scattered to list here. I have begun writing a monograph study of the subject, 'An early modern security state: martial law and garrison government in the English Kingdom of Ireland, 1556–1641'.

11 Viceroyalty: Sir George Carey (1603–5), as well as Chichester and St John (above). Munster: Henry, Lord Danvers (1607–15), and Donough, earl of Thomond (1615–24). Connacht: Richard, earl of Clanricarde (1604–16) and Sir Charles Wilmott (1616–44).

12 For example, Sir Toby Caulfield, Sir Richard Wingfield, Sir Oliver Lambert, and Sir Henry Power.

13 Gráinne Henry, *The Irish Military Community in Spanish Flanders, 1586–1621* (Dublin, 1992); Jerrold Casway, 'Henry O'Neill and the formation of the Irish regiment in the Netherlands, 1605', *Irish Historical Studies*, 18 (1973), 481–8; Benjamin Hazard, '"A new company of Crusaders like that of St John a Capistrano": Interaction between Irish military units and Franciscan chaplains, 1579–1654', in Garcia Hernan and Recio Morales (eds), *Extranjeros en el Ejército: Militares Irlandeses en la Sociedad Española, 1580–1818* (Madrid, 2007), pp. 181–97; Ciaran O'Scea, 'Caracena: champion of the Irish, hunter of the Moriscos', in Morgan (ed.), *The Battle*, pp. 229–39.

14 Bodleian Library, Oxford (Bodl.), Carte MS 63, Jacob to Northampton, 30 November 1613, fols 96r–97v.

15 The National Archives (TNA), London, SP 63/241/190, Abstract of certain papers concerning Ireland, n.d., after August 1625 (summarised in *Calendar of State Papers Relating to Ireland (Cal. SP Ire.), 1625–32*, pp. 71–6).

16 Glyn Redworth, *The Prince and the Infanta: The Cultural Politics of the Spanish Match* (New Haven and London, 2003).

17 As note 15 above.

18 *The Manuscripts of the Earl Cowper, K. G.*, Preserved at Melbourne Hall, Derbyshire (HMC, 3 vols, London, 1888–9), vol. ii, pp. 229–30.

19 *Cal. SP Ire.*, ed. H. C. Hamilton, E. G. Atkinson, and R. P. Mahaffy (24 vols, London, 1860-1912), *1615-25*, pp. 19-22. For Tyrone's actual movements, see Micheline Kearney Walsh, *Destruction by Peace: Hugh O'Neill after Kinsale* (Armagh, 1986), pp. 117-26, 129-40.

20 Brian Donovan and David Edwards, *British Sources for Irish History, 1485-1641: A Guide to Manuscripts in Local, Regional and Specialised Repositories in England, Scotland and Wales* Irish Military Community (IMC), Dublin, 1997, p. 43.

21 Bodl. Carte MS 61, fol. 523.

22 *Report on the Manuscripts of the Late Reginald Rawdon Hastings* (HMC, 4 vols, London, 1928-47), vol. iv, p. 48.

23 Canny, *Making Ireland British*, pp. 432-5, which brings to light for the first time material recorded in the Minute Book of the Ironmongers' Company 1609-17 (Guildhall Library, London, MS 17,278/1).

24 *Cal. SP Ire.*, *1615-25*, p. 23.

25 Ibid., pp. 6-10; David Stevenson, *Highland Warrior: Alasdair MacColla and the Civil Wars* (Edinburgh, 2003), pp. 30-1, 35-51.

26 Raymond Gillespie, *Conspiracy: Plots and Plotters in Ulster in 1615* (Belfast, 1987); Stevenson, *Highland Warrior*, pp. 39-40.

27 *Cal. SP Ire.*, *1615-25*, pp. 23, 140.

28 Ibid., p. 262.

29 National Library of Ireland (NLI), Dublin, MS 12, 813/1, p. 175; NLI, MS 12,813/2, pp. 210, 219, 232; *Lismore Papers, by Richard Boyle, Earl of Cork*, ed. A. B. Grosart (10 vols, London, 1886-8), vol. i, p. 29. The Dungarvan disturbances can be traced back several years: see Margaret Curtis Clayton (ed.), *The Council Book for the Province of Munster, c.1599-1649* (IMC, Dublin, 2008), pp. 263-4.

30 Clayton, *The Council Book, 1611-14*, pp. 337-8, 454; *Report on the Manuscripts of the Marquess of Downshire, preserved at Easthampstead Park, Berkshire* (HMC, 4 vols, London, 1924-40), vol. v, pp. 182-3.

31 *Cal. SP Ire.*, *1615-25*, pp. 262, 267-8.

32 Clarke, the main authority on the subject, has noted this (Aidan Clarke, *The Graces* (Dublin, 1968), pp. 16-17; Clarke, 'The Army and politics'), but subsequent writers have not.

33 Of course, Spanish plans were indeed centred on Ulster. In December 1625, Philip IV was advised by a leading councillor 'it would be easier and more feasible through Ireland *and the north* [my italics], where the Catholics are more numerous and more friendly towards Spain': cited in Óscar Recio Morales, *Ireland and the Spanish Empire, 1600-1825* (Dublin, 2010), pp. 105-6.

34 NAI, Catalogue and Index of Fiants, Charles I, nos. 238, 359.

35 *Lismore MSS*, vol. ii, pp. 169-70, 173.

36 *Cal. SP, Ire.*, *1615-25*, p. 511; *1625-32*, p. 14.

37 Robert Hunter, 'The Ulster Plantation in the Counties of Armagh and Cavan, 1608-41' (Ph.D. thesis, Trinity College Dublin, 1969), chapter 5, is essential reading for these developments.

38 British Library (BL), London Add. MS 11,033, Petition of Munster merchants, 27 June [1627], p. 84; Marsh's Library, Dublin, MS Z3.2.6, item 74, Warrant for the lord president, 8 April 1627.

39 Edwards, *The Ormond Lordship*, pp. 287–8.

40 TNA, SP 63/247/1188, Extract of letter, Esmond to Falkland, 28 October 1628. The army was also heavily quartered in parts of Wicklow, in case of an O'Byrne revolt, albeit in this case the measures taken were as much to do with the administration's ongoing antagonism towards the old Gaelic dynasty as any necessary precaution against invasion. See BL, Add. MS 18,824, nos. 11, 36.

41 Clarke, *The Graces*, p. 23.

42 *Cal. SP, Ire., 1625–32*, pp. 25–37, 39–40; Gilbert Library, Dublin, Gilbert MS 169, fol. 119.

43 BL, Sloane MS 3827, fols 163r–164v.

44 *Cal. SP, Ire., 1625–32*, p. 297.

45 Gilbert MS 169, fol. 127.

46 Ibid., fol. 194.

47 TNA, SP 63/254/49, Memorandum concerning Ireland, 26 July 1633.

48 For some time I thought I was the first to discover this, only to learn I am not! The late Bob Hunter got there before me, in his exemplary unpublished dissertation (Hunter, 'The Ulster plantation in the counties of Armagh and Cavan', chapter 6). I have here attempted to augment his account with some additional references from the original source and some fresh genealogical information.

49 Bodl., Carte MS 67, fols 6r–11r.

50 Ibid., fol. 8v.

51 Ibid.

52 Ibid., fol. 8v.

53 Ibid.

54 Ibid., fol. 10r; Shortly before it erupted, Captain Neal O'Neill, a close adherent of the exiled earl of Tyrone, had been in Ulster, ostensibly to raise troops for Flanders, but possibly also to make connections on his master's behalf. Ibid., fol. 7v. For Captain Neal (or Niall) O'Neill and the 3rd earl of Tyrone see Jerrold I. Casway, *Owen Roe O'Neill and the Struggle for Catholic Ireland* (Philadelphia 1984), p. 45.

55 My thanks to Kenneth Nicholls for some of this information.

56 *Cal. SP Ire., 1633–47*, pp. 77, 102.

57 Ibid., p. 110.

58 Strafford MSS, 16, Stewart to Wentworth, 7 March 1636.

59 It is difficult to determine the precise origins of the Wexford troubles. In autumn 1634, Wexford was reported as having suffered very little stealing or banditry *that summer* – unlike, by implication, the previous summer: Strafford MSS, 14, Esmond to Wentworth 26 October 1634.

60 Strafford MSS, 15, Esmond to Wentworth, 30 May 1635.

61 Strafford MSS, 16, Esmond to Wentworth, 20 December 1636.

62 BL, Harl. MS 430, fol. 406.

63 Strafford MSS, 17, John Bowell to Wentworth, 13 February 1638.

64 The answers of Teige O'Lawlor *et al.*, n.d. (Bodl. Carte MS 176, fols 14r–15r).

65 *Cowper MSS*, vol. ii, pp. 229–30. For the troubles in Offaly and MacCoughlan's country during spring/summer 1638, see NAI, MS 2448, pp. 57–8.

66 *Manuscripts of the Earl of Egmont* (HMC, 3 vols, London, 1920–3), vol. i, pp. 105–6.

67 Ibid., pp. 111–12.
68 Strafford MSS, 10a, Wentworth to Lord Clifford, 2 June 1639, pp. 332–3. This was in addition to Antrim's regiment stationed near Carlisle.
69 NAI, Catalogue and Index of Fiants, Charles I, nos 842, 2479, 3091.
70 Ibid., nos 3136, 3246. Peisley's brothers Bartholomew and Francis were heavily involved in Wentworth's acquisition of land in Counties Kildare, Wicklow and Sligo, for example, Donovan and Edwards, *British Sources*, pp. 275, 286.
71 TCD, MS 808, fol. 137v. For the circumstances of Wentworth's impeachment, see especially Clarke, 'The breakdown', pp. 277–85, and Perceval-Maxwell, *The Outbreak*. That the charges against Wentworth were hurriedly prepared, and thus failed to give detailed corroboration of the martial 'tyranny' he was accused of, should not detract from the fact that the actions of the provosts marshal and other military personnel were used to instigate the most damaging charges against him.
72 NLI, Doneraile Papers, MS 34,129 (3).
73 NLI, De Freyne MSS, PC 12,084, item 16, Warrant of Lords Justice and Council to Teige O'Connor, 21 September 1641. I wish to thank Tom Desmond of the National Library Manuscript Reading Room for enabling me to consult this document prior to the transfer of all packing case material from Kildare Street to new stores. For the background to developments in Sligo, see Mary O'Dowd, *Power, Politics and Land: Early Modern Sligo 1568–1688* (Belfast, 1991), pp. 105–30.
74 NLI, Prior Wandesford MSS, 'The case concerning the territory of Idough', n.d., [August–September 1641].
75 TCD MS 834, Deposition of Roger Holland, 4 March 1642, fol. 120r.

7

News from Ireland: Catalan, Portuguese and Castilian pamphlets on the Confederate War in Ireland.[1]

HIRAM MORGAN

During the Irish wars of the 1590s, printed news on the continent about developments in Ireland emanated from the Roman press of Bernandino Beccari.[2] Surprisingly, in the more advanced media environment of the 1640s, with Papal representatives based at Kilkenny and prominent in Irish affairs, Italian printers of news paid little attention to Irish affairs. In the 1640s, most of the printed news and opinion about Ireland in Catholic Europe came from the home of so many of the Irish exiles – the Iberian Peninsula. In addition to featuring in general news, at least a dozen published items related to developments in Ireland. These Iberian publications fall naturally into three groups – pamphlets from the 'rebel' city of Barcelona, all dating from 1641 and 1642: a range of material from Lisbon, the capital of the newly restored kingdom of Portugal, dating from the early and middle 1640s; and more pamphlets from Castile, consisting mainly of re-publications of Irish Catholic Confederate material.

These publications provide the opportunity to discover new factual material relating to the Irish situation, which has not survived in repositories in Ireland or Britain. Even more interesting from an historical point of view is the possibility of comparison with rebellions against the Spanish multiple-monarchy going on in the peninsula, not dissimilar to the struggle in the three Stuart kingdoms, though finding analogies has not proved straightforward. On the other hand, the Catholic reception of the news of the killings of Protestants in Ireland is very apparent in these pamphlets, as is the changing allegiance of the Irish in continental geo-politics.

The 1640s constitute the high point of the so-called 'general crisis of the seventeenth century'. Forty years ago, Aidan Clarke applied the general crisis theory in an Irish context to explain the outbreak of the 1641 rebellion as the reaction of alienated nobility in the rapidly integrating Stuart states.[3] In fact, it is quite striking how the Irish, through their experience of migration and exile, appeared at many of the nodal points in the crisis-racked European system, not only in the Stuart monarchy, but also in the Habsburg one. In Spain, a number of leading figures made the connection between the experiences of both monarchs.[4] The Count-Duke of Olivares, Philip IV's chief minister, knew that *La Monarchia Española* faced a challenge similar to that engaging the government of Charles I. He discussed the matter with the Stuart ambassador, Sir Arthur Hopton, when Charles I's troubles began in Scotland, and boasted that Philip IV would not end up surrendering to his subjects in such an ignominious fashion. Ironically, within a few short years he would end up being sacrificed to avoid exactly that scenario.[5] In the *Nicandro*, a political testament, written just before his fall, Olivares described these developments as universal, providential, maybe even the beginning of the end of time:

> We have seen the whole North upset and altered, its rivers running with blood, its populous provinces wasted; England, Ireland and Scotland burning in civil wars, an emperor of the Turks attacked in the streets of Istanbul, the Ottomans scorched in civil wars, afterwards the Persians. China invaded by the Tatars, Ethiopia by the Turks, the kings of India between the Ganges and Indus con-sumed in similar fashion. Which province has not in its way – if not affected by war, then by earthquakes, epidemics and famines – felt the rigour of this universal deluge? What blame then attaches to the Duke when the world is subject to such misadventures?[6]

Certainly Spain, with a revolt in the Philippines and a conspiracy in Mexico, faced a series of interlocking problems, nearly as catastrophic for Philip IV in Castile as for Charles I in England. The key difference, however, was that the central component of the Spanish monarchy did not collapse under the strain. Rather than religion aggravating relations between court and country, the strain from long years of war in the Low Countries and Germany eventually reached breaking point in Catalonia in 1640. In the same way as the Scottish situation brought forward the crisis in Ireland, the demands of Madrid on the increasingly recalcitrant Portuguese for an army to suppress Catalonia pro-voked a revolution in Lisbon. These linked nationalist revolts represented the outworking of a crisis at the centre between supporters and opponents of Olivares, his war policy and its accompanying centralising defence and taxation policies. Nonetheless, the centre survived. Castile, unlike England, retained an ultra loyal and conservative church and a compliant Parliament, enabling Philip IV to struggle on by sacking Olivares and taking personal control of the war against the French and their allies, the Catalans and Portuguese.[7]

Not only did the crises in the Stuart and Habsburg monarchies exhibit similarities in structure and process, but also in effect. One of these was the development of a mass print media, in London in particular, as well as on a smaller scale in Barcelona and Lisbon. Lively presses developed rapidly in

Catalonia and Portugal following their revolts from Castile, as they kept tabs on the respective developments of their situations.[8] In Castile, however, the media remained conservative. Its printed publications, emanating mostly from the presses of Seville, came in the older form of relations about royal events, military victories or prodigies. Because of the lack of news-sheets and gazettes, the private circulation of news to friends and subscribers by court gossips such as Pellicer and Barrionuevo remained important in Castile.[9] These diverse printing scenarios pose questions about whether these publications were propaganda-led, driven by demand or prompted by the sheer novelty of publishing something out of the ordinary.

One notable aspect of this reportage is how strongly Ireland features in Iberian news. News from Ireland came through diplomatic channels, mercantile links and from travellers such as churchmen, students and soldiers. The information might be their own or it might come already digested in manuscript or printed form. In Iberia, news spread from the ports, leaked from official sources or disseminated in the first instance in the Irish community and then into wider society. Increasingly, the news formed part of the media industry, with information copied and translated from news-sheets already in circulation in London, Amsterdam, Paris or even Kilkenny.

I

Barcelona publications indicate a strong interest in Irish events at a time ironically when Irish regiments in the service of Spain were heavily involved in the attempted suppression of their revolt. John O'Neill, earl of Tyrone, commander of an Irish tercio, had already died leading his troops bravely against the heights of Montjuich in a failed attempt to retake the city.[10] Word of the Irish rebellion of 23 October 1641 first appeared under the title 'Extraordinary News' in a pamphlet printed in Catalan in Barcelona on 17 November, alongside a piece welcoming the victory of the anti-Spanish Pope Urban VIII against the Farnese at Castro. The publication set these events in the context of certain astrological predictions recently made in Constantinople.[11] The Catalan pamphleteers maintained their interest in the developing Irish situation and in April 1642 they advertised more 'Extraordinary News', including a copy of an oath sworn by the rebels, printed side by side with the articles of surrender of the town of Collioure to the Franco-Catalan forces.[12] The juxtaposition of these two news items is interesting but merely coincidental. The Irish part consisted of a translation of a pamphlet in French, allegedly printed in London, which had come into the hands of the printer via Paris. The original French pamphlet does not survive, though there is a contemporary version in English, entitled *A Declaration Sent to the King of France and Spain from the Catholiques or Rebells in Ireland*, which differs significantly in places, as the translator Robert Codrington obviously intended his publication to be used as counter-propaganda.[13]

But why go to the trouble and expense of translating, printing and selling a tract already available in a similar romance language? Certain aspects of this tract would surely have interested the Catalan insurgents. It drew attention to the contemporary efforts of the earls of Antrim and Clanricard to stand neutral in the developing conflict on account of their having estates in England. In Catalonia, grandees with links to Court had retreated to Madrid, abandoning their Catalan estates, and now many nobles experienced fresh doubts as their fledgling state moved into the orbit of the French.[14] The insurgents in both countries needed to maintain the discipline of their forces in what at times appeared to be little more than a jacquerie.[15] The article in April 1642 published the Irish decree to prevent attacks on friends and non-combatants, alongside the oath taken by Irish Catholics, similar in intent to that taken by the insurgents in Catalonia.

The other two Barcelona printings appeared in Castilian. The first was *Requesta de las dos cameras del parlamento de Inglaterra, presentado al rey de la gran bretana, para impeder su viaje en Irlanda: con su resquesta*, a translation of *The Petition of the Lords and Commons Presented to his Majestie by the Earle of Stamford, Master Chancellour of the Exchequer, and Master Hungerford, April 18. 1642.*[16] It began with a short preface containing language of the general crisis: 'Between the mutations that happen in the world, of the sort that novelty can entertain, not much is more considerable than what is starting in England.' The *Requesta y repuesta* proceeded to show the English Parliament demanding that Charles I decline from leading an army in person into Ireland on the alleged grounds of fears for their monarch's safety, and the king in turn scolding a perceived lack of impetus on the same matter by Parliament. In reality, Parliament feared the King might actually use the army against his opponents in England. This would have resonated with the Catalans, where the King, having taken personal charge of the war, faced increasing opposition to the urgent need to recruit large forces in Castile itself. Perhaps the publishers hoped to encourage potentially rebellious subjects elsewhere in the peninsula by pointing to the English example.[17]

The third Irish item from Barcelona is another translation into Castilian, this time of the manifesto of the Catholic gentry of Galway, entitled *Manifiesto de los principales cavalleros catolicos del Condado de Galuay, y otros de la Prouincia de Connact en Irlanda: Contiene las rezones, por las quales no pueden quedar neutros, como son solicitados por su Gouernador a la instancia del Parlamento de Inglaterrra*, which does not survive in Irish or British records.[18] This highlighted the importance of neutrals, as the war in Ireland became more critical, in particular the failure of the earl of Clanricard to commit himself to the Catholic cause, which the tract attributes to his landed interests in England and his heeding promises from the English Parliament. But why was a piece about Galway politics being published by Catalans, in the language of their oppressors. The tract's evident support for the independence of the Irish state presumably found a resonance in Catalonia, where all classes held grievances against Madrid.[19] Of course, the focus on the vexed issue of neutrality might have been intended to pressurise those in Castile and Catalonia who where trying to stay neutral, or even the Irish whose loyalty to Spain could no longer be taken for granted. Nonetheless, Hugh O'Donnell, earl of Tyrconnell, commander of another Irish tercio, underlined the steadfastness of the latter group, when he was killed in a Spanish naval assault on Perpignan in the late summer of 1642.[20]

II

The only extant copy of this Galway Manifesto, published in Barcelona, is in the National Library in Lisbon. Its presence there is symptomatic of the great interchange between the insurgent parts of the peninsula. Although pursuing their own agendas, these regions remained very much aware of how developments elsewhere in the multiple-monarchy affected them. In the case of this Barcelona-published manifesto, the question of neutrals and those of equivocal loyalty surely struck a chord with those engaged in the struggle in Portugal. A number of its noble families were divided in their loyalties between King and country and the question of neutrals also surfaced in pamphlets published by the Irish in Lisbon. The Duke of Braganza, a courtier in Madrid and the largest landowner in Portugal, quickly jumped on the nationalist bandwagon. The rest of the nobles attempted to stage a counter-coup, which was discovered and stamped out. Most of these who had chosen court over country fled to Madrid, with their return dependent on the army of Philip IV.[21] Although Braganza was established as King and most of the country liberated, success could not be guaranteed. The Portuguese urgently sought international recognition from their ancient allies, France and England. A pre-existing dispute over the *patronato*, which had seen the country placed under an interdict, hampered support from the Papacy. The rapid establishment of an embassy in London, alongside the additional fact that, as a major hub of Atlantic trade, Lisbon received news from all parts, meant the Portuguese were very *au fait* with developments in the Stuart kingdoms.

The gazette established in Portugal after the Restoration, therefore, published not only national news, but also a wide selection of foreign reports. Ireland often figured in these accounts, sometimes as part of larger bulletins about the crisis facing the Stuart monarchy and sometimes as stand-alone items. Portuguese editors proved sympathetic to the Irish cause, both as fellow Catholics and fellow insurgents. The December 1641 issue, which celebrated the grand welcome the Portuguese delegation received from the authorities in London, also reported on the regime's deepening troubles. The pamphlet described Puritan moves in London to remove images and crosses from churches as well as informing readers that the Irish had 'killed by the sword a great number of Protestants and had taken cities, towns and forts'. As a result, Parliament was now in the process of appointing the earl of Leicester as governor of Ireland and ordering the intervention of General Leslie from Scotland.[22]

A steady stream of Irish items appeared in the Portuguese press over the next year, which recorded the successes of Phelim O'Neill, the arrival of Leslie in Ulster, the Parliamentary expedition to Galway, the ebbing of Irish fortunes, the meeting of the Confederates at Kilkenny and the much-heralded arrival of Owen Roe from the continent.[23] Two items in particular stand out. The *Gazeta do mes de Abril* republished and rendered into Portuguese a petition out of a French gazette, in which the Confederate Catholics of Ireland demanded from Charles I the same rights accorded to the Scots. Not only did they, as Catholics, want liberty of conscience and control of the church, they also sought recognition of native rights with regard to offices, lands, commerce and Parliament – all matters with which the Portuguese could empathise.[24]

The Lisbon gazette for June 1642 throws up an even more interesting issue. It reported on the book composed by Dr Henry Jones from witness state-ments of English and Scottish refugees and published by order of Parliament, entitled *A Remonstrance of Divers Remarkable Passages Concerning the Churche and Kingdom of Ireland*.[25] The Portuguese newspaper, or its correspondent in London, took an entirely different line in this first major report on the atrocities committed against Protestant settlers by Irish Catholics, focussing on a list of what were obviously considered Irish Catholic successes rather than the horrible instances of sectarian and ethnic cruelty in the aftermath of rebellion. These included the following stories: that a soldier killed fifty English settlers, converted to Catholicism by an Irish priest, as he said that they would only backslide;[26] that Fr Ross MacGeogeghan (referred to as Frey Roque de Avis and identified as a Dominican who had resided in Lisbon for 18 years), on taking possession of his bishopric of Kildare and wanting to re-consecrate his church, dug up the bones of the Protestant bishops and six others buried there; that the Irish knight Edmund O'Reilly, having killed the bishop of Kilmore in his own house along with his wife and two sons, sent word to Edmund MacSweeney, the Catholic Bishop, to take charge of the place;[27] and finally that all the prelates and doctors of Ireland meeting in the Convent of Our Lady at Multyfarnhan had debated what to do about the Protestants being thrown out of the country, and after discussing various options they resolved to let them depart with some of their belongings.[28]

The *Gazeta*, in effect, turned Jones's propaganda on its head. It should be remembered that, even though Portugal sought to renew an alliance with England, public opinion remained Counter-Reformation Catholic and part of the Catholic International. The Portuguese had been the object of attack at home and abroad by Dutch and English Protestants since 1580 and had long been subjected to sermons and literature about the sufferings and martyrdoms of Catholics in Northern Europe. Indeed, Philip O'Sullivan Beare painted a similar picture about developments in Ireland in his *Historiae Catholicae Iberniae Compendium*, published in Lisbon in 1621.[29]

The same appeal to Catholic opinion, evident in the Irish items in the early years of the *Gazeta*, is apparent in the three pamphlets from the mid 1640s about the war in Ireland published in Lisbon – two in Portuguese and one in Castilian. These were more substantial and analytical than anything previously published in Portugal or indeed anywhere elsewhere on the peninsula. They were written by Catholic Irishmen living in Portugal, where a well-established Irish community of clergy and merchants existed, especially in Lisbon. Trade links with Ireland had remained open and the first of these pamphlets – *Relaçam sumaria & verdadeira do estado presente do Reyno de Irlanda* – claimed to be derived from letters and information received from high-ranking people and trustworthy individuals travelling out of Ireland. The anonymous author probably also derived source material from news which had already appeared in the Lisbon gazette.

The *Relaçam Sumaria*, published in January 1644, was a fragmentary compilation of information, parts of it inaccurate, exaggerated or apocryphal, intended to explain the outbreak and early stages of the Irish war fought for religion and country.[30] The author highlighted the issue of religion, giving a different, more religiously charged, version of the Irish petition to Charles I printed earlier in the Portuguese press. When Irish Catholics realised that the King could not protect them against the Puritan Parliament of England, they secretly plotted a revolt. Better to die with honour than live without it, and, as they fought for the faith, they did so in expectation of God's assistance. The revolt made miraculous progress, despite limited resources and lack of arms and training, helped by the return of Irish veterans who had seen continental service. The author named Thomas Preston, Gerald Barry and John Burke but most notably Owen Roe O'Neill. The reproduction in Latin and Portuguese of the letter from Pope Urban VIII granting O'Neill and his allies a plenary indulgence for the war against heretics served to confer authority on both the Ulsterman and his cause. The pamphlet noted the arrival of the Papal nuncio, Pierfrancesco Scarampi, in July 1643, commenting that 'much good is expected of his coming and being in this kingdom', and rehearsed Irish Catholic military successes, giving descriptions of the religious banners under which they fought.

The whole question of loyalty for a service nobility, forced to choose between King and country, undoubtedly interested a Portuguese audience. The author was congratulated those English and Scots Catholics who had joined the Irish cause, while heaping opprobrium on six Irish peers who behaved scandalously by staying neutral or actively fighting against their countrymen. The list of trimmers or outright traitors – either misguided Catholics or raised Protestants in England – included the earls of Clanricard, Ormond, Thomond and Barrymore, as well as the barons of Lixnaw and Inchiquin. The author predicted a nasty end for the latter, a declared enemy of his country and a notorious heretic.

The other interesting aspect of this pamphlet revolves around the discussion of the 1641 massacres and other sectarian aspects of the conflict. The writer obviously considered the killing of heretics to be meritorious, as well as either edifying or exhilarating for his readers. According to this text, the conspirators discussed 'whether it was better to kill in the first encounters all the heretics of whatever nationality, sex or condition, without respect to kinship or followers'. The ecclesiastics argued that only those who resisted should be killed, whereas the gentry held that all heretic males capable of bearing arms should be dispatched. The gentry justified their argument by the example of Philip III's failure to kill Morisco males, who being expelled merely continued as pirates against Christians. The view of the gentry was accepted, with planter Protestant women and children, in accordance with natural law, being evicted from the country. The pamphlet went on to tell approvingly the story of the many heretics dispatched by the Talbot brothers, and to claim that a new law directed that any Protestant captured and thrown out of the country would be branded if they dared to return. Indeed, this account, by claiming that over a 100,000 heretics had already been killed, accepted English Protestant propaganda as it made the success even more glorious to Catholic eyes. The author celebrated the restoration of Catholic worship – and even supplied three Latin couplets of a poem marking the purging of the poison of heresy from Ireland. This pamphlet, which ended with a 500-year-old prophesy about the destruction of the perfidious English and their country, caused consternation amongst many of the English in Portugal.[31]

The following year, a pamphlet written by Mercurio, entitled *Mercurius Ibernicus*, referred to the annoyance caused to the members of the English community and argued that they should be treated with the same courtesy afforded to anyone, even enemies. Nonetheless, this pamphlet intended to create a positive image of Ireland in the minds of Catholics and of the Portuguese in particular. Instead of dwelling on the massacres which accompanied the revolt, Mercurio interpreted the alleged apparitions and prodigies which attended the uprising as signs of God's favour. These signs included the heroic resistance led by Lady Plunkett against the odds when confronted by the besieging forces of that 'heartless and fiery man', Charles Coote. This list of marvels was of course to be expected in an island, formerly called, of the saints. Even if some continued to doubt these prodigious events, the Irish kingdom's perseverance in Catholicism despite being ruled by heretical, avaricious and base-born neighbours, represented the greatest miracle of all.

Of the three Lisbon publications, this pamphlet, written in Castilian, ironically made the most overtures to a Portuguese audience. It sought to correct falsehoods about Ireland, oftentimes the result of ignorance and lack of information rather than malevolence. Surely, Mercurio averred, the Portuguese of all people had enough political astuteness to recognise such attempts at national denigration. He asserted that the stereotyping of Ireland and the Irish had to do with English attempts to conquer and subdue the island and its inhabitants. Mercurio added a further, more practical cause for this bad image abroad: 'Since the Irish write with particular letters and characters that have more similarity with Greek than Latin, which only they understand, they are often left exposed to the fables that their enemies invent about them and since writers of other nations did not understand our alphabet, they took up the lies the English published about us which are due to the natural hate they always bore us, something that is very common between neighbouring nations (cosa muy ordinaria entre naciones vezinas)'.

Mercurio reminded his readers of the Portuguese priest who bravely ministered to Hugh MacMahon, one of the Irish conspirators of the rising, before his execution in London. He also sought to explain how the Irish did not have a native King of their own for so many years, even though the country historically had more native kings than anywhere else in Europe, when the Portuguese 'did not have the patience to be 60 years without their own king'. He put this down to provincial and racial divisions within Ireland, as well as rivalries between its leading families encouraged by the English. Yet Ireland, with its temperate climate and exploitable resources, was a country worth fighting for. Mercurio went on to outline the constitution of the Irish Catholic Confederation and its political and military structures, praising the nobility of the office-holders and the other major servitors of the state. The writer also trumpeted the victories of the Irish in the defence of Catholicism, especially those won by Preston, Castlehaven and Owen Roe O'Neill. Mercurio clearly preferred the general of Ulster, 'whose ancestors were kings of Ireland when St Patrick came to that kingdom' for more than just his military skills.

By the time a third pamphlet – the *Relaçam dos successos* – appeared in 1646, it was providing a news update from Ireland, based on the assumption that the readers already knew about the early stages of the war.[32] The update began with an account of the Catholic Confederation's negotiations with King Charles I, which the pamphleteer thought had been successfully concluded. The upbeat assessment claimed that even though the confederates had been forced to concede toleration of worship in two cities 'it is expected that with the arguments and preaching of the Priests and other Catholic clergy, these Protestants would be reduced, as many have been reduced this year and in the previous years'. This pamphlet highlighted Owen Roe O'Neill's overwhelming victory over the Scots at the battle of Benburb;[33] described the victories of Alasdair MacColla, comparing his campaign in Scotland to Hannibal's in Italy; and commented on the King's mounting difficulties, and the concomitant dangers to English Catholics, which followed on from losing the first round of the English Civil War. Most importantly, the *Relaçam dos successos* concluded with a reproduction of a long letter which Cardinal Rinuccini sent to his home archdiocese of Fermo after his arrival as nuncio to the Catholic Confederation in 1645. This letter sang the praises of Ireland and the Irish, comparing them favourably with other Europeans. Like the work of Mercurio, the publication of this pamphlet formed part of an effort by the Irish in Lisbon to counteract negative English representations of their homeland and its people. However, the approach here was made more strategic and instrumental, coming as it did independently and authoritatively from the Pope's special envoy.

These three tracts do not name their writers, though there are two obvious candidates. The first is Kerryman Dominic O'Daly who, with the permission of Philip IV and the patronage of a number of rich Portuguese, first established an Irish Dominican monastery and then more recently a nunnery in Lisbon. As confessor to the new Queen of Portugal and a diplomat in royal service, he travelled to Rome and Paris to make to representations on behalf of the restored Portuguese state. In the later 1640s, he tried to tempt King João IV to consider taking on the sovereignty of Ireland in return for Irish soldiers to serve in the Portuguese army and Irish colonists to resettle Brazil. In 1655, he published *Initium, Incrementa, et Exitus Familiae Geraldinorum Desmoniae Comitum* (Lisbon, 1655) about the fall of the Desmonds of Munster and the persecutions of Catholics which had followed, concluding with the many martyrdoms suffered and prodigies witnessed during the recent Cromwellian invasion.[34] Having established good relations with the Stuart court in exile, he then used his diplomatic experience to help negotiate the marriage of Charles II to Catherine of Braganza, though he cannot have been too pleased with the dispatch of Lord Inchiquin, recently converted to Catholicism, to assist the Portuguese in the continuing war against Spain.[35]

The other candidate, especially for the *Mercurius Ibernicus* pamphlet, is Cornelius O'Mahony S. J., a Cork-born theology professor at the University of Evora, and priest at St Rocque's in Lisbon. The *Mercurius* uses some of the same ideas and sources as O'Mahony's infamous book, entitled *Disputatio Apologetica de Iure Regni Hiberniae* (Lisbon, 1645). They both came out in the same year, both concluding with similar back-handed remarks about the future survival of the Stuart Dynasty.[36] In this same regard, one cannot help wondering if the cherubic winged-figure crushing the snake of heresy used as the printer's symbol on the title-page of the *Disputatio* book is supposed to represent Mercury.

O'Mahony wrote his book to rally opposition to the proposed compromise between the Irish confederates and the royalists, favouring instead a Catholic Ireland entirely separate from England. O'Mahony was influenced by recent constitutional developments in the peninsula, especially in Portugal. He thought it entirely lawful that first Catalonia and then Portugal should assert their right to self-determination, though he hesitated to mention that Ireland had a far better right to depose its heretical king than either of them had to get rid of their legitimate one. In referring directly to the independence bids of these dependent kingdoms, he clearly preferred the Portuguese example of having a native aristocrat as king rather than the Catalan approach of transferring sovereignty to another monarch.[37] This in turn facilitated the exhortation he made to his fellow countrymen to select 'a Catholic king, an indigenous or native-born Irishman who will be able to govern them as Catholics'.[38] O'Mahony climaxed by arguing that Ireland must not only rid itself of its heretic king but also expunge all heretics from the island. 'Already you have killed 150,000 of the enemy during these four or five years from 1641 to 1645, when I am writing these words . . . It remains for you to kill the remaining heretics or expel them from the territory of Ireland, lest the infection of their heretical errors should spread more widely in our Catholic country.'[39]

In 1647, the public hangman in Kilkenny burned O'Mahony's famous justification for Irish separatism on the orders of the Supreme Council of the Confederation. Far from assisting the opposition of Rinuccini and Owen Roe to the proposed Ormond Peace with Charles I, the book was used against them as evidence of their alleged ambitions. On discovery that the work was not published in Frankfurt as stated on the title-page but 'printed here by a religious man of the Company of Jesus, called Cornelius of St Patrick', an English priest in Lisbon brought the book to the attention of the Portuguese King. The reason given for the subsequent royal prescription is compelling: 'because the end and intent of this book is to prejudice the obedience which the subjects of my brother the King of England owe unto him as their true King and Lord, and I resent that so bold an attempt should be committed in my kingdom'.[40] In other words, ignoring the advocacy of mass murder, the Portuguese crown believed that this Irish assertion of national rights printed in Lisbon might damage relations with England. The unspoken assumption must be that the crown, like the people of Portugal, had no problems about the idea of liquidating heretics. As evident from the rest of the Portuguese coverage of Irish events, there was wholehearted agreement with persecuted co-religionists taking the opportunity to kill Protestants. It was not considered an atrocity. Quite the contrary, it was a positive good – the necessary cleansing of a divisive and demonic element which threatened to destroy human society.

III

Given the long-standing Spanish connections with Ireland, one might have expected extensive Castilian reporting on developments there but that is not the case. The fact that leading Irish Catholics such as O'Daly and O'Mahony, formerly so closely associated with the Spanish monarchy, willingly supported the Portuguese rebels seriously worried the authorities in Madrid. O'Daly informed the Portuguese King that after the first Irish troops went into French service in 1638, 'the earls of Tyrone and Tyrconnell were thinking of abandoning Spain before passing into Catalonia where they were killed'.[41] Even as far off as Mexico, where the ex-Olivares man William Lamport was accused of conspiring to lead a break-way Creole state, the loyalty of the Irish to the Habsburgs could no longer be taken for granted.[42] Basically, the crisis of confidence confronting the Spanish service nobility affected the Irish as well. Yet the knock-on strategic consequences of the crisis meant the Spanish monarchy urgently needed Irish manpower for its army. The limited response in Castile, however, to the developing Irish situation was primarily because of the nature of the news media there, with output restricted to the occasional populist tabloid, pro-government, semi-official and official publication. Indeed, the more frequent and voluminous material being printed in Lisbon and Barcelona was penetrating into Castile, bringing with it amongst other things news about events in Ireland.[43] The principal publications in Castile came off the presses of Juan Gomez de Blas, an innovative journalist, who eventually came to be recognised as the chief printer of Seville.[44]

The first Castilian notice of the war, entitled *Relacion verdadera de la insigne Vitoria*, appeared in the first months of 1642, the work of a well-informed Spaniard with as much knowledge of England and Scotland as Ireland, who had over-reacted to rumours of a complete Catholic victory. The pamphlet traced the development of the crisis from a neo-Catholic attempt to impose the prayer book on Scotland, through the Scottish defeat of King Charles, the raising of an army in Ireland under Antrim and Puritan fears of that army leading to the execution of the earl of Strafford in May 1641. With the empowered Parliament threatening to impose penal laws on Ireland, the nobles there had no option but 'to take up arms and throw off the heretical yoke'. The author likened the resulting revolt to the Sicilian Vespers, when that island suddenly rose up against their French oppressors in the days of another King Charles. This anti-French historical analogy conveniently ignored more recent and closer-to-home anti-Castilian events in Barcelona and Lisbon. The pamphlet ended with Phelim O'Neill preparing his forces to resist a counter-strike from Scotland, having already allegedly succeeded in capturing Dublin. It was surely providential, the writer averred, that the soldiers, prevented by English Parliamentary pressure from joining the Spanish army, had succeeded in winning back their own country for Catholicism.[45]

In this same context, the *Manifiesto de Los confederados Catolicos de Irlanda* was republished in Seville, a full version of the Irish Catholic articles addressed to Charles I, which appeared in summary form about the same time in the Portuguese press. A translation of the oath taken by the Irish rebels, reported about the same time as 'Extraordinary News' in Barcelona, accompanied the articles. With Castilian politics in tumult, the document presented a seemingly radical message: dutiful subjects – good Catholic ones – demanding from their prince the same rights to liberty of conscience and free exercise of religion as the Scots had won after invading England. The Catholic Irish, however, emphasised their commitment to the royal pre-rogative and rejected the revolutionary powers the English Parliament claimed for itself. Rather than avengers of the zealous officials who had provoked their action, they posed as humble petitioners for concessions from a pious and moderate prince. In these respects, the Irish Catholics were not unlike the loyal monarchists of Castile who wanted rid of Olivares but who would otherwise willingly follow the King.

The Spanish state as the self-proclaimed international standard-bearer of Catholicism had no option but to support the Irish Catholic rebels, in the hope that their rapid success which would free up troops for Habsburg recruit-ment needs. To this end, the Spanish authorities reluctantly agreed to allow Owen Roe O'Neill and hundreds of other veterans of the Spanish service in Flanders to depart for Ireland. Spanish ministers were pleased to discover from the Irish delegation arriving later in 1642 that the newly established Catholic Confederation of Kilkenny would release troops for Spanish service in exchange for money and arms.[46] The failure of the confederates, however, to secure a comprehensive peace settlement for much of the 1640s, or achieve total military victory, hindered large-scale recruitment.

The nearest they came was recorded in the next Irish issue from the Castilian press in 1647, entitled *Relacion verdadera de las felizes vitorias*. Juan Gomez de Blas produced this tract from two items, no longer extant, published in English in Kilkenny. The great victory at Benburb won by Owen Roe O'Neill, referred to here as 'Don Eugenio O Neil' and remembered to Spanish readers for his heroic defence of Arras and Douai against the French, provided the centrepiece. The pamphlet presented Benburb as a vicarious Spanish victory at a time when things were going badly for Spain's own armies on the inter-national front. Set in the context of civil conflict in England, whose miseries the writer regarded as something of a consolation for war-stressed Spain, it described the campaign of Owen Roe to save the Confederacy from the false peace moves of the traitorous marquis of Ormond and the approaching British army led by General Munroe. Unfortunately, for the confederates, as the writer noted at the time, Owen Roe failed to follow up on the victory.[47] Thus, any prospect of Spain's recruiting agents, already frustrated by French counter offers in Kilkenny, benefiting from Confederate military success proved illusionary.

Ironically, large numbers of Irish troops only became available for Spanish service following the Cromwellian conquest in the early 1650s. The English authorities, anxious to rid Ireland of military veterans, facilitated the transport of as many as 40,000 men from 1652 to 1654. With Irish troops in Spanish service increasingly prone to defection to the French because of poor conditions and lack of pay, the relationship was under stress. Cromwell declaration of war against Spain in 1655 served to rejuvenate and clarify Spanish views of Ireland and the Irish. A Castilian pamphlet from 1657 rehearsed in tabloid fashion a set of draconian decrees passed against Irish Catholics by the Cromwellian regime in Ireland, accompanied by the re-publication of a letter from the head of the Franciscans in Ireland. This pamphlet, published in other provincial centres as well as Seville, was blatant anti-English propaganda. The featured decrees included the forced transportation of Irish youths to the West Indies, the mistreatment of the Catholic clergy and the residence restrictions imposed on the Irish, as well as oddities such as the regulations governing what hats the Irish could wear in order to shock the status-conscious Spaniards.[48]

IV

What conclusions can be reached about these various Ibernian publications relating to the mid-seventeenth century wars in Ireland? Plainly, a broadly similar crisis affected the multiple Stuart and Habsburg monarchies, which contemporaries recognised and to which the media reacted. The press throughout the peninsula clearly took a particular interest in Ireland, political as well as commercial. In Castile, the Spanish state had an evident self-interest in the fate of the Catholic Irish, both as potential political allies and as a source of manpower, but Spain's declining power made it increasingly less attractive to the Irish. In Catalonia and Portugal, newsletters relating to Ireland may have sought to sell copy about analogous independence struggles going on simultaneously. If so, the first phase of information globalisation actually reflected the fact that all politics are local. Furthermore, Irish-related publications put out in Barcelona and Lisbon in Castilian may well have been aimed at neutrals and malcontents inside Castile itself. Indeed, some of publications from the more muted presses of Seville also fall into this category.

Unsurprisingly, no publication focussed on the contemporary struggle in Calvinist Scotland, nor indeed is there a great deal about events in England until the trial and execution of the King at the end of the decade.

The commercial instincts of the publishers, as well as the political reasons behind their publications, are important in this regard. The Irish in the peninsula created a demand for news from home – there were after all several thousand Irishmen in the army, at court, at colleges and universities, in the clergy and in the almshouses. Nonetheless, the main targets of these Irish-orientated publications, including those by Irish authors, were local fellow Catholics interested in the successes and failures of their co-religionists. Iberian Catholics were well aware of the Irish residing amongst them, fighting for them and taking their charity. Fed on a diet of anti-Protestant rhetoric and victims themselves from time to time of Protestant aggression, they were pleased to hear of the providential success of the Irish in 1641 and of the prodigies which accompanied their revolt. They saw events in Ireland not as a massacre or atrocity but as a veritable triumph for human rights. By the same token, on account of their heretical religions and relative absence in the peninsula, Catholic readers had little interest in the English and even less in the Scots.

These findings on Iberian publications about the Confederate War in Ireland and its aftermath are preliminary and the results merely suggestive. This paper may provide the impetus for a project to examine all continental news relating to events in Ireland during this period, and the republication of such news items elsewhere, either whole or in edited form. Improved news circulation is definitely one of the observable phenomena relating to the General Crisis. Indeed, not only were national public spheres greatly enhanced at this time but an international one came into being as well. This had important results, particularly for the history of ideas. Before the mid-seventeenth century, most political thought was confined to specific issues in time or place but after that watershed political ideas came to be framed in terms of general principles. Might this have something to do with the globalisation and contemporaneity of news? It is interesting in this regard that the first attempt at writing a history of the general crisis, as noted by Parker and Smith, was by an Italian in the 1650s using French newspapers.[49]

NOTES

1 The original version of this paper was given at 'From across the Channel: Contemporary Readings of the English Revolution', a workshop at Consejo Superior de Investigaciones Científicas, Madrid, organised by Angel Alloza and Glyn Redworth on 14 April 2010. Funding to complete the paper came from the UCC Humanities Platform under PRTLI4. The author wishes to thank Eoin O'Neill for his assistance as well as Anita Howard, John Barry, James Amelang, Stephen Boyd and Mitchel Leimon.

2   See Hiram Morgan, 'Policy and propaganda in Hugh O'Neill's connection with Europe', in Thomas O'Connor and Mary Ann Lyons (eds), *The Ulster Earls in Barque Europe* (Dublin, 2010), p. 18.

3   Aidan Clarke, 'Ireland and the general crisis', *Past and Present*, 48 (1970), 79–99.

4   Geoffrey Parker and Lesley Smith, *The General Crisis of the Seventeenth Century* (London, 1997), esp. chapter 1. See also Parker's comparative essay 'The crisis of the Spanish and Stuart Monarchies in the mid-seventeenth century: local problems or global politics', in C. Brady and J. Ohlmeyer (eds), *British Interventions in Early Modern Ireland* (Cambridge, 2005), pp. 252–79.

5   J. H. Elliott, *The Count-Duke of Olivares: The Statesman in an Age of Decline* (New Haven, 1986), pp. 530, 596.

6   Elliott, *Memoriales y cartas del conde duque de Olivares* (2 vols, Madrid, 1978–80), vol. ii, p. 275.

7   R. A. Stradling, *Philip IV and the Government of Spain 1621–1665* (Cambridge, 1988), pp. 120–85.

8   Henry Ettinghausen has published the pamphlets and news-sheets which poured from the Catalan presses in four facsimile volumes. Henry Ettinghausen (ed.), *La Guerra dels Segadors a través de la premsa de l'època* (4 vols, Barcelona, 1993). There is scope for a similar study on Portugal where a monthly gazette digested national and international news in the early years of the Restoration.

9   For the general situation of the news media in Spain, see Henry Ettinghausen, 'The news in Spain: *relaciones de sucesos* in the reigns of Philip III and Philip IV', *European Political Quarterly*, 14 (1984), 1–20, and Henry Ettinghausen, 'Politics and the press in Spain', in Brendan Dooley and S. A. Baron (eds), *The Politics of Information in Early Modern Europe* (London, 2001), pp. 199–215.

10 R. A. Stradling, *The Spanish Monarchy and Irish Mercenaries: The Wild Geese in Spain, 1618–68*, (Dublin, 1994), pp. 115–16.

11 Each of these Barcelona pamphlets carried a unique image on its cover. This one, with a feather quill indicating to the reader that it is 'from our correspondent', represents neatly and quite by accident the shift from manuscript to print in the dissemination of news. *Noues extraordinaries de 17 de noembre de 1641: contenent los articles del rendiment de la Fortalesa de Castro pressa sobre lo Duc de Parma per les armes del Papa: la rebolucio dels Catholics de Irlanda* (La casa de Iaume Mathevat, Barcelona, 1641).

12 *Nouas extraordinarias vingudas de Paris de tretze de Abril de mil sis cents quaranta y dos : en las quals se dona auis de las lleys nouament fetas y establertas ab los Catholichs de Irlanda ques ere[n] mesclats ab los solleuats . . . la presa de Coblliure, ab los pactes ques feren en son rendiment, impressas en Llondres [sic] en llengua Francesa y traduydes en nostra vulgar llengua Cathalana* (La casa de Iaume Mathevat, Barcelona, 1642).

13 *A Declaration sent to the King of France and Spayne, from the Catholiques or Rebells in Ireland: with a Manifesto of the Convenant or Oath they have made and taken for the Defence of the Catholique League against the Protestants in that Kingdome. Wherein is Discovered their Treacherous Practizes under the Pretence of Religion and their Bloody Actions full of Cruelty and Barbarism. Published in*

Paris, April the 24 1642. And Translated out of French by R.C. Gent (I.T., London, 1642). Whereas the Catalan tract begins 'Irlanda estant encara en su llibertat, y exemptats dels Paysos subjectes a la dominacio del Rey de la gran Bretanya', Codrington has 'Ireland being to this day the Sole Right and a country subject to the government of the King of Great Britaine'.

14 J. H. Elliott, *The Revolt of the Catalans: A study in the Decline of Spain, 1598–1640* (Cambridge, 1963), pp. 313, 453, 534–5; Stradling, *Philip IV*, p. 120.

15 Stradling, *Philip IV*, p. 180.

16 *Requesta de las dos camaras del Parlamento de Inglaterra presentada al rey de la Gran Bretaña para impedir su viaje en Irlanda, con su respuesta* (La emprenta de Iayme Romeu, Barcelona, 1642). This does not appear in Ettinghausen's collection of Catalan tracts and newsletters. For the original see *The Petition of the Lords and Commons Presented to his Majestie by the Earle of Stamford, Master Chancellour of the Exchequer, and Master Hungerford, April 18. 1642* (Robert Barker, London, 1642).

17 Olivares was himself worried that the some of the Catalans pamphlets had been actually written in Madrid! See Elliott, *Revolt of the Catalans*, pp. 472, 526–7.

18 *Manifiesto de los principales cavalleros Catolicos del condado de Galuay, y otros de la Prouincia de Connact en Irlanda: Contiene las razones, por las quales no pueden quedar neutros, como son solicitados por su gouernador a la instancia del Parlamento de Inglaterrra* (La emprenta de Iayme Romeu, Barcelona, 1642). This does not appear in Ettinghausen's collection of Catalan tracts and newsletters.

19 Elliott, *Revolt of the Catalans*, pp. 72–3, 222, 486–8.

20 Stradling, *Spanish Monarchy and Irish Mercenaries*, pp. 115–16.

21 Stradling, *Philip IV*, pp. 182–5.

22 *Gazeta do mes de Dezembre de 1641* (Officina de Lourenco de Anveres, Lisbon, 1641).

23 *Gazeta do mes de Noviembre de 1642* (Officina de Lourenco de Anvers, Lisbon, 1642).

24 *Gazeta do mes de Abril de 1642* (Officina de Domingos Lopez Rosa, Lisbon, 1642).

25 *A Remonstrance of Divers Remarkable Passages concerning the Churche and Kingdom of Ireland, Recommended by the Lords Justices, and Councell of Ireland, and Presented by Henry Jones, Doctor of Divinity, Agent for the Ministers of the Gospel in that Kingdom, to the Honourable Houses of Commons in England* (Godfrey Emerson & William Bladen, London, 1642).

26 The *Remonstrance*, p. 72 says that the priest, Hugh Maguire, having managed to reconcile forty or fifty English and Scottish Protestants to the Faith, swearing them to accept the Pope as supreme head of the church and the real presence in the Eucharist, had killed them himself lest they should relapse into heresy.

27 The *Remonstrance*, p. 36 had of course noted the survival of Bishop Bedell and his family, and that they were in custody having been spoiled by the rebels.

28 *Gazeta do mes de Junho de 1642* (Officina de Domingos Lopez Rosa, Lisbon, 1642).

29 On this book see Morgan, ' "Making Ireland Spanish": the political writings of Philip O'Sullivan Beare', in Jason Harris and Keith Sidwell (eds), *Making Ireland Roman: Irish Neo-Latin writers and the Republic of Letters* (Cork, 2009), pp. 86–108.

30 *Relaçam sumaria & verdadeira do estado presente do Reyno de Irlanda, tirada de muitas cartas de pessoas graves, & de informaçoens de alguns homens de credito, que vieraõ de lá estes dias* (Paulo Craesbeeck, Lisbon, 1644).

31 As noted at the start of *Mercurius Ibernicus, Que relata algunos casos notables, que sucedieron en Irlanda, despues que tomó las armas por defender la religion Catholica. Con una breve noticia del estado prezente de aquel reyno* (La officina de Domingos Lopes Rosa, Lisbon, 1645).

32 *Relaçam dos svccessos do reyno de Irlanda com as capitulaçoes das pazes entre os Catholicos Irlandeses* (Lisbon, 1646).

33 The author of this pamphlet stated that 'a report of this illustrious victory has been published in English here in Lisbon'. I have not been able to find this.

34 Translated, with memoir and notes, by C. P. Meehan as *The Fall, Rise and Exit of the Family of the Geraldine to which is Added is the Persecutions Inflicted on the Irish People by the English Collected out of Various Works and Written in Latin by Fr Dominicio de Rosario O'Daly, printed by Craebeck, Lisbon 1655* (Dublin, 1847 and 1878).

35 The expert on this cleric cum politician is Margaret MacCurtain – see her article 'Dominic O'Daly, Irish diplomat', *Studia Hibernica*, 5 (1965), 98–112 and her thesis on O'Daly, held in library of Dominican friars at Tallaght. He also features in the compendium of Portuguese sources on Ireland: M. Conçalves da Costa, *Fontes Inéditas Portuguesas para a historia de Irlanda* (Lisbon, 1981), pp. 42–8, 309–10.

36 Constantinus Marullus, *Disputatio Apologetica de Jure Regni Hiberniae pro Catholicis Hiberniis adversus haereticos Anglos* (Frankfurt, 1645).

37 Conor O'Mahony, *An Argument Defending the Right of the Kingdom of Ireland* (1645), translated by John Minahane (Athol Books for Aubane Historical Society, London, 2010), p. 181.

38 Ibid, p. 185.

39 Ibid, pp. 200–1

40 Royal Decree of 5 December 1647 as quoted in J. P. Conlon, 'Some notes on the 'Disputatio Apologetica', *Bibliographical Society of Ireland*, 6/5 (1955), 69–77.

41 Da Costa, *Fontes Inéditos*, p. 306.

42 The pioneering work on this subject was done by Fabio Troncarelli in *La Spade e la Croce: Guillen Lombardo e l'inquisizione in Messico* (Rome, 1999).

43 For instance the Biblioteca Nacional de Espana in Madrid has a copy of the Lisbon-published *Relaçam sumaria* (1644) and four copies of the *Mercurius Ibernicus* of 1645.

44 Ettinghausen, *Political Quarterly*, pp. 12–13.

45 *Relacion verdadera de la insigne vitoría que los Catolicos del Reyno de Irlanda han obtenido contra los Ingleses que no son Catolicos Romanos: dase quenta del estado de la religion Catolica en la Gran Bretaña y grandes mudãças de aquella monarquia, causadas de la diuersidad de heregias* (La casa de Juan Gomez de Blas, Seville, 1642; J. T. Gilbert (ed.), *History of the Irish Confederation and the War in Ireland* (7 vols, Dublin, 1882–91), vol. v, pp. 25–9. Bellings' account of Benburb was probably partly based on the same sources as those edited by Blas.

46 Stradling, *Spanish Monarchy and Irish Mercenaries*, pp. 43–4.

47 *Relación verdadera de las felizes vitorias qve han obtenido los Catholicos Confederados de el Reyno de Irlanda contra los Ingleses y Escoceses.* (La casa de Juan Gomez de Blas, Seville, 1647).

48 *Relacion de los diez y siete decretos, que Oliuerio Cromuel ha mandado publicar en Dublin Corte de Irlanda, para que se obseruen y guarden inuiolablemente en los Catholicos de aquella ciudad, y demas partes de aquel reyno. Refierese vna copia de carta escrita al . . . Padre Fray Pedro Manero, General que fue de la Sagrada Orden de San Francisco, por los padres que han sido prouinciales en . . . Irlanda* (La casa de Iuan Gomez de Blas, Seville, 1657). Also published in Granada and Zaragoza under title 'Relacion de los nuevos decretos'.

49 Parker and Smith, *General Crisis*, p. 1.

8

Performative violence and the politics of violence in the 1641 depositions

JOHN WALTER

In January 1644, George Burne, an English captive, deposed about his experiences during the 1641 rising in Ireland.[1] Burne numbered and named those he had seen killed and those about whose killing he had heard, but his deposition, as recorded, did not detail the manner of their death. Forced along with other English captives to attend a sermon at Dungannon, he heard (in what language?) the preacher, an Irish friar, take as his text the Old Testament story of Judith and Holofernes. This story of the defeat of an Assyrian conqueror had obvious parallels with Catholic native experience. By contrast, the focus on the beheading of Holofernes must have resonated with the experiences of the friar's English auditors, since multiple beheadings marked the extension of English rule and featured prominently in the killing of English settlers in 1641 and thereafter. According to Burne, the partial collapse of the upper chamber, killing many of the Irish present, rudely interrupted the friar's sermon, but he and the rest of the English by 'the Mercy and providence of God' emerged unhurt. Thereafter, his deposition records, at second hand, a tale of murders, drownings and rape. Burne's recounting of his experiences and their recording encapsulates both the problems and promise of the 1641 depositions.

In 1995, Nicholas Canny shrewdly observed that, 'the thrust of scholarly endeavour has been to explain why 1641 occurred, rather than the consideration of what happened'.[2] Since this observation, there has been a steady swell in the number of works on the rising signalling a renewed interest in the value of the 1641 depositions for establishing what happened in Ireland in 1641. Of course, the politically charged nature of the events that the depositions described, and of the process by which that evidence was assembled, rendered problematic historians' use of the depositions for a long time. The victims of violence testified within the discourse of godly suffering and racialised representations of the native Irish as duplicitous, barbarous and savage.[3]

The almost complete absence, until the judicial examinations of the 1650s, of evidence from those committing or accused of committing acts of violence against English and Scottish settlers reflects the more common situation in which crowds are often rendered silent by unequal access to the historical record, or have their actions evidenced by elites whose testimony reveals more about their own preconceptions than the reality of the crowd's actions. Thus, historians of the violence in the 1641 rising have to recover what the attackers did, what they thought they were doing and why from the hostile testimony of overwhelmingly Protestant deponents.

But the fact that in the past, authority was the first 'historian' of popular violence means that students of popular politics always have to work against the grain of bias in their primary sources. A shared interest between authority and the victims of crowd actions in denying the legitimacy of popular protest saw that the standard sources in early modern England often represent crowds in terms of the contemporary trope of a 'many-headed monster', given to irrational violence. This helps to explain why, in trying to read the meaning of crowd actions in the surviving evidence, historians examine descriptions of *what* they did and *how* they did it.

Under the influence of anthropology, historians have increasingly focused on the ritualised and symbolic nature of crowd behaviour, to explore the evidence this provides of the ideas informing crowd actions.[4] In seeking to answer Canny's question of what really happened in the rising, this chapter concentrates on the 'performative violence' in the 1641 depositions, in an attempt to get behind the biases in the archive and to recognise the statements made through the violence. In doing so, it seeks to bring together and to build upon the findings of the distinguished group of historians whose work has done so much to recover the value of the 1641 depositions.[5] Taking inspiration from the body of work associated with the new social history of politics in early modern England, it offers a comparative perspective on the meaning of the pattern of violence in the Irish rising, questioning in the process the appropriateness of the influential model of a two-part rising of a political elite and peasant fury. This chapter argues that, while both sections of Irish landed and urban society became entangled in the violence, popular participation suggests a greater level of popular *political* engagement.

Striking dissimilarities exist between the nature of the 1641 depositions and the equivalent body of English evidence, particularly with regard to the often tightly compressed nature of the evidence *as recorded* in the depositions. Evidence taken as part of legal proceedings by commission in England often contains much more detail. Depositions before local commissions operating under equity courts like Star Chamber, and answering to lists of interrogatories drawn up by both prosecutor and defendant, could be extremely prolix. Each case would involve a number of deponents testifying about the same event, thus allowing some comparative evaluation of the evidence. (By contrast, the Irish evidence is largely free of the legal formulae and hackneyed descriptions of violence that mar the English records). Significantly, the prolixity of the English material permits a narrativity often missing from the abbreviated recital of events in many of the 1641 depositions. This comparative silence in the Irish records means that, despite their sheer volume, they are often missing the sometimes revealing micro-sequencing and intersecting specificities of space, place and time in rendering the event as *process*, rather than merely outcome, which can reveal much about both the nature of the violence and the ideas animating it. Violence is both an event and an act.

The commissioners 'for the despoiled subject', who collected the depositions during the 1640s, were required 'to reduce to writinge All the Examinacions'.[6] Familiar problems occur in reading the 1641 depositions in relation to the process by which oral testimony was turned into written evidence, in the slippages between what was recorded and what was said and between what was remembered and what was recounted. Work by social psychologists also suggests that more attention needs to be given in work on 1641 to the impact of the trauma of violence on the forming and recall of memory.[7] Problems of language also persist, particularly on what was lost (or gained) in translation, with deponents testifying in English about exchanges with Gaelic-speaking attackers.[8] Moreover, the history of the power dynamics implicated in the taking and making of the record is as yet unrecovered, and possibly irrecoverable. Discussions of sexual violence recognise the gender dynamics and their possible consequences for women of deposing in what appears to have been an all-male environment, where notions of female honour, modulated by marital status and class, possibly led to self-censorship.[9] By contrast, no debate has taken place of how early modern constructions of masculinity might have shaped what men chose to say to other men. For example, the premium placed on men's ability to defend themselves and their dependants may have led some men to emphasise, or exaggerate, the degree of overwhelming violence they faced, as an explanation for their abandoning or failing to fulfil their role as protectors of their dependants.

In his influential essay on the anthropology of violence, David Riches noted that the uses of violence can be both instrumental and symbolic. Violence serves as an easily accessible and economical means to transform society and as an 'excellent communicative vehicle' with which to make symbolic statements.[10] Similarly, Donald Horowitz, whose analysis of modern atrocities provides many points of comparison with the pattern of violence in Ireland in 1641, argues that 'the deadly ethnic riot is a passionate but highly patterned event'.[11] A 'thick description' of the ritualised and symbolic patterning to crowd behaviour can then provide evidence of the ideas informing violence. It is the dramaturgy of the 1641 violence that this chapter seeks to recover.

Paradoxically, the resort to violence raises issues of legitimacy. As in early modern English protests, Irish rebels sought legitimacy for their actions in the claim that they acted by royal commission as agents of legitimate authority.[12] But, as in England, prophecy and rumour also played important roles in justifying violence.[13] Rumour's role was to 'justify the violence that is about to occur', by crystallising fears about the dangers from the 'target group' and projecting onto future victims the 'very impulses' the performers of violence will themselves demonstrate. As Riches notes, violence as a tactical pre-emption offers the ultimate defence for all violent acts.[14] Events in Ireland in 1641 mirrored precisely the pattern found by Horowitz, where the common form of 'violence-triggering rumour' took the form of an impending take-over by the 'target group'. One leader of the rising gave pithy expression to this idea: 'the English thought to cut the throats of the Irish for the[i]r religion but the Irish would prevent them & cut there throats first for there religion.'[15] Rumours spoke of the violence done to Catholics in England and predicted that the same would happen in Ireland.[16] The *reported* words of the rebels seem marked by the same *rhetoric* of violence to be found in the English records. In England, violence was normally directed against property rather than persons. Anti-popery, however, provoked acts of extraordinary violence, with some Protestant troops assembled to fight the Scots killing officers they suspected of being Catholics.[17] In sixteenth-century England, rebels had killed few people, but in the 1640s the explosive mix of religious and ethnic differences did lead to a succession of atrocities.[18] In Ireland, anti-Protestantism played the larger role in legitimising *and* shaping the pattern of violence in 1641. Thus, acts of real and symbolic violence reflected the confessional nature of the conflict.

In contrast to England, the stripping of those attacked emerged as a common and distinctive pattern in the Irish violence of 1641. A variety of reasons might explain this but the ubiquity of the tactic suggests deeper motives. According to Nicholas Canny, stripping 'also must have had a psycho-sexual aspect' and was carried out with 'such ritualistic fervour' to degrade and dehumanise.[19] The English and Scottish victims certainly did not share the alleged relaxed attitude of the native Irish to nakedness.[20] The English church court punishment of standing 'bare-legged' in a sheet before the parish suggests that even to be seen publicly in a shift was shameful.[21] A woman in that state of undress might also signify 'bodily and sexual vulnerability'.[22] Thus, stripping always carried with it strong notions of humiliation and dishonour especially where class and gender intersected.[23] Stripping, therefore, should be seen as part of that process by which victims became depersonalised and vulnerable to violence.

Name-calling might also be a prelude to physical violence. Deponents complained of such abuse: 'wee were not Christians & . . . were noe better then doggs'.[24] This pattern of 'derogatory naming' proved ominous. One friar reportedly told his listeners that it was 'as lawful to kill an Englishman as a dog', a threat repeated in other depositions.[25] In early modern culture, attitudes towards dogs reflected their reputation as filthy, greedy, beastly animals that, like other unclean beasts, would be excluded from salvation at the Resurrection. What in the early modern English context Erica Fudge has called the figurative 'making-animal' of the victim served to signal their exclusion from humanity and thus from normal prohibitions on violence. Being herded like animals – 'driven like hogs' or 'brought or rather driven like sheepe or beasts to a Markett' – served to distance and dehumanise victims, lessening restraints on aggression or atrocity.[26] As one deponent claimed to have been told, 'they would make no more conscience nor care to kill him then they would doe of a pigg or a sheepe'.[27]

It is important not to fall into the trap of over-explaining the killing of victims in 1641 or of underestimating the violence involved in the more common acts of robbery. Apparently, the majority of killings did not involve performative violence, at least as reported. But, as Horowitz has observed, the manner of killing in atrocities was selected to show that the victims no longer counted. Setting aside the pattern of wounding and torture designed to extract money and information, much of the killing that did take place involved hangings and beheadings, as well as sometimes repeated stabbings and mutilation with *skeans*, in what has been called 'the ritual of multiple killings'.[28] It may be significant that the skean took on a symbolic significance for both the Irish and their victims. For the English, the skean became synonymous with Irish violence and for the native Irish it apparently became the watchword to signal the start of a massacre.[29]

The choice of hanging was possibly intended to mimic the actions of authority and thus to lay claim to a socially sanctioned violence. In early modern English crowd violence, mimesis of the judicial procedures and punishments of the state and church courts often shaped protests, though primarily through *displaced* violence, for example hanging figures in effigy. The striking reference to the hanging of an English woman in which an Irish woman walked before her, bearing a white staff and taunting her by 'saying she would be sheriff for that turn', suggests a parodic inversion of the administrative processes of English rule and perhaps an echo of the customary homo-social ordering of rites of passage where, for example, women bore women to their burial. The compressed nature of the depositions means that few details of hangings survive, though the frequent references to placing victims in the stocks and to the haltering and dragging of victims by ropes to their execution might also suggest a mimesis of the judicial process.[30] The beheading and public display of the heads of Protestant victims directly parroted English policy for the punishment of rebels.[31]

One group of murder victims, Protestant ministers, attracted rites of violence which drew on the association between preaching and Protestantism. An episode at Disart Castle, Queen's County brings out the parodic quality of the violence inflicted on ministers. According to a deponent present in the castle, the attackers killed Robert Brereton, the minister there, while he knelt at prayer and then used him 'spightfully, for after he was dead, they sett his Corpse (all goared in blood) sitting in a chaire, & put his Bible into his handes, Comanding him for to preach'. They then set his corpse and that of his murdered patron, William Piggot, in chairs, 'one against another face to face'. Brereton's killers, 'triumphing over his dead Corps with spitefull and malitious words . . . [and] *calling him puritan & round head*', placed a potato in his mouth and 'in derision of his function they tore a Leafe out of a Bible . . . & put [it] unto the said Brereton's hand . . . bidding him to preach to his patron.'[32] Something similar happened in a later episode at Kildare, where the rebels reportedly displayed the decapitated head of the minister, Thomas Bingham, in the market place.[33]

Existing work has shown how rebels frequently attacked clergymen because of their role as landowners and moneylenders. Further research, which restores their distinctive *religious* identity and explores how they envisaged their clerical role and the implications of this for their relationships with their Irish neighbours, might help to explain the selection of particular individuals as victims.[34] But ministers were also targeted as a *symbol* of an alien religion and rule. The ritualised nature of this violence and the manipulation of the symbols of Protestant worship indicate a ready grasp of the defining differences between Catholics and Protestants in their worship. A gentleman deponent recounted how he had been told that before Mr Oliphant, whom he described as 'a constant preaching minister', was hanged 'a great multitude' surrounded him 'singing *with derideing voices* . . . some of the psalmes'.[35] Psalm singing, often associated in particular with puritan liturgical preferences, defined Protestant worship. Thus, the wife of a skinner at Waterford had the 'singeinge Psalmes' torn from her bible.[36]

Beheadings were represented in the depositions as moments of blind violence. The significance accorded the head in early modern constructions of the body undoubtedly added to the horror and revulsion these reports created. As Clodagh Tait and David Edwards argue, the belief that the head was the repository of personality and site of the soul gave decapitation considerable symbolic value. Defacing and ritually displaying the head was a deliberate act of humiliation.[37] In medieval England, however, the beheading of unpopular government officers represented a claim by crowds to exercise a form of popular justice on those they perceived to be traitors to king and commonwealth.[38] Did beheading carry a similar claim to agency in Ireland in 1641? Whatever the arguments about beheadings as an aspect of (earlier) interpersonal violence in Ireland, the beheading of victims in 1641 and the public display of their heads certainly reflected a grim copying of the terror tactics employed in the imposition of English rule.[39] At Ross in County Wexford, the insurgents hung the heads of two Englishmen on the town gates, 'as trophies of their victories *calling them by the name of Traytors*'.[40] That in England this form of popular justice had died out by the end of the fifteenth century and later became associated with depictions of Irishness on the London stage, meant that beheadings by the rebels (but not of course by the state) could be advanced by Protestant polemicists to underscore the savage and barbaric nature of the native Irish.[41]

Even (indeed especially) after death, violence continued to be performed on the bodies of victims. Disarrangement of the body carried humiliation into the grave. A Protestant shoemaker from Kilkenny, drawing on the eye-witness account of his Irish apprentice, deposed about the killing of one Captain Chambers, who was subsequently buried naked in a ditch with his severed head and genitals placed between his legs.[42] Reports of genitalia being cut off occur in a number of depositions. At Disart Castle, Mary Piggot witnessed the murder of her husband in front of her eyes and his 'private partes . . . slitted & scarred'.[43] Castration also had biblical resonances which emphasised the victim's intended exclusion; according to Deuteronomy 23:1, 'He that is wounded in the stones, or hath his privy member cut off, shall not enter into the congregation of the Lord.' The act of castration also mimicked the official punishment of traitors in Ireland in which, as part of the punishment of being hung, drawn and quartered, the removal of the privy members symbolised the erasure and damnation of a lineage.[44] The sexualised display of naked bodies clearly had a similar shaming purpose. According to the deposition of a merchant's wife, at the massacre at Sligo gaol the attackers cut the bodies of their victims into pieces and, 'placd some of the dead bodyes of the naked murthered men upon the naked bodyes of the women in a most immodest posture not fitt for chast eares to heare'. Something similar reportedly happened after the massacre at the mines in Knockanaderrick.[45]

In this way, the violence in 1641 reflected the pattern to be found in other atrocities, past and present. As Horowitz has observed, killings might begin as exemplary but end as euphoric, with what he calls a 'sadistic gaiety', a 'playful, light-hearted cruelty common in the handling of the bodies', marking such violent episodes.[46] In Galway, in April 1642, eye-witnesses reported that 'the Irish people of Err Connaght', carried a man's head up and down on the point of a pike to the accompanying cries of 'the head of an English Dogg'. Several people took turns to fling the head in the air, with 'a great Lustie Irish woman' picking it up by the hair and throwing it as high as she could. They then kicked and tumbled the head 'lyke a football in the streets'. In a scene reminiscent of certain continental episodes, clergy and friars employed counter-ritual to prevent further violence, processing through the town, 'in their vestments with tapers burneing, and the Sacrament borne before them', earnestly exhorting the killers to shed no more blood.[47] Behind what Alain Corbin has called 'ceremonious mutilation' was a further mimesis of the state policy.[48] A punishment favoured by the Court of Castle Chamber at Dublin involved the slitting of noses and cutting of ears, on occasion ordered to be self-inflicted.[49] An exchange between a rebel and a Protestant minister brings out the possible layers of meaning behind these mutilations: 'Remember how you English have served us? Howe they slitt our noses and scarrd our faces?'[50] Thus, the exhumation and mutilation of the recently buried body of the Bishop of Limerick may have been intended as a parody of government-prescribed violence.[51]

The disposal of the bodies of the victims offered one last chance for making a statement. The desecration of Protestant bodies was intended to taunt and humiliate the victims, to demonstrate their powerlessness, and to deny them honourable burial. Deponents persistently complained about the refusal to allow proper burial and the exposure of victim's bodies to the ravages of birds and animals.[52] According to one deponent, the rebels would eventually allow the bodies of their victims to be buried in ditches, but in a deliberate inversion of customary practice 'they must ever be layd with there faces downeward . . . that they might have a prospect and sight of hell only'.[53] In what Clodagh Tait has called the 'politics of disinterment', the attack on churches involved the desecration of the Protestant bodies buried there.[54] Protestant bodies represented a source of confessional contamination. Their disinterment, desecration and disposal symbolised that Protestants were, 'God's enemies for whom there was no hope of resurrection and therefore no place in God's acre'.[55] In this instance, as Horowitz has noted for modern atrocities, performative violence was intended to communicate the alien and worthless status of the target group and their illegal occupation of space and place.[56]

Attacks on sacred space, through the widespread desecration of churches, also challenged Protestant notions of holiness.[57] The insurgents destroyed church interiors, and sometimes the buildings themselves. At Tesaran in King's County, the assailants pulled down the pulpit and threw it outdoors, together with the seats and communion table. At Belturbet, County Cavan, the rebels reportedly burnt the seats, bible and church books, leaving the interior 'much defaced and blackened . . . with fyer'. At Powerscourt, County Wicklow, the pews, pulpits, chests, and bibles were burnt 'with extreme violence and triumph & expression of hatred to religion'.[58] The patterning to this desecration and destruction suggests that the attackers understood the priorities within Protestant worship, especially the importance of the pulpit. At Kilkenny, the perhaps aptly named William Lawlis, allegedly 'belt[ed] the pulpytt in Sct. Maryes church to peecs'.[59]

Above all else, the insurgents targeted the Protestant bible.[60] One man seized Edward Slacke's bible and, 'laying the open side in a puddle of water lept and stamped upon it, Saying a plague on't. This booke hath bred all the quarrel . . . and they hoped within 3 weeks all the bibles in Ireland should be used as that was or worse & that none should be left in the Kingdome.' Burning bibles he had confiscated, John O' Maloney, 'Chaplain Maior of the Catholique Army', reportedly said that, 'he was sworne to burne all the Protestant Bibles that came to his hands'.[61] The significance of the pulpit bible, the most common piece of interior decoration after the communion silver, made it an obvious target. In the attack on Newtown church in Fermanagh, proceeded by a piper, the leader, 'noe sooner entred, but in Contempt of god & his sacred worde, he went up into the pulpit, and tooke downe the English bible that was ther & Rent & tore the same in peecs'.[62] At Mountrath, County Laois, rebels who tore apart two bibles did so, 'with most horrible indignation telling the English dogges . . . [they] should never come to howle there more'.[63]

Bibles were not simply seized and destroyed but often subjected to public desecration and destruction. At Belturbet, 'all the protestant bookes as bibles and the rest, that were not of the Romish stampe and party were burned in great heapes at the high Crosse'.[64] Destruction necessarily involved desecration, but sometimes this went further. A fellow gentleman told John Parrie an episode which employed a well-understood signifier of contempt within the early modern gestural code to challenge notions of holiness: 'Opening the sacred bible [its attacker] pist upon the same, saying if I could doe worse with it I would.'[65] At Fethard castle, assailants cut the pulpit cloth, tore up the minister's books, called for a piper and then trampled the papers under their feet as they danced.[66] A County Monaghan gentleman witnessed the rebels' hostility to the bible. Whenever they came upon bibles and other Protestant books, he saw them rip them apart and play football with various pieces.[67]

Fire and water were both used in the destruction of bibles and churches.[68] In an episode at Lismore in January 1642, a rebel opened the New Testament, spread it on the fire with 'his foot upon it, that it might be burnt sooner'.[69] Insurgents in County Wexford burnt bibles before the faces of their Protestant owners, reportedly 'saying in disgrace and contempt of religion, what will you doe now your bibles are burnt'.[70] Fleeing with two chests of his divinity books, the minister John Sharp was allegedly stripped naked and forced to trample the books in the water before his attackers 'tossed many of them in the wynd'.[71] In County Cavan, two men reportedly, 'did often take into their hands the protestant bibles & wetting them on the durty water did 5 or 6 severall tymes' dash them into the faces of their Protestant victims, 'saying come I know you love a good lesson. Here is a most excellent one for you & come to morrow & you shall have as good a sermon as this.'[72]

The use of fire and water to remove sources of Protestant pollution had symbolic associations with acts of purification in liturgical practice that made their use in episodes of confessional violence in England and on the Continent particularly appropriate.[73] Attacks, therefore, on Protestant ministers, churches, pulpits and bibles in Ireland can be read not simply as acts of desecration, but as acts of reformation. The compressed nature of many of the 1641 depositions, however, makes it impossible to establish the full extent of possible symbolic and ritual display in these acts of violence. Nonetheless, the vignette of a group of men on the Cork coast throwing the bibles they had found in Protestant houses onto the strand and stoning them carries obvious overtones of Old Testament punishment.[74]

An influential essay by David Riches, on the anthropology of violence, highlighted how the meaning of performative violence is contested in a negotiation between performer, victim and witness. To this, we might add audiences. Both the act of deposing and the shaping of the events described therein can be seen as a form of competitive 'othering'. Opponents of iconoclasts in England sought to represent their actions as vandalism. Protestant deponents in Ireland, while anxious to emphasise attacks on the central Protestant text of the bible, could also employ a language of criminality to refer to the wanton destruction of churches. After the attack on Kilkenny cathedral, one deponent described the chalice, surplice, church ornaments and books as having been 'robbed'. Similarly, the curate at Whitchurch, talked of the church being 'robbed and forcibly dispoyled of its ornaments and utensills' and gave a monetary value to the goods removed.[75] The objects he listed, including church bible, books of common prayers, surplice and pulpit cloth, were all of course symbols of Protestant worship. To describe these actions as acts of theft doubtless reflected an understanding of the role of the Commission for the Despoiled Subject to secure compensation, but the deponents perhaps also sought to deny, implicitly or otherwise, the motive of the attackers.

In the context of the early modern mental world, a belief in the providentialist God of the Old Testament complicated the contest over the meaning of violence. This made God a party to the struggle over the meaning and legitimacy of violence. A sensitivity to the signs and wonders that could provide evidence of God's judgements made Protestant deponents acute readers for meaning in the violent events they experienced. For some deponents, these might be found in personal histories, where escape from otherwise random violence could be attributed to divine intervention. Reports of strange happenings, however, that could be read as signs of God's disapproval often accompanied the larger-scale atrocities. Thus, for example, the bodies of drowned Protestants refused to sink or re-surfaced, and continued to bleed long after their murder, before reappearing as spectral figures calling for revenge at the sites of massacre.[76] Those guilty of their deaths became distracted or found the limbs that delivered the fatal blow attacked by mysterious ailments. A murderer of a minister, for example, acquired an 'unnaturall & odious smell & odoure'.[77] Seeds in the gardens of those implicated in the violence failed to germinate, while rivers emptied of fish following the mass drowning of Protestants, triggering attempts by friars going 'in great companies in procession . . . to sanctify the water'.[78] Fast-flowing streams appeared unable to sweep away the upright bodies of murdered men and women, while waters turned the colour of blood when Catholics took mass at formerly Protestant sites.[79]

In one of the more infamous episodes of performative violence, the rebels reportedly tried and executed 'English' livestock, 'with all derision and scoffing carriage used to bring a booke before the Cowe or sheepe of English straine . . . and asked them whether they could reade'?[80]

> In contempt & derision of the English Lawes [they] did ordinarily & commonly prefer *or seeme to prefer* bills of inditement & bring the English breed of Cattle to be tried upon Juries & having on their fashion arraigned those Cattle then their scornfull Judge . . . would say they looke as if they could speake English, give them the booke, to see if they can read, pronounceing the words legit an non [i.e. reads not] to the Jury. And then because they stood mute & could not read hee would . . . pronounce Judgment and centence of death against them.[81]

Although there are few references to such mock trials, the episode merits serious analysis for what it reveals of the social creativity of those engaged in the rising. In the run-up to civil war, English protesters engaged in similar episodes of street theatre. Reluctant troops, for example, recruited to fight in the unpopular Bishops' Wars against the Scots enthusiastically staged mock trials to arraign and punish figures of popular hate in the Laudian church. They also held kangaroo courts, modelled on the procedures of the unpopular church courts, in which they made sophisticated and subtle criticisms of what they perceived as Laudian perversion of the English church.[82] In putting 'English' livestock on trial, the Irish rebels focused attention on one of the major symbols of their loss of land. The large-scale destruction of livestock more frequently noted in the depositions might then be compared to the mass slaughter of deer as hated symbols of aristocratic emparkment that took place in England in the early stages of the civil war.[83] It might also be seen as part of a broader European tradition in which the trial and execution of animals was used to make symbolic and extra-judicial statements.[84]

In this instance, the rebels mimicked the practice of 'benefit of clergy', a corruption of an earlier legal practice by which the clergy in medieval England could claim exemption from trial in the secular courts. The ability to read Psalm 51, popularly known as 'the neck verse', could mitigate or avoid punishment. In parodying the procedures of the English-imposed law courts, the participants in this episode staged a piece of street theatre that both mocked and criticised English law. This performance, therefore, might be read as a criticism of the recent extension of the assizes into areas like County Mayo. According to another deponent, also from Mayo, 'the Rebells say That they ment to Roote out both the English and the Scottish because they had gotten all from them by their Corts and assizes'.[85] It also serves as a reminder of a cultural patterning to the violence, in which apparently all things English became targets for Irish hostility: the English language, place names and even English dress in reaction to English-imposed sumptuary laws.[86] Ethnic, as well as religious, differences also played a role in the shaping of violence. Presumably, Irish-only speakers who found themselves before the English courts found themselves as disadvantaged by their enforced 'muteness' as 'English' cattle.

As David Riches argues, one of the key values of violence as a social and cultural resource is that it can, 'strikingly dramatize important social ideas'.[87] The coincidence of the (incomplete) establishment of a Protestant church with the extension of English rule fused social, economic, political and ethnic tensions in a cultural conflict that found expression in anti-Protestantism. The parallel development of a post-Tridentine Catholicism promoted by continentally trained priests and members of the religious orders, especially the Franciscans, added the language of heresy to all this: Protestants were 'no Christianes but heretickes'.[88] Not all priests and friars called for the destruction of Protestants, and further analysis is required of the processes of accommodation.[89] The optimistic assessment of Nicholas Canny, however, that the Catholic clergy directed their hostility towards Protestant property and not persons needs to be revisited.[90] Franciscans' identification of Protestants with devils made their beliefs, their buildings and their behaviour literally diabolical. Reported speech in the depositions suggests that the Franciscans found a receptive audience.[91] Protestant worship was in effect devil worship – 'all that went to church went to the divell, for god had nothing to do with them nor they with him' – while the bible 'was the word of the divell' and there was 'nothing in that booke but *the* devils Inventions'.[92]

The aggressive 'othering' implied in such labelling had the obvious consequence of removing Protestants from the protection of a Christian-derived moral code. In one case, a victim used the protean early modern language of neighbourliness and moral community, telling his attackers that God would punish them 'for taking away *neighbours* goods'. They responded that, 'protestants were noe neighbours of theirs, but they were hereticks & therefore [it was] noe breach of Conscience to take away their goods'.[93] Attacks against Protestants could be reframed as 'holy violence' performed by the just on the wicked.[94] Violence might then become a moral and legitimate act. According to one deponent, priests claimed that it was 'no sin to kill the protestants whoe are damned creatures'.[95]

Of course, a whole range of grievances, local, personal and general went into the making of 1641. Nonetheless, despite these various inflections, confessional conflict clearly ran through the 1641 rising, aligning it with the 'didactive' violence of much of continental Europe.[96] Evidence in the depositions illustrates that this message was not lost on its victims. In turn, English printed reports, with their preference for the more lurid accounts of hearsay evidence, also fore-grounded attacks on sacred spaces, texts and bodies.[97] This raises the interesting question as to what extent deponents selected out religious violence precisely because of the potency of the black legend of anti-popery, as well as by their knowledge of the Bible, reading, as Aidan Clarke notes, in the Book of Revelation of 'the dead bodies of martyrs' refused burial and left to lie in the streets of Sodom.[98] At the same time, and perhaps not incidentally, this emphasis might downplay or avoid granting legitimacy to those other potent symbols in early modern rebellions of land, liberty and *patria*. As in England, religion could serve as a common metaphor for a wider range of grievances, which cut across sectional and class divisions. Thus, religion as an ideology of revolt in 1641 could subsume and explain the economic and political grievances arising from the experiences of plantation, colonisation and the loss of political autonomy. Its unifying role in 1641 bears out Horowitz's acute observation that 'what observers separate out for analysis the participants regularly put together for action.'[99]

A focus on symbolic and ritual statements in episodes of violence in 1641 suggests a pressing need to revisit and revise the understanding in the current historiography of the rising as a two-tier protest, with a popular movement which ran beyond the control of the elite.[100] Fathering political violence on the 'many-headed monster' of the people was a common ploy in English rebellions of this period and much more work needs to be done on the social identity of the attackers in 1641. The division between the elite and the 'people' ignores the critical role of the socially intermediate groups of property-owning local and urban officeholders, stressed in recent work on English rebellions. On reading the depositions, the idea that the violence can be attributed primarily to popular fury does not seem to hold up. It is already beginning to be challenged, but it is possible to go further.[101]

Much of the focus of this paper will be familiar to Irish historians of 1641 but its implications for our understanding of early modern Ireland have yet to be fully realised. Much recent work on popular violence in early modern England argues that crowd actions were necessarily political and reflected a claim to a popular agency. This, in turn, reflected a larger political awareness running from the politics of subsistence to the politics of the post-Reformation state and church. Popular agency represented in part an outgrowth of a political culture informed by both civic humanism and Protestantism. It was also the product of the particular structures of the English monarchy that made self-government at the King's command a political necessity, and required the popular policing of market, church and state. This created, in effect, a negotiated state, which offered legitimation for popular agency in the public transcripts that authority created and publicised to secure consent to its rule. In England in the 1640s, Parliament, print and pulpit combined to radicalise this popular political culture.[102] Presumably, the complex political and social relationships in early modern Ireland, with an increasingly anglicised administration itself a source of political tension, offered more limited space for any such development. In Ireland, the state as aggressor rather than (as in England) educator played the larger role in 1641. Nevertheless, developing work on the negotiation of authority, and on the politics of the crowd in pre-1641 Ireland, suggests that violence in 1641 may be better understood when seen less as a climacteric event and more in the context of a continuum of political and social violence.[103] The implications of the ability of crowds to make statements through performative violence, as well as the political nature of the statements voiced by the rebels (not discussed in this paper, but in which the Commissions took an especial interest) require further research to explore the social depth to the *politics* of the popular violence that took place in 1641.

NOTES

1 Trinity College Dublin (TCD) MS 839, fols. 38r–39v.
2 Nicholas Canny, 'What really happened in Ireland in 1641', in Jane Ohlmeyer (ed.), *Ireland: From Independence to Occupation* (Cambridge, 1995), pp. 24–42, at p. 26.
3 Joseph Cope, 'Fashioning victims: Dr Henry Jones and the plight of Irish protestants, 1643', *Historical Research*, 74(186) (2001), 370–91; Cope, *England and the 1641 Irish Rebellion* (Woodbridge, 2009); Kathleen Noonan, ' "The cruel pressure of an enraged, barbarous people": Irish and English identity in seventeenth-century policy and propaganda', *Historical Journal*, 41(1) (1998), 151–77; Noonan, ' "Martyrs in Flames": Sir John Temple and the conception of the Irish in English Martyrologies', *Albion*, 36(2) (2004), 223–55.
4 John Walter, *Crowds and Popular Politics in Early Modern England* (Manchester, 2006), chapters 1 and 2.
5 For a selection, see Nicholas Canny, 'The 1641 depositions as a source for the writing of social history: County Cork as a case study', in P. O'Flanagan and C. Buttumer (eds), *Cork History and Society* (Dublin, 1993), pp. 249–308; Canny, 'Religion, politics and the Irish Rising of 1641', in Judith Devlin and Ronan Fanning (eds), *Religion and Rebellion* (Dublin, 1997), pp. 43–68; Canny, *Making Ireland British 1580–1650* (Oxford, 2001), pp. 461–550; Aidan Clarke, 'The genesis of the Ulster rising of 1641', in Peter Roebuck (ed.), *Plantation to Partition: Essays in Ulster History in Honour of J. L. McCracken* (Belfast, 1981), pp. 29–45; Clarke, 'The 1641 depositions', in Peter Fox (ed.), *Treasures of the Library: Trinity*

College, Dublin (Dublin, 1984), pp. 111–22; Clarke, 'The commission for the despoiled subject, 1641–7', in Brian Mac Cuarta (ed.), *Reshaping Ireland 1550–1750: Colonization and Its Consequences* (Dublin, 2011), pp. 241–60; Robin Clifton, ' "An indiscriminate blackness"? Massacre, counter-massacre, and ethnic cleansing in Ireland, 1640–1660', in Mark Levene and Penny Roberts (eds), *The Massacre in History* (New York and Oxford, 1999), pp. 107–26; Raymond Gillespie, 'Mayo and the rising of 1641', *Cathar Na Mart*, 5(1) (1985), 38–44; Gillespie, 'The murder of Arthur Champion and the 1641 rising in Fermanagh', *Clogher Record*, 14(3) (1993), 52–66; Gillespie, 'The end of an era: Ulster and the outbreak of the 1641 rising', in Ciaran Brady and Raymond Gillespie (eds), *Natives and Newcomers: Essays on the Making of Irish Colonial Society 1534–1641* (Dublin, 1986), pp. 191–212; Brian Mac Cuarta (ed.), *Ulster 1641: Aspects of the Rising* (Belfast, 1993); Brian Mac Cuarta, 'Religious violence against settlers in south Ulster, 1641–2', in David Edwards, Pádraig Lenihan and Clodagh Tait (eds), *Age of Atrocity: Violence and Political Conflict in Early Modern Ireland* (Dublin, 2007), pp. 154–75; Charlene McCoy and Micheál Ó Siochrú, 'County Fermanagh and the 1641 depositions', *Archivum Hibernicum*, 61 (2008), 62–136; Bríd McGrath, 'County Meath from the depositions', *Ríocht na Midhe*, 9(1) (1994/1995), 24–41; M. Perceval-Maxwell, *The Outbreak of the Irish Rebellion of 1641* (Montreal, 1994); Brendan Scott, 'The 1641 rising in the plantation town of Belturbet', *Breifne*, 10(40) (2004), 155–75; Scott, 'Reporting the 1641 rising in Cavan and Leitrim', in Brendan Scott (ed.), *Culture and Society in Early Modern Breifne/Cavan* (Dublin, 2009), pp. 200–14.

 6 Clarke, 'Commission'; TCD MS 812, fol. 1r.

 7 Inga Volmer, 'A comparative study of massacres during the wars of the three kingdoms, 1641–53' (Ph.D. dissertation, University of Cambridge, 2006), p. 24.

 8 On which, see Renato Rosaldo, 'From the door of his tent: the fieldworker and the inquisitor', in James Clifford and George E. Marcus (eds), *Writing Culture: The Poetics and Politics of Ethnography* (Berkeley and Los Angeles, 1986), pp. 77–97.

 9 Mary O'Dowd, 'Women and war in Ireland in the 1640s', in Margaret MacCurtain and Mary O'Dowd (eds), *Women in Early Modern Ireland* (Edinburgh, 1991), p. 101; Dianne Hall and Elizabeth Malcom, ' "The rebels Turkish tyranny": understanding sexual violence in Ireland during the 1640s', *Gender and History*, 22(1) (2010), 55–74.

10 David Riches, 'The phenomenon of violence', in David Riches (ed.), *The Anthropology of Violence* (Oxford, 1986), p. 25.

11 Donald H. Horowitz, *The Deadly Ethnic Riot* (Berkeley and London, 2001), pp. xiv, 1–2.

12 Thomas Fitzpatrick, 'The Ulster civil war: "The King's Commission" in the County Cavan', *Ulster Journal of Archaeology*, 2nd ser., 13(3–4) (1908), 133–42, 168–77; 15(1–3) (1909), 7–13, 61–4.

13 TCD MS 835, fols 238v–96, MS 810, fol. 92r; Keith Thomas, *Religion and the Decline of Magic* (Harmondsworth, 1973), pp. 461–514.

14 Horowitz, *Deadly Ethnic Riot*, pp. 82, 74–5, 155–8, 528–9; Riches, 'Violence', pp. 5–6.

15 TCD MS 833, fol. 11r.
16 Perceval-Maxwell, *Outbreak*, pp. 221–2, 234, 290; Mac Cuarta, 'Religious violence', pp. 156–8; Raymond Gillespie, 'Faith, family and fortune: the structures of everyday life in early modern Cavan', in Raymond Gillespie (ed.), *Cavan: Essays on the History of an Irish County* (Blackrock, 1995), p. 107; McCoy and Ó Siochrú, 'County Fermanagh', pp. 84, 94–5; TCD MS 812, fol. 28r; MS 815, fol. 295r; MS 816, fol. 97v; MS 817, fols 37v, 140v; MS 818, fols 110r–113v; MS 833, fol. 11r; MS 835, fols 133v, 210v.
17 I am preparing an article on these exceptional episodes involving the killing of officers by their troops.
18 Mark Stoyle, 'The road to Farndon Field: explaining the massacre of the royalist women at Naseby', *English Historical Review*, 123 (2008), 895–923; Will Coster, 'Massacre and codes of conduct in the English civil war', in Levene and Roberts (eds), *Massacre*, pp. 89–105.
19 Canny, *Making Ireland British*, pp. 542–3; Canny, 'What really happened', p. 32.
20 S. J. Connolly, *Divided Kingdom: Ireland 1630–1800* (Oxford, 2008), p. 47; Marjo Kaartinen and Anu Korhonen (eds), *Bodies in Evidence: Perspectives on the History of the Body in Early Modern Europe* (Turku, 1997), p. 177.
21 Martin Ingram, *Church Courts, Sex and Marriage in England 1570–1640* (Cambridge, 1987), pp. 54, 249, 257–8, 336.
22 Garthine Walker, *Crime, Gender and the Social Order in Early Modern England* (Cambridge, 2003), p. 54; Hall and Malcom, ' "Rebels Turkish Tyranny" ', p. 66.
23 Gillespie, 'Destabilizing Ulster', p. 120.
24 TCD MS 833, fol. 235r; MS 830, fol. 169r; MS 836, fol. 40v; McCoy and Ó Siochrú, 'Fermanagh', p. 117.
25 Mac Cuarta, 'Religious violence', p. 162; Canny, *Making Ireland British*, p. 490.
26 TCD MS 836, fols 2r, 95r, 101v; TCD MS 812, fol. 212r, MS 814, fol. 162v; Canny, *Making Ireland British*, 485.
27 TCD MS 831, fol. 191r; Erica Fudge, *Brutal Reasoning: Animals, Rationality, and Humanity in Early Modern England* (Ithaca and London, 2006), pp. 70–1; Alain Corbin, *The Village of Cannibals* (Cambridge, 1992), pp. 75–7.
28 TCD MS 831, fol. 119r; Edwards, Lenihan and Tait (eds), *Age of Atrocity*, p. 21.
29 Stoyle, 'Farndon Field', pp. 905–6; G. S., *A Briefe Declaration of the Barabarous and inhumane dealings of the Northerne Irish Rebels . . .* (London, 1641), pp. 2–3.
30 Connolly, *Divided Kingdom*, p. 48; TCD MS 836, fol. 52r; MS 815, fol. 186r.
31 TCD MS 836, fol. 71r; David Edwards, ' "Some days two heads and some days four" ', *History Ireland*, 17(1) (2009), 18–21.
32 TCD MS 815, fol. 381r, fols 421r–v, 439v.
33 TCD MS 812, fols 203r–v, 220r.
34 Connolly, *Divided Kingdom*, p. 41.
35 TCD MS 831, fol. 175v.
36 Christopher Marsh, *Music and Society in Early Modern England* (Cambridge, 2010), chapter 8; TCD MS 820, fol. 50v.
37 Clodagh Tait, *Death, Burial and Commemoration in Ireland, 1550–1650* (Basingstoke, 2002), p. 75; Edwards, ' "Some days Two Heads" ', p. 19; TCD MS 821, fol. 44r.

38 John Watts, 'Public or plebs: the changing meaning of "The Commons", 1381–1549', in Huw Pryce and John Watts (eds), *Power and Identity in the Middle Ages: Essays in Memory of Rees Davies* (Oxford, 2007), pp. 242–60.

39 Kenneth Nicholls, 'The other massacres: English killing of Irish, 1641–2', in Edwards, Lenihan and Tait (eds), *Age of Atrocity*, p. 188; Edwards, '"Some days Two Heads"', pp. 18–21.

40 TCD MS 818, fol. 26v (my emphasis).

41 Patricia Palmer, '"An headless Ladie" and "a horses loade of heades": writing the beheading', *Renaissance Quarterly*, 60(1) (2007), 25–57.

42 TCD MS 812, fols. 47v, 213r, 214r–v, 247r.

43 TCD MS 815, fols. 412r–v.

44 Barra Ó Donnabháin, 'Monuments of shame: some political trophy heads from medieval Dublin', *Archaeology Ireland*, 9(4) (1995), 13; Tait, *Death*, p. 31.

45 TCD MS 831, fol. 74r; MS 830, fols 37r, 120r–2r; MS 821, fols 194r–v.

46 Horowitz, *Deadly Ethnic Riot*, pp. 2, 114, 536.

47 TCD MS 830, fols 134r–47v, 226r, 233r–6v, 256r; Peter Burke, 'The Virgin of Carmine and the revolt of Masaniello', *Past and Present*, 99 (1983), 3–21.

48 Corbin, *Village of Cannibals*, p. 77. I am grateful to Clodagh Tait for this suggestion.

49 *Manuscripts of the Earl of Egmont* (HMC, 3 vols, London, 1920–3), vol. 1, pp. 11, 20, 22–3, 28, 33, 37.

50 TCD MS 831, fol. 192v.

51 TCD MS 829, fols. 180r–v.

52 Gillespie, 'Champion', p. 59; TCD MS 814, fols 157r–8v; MS 815, fol. 217r.

53 TCD MS, 809, fol. 12r; Tait, *Death*, p. 83; TCD MS 814, fol. 178r.

54 Tait, *Death*, pp. 31, 81; TCD MS 812, fols 219 r–v; MS 813, fols 260r, 285v, 385r–v; MS 814, fols 231v, 241r; MS 815, fols 183r; 191v–2r; MS 818, fol. 24v; MS 820, fols 56r, 312–5v; MS 829, fol. 81r; MS 835, fol. 238v; MS 836, fol. 109r.

55 Tait, *Death*, pp. 83, 85–96.

56 Horowitz, *Deadly Ethnic Riot*, pp. 121–2. Cf. Canny, 'Religion', p. 57.

57 TCD MS 836, fol. 111r; MS 839, fols 136r–v.

58 TCD MS 834, fols 109v, 131v; MS 811, fols 47r–8v, 174r–5v; MS 814, fols 240r–1v; McCoy and Ó Siochrú, 'Fermanagh', pp. 112–3.

59 TCD MS 812, fol. 247v.

60 Mac Cuarta, 'Religious violence', pp. 171–2.

61 TCD MS 835, fol. 170r; MS 834, fol. 119r; MS 834, fol. 103r; MS 810, fols 244r–v.

62 TCD MS 835, fols 109r, 176r; Raymond Gillespie, *Devoted People: Belief and Religion in Early Modern Ireland* (Manchester, 1997), p. 93.

63 TCD MS 815, fols 217r–v; MS 817, fol. 35r–v.

64 TCD MS 833, fols 275r–81v; MS 817, fol. 38r.

65 TCD MS 836, fol. 64r; John Walter, 'Gesturing at authority: deciphering the gestural code of early modern England', in M. Braddick (ed.), *The Politics of Gesture: Historical Perspectives* (*Past and Present*, Supplement, 4, 2009), pp. 96–127.

66 TCD MS 815, fols. 253r, 374r–8v; MS 818, fol. 88r; MS 820, fols. 20r, 50v; MS 836, fol. 49r.

67 TCD MS 834, fol. 132r.

68 TCD MS 811, fol. 170r; 813, fols. 330r, 380v; MS 814, fols. 161r; MS 815, fols. 217r, 223r, 240r, 253r, 295r; MS 820, fol. 44r; MS 823, fol. 169r.

69 TCD MS 820, fol. 20r.

70 TCD MS 818, fols. 25r, 124r.

71 TCD MS 816, fol. 144v.

72 TCD MS 833, fol. 1v.

73 Natalie Zemon Davis, 'The rites of violence: religious riot in sixteenth-century France', *Past and Present*, 59 (1973), 57–85; Margaret Aston, 'Rites of destruction by fire', in Margaret Aston, *Faith and Fire: Popular and Unpopular Religion 1350–1600* (London, 1993), p. 300.

74 TCD MS 824, fol. 149r. Cf. Alastair Bellany, 'The murder of John Lambe: Crowd violence, court scandal and popular politics in early seventeenth century England', *Past and Present*, 200 (2008), 37–76, at 73.

75 TCD MS 812, fol. 203v; MS 820, fol. 211r.

76 TCD 836, fols 89r–v, 95v–6r, 102v–3r MS 833, fols 98v–9r, 129v; MS 809, fol. 10v; MS 833, fols 161r, 278v; MS 834, fol. 160r.

77 TCD MS 812, fol. 203r; MS 815, fol. 197v; MS 831, fol. 74v; MS 837, fols 11r–v.

78 TCD MS 821, fols 31r; MS 814, fol. 218r; MS 833, fols 105r–6v 156r–v, 217v; MS 831, fol. 73v.

79 TCS MS 833, fols 220r–v; MS 836, fols 97r, 98v.

80 TCD MS 831, fol. 169r.

81 TCD MS 831, fols. 190r–v. I am very grateful to Eamon Darcy for bringing this to my attention.

82 John Walter, '"Abolishing superstition with sedition"? The politics of popular iconoclasm in England, 1640–1642', *Past and Present*, 183 (2004), 79–123, at 109–11.

83 Daniel C. Beaver, *Hunting and the Politics of Violence before the English Civil War* (Cambridge, 2008).

84 E. P. Evans, *The Criminal Prosecution and Capital Punishment of Animals* (London, 1906); Darren Oldridge, *Strange Histories: The Trial of the Pigs, the Walking Dead, and Other Matters of Fact* (London, 2005), pp. 40–55.

85 TCD MS 831, fol. 183v. I am indebted to Clodagh Tait for this observation.

86 TCD MS 833, fol. 232v; MS 834, fols 111r–v, 112r, 132r;. MS 814, fol. 162v; Mac Cuarta, 'Religious violence', p. 154; Bernadette Whelan, 'The weaker vessel? The impact of warfare on women in seventeenth century Ireland', in Christine Meek and Catherine Lawless (eds), *Studies in Medieval and Early Modern Women, 4: Victims or Viragoes* (Dublin, 2005), p. 125; Canny, *Making Ireland British*, pp. 486–7; Ann Rosalind Jones and Peter Stallybrass, 'Dismantling Irena: the sexualising of Ireland in early modern England', in Andrew Parker *et al.*, (eds), *Nationalisms & Sexualities* (New York & London, 1992), pp. 157–71.

87 Riches, 'Violence', p. 25.

88 Ian W. S. Campbell, 'John Lynch and renaissance humanism in Stuart Ireland: Catholic intellectuals, Protestant noblemen, and the Irish *respublica*', *Éire-Ireland*, 45(3–4) (2010), p. 37; Colm Lennon, 'Taking sides: the emergence of Irish Catholic ideology', in Vincent P. Carey and Ute Lotz-Heumann (eds), *Taking Sides? Colonial and Confessional Mentalities in Early Modern Ireland* (Dublin, 2003), pp. 92–3; TCD MS 833, fol. 187r.

89　Joseph Cope, 'The experience of survival during the 1641 Irish rebellion', *Historical Journal*, 46(2) (2003), 295–316.

90　Canny, *Making Ireland British*, pp. 488–90, 546–7; Canny, 'Religion', pp. 55–6;

91　Edwards, Lenihan and Tait (eds), *Age of Atrocity*, p. 25; Mac Cuarta, 'Religious violence', pp. 157, 169; Gillespie, *Devoted People*, p. 1.

92　TCD MS 836, fol. 49r; MS 835, fol. 210r; MS 832, fol. 63v; MS 811, fol. 40r; MS 820, fol. 50v; MS 815, fol. 381v. Mac Cuarta, 'Religious violence', p. 170.

93　TCD MS 813, fols 287r–288v; MS 817, fol. 202r.

94　Horowitz, *Deadly Ethnic Riot*, p. 528; Alexandra Walsham, *Charitable Hatred: Tolerance and Intolerance in England, 1500–1700* (Manchester, 2006), p. 140.

95　TCD MS 816, fol. 8v.

96　For the 'didactive' intent behind French religious violence, see Barbara Diefendorf, *Beneath the Cross: Catholics and Huguenots in sixteenth-century Paris* (New York and Oxford, 1991); Zemon Davis, 'Rites of violence'.

97　Clarke, 'The 1641 rebellion', p. 155; Cope, *England and the 1641 Irish Rebellion*, pp. 82–3; Noonan, 'Martyrs in Flames', pp. 240–1; Henry Jones, *A Remonstrance of Divers Remarkable Passages Concerning the Church and Kingdome of Ireland . . .* (1642), p. 8.

98　Aidan Clarke, 'The 1641 rebellion and anti-popery', in Mac Cuarta (ed.), *Ulster 1641*, p. 155.

99　Horowitz, *Deadly Ethnic Riot*, p. xiv.

100　This distinction runs through Nicholas Canny's writings on 1641 and is given full expression in his chapter 8 of his *Making Ireland British*. See also Michael Perceval-Maxwell, *Outbreak*, p. 227; Scott, *Cavan*, p. 208; Simms, 'Violence in County Armagh, 1641', in Mac Cuarta (ed.), *Ulster*, p. 135.

101　McCoy and Ó Siochrú, 'Fermanagh', 67.

102　Walter, *Crowds*, pp. 1–26, 196–217; Walter, 'Politicising the popular? The "tradition of riot" and popular political culture in the English revolution', in Nicholas Tyacke (ed.), *The English Revolution c. 1590–1720: Politics, Religion and Communities* (Manchester, 2007), pp. 95–110.

103　Raymond Gillespie, 'Negotiating order in early seventeenth-century Ireland', in Michael J. Braddick and John Walter (eds), *Negotiating Power in Early Modern Society: Order, Hierarchy and Subordination in Britain and Ireland* (Cambridge, 2001), pp. 188–205; W. Sheehan and M. Cronin, *Riotous Assemblies: Rebels, Riots and Revolts in Ireland* (Cork, 2011); Clodagh Tait, 'Riots, rescues and "grene bowes": Catholics and protest in Ireland, 1570–1640' (forthcoming).

9

Atrocities in the Thirty Years War

PETER H. WILSON

At 7a.m. on Tuesday 20 May 1631, following a pre-arranged signal, 18,000 imperial and Catholic League troops converged on the Protestant city of Magdeburg in five assault columns. After an hour's stubborn resistance, one detachment broke through a lightly held sector, and organised defence soon collapsed. A fire began around the point of entry and soon spread, engulfing the city and consuming 1,700 of its 1,900 buildings. Discipline broke down as the attackers dispersed to plunder before their prize literally went up in smoke. Sufficient men remained under orders to save the cathedral, where around 1,000 people had sought shelter, while the monks of the city's only Catholic monastery rescued another 600 women. Nonetheless, around four-fifths of the 25,000 inhabitants were dead by the time order was restored a few days later.[1]

Magdeburg's destruction immediately attracted wide attention, with at least 205 pamphlets appearing before the year was out.[2] The event profoundly affected the contemporary perception of the Thirty Years War (1618–48), becoming the centrepiece in accounts of generalised brutality. English-speaking readers were informed by works such as Dr Vincent's graphically illustrated *Lamentations of Germany* (1638), which in turn influenced the reception of the horrors of Britain's own civil wars and the Cromwellian campaigns in Ireland.[3]

This paper focuses on the continental experience of the Thirty Years War, rather than contemporary British perceptions which have already received some attention.[4] Magdeburg looms large in how the war has been interpreted. Friedrich Schiller already devoted considerable space in his history of the war to describing the assault and its violent aftermath.[5] The appearance of his account in 1791 on the eve of another prolonged and destructive conflict (this time against Revolutionary and Napoleonic France) gave Schiller's history an immediate contemporary resonance and cemented the association in the German popular consciousness between the Thirty Years War and national disaster. The war became a byword for unlimited, pointless violence that broke all bounds and left a beautiful land desolate and despoiled. There was a general sense that the country had plunged into an abyss as the war spiralled out of control, with any initial political or religious objectives smothered in an orgy of destruction. Gustav Drosyen (1808–86), in his biography of Gustavus Adolphus of Sweden, labelled this process the 'Magdeburgisation' (*Magdeburgisierung*) of the war.[6] Nationalists were quick to relate the loss of control with foreign intervention, which was blamed for much of the violence. The image of the 'Martyrdom of Magdeburg' which appeared in prints and songs of the 1630s was now applied to the entire nation, presenting the Thirty Years War as a necessary sacrifice to prepare Germany for national redemption in the form of Prussian-led unification in 1870. Reliance of writers elsewhere on German scholarship perpetuated this interpretation, and made the war a benchmark to judge later conflicts. A recent general history of massacres argues the sack of Magdeburg involved slaughter not seen since Ghengis Kahn and Tamurlaine, making it 'the worst destruction of a single community' prior to the 'Rape of Nanking' in 1937.[7]

The nationalist gloss has long fallen from fashion, but many still explain the level of violence in the Thirty Years War by presenting it as the culmination of a supposed 'age of religious wars'.[8] Religious fervour allegedly propelled people to fight, while sectarian hatred ensured conflicts were especially bloody. A parallel explanation stresses the mercenary composition of the armies composed of men lacking loyalty or discipline, who showed no mercy and plundered their way across the land without regard to friend or foe.[9] These two perspectives are often combined,[10] yet are inherently contradictory since those who did the killing are supposed to be indifferent to all ideals, including religion.

Before exploring the thorny problem of motives, it is helpful to consider the still-difficult but slightly more tractable problem of definition. The specialist theoretical and historical literature identifies 'atrocity', 'massacre' and 'genocide' as three key concepts, but unfortunately differs widely on their meaning.[11] At least the lack of agreement pinpoints three issues useful in understanding atrocities during the Thirty Years War. The first is *scale*: when does killing transform into massacre? This involves not only the number of victims, but also perpetrators. Second, there is the question of *intent*, which is frequently used to distinguish massacre from genocide. The latter is usually defined as the deliberate, systematic destruction of a racial or cultural group, thus entailing both deliberate intent and considerable scale. Massacre, by contrast, is defined as the ruthless and indiscriminate killing of large numbers of people. While this implies scale, it leaves open whether a massacre results from cold-blooded premeditation, or follows from some unintended hot-blooded escalation of violence. The third issue concerns the *legitimacy* of mass killing in relation to war making. This question much excised twentieth-century commentators struggling to decide whether acts like the strategic bombing of Dresden or Hiroshima constituted massacre or simply brutal, but legitimate military necessity. These questions are usually answered by reference to the alleged purpose of such acts: whether they were carried out as elements of military strategy intended to end a war quickly by breaking the enemy's will to resist, or simply to kill large numbers of people.

Seventeenth-century Europeans were already aware there are no clear answers to these questions. The ambiguities were present in their language of war and atrocity. The German word for battle is *Schlacht* – literally 'slaughter'. In some parts of Germany, a butcher's shop is still called a *Schlächterei*; a word which can also denote massacre. As Mark Greengrass has noted, the word 'massacre' derives from the old French for butcher's block and was already used in its modern sense as early as 1545.[12] The expression rarely appeared in seventeenth-century Germany, and indeed was still missing in nineteenth-century specialist military literature.[13] Seventeenth-century Germans used 'Schlacht' to denote legitimate slaughter in the sense of battles between armies acting, at least ostensibly, on behalf of properly constituted authorities. Two terms existed for what were considered abuses of legitimate violence. The most common was *Excess*, an elastic term indicating transgression of accepted norms. Its use gradually became more precise, so that by the later seventeenth century it generally meant breaches of military regulations forbidding robbery and other forms of extortion. *Kriegsgreuel* denoted far more serious transgressions involving physical violence, bloodshed and barbarity. This term is usually translated as atrocity. Massacre as understood today was subsumed as an atrocity on a large scale involving multiple deaths. There was no contemporary equivalent for genocide, a term not coined until 1944. Furthermore, as will be shown, there were countless excesses, numerous atrocities and massacres, but no acts of genocide in the Thirty Years War.

Any discussion of what actually occurred is clouded by the virulent sectarian polemic which accompanied the fighting. The war encouraged a rapid expansion of print culture, including Europe's first regular press, as well as a flood of partisan pamphlets often interpreting events through the *Book of Revelations* and other biblical texts. A good example is the widespread popular reception of the invading Swedish king, Gustavus Adolphus, as an avenging 'Lion of the North' sent by God to save Protestant Germany from 'the horror of the papists' and the 'tyranny of the tyrannical Emperor Ferdinand II' as one pastor put it in his church record.[14] Such views, however, remained restricted to a militant minority, especially junior clergy and exiles, who rarely influenced policy. Rulers certainly pursued confessional objectives, but these did not extend to the physical extermination of those holding contrary beliefs, still less to the destruction of other ethnic groups. Confessional conformity was a priority, because it was widely held to be a foundation for political stability. It was to be achieved, not through killing, but the expropriation and exile of a politically as well as confessionally hostile elite. Mere adherence to the 'wrong' religion was not itself an automatic death sentence in the case of defeat.[15]

The seventeenth-century concepts of excess and atrocity were defined in relation to prevailing norms. These are central to any understanding of violence in the Thirty Years War, but are missing from the received picture of the war presented in later literary and scholarly accounts which convey a sense of violence exceeding all bounds. One recent study concludes violence was all-pervasive, with no aspect of early modern life that was not a 'theatre of horror'.[16] This immediately raises the question, however, of how contemporaries judged violence. What was their threshold of horror? When did violence become atrocity? Such questions were vital to those experiencing the Thirty Years War. While not a religious war, it was nonetheless fought in an age of faith in which the fate of one's immortal soul was a matter of direct personal concern. How one acted was also a matter of immediate worldly significance as the judgement of others was a key determinant of personal and collective honour.[17]

Above all, such questions concerned soldiers whose purpose required them to break the fundamental Christian commandment not to kill. The widespread critique of soldiers as hired killers was a major factor in their social ostracisation and low social status.[18] Aristocrats' association with martial values was also under sustained attack from contemporary ideologies, such as the urban burghers' claims for the collective nobility of their towns, and the humanist ideal of the nobility of virtue and learning[19].

Soldiers' concerns were addressed through the discourse on 'just war' that drew on classical and particularly early Christian texts, and established three criteria for violence to be legitimate.[20] A just war had to be waged with the 'right intent', usually defined as upholding justice and defeating evil. This was buttressed by reference to ideas of natural law that included a right of self-defence. Second, a just war had to be conducted by the 'right means', which were identified in the late sixteenth century by a variety of customary and written laws. The latter included the 'articles of war', notably the set approved by the *Reichstag* (imperial diet) in 1570 as part of the laws of the Empire. The imperial articles served as the basis for military codes issued later in the German territories, as well as other countries, including the famous Swedish articles of 1621 and 1632.[21] The articles defined soldiers' duties, specified correct behaviour, as well as punishments for transgressions, and identified illegitimate targets, chiefly children, women, the elderly, clergy and others considered incapable of defending themselves.

The articles also stressed the third criterion for just war by emphasising soldiers' subordination to a properly constituted authority. This aspect was the most political, since all early modern wars were ultimately conflicts over who or what constituted a proper authority in a given area.[22] Much of the recent theoretical literature emphasises this connection, arguing that states, especially those collapsing or under pressure, are the primary instigators of massacres and genocide. Even well-ordered, stable states can facilitate atrocity simply by failing to intervene when it is committed elsewhere.[23]

The concept of just war led people to distinguish between the legitimate application of force by a proper authority (*potestas*) and illegitimate violence (*violentia*).[24] Such distinctions were important to the self-image and hence also to the legitimacy of rulers such as Emperor Ferdinand II and Duke (later Elector) Maximilian of Bavaria.[25] The purpose of war, so the arguments ran, was to restore peace by forcing opponents to abandon their evil intentions. War was thus constrained by limited objectives, framed with reference to Christian morality and princely rights enshrined in the imperial and territorial constitutions.

It is important not to see these ideas as simply imposed from above in some form of one-way communication between rulers and an inarticulate mass of subjects. Naturally, rulers' attitudes to violence reflected their own sense of social distinction and political superiority. Yet, the legitimacy and hence effectiveness of such views depended not merely on the media through which they were conveyed to their own subjects and their peers amongst rulers elsewhere, but also how these audiences received them. In short, elite attitudes enjoyed validity through their correspondence with widely held beliefs about what the world should be like. This is manifest through the relative ease by which some laws were upheld with minimal official effort, whereas others required sustained intervention at local level, or proved unenforceable.[26] Thus, as Michael Kaiser has argued, we need to understand violence as social practice in which the norms for what was considered acceptable were defined by society as a whole, and not merely those wielding official authority.[27]

The theoretical literature on massacre stresses the significance of propaganda as conditioning people to transgress accepted norms by identifying a clear enemy who poses such a threat that they must be physically exterminated. Sectarian polemic provides the chief evidence for the received view of the Thirty Years War as a religious conflict. The outbreak is explained as the result of progressive confessional polarisation propelling first the Empire, and then the rest of Europe inevitably towards general war. This argument is usually backed up by reference to the process of confessionalisation initiated with the Reformation that led to the formation of distinct Catholic and various Protestant identities by the 1580s. These allegedly overrode all other foci for identity, such as the Empire, ruling dynasty, nationality, community, gender or social status, to divide the population starkly from prince to peasant into mutually hostile confessional groups. Perceiving the world solely through confessional stereotypes, we are told that both rulers and ruled were no longer able to communicate across the sectarian divide, opening the door to mis-understanding, suspicion, paranoia and ultimately war.[28]

Unfortunately, it is far easier to analyse the content of this largely clerical discourse, than to identify links between it and acts of violence. Certainly, key decision-makers often despised those holding contrary religious beliefs. A number of them, notably Gustavus Adolphus, Ferdinand II and Elector Friedrich V of the Palatinate, felt personally summoned by God to take par-ticular actions. Yet, it is also significant that the virulence found in clerical polemics rarely translated into internal state papers or official propaganda that routinely legitimised policy by reference to the imperial and territorial constitutions. Suspicion and misunderstanding undoubtedly contributed to the outbreak of the Bohemian Revolt in 1618 and the subsequent spread of the conflict throughout the Empire. Fear, however, often arose from political calculations about what others might do, rather than pure sectarian hatred. More importantly, the contending parties negotiated throughout the war. Contrary to the popular perception, the soldiers alone did not rule.[29] Indeed, it could not be otherwise without compromising the legitimacy of rulers' presentation of military operations as the application of *potestas* (armed might) to force their opponents to accept a reasonable settlement. This reflected the early modern belief that peace could only be secured through mutual reconciliation. Amity, not annihilation, remained the goal. The enemy might be heretics, but they were still Christians who should be persuaded to see the error of their ways.

These considerations are important, because they explain the absence of a clearly articulated image of the enemy outside militant polemics. Individuals might be motivated by personal grudges or desires for revenge, especially officers who changed sides after falling out with their earlier employer. But the very fact that many did change sides indicates the fluidity of boundaries between opposing forces. Armies did have predominant confessional char-acters, but always contained at least a minority of dissenters. This was most obvious in the imperial army. The emperor wanted to present himself as standing above religious strife and appointed numerous Lutherans and even some Calvinists to senior positions. Perhaps more significantly, the rank and file who did the actual killing were often dissenters and included large numbers of enemy prisoners pressed to make up numbers.[30]

Even where official propaganda did promote an abstract image of the enemy, defined generally by nationality (as 'the Spanish' or 'the Swedes') rather than religion, such constructs were soon dissolved by the experience of actual encounters with soldiers. Individuals and communities soon discovered their own rulers' troops behaviour often corresponded more closely with the official image of the enemy than the foreign invaders they had actually met.[31] Eye-witness accounts and local records detail the war as a succession of alien intrusions into settled communities. Soldiers are usually identified by the name of their commander or unit; less often by the nationality of the power they served, and only very rarely by their religion.

Far from sharpening the image of an enemy, much of the clerical discourse blurred distinctions between friend and foe. Clergy of all faiths presented the war as divine punishment for the sins of their flocks. Parishioners were exhorted to hasten the return of peace, not by exterminating unbelievers, but by reflecting on the enemy within in the form of their own immorality and lack of faith.[32] Some clergy did advocate action that was more robust. A notable case is Domenico à Jesu Maria (1559–1630), a barefoot Carmelite credited with persuading the imperial and Catholic League generals to begin their attack at White Mountain which crushed the Bohemian Revolt in 1620.[33] The actual influence of such individuals was limited, though they did their best to magnify their own role through their writings. Most of them simply accompanied the troops as army chaplains. Rather than instigating atrocities, they explained breaches of discipline by their own side as divine retribution for the sins of the enemy.[34] Active exhortation was frowned upon; something which has so far frustrated a long campaign for Domenico's beatification. A far more acceptable role for clergy was as so-called 'innocent victims' of atrocities, exemplified by Fidelis of Sigmaringen (1578–1622), a Capuchin murdered in a Protestant massacre in the Valtellina. Fidelis' beatification, backed initially by Ferdinand II, was finally realised in 1746. Again, though, it is noteworthy that such figures appeared in official statements and popular culture as protectors from, not instigators of violence. Fidelis, for example, was credited with having saved an imperial garrison by preventing the explosion of its powder magazine six months after his death.[35]

The question of intent highlights the role of those taking the decisions to commit atrocities. Many were horrified by Ferdinand II's decision to execute twenty-eight Bohemian rebels (including one ritually executed after he had already committed suicide in prison!) in the Prague 'Blood Court' of June 1621. The emperor's authorisation of Wallenstein's murder in 1634 was equally shocking.[36] These killings, however, were controversial acts of political justice rather than what contemporaries called atrocities. In contrast with twentieth-century experience, seventeenth-century rulers were rarely directly involved in sanctioning atrocities or massacres. This is partly explained by the preceding discussion of how war was legitimated and the ends to which it was directed. A further reason lies in the nature of military command. While a few rulers commanded in person, like Gustavus Adolphus, or sometimes accompanied their troops, like Maximilian of Bavaria or Johann Georg of Saxony, most were not involved in operational decisions, which were devolved to generals and other officers in the field.

In a number of instances, atrocities were instrumentalised as a deliberate element of military policy. The worst case in continental Europe in terms of fatalities was not part of the Thirty Years War: Louis XIII hastened the end of the final Huguenot rising by ordering the execution or exile of all 3,000 inhabitants of Privas on 26 May 1629.[37] The same policy was employed by generals in the Thirty Years War on at least two occasions. Wallenstein ordered the execution of the 400 or so surviving defenders of Breitenberg on 29 September 1628 to intimidate the remaining Danish garrisons on the mainland into surrendering. The Swedes repeated the tactic in January 1644 during their invasion of the Danish peninsula when they massacred the sixty men holding the Christianpreis Fort outside Kiel.[38] In both cases, the policy worked as other garrisons swiftly capitulated.

Many other towns and fortresses were threatened with similar consequences to undermine their resistance. Massacres often ensued if the besiegers broke in, though few commanders admitted to sanctioning such violence. Most were reticent, offering only brief or cryptic statements.[39] It is likely that few intended further civilian or military deaths once the enemy's resistance had been overcome. Certainly, wanton destruction was counter-productive. The whole point of the prolonged imperial blockade of Magdeburg from 1628 and the subsequent lengthy siege in 1631 was to force the city to allow the emperor's forces to garrison what was a rich commercial and strategic base. Furthermore, death and destruction directly challenged a commander's authority, as a gross breach of military discipline and of the articles of war. The situation was often akin to mutiny and desertion, and indeed indiscriminate plundering and killing of civilians often accompanied both of these.[40]

Most commanders refrained from intervening to prevent a sack once a town had been taken. At best, units still under orders were moved to protect valuable assets or as yet untouched districts where civilians had sought shelter, as in the case of Magdeburg's cathedral and Premonstratensian monastery. As Tilly discovered, such inactivity attracted hostile public comment damaging his reputation. Like princes, commanders were expected to display clemency to defeated foes and to treat prisoners and civilians with civility. This explains why they downplayed breaches of discipline. A sack was usually legitimated through the customs of war, which permitted soldiers to plunder a town captured after refusing earlier offers to surrender. This featured at Magdeburg, as well as Mansfeld's sack of Ladenburg in 1622, Tilly's sack of Neubrandenburg in 1631 and that by the Swedes at Donauwörth a year later to give just a few examples.[41] The other favourite excuse was to claim mitigating circumstances, usually that most of the deaths had been caused by the explosion of a powder magazine in the final stages of the assault, rather than as cold-blooded murder afterwards. This reason was cited after Tilly's army sacked Münden in June 1626 where 1,000 inhabitants and all 800 of the garrison were said to have perished.[42] It also featured at Magdeburg where the uncontrolled spread of the fire was attributed to the ignition of an apothecary's house used by the defenders to store powder. Indeed, exploding powder magazines were a common explanation for heavy losses and especially to excuse battlefield defeats. Thus, the resistance of the Margrave of Baden-Durlach's army collapsed at Wimpfen (1622) after a powder wagon blew up, while the initially successful Swedish assault on the Albuch hill at Nördlingen (1634), allegedly failed after the explosion of the magazine in a captured redoubt.[43] Such explanations cannot be dismissed entirely in an age of black powder weaponry, but they were undoubtedly a convenient way to shed responsibility for what was considered excessive violence and it is noteworthy that the scale of the Privas casualties was subsequently blamed on an exploding magazine.[44]

In contrast to the French Wars of Religion, as well as many twentieth-century massacres, civilians, militia and paramilitaries did not feature prominently amongst the perpetrators in the Thirty Years War. Civilians did participate, but less frequently and far less bloodily than military personnel. Most able-bodied males were at least theoretically liable for military service through the militias which existed in virtually all German territories. A significant proportion – perhaps one in ten – underwent some military training and many served when militia units were mobilised after 1618.[45] The possession of weapons, including firearms, and familiarity with them, extended more widely still. Other paramilitary and semi-regular units existed, notably the burgher guards in towns and imperial cities. All these forces were defensive. Some militia were used to supplement professionals in the field and the 'little war' of outposts and raids which ran parallel to the main operations. Militias, however, were rarely in the asymmetrical power relationship, which would have permitted them to harm helpless enemies. They were far more likely to fall victim to military violence, like the 4,000 Württemberg militia left guarding the Swedish baggage slaughtered by the victorious imperialists after Nördlingen.[46] Others perished in massacres following the failed defence of their home town, like many of Magdeburg's armed citizens.

Partisans represented another area of civilian involvement. Their role was more ambiguous, since they were organised locally, often without official support or approval. Subjects were encouraged to guard their communities and, sometimes, were offered a bounty for each marauder they killed.[47] Nevertheless, there was a general reluctance to endorse spontaneous popular mobilisation. Whether authorised or independent, partisans operated sporadically according to circumstances beyond their control. Most acted to defend their home areas, to take revenge for past atrocities or opportunistically to sustain or enrich themselves. Again in contrast to twentieth-century conflicts, the targets were nearly always soldiers, not other civilians. They attacked stragglers, or small detachments of troops, frequently with considerable ferocity.[48] Soldiers responded brutally, destroying entire villages and killing any inhabitants they found.[49]

While cruel and bloody, such actions were not always condemned as atrocities. Peasant resistance was often caught in a cycle of brutality generated by ostensibly legitimate military action. Systematic destruction of life and especially property was a recognised, if extreme, element of regular warfare used to pressure opponents into agreeing terms. It was justified by arguments similar to those accompanying strategic bombing during World War II, as a necessary evil to hasten the end of the war and thereby save more lives.[50] The Swedes employed this tactic during their invasion of Bavaria in spring 1632 and again against the Westphalian territories in 1646, while imperial raiding parties informed the Saxon elector in 1632 that he could dispense with candles for his banquets as they would light them by burning his subjects' homes unless he changed sides.[51]

Civilians were also linked more indirectly with atrocities committed by soldiers. Much civil-military violence arose as the largely unintended consequence of soldiers' search for sustenance. While supply arrangements were not as rudimentary as depicted in the secondary literature, armies were nonetheless expected to maintain themselves largely at the expense of the areas in which they were operating. The line between official requisitioning and private plunder was extremely fluid. Plunder was an accepted military perquisite, sanctioned by the customs of war and the law of conquest.[52] It was practised by all ranks, but was expected to be kept within bounds so as not to undermine the viability of the civil economy upon which both war and the state ultimately depended. The arrival, however, of even a small detachment could spell disaster for communities which struggled to produce a surplus even in good peacetime years. Plundering and requisitioning were the primary sparks for popular resistance and the main source of civil–military violence. This was recognised in the war's literary classic, Grimmelshausen's novel *Simplicissimus*, with its famous scene of a raid on the hero's farm where each of the soldiers 'fell to his appointed task: which was more or less death and destruction'.[53]

Plunder and requisitioning, however, only functioned thanks to civil involvement, not only as producers, but also to fence, purchase and consume stolen goods. The wider military community of non-combatant camp followers was equally involved, both in procuring, distributing and consuming goods for the army, as well as using violence, if necessary, to do so. Camp followers joined soldiers and often local civilians as well in plundering towns during a sack, or corpses, the wounded and stragglers after a battle.[54]

All types of soldier participated in excesses and atrocities, including men ravaging their own region. One recorded in his diary following the sack of Magdeburg that 'it troubled my heart that the city burned so terribly, because it is a beautiful place and because it is my homeland'; yet noted with approval that his wife returned safely from her plundering trip, and was happy to accept the stolen money his comrades brought back.[55] Contemporary accounts, however, were far more likely to blame northern or eastern Europeans for acts of violence. Their role requires careful analysis given the general attitude to the war as a violent intrusion, disrupting the Empire's tranquillity. All the contending parties within the Empire used late humanist patriotic language equating their opponents with 'foreign tyranny'. Thus, the Bohemian rebels tried to distinguish between 'those Catholics who are our dear friends' whom they hoped would remain neutral, and 'evil Jesuits' who were stirring trouble on behalf of 'the Roman See, a foreign power'.[56] Underlying this was a general belief common to both sides that brutality was something that happened elsewhere; hence the sense of transgression when it occurred within a civilised Christian country. Long before the Enlightened 'invention of eastern Europe,'[57] central Europeans had a sense of a wild East; something that was magnified by the Empire's role as Christendom's bulwark against the Muslim Ottoman Turks. For over a century the Turks had been associated with extreme barbarity and the accusation 'behaving like (or worse than) the Turks' was used to identify those perceived as breaching all taboos.[58] Barbarity was thus considered a natural attribute of Eastern Europeans and others inhabiting the continent's outer fringes, such as the Finns, Lapps and Scots who served in the Swedish army.

There were also practical reasons, however, why such soldiers feature disproportionately in accounts of atrocities. As foreigners, they were more likely to stand out than Germans, perhaps encouraging writers to highlight their involvement. Their difficulties with the German language would have made it harder for them to convey their demands, increasing the likelihood of violent encounters. Perhaps more importantly, men from these regions were recruited for the kinds of tasks where atrocities were most likely to be committed. The Finns, for instance, were used as assault troops to spearhead attacks and deliberately fostered a fearsome reputation as an element of psychological warfare, including their war-cry 'Hack 'em down'.[59] Transylvanians, Poles (generally called 'Cossacks') and men from the Balkans (invariably called 'Croats') were recruited as light cavalry used for raiding, foraging and harrying defeated armies. They were outsiders, even in their own army, and were viewed with disdain by infantry and heavy cavalry officers. Shoddy treatment perhaps fostered a sense that they were beyond the legal constraints binding other soldiers. More immediately, they were often paid and fed differently, and usually expected to find their own sustenance. They generally arrived ahead of the main army and so would have a better chance of seizing plunder.[60]

Events like the sack of Magdeburg convey the impression that civilians were the war's principal victims, but it is worth remembering that thousands of soldiers suffered in what can be considered atrocities. Up to 1.8 million soldiers died during the war, of whom at least 450,000 were killed in major battles and sieges.[61] Casualties were highest in the closing stages of battles when, generally, one side lost cohesion and tried to escape. Even armies which withdrew in good order, such as the imperialists after Lützen (1632), usually abandoned many of their wounded on the battlefield. The wounded were often killed by soldiers and civilians searching the field for plunder, or simply left to die. Croats, Cossacks and other light cavalrymen were sent in pursuit of enemy units, which lost their ability to resist when their men broke ranks to escape. Massacres frequently followed, such as after the battle of Stadtlohn (1623) where the imperial Croats and Cossacks ruthlessly cut down Christian von Halberstadt's raw recruits who had fallen to their knees to beg for mercy. Around 6,000 were killed, or one in three – long after locals told tales of their ghosts still trying to escape.[62]

The presence of clergy, women, the young and elderly among civilian victims in contemporary accounts is problematic. Military regulations expressly forbade soldiers from harming these groups, often extending the general category of 'women' by identifying 'virgins' and expectant mothers as worthy of particular protection. Their presence amongst the victims magnified the sense of outrage – a point to which we will return below.

The Thirty Years War offered little scope for the role of bystander, in contrast to more recent massacres and genocide which occurred in the midst of communities where at least part of the population has knowingly chosen to remain in the vicinity, without intervening or participating. Twentieth-century massacres and genocide have often involved sustained, systematic killing over prolonged periods – years in the case of the Nazi Holocaust. By contrast, atrocities in the Thirty Years War were rarely coordinated and usually lasted hours, or a few days at the most. Order was restored in Magdeburg after four days of looting and this was noted as exceptionally long. Killing tended to encompass anyone in the vicinity who was not amongst the perpetrators, and was often extended to infighting amongst the latter as well. The image of drunken soldiers fighting over plunder was a stock motif of contemporary genre painting and polemics used to emphasise the perpetrators' depravity.

These considerations draw our attention to the context in which atrocities occurred. What might be labelled the 'geography of atrocity' is an aspect often overlooked. Location helps explain why victims and perpetrators encountered each other, shaped how events unfolded and often how the killing took place.

There were two main types of location. Settlements and fortified towns con-centrated civilians and defending garrisons in a small area from which there was frequently little chance of escape. Malnourishment and disease often weakened their ability to resist attackers, whilst the confinement greatly increased the likelihood of death through plague. This magnified the overall sense of disaster, for instance at Mantua which suffered the second worst sack of the war (in 1630). There was also the risk of fire, which proved the biggest killer at Magdeburg where most of the dead had suffocated hiding in their cellars.

By contrast, atrocities committed in open ground rarely affected civilians other than those already associated with the army as camp followers. Mass killing in these locations usually affected fleeing or surrendering soldiers whose escape was blocked by some physical feature, such as the river which trapped Christian von Halberstadt's army at Stadtlohn. This experience is very similar to that noted for massacres during the English Civil War.[63]

Just as certain troop types featured amongst the perpetrators, so did others among the victims. Infantrymen predominated, since they were less able to escape than their mounted comrades, and were more vulnerable if their unit lost formation. They also made up the bulk of fortress and civic garrisons. Units that retained cohesion in the face of defeat were usually able to negotiate surrender. Prisoners might be plundered, but they were rarely killed in cold blood after they had been granted 'quarter' (mercy), as to do so brought deep dishonour. This point needs particular emphasis, given how this war is usually interpreted as a religious conflict. It certainly sets the Thirty Years War apart from later, ideologically charged conflicts where the cold-blooded execution of prisoners was the norm (such as the Carlist War of 1833–39, or the Mexican Revolution of 1910–20).[64]

The rules governing surrender highlight the central issue in defining atrocity; namely at what point did the use of force cease to be legitimate? Many contemporary observers considered the encounter at Chumik Shenko on 31 March 1904 to be a massacre. A force of 1,300 British and Indian Army, soldiers, equipped with magazine rifles and Maxim machine guns, killed 500 of 900 Tibetans carrying swords and matchlocks in a matter of minutes. One British machine gunner noted in his diary 'I got so sick of the slaughter I ceased fire.'[65] Seventeenth-century soldiers did not admit revulsion so readily, but their commanders were still clearly concerned not to be seen to use excessive force.

It has been plausibly suggested that some commanders may have permitted massacres to preserve their credibility by making good earlier threats to sack a town if it refused to surrender.[66] It is also possible that certain units used extreme violence to live up to their reputation and maintain an aura of terror. This would bring practical benefits by reducing the likelihood of serious resistance. From contemporary diaries and other accounts, it seems that peasants were far more likely to flee their homes at the news of the approach of Croats, Poles or others noted for brutality, thus making plunder easier. Studies of more recent atrocities, however, suggest that violence often derives from peer pressure linked to group solidarity, for example encouraging new recruits to bloody their hands as a ritualised induction into the unit.[67]

The choice of victims and the character of the violence indicate that this pressure also applied in the seventeenth century. Some soldiers came directly from the military community, as children or orphans raised in the camp. The vast majority, however, grew up in towns and villages prior to enlisting, meaning we should not over-emphasise civil–military antagonisms. Nonetheless, their status as soldiers set them apart from settled civilian life, something that was reinforced by the jurisdiction of martial law, distinctive forms of dress, slang, rituals and other cultural aspects fostering a separate identity. This also distinguished them from militiamen who were rarely deployed far from home and usually longed to return there as soon as possible. The presence of soldiers as a distinct community was not in itself unusual in a society characterised by a multitude of corporate groups. As indicated above, however, soldiers were generally despised and it is clear that much of their violence was a means to retaliate and assert superiority over people who shunned them.[68]

Two forms of evidence support this. First, serious violence and especially massacres were often excused by citing previous provocation from the enemy. The most frequent form was deliberate taunts from enemy units, and especially from besieged towns summoned to surrender. This occurred at Magdeburg where, for instance, the defenders named one bastion 'Defy Tilly'. Repeated refusals to surrender, exceptionally prolonged resistance and the use of weapons or tactics considered unfair all feature as mitigating circumstances cited to excuse soldier's behaviour.

The second is the form of violence which indicates that the purpose was not merely to kill, but to make the victims suffer and to desecrate them after death. At its mildest, this involved the wanton destruction of things dear to the victims – something which also explains iconoclasm. Worse, figures of authority and status were humiliated by the theft of their clothes or being compelled to perform menial or disgusting tasks, while husbands and families were forced to watch gang rape. Killing often took laborious forms, such as disembowelling or roasting alive. Corpses were mutilated or denied Christian burial.[69]

These considerations offer only partial explanation for events which often seem as incomprehensible to us as to seventeenth-century observers. A key factor defining atrocity for contemporaries was a lack of proportion between the level of violence and the perceived slight that ostensibly caused it. A party of unidentified soldiers beat a road mender to death near Dortmund in May 1634 simply because he was unable to give them directions.[70]

The evidence for atrocities is notoriously problematic, since much depends on the perspectives of those reporting it. Some eye-witnesses failed to mention peaceful encounters with soldiers, while others omitted or underplayed painful experiences.[71] Much of the writing is characterised by stock phrases and vignettes, often repeated verbatim or literally pasted in, as in the case of newspaper cuttings inserted into diaries. Typically, examples include references to babies impaled on pikes or ripped from their mother's womb, as well as captives led by their entrails. Sister Junius of the Heiliggrab Convent in Bamberg readily believed that blood ran down the walls of nearby Würzburg as its garrison was massacred by the Swedes in October 1631. She also recorded that the defenders had been cut down whilst at prayer in the fortress chapel, an accusation frequently associated with massacres following assaults.[72]

Such evidence underscores this essay's central argument that society's norms remained in place despite the conflict. Particular incidents, real or alleged, were highlighted precisely because they were still shocking. The same applies to incidents of cannibalism, which almost certainly never happened in practice, but symbolised the fear that the war was exceeding all bounds.[73]

This point is reinforced by the place of atrocities in official propaganda. All the principal belligerents accused their opponents of breaking the bounds of commonly accepted behaviour. Unlike twentieth-century propaganda, there was little attempt to use atrocity allegations for ideological mobilisation by fanning hatred of a demonised enemy. Rather than being directed at the home audience, propaganda was intended to rally foreign support and to mask one's own failings or bad behaviour.

The Magdeburg campaign provides a good example. The Swedes had landed uninvited in Pomerania in June 1630 and were widely perceived by Protestants and Catholics alike as foreign invaders whose presence re-ignited a conflict largely settled by 1629. Despite the poor condition of the imperial army, Gustavus Adolphus failed to break out of his Pomeranian bridgehead. Nearly half the original invasion force was dead within six months, mainly through exposure to unfamiliar microbes. Thousands more died over the following year, pushing total Swedish losses to 50,000. Even with French financial backing, it was obvious that under-resourced Sweden could not sustain war in the Empire without German collaboration. To his disgust, the Protestant princes, including his Brandenburg in-laws, convened in Leipzig in February 1631 in an effort to interpose themselves between Sweden and the emperor. Other than the Pomeranian town of Stralsund, only the fugitive Protestant administrator of the (unofficially) secularised archbishopric of Magdeburg had openly declared for Sweden. More were prepared to do so, but only if Gustavus Adolphus could achieve a clear victory over the imperial armies occupying their lands. Gustavus, however, was reluctant to risk battle whilst he remained outnumbered. Any reverse would discourage his potential supporters and embolden the emperor to disarm the members of the neutral Leipzig Convention.

It is within this context that we must place the three massacres which took place in the first half of 1631. The first occurred at Neubrandenburg on 19 March during Gustavus' attempt to punch through the imperial cordon containing him in Pomerania. The town was held by 750 Swedish troops whose commander refused surrender because he thought Gustavus was marching to his relief. In fact, the King authorised surrender two days earlier, but the letter was intercepted without, it seems, being passed onto Tilly's assault force, which stormed and sacked the town. Though far from decisive, the loss of Neubrandenburg was a serious setback given that the Protestant princes meeting in Leipzig had not yet reached a decision. Swedish accounts swiftly appeared, claiming that only fifty defenders had been spared, while the rest were cut down during a church service. The latter reference was clearly a ploy to generate outrage and was believed by members of the Swedish army.[74] The Swedes omitted to report their execution of 300 wounded left in the town when Tilly retreated a few days later.[75]

Hoping to distract Tilly from Magdeburg, which was now under close siege, Gustavus moved east to Frankfurt on the Oder, a university town belonging to his brother-in-law, the still neutral elector of Brandenburg. After initial stubborn resistance from the 6,400 strong imperial garrison, the town was stormed and sacked on 13 April. Many of the defenders escaped, but 1,700 were killed, along with many of the town's Protestant inhabitants. Significantly, Swedish soldiers responded to the defenders' appeals for 'quarter' by crying 'Neubrandenburg quarter!', and the general breakdown of discipline was subsequently presented as a legitimate reprisal for the earlier alleged atrocity.[76] Gustavus spent the next ten weeks intimidating his brother-in-law into an alliance, eventually achieved when the entire Swedish field army trained its artillery on the electoral palace.[77]

In the meantime, Magdeburg was taken and sacked by Tilly's army. Magdeburg's loss exposed Gustavus' military weakness and inability to protect his allies. He had sent a trusted officer, Colonel Dietrich von Falkenberg (1580–1631), to assume command of the city's own forces in October 1630, but otherwise did little to help it. The Swedish alliance split opinion in the city where many preferred an arrangement with neutral Saxony to collaboration with either Gustavus, or his puppet, the Protestant administrator, who was clearly pursuing his own agenda. Falkenberg deliberately frustrated attempts by some councillors to accept Tilly's offer of surrender, claiming falsely that Swedish assistance was expected within hours. The magnitude of the subsequent disaster conveniently rescued Gustavus from political embarrassment by distracting attention from his own less-than-heroic part in the city's demise. Protestant militants and pro-Swedish apologists rapidly disseminated tracts playing on the city's past defiance of Emperor Charles V (in 1548–51), and on its name, literally 'maiden's castle', to present an image of a virgin who preferred to immolate herself than suffer rape at the hands of the papists.[78]

Magdeburg thus replaced Neubrandenburg on a far larger scale as a convenient way to deflect criticism of Gustavus' failure and to persuade neutral princes that the emperor could not be trusted. It also served to mask later Swedish atrocities: during the sack of Würzburg in October 1631, Swedes cried 'Magdeburg quarter!' as they cut down the surrendering garrison and inhabitants.[79]

What is striking about the Thirty Years War is that such a cycle of atrocity and counter-atrocity did not produce escalating violence. Far from 'degenerating' into meaningless, generalised brutality, atrocities blighted the war from the outset.[80] Individuals may well have been brutalised by their experience, but it would be wrong to present the whole conflict following a simple trajectory of ever-greater destruction. It was waged with varying intensity across time and space, with much of the later stage characterised by more orderly civil-military relations than those during the peak of 1631–41.

Magdeburg's experience is both misleading and instructive. The drama of the siege and the scale of horror following the assault encouraged later writers to generalise from this one event. Closer inspection reveals that the deaths were largely unintended. Second, amidst the horror contemporaries still recognised a threshold distinguishing atrocities from other acts of violence. Magdeburg attracted such attention precisely because it was so exceptional. The outrage at such atrocities indicates the persistence of civil order and social norms despite the widespread belief that they had disappeared.[81] Third, these norms constrained violence through their place in the language of political legitimacy. The boundary defining what was permissible remained contested, but the fact that accusations of atrocities had propaganda value indicates an underlying consensus on what constituted proper behaviour. Nonetheless, the rhetoric of atrocity, fuelled by the prodigious development in print media across the period, along with the war's length and the widespread experience of it as a succession of disturbing encounters, all contributed to the lasting impression of fearful, generalised violence which shaped interpretations of the conflict until now.

NOTES

1 M. Puhle (ed.), *Gantz verheert! Magdeburg und der Dreißigjährige Krieg* (Magdeburg, 1998); H. Medik, 'Historical event and contemporary experience: the capture and destruction of Magdeburg in 1631', *History Workshop Journal*, 52 (2001), 23–48; and the two articles by M. Kaiser, ' "Excidium Magdeburgense": Beobachtungen zur Wahrnehmung und Darstellung von Gewalt im Dreißigjährigen Krieg', in M. Meumann and D. Niefanger (eds), *Ein Schauplatz herber Angst* (Göttingen,

1997), pp. 43–64, and 'Die "Magdeburgische Hochzeit" (1631)', in E. Labouvie (ed.), *Leben in der Stadt: Eine Kultur- und Geschlechtergeschichte Magdeburgs* (Cologne, 2004), pp. 196–213. Eye-witness accounts in K. Lohmann (ed.), *Die Zerstörung Madgeburgs von Otto von Guericke und andere Denkwürdigkeiten aus dem Dreissigjährigen Krieg* (Berlin, 1913); E. Neubauer (ed.), *Magdeburgs Zerstörung 1631: Sammlung zeitgenössischer Berichte* (Magdeburg, 1931); R. Volkholz (ed.), *Jürgen Ackermann, Kapitän beim Regiment Alt-Pappenheim, 1631* (Halberstadt, 1895); H. Wäschke (ed.), 'Die Belagerung und Zerstörung Magdeburgs', *Geschichtsblätter für Stadt und Land Magdeburg*, 41 (1906), 318–27.

2 W. Lahne, *Magdeburgs Zerstörung in der zeitgenössischen Publizistik* (Magdeburg, 1931); M. Schilling, 'Der Zerstörung Magdeburgs in der zeitgenössischen Literatur und Publizistik', in *Konfession, Krieg und Katastrophe*, Verein für Kirchengeschichte der Kirchenprozinz Sachsen (Magdeburg, 2006), pp. 93–111.

3 For a survey of English sources on the war, see E. A. Beller, 'Contemporary English printed sources for the Thirty Years War', *American Historical Review*, 32 (1927), 276–82.

4 B. Donagan, 'Codes of conduct in the English Civil War', *Past and Present*, 118 (1988), 65–95, at 65–73; I. Roy, ' "England turned Germany?" The aftermath of the Civil War in its European context', *Transactions of the Royal Historical Society*, 5th series, 28 (1978), 127–44.

5 F. Schiller, *Geschichte des Dreißigjährigen Krieges* (DTV edition, Munich, 1966), pp. 146–54.

6 G. Droysen, *Gustav Adolf* (2 vols, Leipzig, 1869), vol. ii, p. 339. Further discussion in K. Cramer, *The Thirty Years War and German Memory in the Nineteenth Century* (Lincoln, Nebraska, 2007), pp. 141–216.

7 B. Bailey, *Massacres and Account of the Crimes against Humanity* (London, 1994), pp. 36–7, 118, which uses Schiller's history as its main source. A typical recent example of the standard view of atrocities during the Thirty Years War is D. Stone, *Fighting for the Fatherland: The story of the German Soldier from 1648 to the Present Day* (Washington, DC, 2006), pp. 26–30.

8 For a critique of this approach, see P. H. Wilson, 'Dynasty, constitution and confession: the role of religion in the Thirty Years War', *International History Review*, 30 (2008), 473–514, and the nuanced case studies in F. Brendle and A. Schilling (eds), *Religionskriege im Alten Reich und in Alteuropa* (Münster, 2006).

9 A representative example of this view is E. v. Frauenholz, *Das Heerwesen in der Zeit des Dreißigjährigen Krieges* (2 vols, Munich 1938–9), vol. i, pp. 14–18 who argues there was no 'grand ideal' to motivate soldiers between the demise of medieval chivalry and the rise of modern nationalism. Further discussion of this point in B. R. Kroener, 'Soldat oder Soldateska?', in M. Messerschmidt (ed.), *Militärgeschichte* (Stuttgart, 1982), pp. 100–23.

10 For example, M. Konnert, *Early Modern Europe: The Age of Religious War, 1559–1715* (Peterborough, Ontario, 2006), pp. 12, 26.

11 J. Semelin, 'Towards a vocabulary of massacre and genocide', *Journal of Genocide Research*, 5 (2003), 193–210; E. Carleton, *Massacres: An Historical Perspective* (Aldershot, 1994); M. Levene, 'Introduction', in M. Levene and P. Roberts (eds), *The Massacre in History* (New York, 1999) pp. 1–38.

12 Mark Greengrass, 'Hidden transcripts: secret histories and personal testimonies of religious violence in the French Wars of Religion', in Levene/Roberts (eds), *Massacre*, pp. 69–88, at p. 69.

13 There are no entries for massacre or atrocity under any of the possible terms in the standard nineteenth-century dictionary, B. v. Poten (ed.), *Handwörterbuch der gesamten Militärwissenschaften* (9 vols, Bielefeld and Leipzig, 1877–80).

14 Martin Feilinger (1573–1635), cited by J. Rullmann, 'Die Einwirkungen des 30 jährigen Krieges auf die Stadt Schlüchtern und ihre Umgegend, aus Kirchenbüchern zusammengesellt', *Zeitschrift des Vereins für hessische Geschichte und Landekunde*, new series, 6 (1877), 201–50, at 207, 214, 240–1.

15 Further discussion in P. H. Wilson, *Europe's Tragedy: A History of the Thirty Years War* (London, 2009), pp. 347–61, 483–8.

16 C. Ulbrich *et al.* (eds), *Gewalt in der frühen Neuzeit* (Munich, 2005).

17 Though focusing on England, Keith Thomas' recent work is useful in highlighting the issues involved: *The Ends of Life: Roads to Fulfilment in Early Modern England* (Oxford, 2009), pp. 148–80.

18 P. Burschel, *Söldner im Nordwestdeutschland des 16. und 17. Jahrhunderts* (Göttingen, 1994), pp. 27–53.

19 N. Schindler, *Rebellion, Community and Custom in Early Modern Germany* (Cambridge, 2002), pp. 12–47, 141–2, 228–33; K. Graf, 'Feindbild und Vorbild: Bemerkungen zur städtischen Wahrnehmung des Adels', *Zeitschrift für Geschichte des Oberrheins*, 41 (1993), 121–54; M. Kaiser, ' "Ist er vom Adel? Ja. Id satis videtur": Adlige Standesqualität und militärische Leistung als Karrierefaktoren in der Epoche des Dreißigjährigen Krieges', in F. Bosbach *et al.* (eds), *Geburt oder Leistung?* (Munich, 2003), pp. 73–90.

20 The literature on this is extensive. For an overview, see G. Parker, 'Early modern Europe', in M. Howard *et al.* (eds), *The Laws of War* (New Haven, 1994), pp. 40–58. Of particular use for the Thirty Years War is P. Piirimäe, 'Just war in theory and practice: the legitimation of Sweden's intervention in the Thirty Years War', *Historical Journal*, 45 (2002), 499–523.

21 Text in Frauenholz, *Heerwesen*, vol. i, pp. 355–424; discussion in W. Erben, 'Ursprung und Entwicklung der deutschen Kriegsartikeln', *Mitteilungen des Instituts für österreichischen Geschichtsforschung*, supplement 6 (1901), 473–529.

22 J. Burkhardt, 'Die Friedlosigkeit der frühen Neuzeit', *Zeitschrift für historische Forschung*, 24 (1997), 509–74.

23 R. J. Rummel, *Death by government* (New Brunswick and London, 1994).

24 R. Pröve, 'Violentia und Potestas: Perzeptionsprobleme von Gewalt in Söldnertagebüchern des 17. Jahrhunderts', in Meumann and Niefanger (eds), *Schauplatz*, pp. 24–42, and his 'Gewalt und Herrschaft in der frühen Neuzeit', *Zeitschrift für Geschichtswissenschaft*, 47 (1999), 792–806.

25 A. Kraus, 'Das katholische Herrscherbild im Reich', in K. Repgen (ed.), *Das Herrscherbild im 17. Jahrhundert* (Münster, 1991), pp. 1–25; R. Bireley S. J., 'Antimachiavellianism, the baroque, and Maximilian of Bavaria', *Archivum Historicum Societatis Jesu*, 103 (1984), 137–59; M. Kaiser, 'Maximilian I. von Bayern und der Krieg', *Zeitschrift für bayerische Landesgeschichte*, 65 (2002), 69–99.

26 J. Schlumbohm, 'Gesetze, die nicht durchgesetzt werden – Ein Strukturmerkmal des frühneuzeitlichen Staates?', *Geschichte und Gesellschaft*, 23 (1997), 647–63.

27 M. Kaiser, '"Ärger als der Türck": Kriegsgreuel und ihre Funktionalisierung in der Zeit des Dreißigjährigen Kriegs', in S. Neitzel and D. Hohrath (eds), *Die Entgrenzung der Gewalt in kriegerischen Konflikten vom Mittelalter bis ins 20. Jahrhundert* (Paderborn, 2008), pp. 155–83.

28 Recent examples of this interpretation include A. Gotthard, 'Der deutsche Konfessionskrieg seit 1619', *Historisches Jahrbuch*, 122 (2002), 141–72; H. Schilling, *Konfessionalisierung und Staatsinteressen 1559-1660* (Paderborn, 2007), esp. pp. 39–40, 349–58, 385–7, 395–9.

29 As asserted by C. V. Wedgwood, *The Thirty Years War* (London, 1957: first published 1938), pp. 362, 373–6, 383.

30 For soldiers' actual relationship to religion, see M. Kaiser, 'Cuius exercitus, eius religio? Konfession und Heerwesen im Zeitalter des Dreißigjährigen Krieges', *Archiv für Reformationsgeschichte*, 91 (2000), 316–53. Further discussion in M. Kaiser and S. Kroll (eds), *Militär und Religiosität in der Frühen Neuzeit* (Münster, 2004).

31 Excellent examples can be found in the diary of Maria Anna Junius, edited by F. K. Hümmer, 'Bamberg im Schweden-Kriege', *Bericht des Historischen Vereins zu Bamberg*, 52 (1890), 1–168; 53 (1891), 169–230. For propaganda see G. Lind, 'Interpreting a lost war: Danish experience 1625 to 1629', in Brendle and Schindling (eds), *Religionskriege*, pp. 487–510; J. Holm, 'King Gustav Adolf's death: the birth of early modern nationalism in Sweden', in L. Eriksonas and L. Müller (eds), *Statehood Before and Beyond Ethnicity* (Brussels, 2005), pp. 109–30.

32 M. Asche and A. Schindling (eds), *Das Strafgericht Gottes* (Münster, 2002).

33 T. Johnson, '"Victoria a dio missa?" Living saints on the battlefields of the Central European Counter Reformation', in J. Beyer *et al.* (eds), *Confessional Sanctity (c.1500–c.1800)* (Mainz, 2006), pp. 319–35; O. Chaline, *La Bataille de la Montagne Blanche* (Paris, 1999).

34 For example, see a Catholic chaplain's account of the 1620 Bohemian campaign: S. Riezler (ed.), 'Kriegstagebücher aus dem ligistischen Hauptquartier 1620', *Abhandlungen der Phil.-Hist: Klasse der Bayerischen Akademie der Wissenschaftern*, 23 (1906), 77–210, at 90–4, 144.

35 M. Ilg, 'Der Kult des Kapuzinermärtyres Fidelis von Sigmaringen als Ausdruck katholischer Kriegserfahrung im Dreißigjährigen Krieg', in Asche and Schindling (eds), *Strafgericht*, pp. 291–439.

36 For the Prague executions, see Wilson, *Europe's tragedy*, pp. 351–2. For Wallenstein's assassination and its public reception, see H. R. v. Srbik, *Wallensteins Ende* (2nd edn, Salzburg, 1952); C. Kampmann, *Reichsrebellion und kaiserliche Acht: Politische Strafjustiz im Dreißigjährigen Krieg und das Verfahren gegen Wallenstein 1634* (Münster, 1992).

37 M. P. Holt, *The French Wars of Religion, 1562-1629* (Cambridge, 1995), p. 187.

38 J. Polisensky and J. Kollmann, *Wallenstein* (Cologne, 1997), p. 138; K. R. Böhme, 'Lennart Torstensson und Helmut Wrangel in Schleswig-Holstein und Jutland 1643–1645', *Zeitschrift der Gesellschaft für Schleswig-Holsteinische Geschichte*, 90 (1965), 41–82.

39 Examples in S. Externbrink, 'Die Rezeption des "Sacco di Mantova" in 17. Jahrhundert', in Meumann and Niefanger (eds), *Schauplatz*, pp. 205–22.

40 The 'Spanish Fury' at Antwerp in 1577 was the most notorious case in continental Europe: G. Parker, 'Mutiny and discontent in the Spanish Army of Flanders 1572–1607', *Past and Present*, 58 (1973), 38–52. Nothing comparable occurred during the Thirty Years War, though desertion was rife: M. Kaiser, 'Ausreißer und Meuterer im Dreißigjährigen Krieg', in U. Brökling and M. Sikora (eds), *Armeen und ihre Deserteure* (Göttingen, 1998), pp. 49–71.

41 *Theatrum Europaeum* (21 vols, Frankfurt, 1662–1738), vol. ii, p. 626; M. Roberts, *Gustavus Adolphus* (2 vols, London, 1953), vol. ii, pp. 476–80; R. Monro, *Monro, his expedition with the worthy Scots regiment called Mac-Keys* (London, 1637; reprint Westport, 1999), pp. 148–51, 244.

42 B. Rill, *Tilly. Feldherr für Kaiser und Reich* (Munich, 1984), pp. 176–7.

43 W. P. Guthrie, *Battles of the Thirty Years War* (Westport, 2002), p. 92; P. Hrncirik, *Spanier auf dem Albuch* (Aachen, 2007), p. 22.

44 A. L. Moote, *Louis XIII* (Berkeley, 1989), p. 203.

45 See Wilson, *Europe's Tragedy*, pp. 139–44 and the literature cited there.

46 L. I. v. Stadlinger, *Geschichte des württembergischen Kriegswesens* (Stuttgart, 1856), pp. 292–3.

47 The Duke of Pfalz-Neuburg offered a 10 taler reward for each dead marauder in 1625: M. Kaiser, 'Überleben im Krieg – Leben mit dem Krieg', in S. Ehrenpreis (ed.), *Der Dreißigjährigen Krieg im Herzogtum Berg und in seinen Nachbarregionen* (Neustadt an der Aisch, 2002), pp. 181–233, at 200. Similar rewards were offered in the neighbouring duchy of Westphalia: see the documents printed in H. Conrad and H. Teske (eds), *Sterbezeiten. Der Dreißigjährige Krieg im Herzogtum Westfalen* (Münster, 2000), pp. 249–69. For partisans in the war, see Wilson, *Europe's Tragedy*, pp. 278, 310, 500, 533, 601–2, 837–8.

48 Graphic examples in Conrad and Teske (eds), *Sterbezeiten*, pp. 51–3; Rullmann, 'Einwirkungen', p. 231.

49 See Monro's account of Swedish reprisals for Bavarian peasant resistance: *Monro*, p. 252.

50 M. Kaiser, ' "Sed vincere sciebat Hanibal": Pappenheim als empirischer Theoretiker des Krieges', in H. Neuhaus and B. Stollberg-Rillinger (eds), *Menschen und Strukturen in der Geschichte Alteuropas* (Berlin, 2002), pp. 201–27.

51 P. Engerisser, *Von Kronach nach Nördlingen: Der Dreißigjährige Krieg in Franken, Schwaben und der Oberpfalz 1631–1635* (Weißenstadt, 2004), pp. 118–20; J. Krebs, *Aus dem Leben des kaiserlichen Feldmarschalls Grafen Melchior von Hatzfeldt 1632–1636* (Breslau, 1926), pp. 14–24.

52 F. Redlich, *De Praeda Militari: Looting and Booty 1500–1800* (Wiesbaden, 1956). For requisitioning, see Wilson, *Europe's Tragedy*, pp. 399–407.

53 H. J. C. v. Grimmelshausen, *The Adventures of Simplicius Simplicissimus*, trans. G. Schulz-Behrend (1668; Rochester, NY, 1993), book 1, chapter 4.

54 For the military community, see J. A. Lynn, *Women, Armies, and Warfare in Early Modern Europe* (Cambridge, 2008).

55 J. Peters (ed.), *Ein Söldnerleben aus dem Dreißigjährigen Krieg* (Berlin, 1993), p. 47.

56 The Bohemian 'Apology' of 25 May 1618, printed in J. C. Lünig (ed.), *Das teutsche Reichs-Archiv* (9 vols, Leipzig, 1710–20), vol. vi, part 1, pp. 133–40.

57 L. Wolff, *Inventing 'Eastern Europe': The Map of Civilisation in the Mind of the Enlightenment* (Stanford, 1994).

58 The extensive literature on anti-Turkish sentiment is summarised by P. S. Fichtner, *Terror and Toleration: The Habsburg Empire Confronts Islam, 1526–1850* (London, 2008), pp. 21–72. It is interesting to note that this prejudice was exported to the New World. For instance, the Peruvians accused their Chilean opponents of behaving 'just like a Turk': W. F. Sater, *Andean Tragedy: Fighting the War of the Pacific, 1879–1884* (Lincoln Nebraska, 2007), p. 299.

59 D. H. Pleiss, 'Finnen und Lappen in Stift und Stadt Osnabrück', *Osnabrücker Mitteilungen*, 93 (1990), 41–94.

60 G. Gajecky and A. Baran, *The Cossacks in the Thirty Years War* (Rome, 1969). The only time when Pastor Feilinger was seriously injured in his encounters with soldiers was during 'Polish and Croat plundering': Rullmann, 'Einwirkungen', pp. 242–3.

61 These figures derive from calculations presented in Wilson, *Europe's Tragedy*, pp. 786–95, which also provides further discussion of mortality during the war.

62 Gajecky and Baran, *Cossacks*, p. 81; Rill, *Tilly*, p. 143.

63 W. Coster, 'Massacre and codes of conduct in the English Civil War', in Levene and Roberts (eds), *Massacre*, pp. 89–105, at 99–103.

64 Further discussion in P. H. Wilson, 'Prisoners in early modern European warfare', in S. Scheipers (ed.), *Prisoners in War* (Oxford, 2010), pp. 39–56.

65 C. Allen, *Duel in the Snows: The True Story of the Younghusband Mission to Lhasa* (London, 2004), pp. 104–28.

66 Kaiser, 'Kriegsgreuel', p. 177.

67 C. Browning, *Ordinary Men: Reserve Police Battalion 101 and the Final Solution in Poland* (London, 1993).

68 R. G. Asch, '"Wo der Soldat hinkömbt, da ist alles sein": military violence and atrocities in the Thirty Years War', *German History*, 18 (2000), 291–309, esp. p. 302; J. G. Theibault, 'Landfrauen, Soldaten und Vergewältigungen während des Dreißigjährigen Krieges', *Werkstatt Geschichte*, 19 (1998), 25–39; M. Kaiser, 'Inmitten des Kriegstheaters: Die Bevölkerung als militärischer Faktor und Kriegsteilnehmer im Dreißigjährigen Krieg', in B. R. Kroener and R. Pröve (eds), *Krieg und Frieden* (Paderborn, 1996), pp. 281–303, and his 'Die Magdeburgische Hochzeit', pp. 205–8.

69 Examples in M. Bötzinger, 'Vitae curriculo', *Beyträge zur Erläuterung der Hochfürstl: Sachsen-Hildburghäusischen Kirchen-, Schul- und Landes-Historie* (Greitz, 1750), part 1, pp. 341–68, esp. p. 363; G. P. Sreenivasan, *The Peasants of Ottobeuren, 1487–1726* (Cambridge, 2004), pp. 285–6.

70 F. Barich, 'Nachrichten aus dem Kirchenbuch der Mariengemeinde, namentlich aus der Zeit des Dreißigjährigen Krieges', *Beiträge zur Geschichte Dortmunds und der Grafschaft Mark*, 23 (1914), 33–74, at 38.

71 A fuller discussion of these problems is in G. Mortimer, *Eyewitness Accounts of the Thirty Years War 1618–48* (Basingstoke, 2002).

72 Junius, 'Bamberg', p. 18. Further discussion in J. Theibault, 'The rhetoric of death and destruction in the Thirty Years War', *Journal of Social History*, 27 (1993), 271–90.

73 F. Julien, 'Angebliche Menschenfresserei im Dreißigjährigen Krieg', *Mitteilungen des Hist. Vereins der Pfalz*, 45 (1927), 37–92.

74 For example, Monro, *Monro*, pp. 148–51. See also, Roberts, *Gustavus*, vol. ii, pp. 476–80; M. Kaiser, *Politik und Kriegführung: Maximilian von Bayern, Tilly und die Katholische Liga im Dreißigjährigen Krieg* (Münster, 1999), pp. 318–21. More reliable reports put total casualties at 250 with the remaining 500 taken prisoner.

75 Rill, *Tilly*, p. 240.

76 Monro, *Monro*, pp. 159–69; W. Watts, *The Swedish Intelligencer* (3 vols, London, 1633–4), vol. i, pp. 51a–4a; E. Zeeh and N. Belfrage (eds), *Dagbok förd I det svenska fältkansliet 26 Maj 1630–6 November 1632* (Stockholm, 1940), pp. 18–19.

77 Elector Georg Wilhelm to Count Adam von Schwarzenberg, 5 July 1631, in J. Kretzschmar, *Gustav Adolfs Pläne und Ziele in Deutschland* (Hanover, 1904), pp. 311–15.

78 For this tradition, see N. Rein, *The Chancery of God: Protestant Print, Polemic and Propaganda against the Empire, Magdeburg 1546–1551* (Aldershot, 2008); J. Finucane, '"To remain unaltered to the courage you have inherited from your ancestors": Magdeburg under siege 1547–1631' (Ph.D., Trinity College Dublin, 2008).

79 Monro, *Monro*, pp. 207–9; Watts, *Intelligencer*, vols. ii, pp. 13a–16a; Engerisser, *Von Kronach nach Nördlingen*, pp. 22–5.

80 For more detail see Wilson, *Europe's Tragedy*, pp. 301–2.

81 A point made by Medik, 'Historical event', p. 42.

10

Why remember terror?
Memories of violence in the Dutch Revolt[1]

ERIKA KUIJPERS & JUDITH POLLMANN

When in April 1572 a string of cities in the Netherlands openly rejected the regime of the Habsburg governor-general, the Duke of Alba, and declared their support for the rebel magnate William of Orange, the Duke began a violent military campaign to force the rebel cities to surrender. In those cities considered to have been the victims of rebel coercion, the citizens were spared as long as they surrendered rapidly. Yet those cities that had invited the rebels in, or refused to accept a Spanish garrison, could be put to the sack.[2] In the towns of Mechelen, Zutphen, Naarden and Oudewater, Habsburg commanders gave their troops free rein to plunder, and hundreds of men, women and children were murdered or died while trying to escape. Many others were tortured and/or raped. A second wave of violence occurred when Spanish troops mutinied over lack of pay in 1576. After Aalst and Maastricht, this 'Spanish Fury' reached Antwerp, where soldiers robbed, tortured and killed significant numbers; the lowest estimate talks of 1,500 dead.[3] Maastricht was ransacked again in 1579 when re-conquered by the Duke of Parma.[4] After this first string of attacks, violence remained endemic, especially in the frontier zones, but killings in urban areas on this scale became less frequent. Even so, rebel troops initiated 'furies' of their own in 1581 and 1582 in Antwerp, Mechelen and Aalst, while according to reports the joint French and Dutch armies killed hundreds of civilians during their sack of the city of Tienen in 1635.[5]

News about the sacks spread rapidly, and was exploited for propaganda purposes. Moreover, the sacks also found a place in the flourishing memory culture that emerged in the course of the Revolt. Surveying the wealth of references to the sacks in this discourse, the American scholar Peter Arnade recently claimed that:

townspeople who were the victims of such violence did not bury the experience. They routinely invoked the memory of past trauma in subsequent upheavals, presenting a community ideal of citizens united by the tribulations of blood and violence . . . As much as these desecrations dramatised the Prince's victory they simultaneously provoked a heightened civic consciousness . . . In the trauma of violence, citizens were forced to confront that which defined them . . . the excessive violence of an urban sack make the lineaments of identity clear to the citizenry.[6]

Yet on closer inspection, this claim proves more problematic than it seems. Undeniably, an extensive memory culture developed around the events of the Revolt.[7] Yet, it seems that among the survivors of the sacks of the 1570s, remembering was by no means as 'routine' as Arnade suggests. Although the sacks became notorious for their cruelty, few individual eye-witness accounts found their way into the public domain. Initially, the sacks also triggered surprisingly little by way of detailed, local forms of commemoration, while some towns never commemorated the local events at all.

Over the past decades, much research has been done to explore how experiences of extreme violence are remembered, and how individuals and communities handle such memories.[8] This body of scholarship has revealed that it is not self-evident for collective memory practices to develop after episodes of extreme violence. Twentieth-century victims of war often had to wait decades for their tales to be heard. While heroes are soon recognised, victims often are not. Moreover, political regimes, communities and individuals often consciously try to conceal or eradicate the past.[9] This is hardly surprising as memories of humiliation, violence and pain can hamper the reconstruction of communities, and the recovery of both social relations and personal identities. Until well into the nineteenth century, many peace agreements literally stipulated 'oblivion'.[10] And even though global policy makers have come to believe in the virtues of 'truth and reconciliation' processes after World War II, when left to themselves survivors of modern atrocities often remain silent. Whether early modern victims responded in a similar way to episodes of extreme violence has never been the subject of systematic enquiry; our findings in the Netherlands suggest that this may well be the case. Yet this also begs the question of why in some cases the collective commemoration of atrocities eventually *did* come into being.

This article will try to answer that question with reference to the survivors of the sacks of the Dutch Revolt. First, under what circumstances did the survivors resume their lives? One important condition for the collective commemoration of violence is the existence of what Aleida Asmann has called a *Solidargemeinschaft* – a community of solidarity.[11] Victims share their experiences with their peers, their community and finally with the world at large, but only with those who are prepared to listen and acknowledge the experiences. This does not always happen in post-war situations, let alone in a situation where the war continues with a threat of further violence, where people have drifted away or are completely preoccupied with survival. As a result, the development of collective memory practices can be much delayed. Moreover, episodes of violence are often associated with issues of political blame and shame within one's own community. This is especially true for civil wars like the Revolt, when disaster might have been prevented had individuals or groups acted differently. Faced with such questions, it can become impossible to arrive at the modicum of consensus required to commemorate violence collectively.[12]

Yet it is also important to consider the nature of the memories themselves. Sacks and massacres did not just incite indignation, but could also create feelings of shame and guilt.[13] Modern research suggests that the first and natural impulse of victims of violence is to remain silent, unless a format can be found through which their tale can take on a meaningful role or contribute to a positive self image. This also pertained to victims in the early modern Netherlands. Initially, people only highlighted those experiences of violence that could be cast in the format of martyrdom or heroism, a process facilitated by the existence of templates for such narratives in the existing media.

Finally, to what extent did the emergence of collective memory depend on the existence of a normative consensus on what is, and what is not, an 'atrocity'? According to Assmann, the total wars of the twentieth century pushed the experiences of victims outside the realm of their own community, and caused an ethical turn that came to insist on recognition and even compensation by society at large. Yet, is this impulse something new?[14] Although sixteenth-century notions of 'natural' justice and crimes against nature differed from our own, the crossing of moral boundaries could result in indignation and even recognition that victims were entitled to compensation. This, in turn, may have contributed to the emergence of collective memories of violence.

I

Although the sacks in the Netherlands produced much public outrage, they were not, in themselves, an unusual or unexpected phenomenon. Leon van der Essen and Geoffrey Parker argue that Alba and his successors simply applied contemporary laws of war to the sacked towns, just as commanders did again in the Thirty Years War.[15] Not only had the cities forfeited their rights by refusing to surrender, the subsequent sack also set an example to others. Initially at least, these exemplary punishments did prove effective – after the sack of Mechelen in 1572, other cities in Flanders and Brabant quickly surrendered and the same happened in the eastern provinces following the fall of Zutphen. Yet famously, this strategy became counter-productive as a result of events at the small town of Naarden in Holland on 1 December 1572. Many people believed that the Spanish commander had accepted the surrender of the city of Naarden. Allegedly, he had promised to save life and limb of the citizens, and even of the rebel troops defending the town. All seemed set for a peaceful handover. Yet once the soldiers entered the city, and called the citizens together to swear a new oath to the King, they turned on Naarden's unarmed inhabitants and killed almost all males in the town, before plundering it completely.[16]

The gruesome fate of Naarden convinced other cities that they would gain nothing by surrendering. Alba was now forced to commit his underpaid troops to a series of long and troublesome sieges. At Haarlem, Alba's commanders spared most of the citizens but showed no mercy to the rebel garrison. This did nothing to dissuade other towns from continuing their resistance, and successfully so; the sieges of Alkmaar and Leiden eventually had to be lifted. By the time Alba departed for Spain, at the end of 1574, his strategy to combat rebellion had clearly failed. Nevertheless, sacks continued to be used as a military tool, as in Oudewater in 1575 and in Maastricht in 1579, while in 1576 mutinying soldiers had already sacked Maastricht and Aalst, before embarking on the infamous 'Spanish fury' in Antwerp.[17]

Unsurprisingly, the sacks of the Revolt attracted a great deal of public attention at the time. Contemporary journals show that such news travelled rapidly, and shocked contemporaries. In 1572 Antwerp, the diarist Godevaert van Haecht reported on the sack of nearby Mechelen in fairly general terms. Yet he noted that 800 of Zutphen's inhabitants had died, and heard reports of the murder of many women and children in Naarden.[18] In Haarlem, a Catholic chronicler also proved horrified by the tales coming from Naarden: 'such murder among the citizens and women and children that the youngest day will call for revenge for God's eyes'.[19] In November 1576, news reached Amsterdam that the people of Antwerp had to dig a pit to bury 6,000 victims of the Spanish Fury, and that another one was in the making.[20]

Small communities could produce a precise body count. Pieter Aertsz thought that 900 male citizens had been killed in Naarden on 1 December 1572; fifty to sixty survived, forty of whom escaped, while others ransomed themselves.[21] Yet in larger communities like Antwerp, with a population of 100,000, estimates of the number of dead varied wildly.[22] The English eye-witness George Gascoigne thought that 18,000 people had died in Antwerp.[23] Historian Emanuel van Meteren, who lived in London but remained well informed about the situation in his native Antwerp, said that while estimates of 4,000–5,000 dead circulated, all that could be said for certain is that about 1,500 soldiers and citizens had been buried in two pits at the cemetery of Our Lady.[24] The chronicler and eye-witness Bernardino de Mendoza noted that while 2,500 bodies had been buried, another 5,000 people had drowned in the river Scheldt or had perished in the massive fire that broke out in the city.[25] Yet, as usual in the pre-modern world, high body counts served as a means to express shock, while the type of casualties also provoked outrage. Thus, Van Haecht's indignation mostly concerned the alleged targeting of women and children in Naarden, even though the men had been the main victims. Other contemporaries focused on the murder of women, children and the bedridden as true proof of the cruelty of the perpetrators, despite occasional lists of the dead which actually suggest more casualties among the men.[26] Foreign news reports confirmed such views. Printmaker Frans Hogenberg found customers throughout Europe for his newsprints about the sacks, just as he had done for many other current political events in the Low Countries and in France. His images often showed panicking citizens in full flight, and desperate women and children at the mercy of cruel assailants.[27] In France, England and Germany, especially, pamphlets also appeared about these 'gruesome murders'.[28]

By the mid-seventeenth century, and especially after the well-publicised horrors of the Thirty Years War, publications exploited the news and propaganda value of cruelty to the full. When the Dutch sacked Tienen in 1635, a major media offensive presented the news to the public in the Southern Netherlands.[29] The sacks also played a key role in later representations of the Revolt, especially in the Dutch Republic, the breakaway state that emerged as a result of the conflict. Tracts and plays, poems and song, prints and paintings from 1600 presented the massacres as compelling evidence of Spanish cruelty, and as an extension of the work of the Spanish Inquisition and the Spanish conquistadores in the Americas.[30]

Long before the emergence of this 'national' discourse in the Dutch Republic, local communities in rebel territory had started to commemorate their war experiences. In those cities with successes to celebrate, a local and elaborate memory culture quickly started to flourish. The city of Leiden immediately instituted an annual day of commemoration to celebrate the lifting of a siege in 1574 and the arrival of bread and fish to feed the famished population, accompanied by plays and a fair. The inhabitants placed inscriptions on public places and recast the 6,000 people who had died during the siege, mostly from plague, as the victims of starvation.[31] Their heroic refusal to surrender was accordingly presented as an active choice for the good cause, celebrated in inscriptions, plays, prints, paintings, local histories and a tapestry commissioned for the city hall.[32] Once Haarlem returned to rebel hands in 1577, a big text screen appeared in the main parish church to commemorate the suffering of the inhabitants, while Alkmaar commemorated its victory with an annual celebration and a series of pictures for the town hall.[33] In the city of Breda, the peat barge used to smuggle rebel troops into the city in 1590 remained on public display.[34]

Yet while such local memory practices flourished in the besieged cities with happy endings to celebrate, the experience was very different in the towns sacked by the Spanish. There, for many decades, public silence was the rule. Although descriptions and eye-witness accounts appeared in print outside the Netherlands very soon after the events, there is only one example from within the Netherlands itself, produced by Pieter Aertsz, who survived the sack of Naarden.[35] Despite the flow of rebel propaganda pouring off presses in the Netherlands, for decades not a single personal account of events at Maastricht, Zutphen, Aalst, Antwerp, Mechelen and Oudewater found its way into the public domain in the Low Countries. The work of the early Revolt historian Emanuel van Meteren did not appear until the late 1590s, while in 1601 Pieter Bor published the second part of his magnum opus on the Revolt, which only covered the years up to 1573.[36]

The silence did not just extend to print. No evidence survives of any commemorative activity relating to the sacks of Zutphen, Aalst and Maastricht: no descriptions in local chronicles, no annual commemorations, no markers in public space, no commissions of artwork at all. In other cities, signs of activity only begin a quarter of a century after the events. A special Mass in Antwerp one year after the Spanish Fury of 1576 was apparently not repeated, and no other commemorative rituals elsewhere until many decades after the sack.[37] Naarden commissioned a painting in 1604 and by the end of the seventeenth century also held an annual day of commemoration.[38] In 1608, Oudewater started commemorating the massacre with an annual memorial service and sermon on the first Sunday on or after 7 August – one of the few Sundays every year when the Reformed communion was also celebrated. From 1615, the States of Holland also began to pay pensions to the remaining survivors – the last one died in 1664, eighty-five years after the event. From 1650, the annual service of remembrance concluded with a collective visit to the newly commissioned commemorative painting in the town hall.[39]

II

In some instances, we do not need to look far for the reasons why communal narratives never come into existence, as the sacks of the 1570s proved to be only the start of a string of such episodes. The town of Aalst, for example, was sacked again in 1579 by disaffected rebel 'malcontents' and in 1582 by the regular rebel army.[40] In 1579, Alessandro Farnese, Duke of Parma, captured Maastricht, which triggered a new wave of violence. Maastricht lost at least half of its population, and decades later the city remained heavily scarred. In 1619, a French traveller, Pierre Bergeron, recalled the 'butchery, pillaging, rape and arson' and noted that the 'traces of cruelty and barbarity of the Spanish' could still be seen throughout the city.[41] Yet, with so many people gone, and Maastricht still contested territory, the chances to reflect on the past remained slim.[42] The city of Zutphen became effectively unliveable, garrisoned by soldiers who demolished empty buildings for firewood. Economic activity ceased for the most part and many Zutphen people left their hometown. With its citizenry dispersed, the town in ruins and continued conflict in the region, there was perhaps no sense that the process of commemoration could begin.[43]

In cities like Maastricht and Aalst, as in Mechelen and Antwerp, public silence was also a political imperative, with memories of revolt oftentimes an unwanted reminder of one-time disloyalty. Maastricht, for instance, only returned to rebel hands in 1632, and was therefore always unlikely to develop a public memory culture around the cruelty of its own Habsburg overlords. This did not mean, however, that memories of Spanish atrocities disappeared altogether from the Southern Netherlands. Histories of Antwerp histories, for example, recalled these horrific events, with the Spanish Fury featuring as the subject of various paintings by the mid-seventeenth century.[44] The Southerners also remembered the 'furies' of rebel troops; both in Antwerp and Mechelen several dozen citizens died heroically while fighting foreign (French and English) rebel troops. Antwerp granted pensions to all the widows and orphans, while inscriptions on sacred images also referred to the Fury.[45]

One might imagine that the use of the memories of this violence should have been most straightforward in the Dutch Republic, where a number of cities developed vibrant local memory cultures. Yet even in cities like Naarden, Zutphen and Oudewater, the politics of memory proved painful and complicated, not least because the citizens often had been intensely divided.[46] Months of riots and civic conflict had rocked Naarden well before the Spanish troops arrived. Members of the elite fled to Utrecht and allegedly incited the Spanish not to spare their compatriots.[47] The rebel garrison also proved a menace in its own right. As Alva's troops approached, moreover, new dilemmas pitched the citizens against each other – should the rebel garrison be asked to go, should the town surrender and under what conditions? In Naarden, the magistrates found they could not initially persuade angry citizens to follow recommendations to negotiate and surrender. The citizens forced the garrison that had already cost them so much grief to stay and fight on.[48] In Oudewater, Catholic survivors blamed their fellow citizens for having provoked Spanish fury, if not divine punishment.[49] During the siege, Calvinist inhabitants staged a mock procession on the city walls to provoke the Spanish troops.[50] While Calvinist historians remained silent on this episode, a tale told by the Catholic priest Ignatius Walvis in 1712, suggests that the memory lived on. Walvis knew 'a reputable person who had heard a very old woman in Oudewater tell repeatedly' of the mock procession with saints' images and a dog with a chalice, which had incited the Spanish to even greater anger, and destroyed the last chance of clemency.[51]

For the survivors of these events, therefore, a central question must have been that of blame. Who had done what, and when, to associate the town with the Revolt? What might have been done to avert the worst?[52] Not surprisingly, it took survivors several decades before they developed a narrative that could be agreed on, which then became the core of their memory culture in the seventeenth century.

III

Those familiar with the findings of modern studies of the psychological effects of traumatic events may not be surprised by this delay. Survivors of extreme violence often try to avoid discussing their experiences, or think it best not to burden new generations with such memories. Indeed, evidence suggests that sixteenth-century survivors also found it extremely painful to recall their experiences. Thus Jean Richardot, who had witnessed the scenes at Mechelen, wrote to a friend four years later that he could not describe his experiences: 'one could say a lot more, if the horror of it did not make one's hair stand on end – not at recounting it but at remembering it'.[53] Survivors of the Maastricht massacre of 1579 were reported to say that 'they said that those who had remained alive had suffered the worst fate'.[54] Studies highlight the sense of shame and guilt felt by the survivors of episodes of extreme violence, irrespective of the actual degree of responsibility of the victim for what happened.[55] Yet in the sixteenth century, outsiders also questioned the innocence of the victims. Even when condemning Spanish cruelties, some contemporaries considered that the cities somehow invited divine wrath. The English soldier, poet and diplomat George Gascoigne, a witness of the Spanish fury of 1576 in Antwerp, made such an assumption. He argued that the ease with which the Spanish troops defeated the local soldiers could only point to one thing:

> I must needs attribute [it] to Gods iust wrath powred upon the inhabitants for their iniquitie, more then to the manhoode and force of the Spanyerdes.[56]

Similar comments emerged in German newsletters.[57] The German caption of one of Hogenberg's prints of the Spanish Fury also emphasised God's rightful punishment for the greed of Antwerp's inhabitants, who had only thought about their profits.

The response of fellow Netherlanders was not necessarily sympathetic either. Although Antwerpers reputedly saved Mechelen's survivors from starvation in 1572 by collecting money and bringing out food, it seems that throngs of local spectators and salesmen routinely gathered around besieged cities, to buy up the plundered goods.[58] Moreover, eye-witness Pieter Aerts noted that although any human should have pitied Naarden's citizens:

nevertheless some people from the surrounding villages did not refrain from adding to the depression and sadness of the poor desolate widows and orphans and to remind them daily of it, and to renew their indignity and shame (in which they had been placed in front of all the world), by making scandalous and infamous songs, and to sing and spit them all through the city of Naarden in the inns and the streets and elsewhere.[59]

But there was a third reason why memory of sacks were often fraught. Of course, contemporaries and historians alike have emphasised the indiscriminate and irrational nature of the violence: the soldiers killed 'young and old, rich and poor, men and women', while they were in a 'rage', a 'fury', a 'frenzy' and operated like 'mad dogs'. In fact, soldiers often operated in a clear, logical and structured manner once they began to sack a town. Sometimes murder was the official policy – in Naarden, for example, the soldiers were ordered to turn on the 400 male citizens who had assembled to renew their oath to the King. Even in the absence of outright orders to kill, there usually was license to do so, with men especially at risk. It was considered much more 'cruel', but not altogether unusual, to kill women, children and old men. Reports survive of rape and of women being sold on, while children might be pressed into service to carry goods for the soldiers. Such crimes, however, were a by-product rather than the point of sacking. As Emanuel van Meteren noted about the sack of Antwerp:

> There was not much mention of rape, because on the first night they were too exhausted or weakened by hunger and labour, and their blood was still heated. The next day they were fully occupied by greed, and after that order was restored.[60]

Although soldiers might appear unruly, they had clear priorities, usually about maximising profits. While much random killing occurred during the sack of a city, this was not the point – quite the opposite in fact. Soldiers used terror, murder and torture to induce citizens who could afford it to 'compose' with them – in other words, to buy their lives by giving up their property. Well aware of the impending risks, many people would bury or hide their valuables. Soldiers tried to force them to disclose the whereabouts of these valuables or find money elsewhere. People sometimes had to borrow or realize other assets (many people had sunk their capital into land or loans). Some of them would be taken as hostages to camps or castles until they could arrange for sales, or could get relatives to come and bring the sums required. In the process of extracting their goods, many of these people suffered physically, yet as long as the soldiers believed money was to be had of them, they were unlikely to be killed.[61] Van Meteren, who was well informed, explained that the rich citizens of Antwerp had no problem 'composing' with the soldiers, but the people who appeared to be 'of some note' [*van eenighen* aensien] yet who had no money suffered most in the Fury. Disbelieving soldiers tried to extract the whereabouts of non-existing wealth from them through threats and torture that included hanging, beating and burning the householders and their children.[62]

Such experiences probably had profound consequences for the survivors, who had negotiated release terms with their tormentors. Victims, in some ways, played an active role in the outcome of the violent negotiations taking place in their household. They had to respond to violent demands, negotiate loans with fellow citizens, assess the risks of refusal, withstand or witness torture and try to protect loved ones from further harm. The descendants of Christine de Bitter in Antwerp reported with pride that she had withstood torture and remained quiet about the whereabouts of most of the family property, and this hopefully also gave her some sense of satisfaction.[63] Those less strong probably experienced unpalatable feelings of failure, guilt and shame, and a sense of complicity in what had unfolded. Evidence shows that painful conflicts sometimes occurred between the survivors. In Antwerp, endless disputes arose over the repayment of the hasty loans that had been arranged, goods that had been given in safekeeping not to be returned, accusations about trafficking in plundered goods, complicity and theft by fellow citizens and so on. Many people found themselves incapable of meeting debts because their own creditors could or would not pay them. A legacy of personal bitterness among the victims, as well as memories of terror, thus marked the lives of the survivors.[64]

The violence probably also had other psychological effects. Research on trauma victims of more recent civil wars suggests that experiences of extreme violence shatter identities and may cause many physical and psychological problems like stress, depression and fear.[65] Occasionally we get a glimpse of such effects in early modern victims. According to one report, Christine Bitter, who had withstood torture and had been left hanging in her own home, 'regained consciousness . . . but never her previous cheerfulness, after the strangulation which weakened her sagacity, and of which her mind forever bore the scar'.[66]

IV

Recounting memories is a way to recovery, yet the ability to talk about painful or terrifying memories requires one to find a semantic category in which to do so. The shared stories must make sense to the listeners, and serve to frame the narrator's social and moral identity.[67] In the sixteenth- and seventeenth-century accounts of the sacks and massacres, two general categories of narrative emerge: one stressing individual or collective heroism, the other emphasising the innocence of the victim and the inhumane cruelty of the aggressor. In both categories, religious interpretations may offer additional significance. Many accounts, once they began to offer details, feature spectacular escapes. A witness account from Oudewater, for example, cited by historian Pieter Bor in 1621, tells of the miraculous escape by the local bailiff, Gerrit Gerritsz Craeyesteyn. By walking through the town with a blanket on his shoulder, the bailiff managed to pass himself off as one of the plundering soldiers. Chased by thirty German soldiers, he spent the night in a ditch, but as his woollen trousers became too soaked and too heavy to wear, he arrived naked in Gouda, was dressed by friends and brought to the Prince of Orange where he reported on the sack.[68]

Women, as already outlined, occasionally claimed heroic roles. In the course of the seventeenth century, courageous women who backed their sons and husbands during the great sieges increasingly obtained a place in the commemorative limelight. By 1650, brave female characters had emerged as icons of the perseverance and courage of the entire community in Haarlem, Leiden, Alkmaar and Utrecht.[69] Women allegedly fought on the walls of Oudewater and Maastricht, but in most later accounts, just as in those produced contemporaneously, these women figured as innocent victims: either as virgins losing their honour, or as mothers, defenceless and often unable to protect their babies from a cruel death. Recurring elements in stories about terror included rape, the murder of babies and the unborn, the undressing of victims, and the merciless killing of defenceless sick or old people. All accounts we found emphasised the innocence of these victims, and the theme recurred in war propaganda produced by both camps. After the violent sack of Tienen in 1635 by French and Dutch armies, Catholic propagandists from the South simply inverted the existing anti-Spanish imagery current in the Dutch Republic by swapping the roles of aggressors and victims.[70] Some accounts also refer to the hand of God; those who prayed were miraculously saved, and their desecrators punished. A seventeenth-century historian of the massacre at Oudewater reported that a soldier, forever haunted by the memory of his cruel deeds, kept being visited by visions of the little children he had murdered: 'God struck his soul in a terrible manner.'[71]

These tales of heroic defenders of liberty or the true faith, and of the victims of devilish cruelty, were the first to make it into the public domain via the popular press. Whether the survivors themselves shaped their narratives to fit such semantic schemes, or whether this was done for them by the authors who first published the accounts, is impossible to establish. A comparison, however, with other sources like petitions or claims for pensions, tax exemptions or compensation for the losses suffered in the course of sieges and sacks, suggests that stressing heroism or innocence was seen as instrumental in achieving recognition. In the North, the new Protestant authorities also proved sensitive to miraculous tales. In 1582, Anna Jans, widow of the Reformed minister of Oudewater who had been hanged two days after the sack in 1575, solicited a pension from the States of Holland. Her request came with an attestation from a burgomaster of Gouda on the condition of the corpse when the rebel army re-conquered Oudewater sixteen months later. According to him, the body remained fully intact, the colour normal, the face not yet hollow, the eyes fresh and bright as if the corpse had been hanging there for only four days, this 'being a divine miracle'. Suitably impressed, the States of Holland responded positively to Anna's request in view of 'her husband's perseverance and the miraculous ways of the Lord with him'.[72]

A precondition for successful claims was the acknowledgement that the experiences of the victims constituted a moral outrage, rather than the result of divine punishment or mere misfortune. In Holland, the emergence of a collective narrative about the Revolt from around 1600 probably facilitated this process. Political and religious divisions within the population were suppressed in favour of a narrative which contrasted Spanish cruelty with the victimhood and heroism of the local population, so offering a meaningful collective semantic framework in which the survivors could fit their tales.

V

International policy makers now believe that it is imperative to offer victims a chance to tell their tales and to bear witness, even if no compensation or retribution may be on offer. The recollection of memories will heal trauma both individually and collectively. Were such options available in the sixteenth and early seventeenth century? As outlined, many obstacles existed to the emergence of public memory cultures of the massacres. Circumstances, however, for the recognition of the suffering gradually became more favourable in Holland, as the area remained in rebel hands and recovered economically before 1600. This can best be demonstrated by the, admittedly quite extraordinary, developments in Oudewater. After rebels recaptured the town in 1576, survivors returned and slowly started rebuilding the place. By the turn of the century, the threat of war had slowly faded into the background. Both local and supra-local authorities recognised the need to support the recovery process. In 1608, the town started to commemorate the events of 1575 with an annual ceremony, while the States of Holland also decided to give a pension to all the survivors. The Oudewater magistrates annually recorded the names of survivors. The first list in 1615 contained 321 names while the last list, dating from 1664, mentions two old women as the only remaining survivors of the sack.[73] We do not know what prompted the States to award the pensions.[74] Although individual people had successfully staked claims for compensation in other cities, this is the first and apparently only instance where all the survivors, without distinction, were considered to have suffered equally by virtue of their presence in Oudewater at the time. Indeed, one woman, still in her mother's womb during the sack, successfully staked a claim for compensation.

The institutional acceptance of claims possibly encouraged the victims to tell their stories. Evidence of survivors telling their stories exists in short marginal comments alongside some of the names on the 1650 list, such as the note stating that one woman 'lay under corpses'.[75] The annual compiling of the list, therefore, may have facilitated the appearance and transmission of individual stories into the public domain in Oudewater. In 1669, almost a century after the massacre, Arnoldus Duin, a local grocer, wrote a very detailed history of the massacre, which illustrates how the Oudewater community had kept the memories of the survivors very much alive. In his introduction, Duin emphasised that Oudewater, now prospering again, should forever remember the tales of ancestral suffering.[76] To this effect, he included a great number of completely 'new' eye-witness accounts and personal stories, which had never appeared in writing before. Some of these again focused on spectacular escapes, the bravery of the citizens, and the demonic cruelty of their assailants. Yet he also included tales, especially by children, which strike a more unusual and more authentic note – precisely because they focus on minor details and sensory experiences. Japikje Pieters, for example, a young girl in 1575, had lived until the 1650s. She reported heartbreaking details, such as her mother's recognition of the clothes of her murdered children at a second hand store in Utrecht. Japikje, severely injured in the sack, hid under a pile of corpses before she was eventually found by a Spanish soldier who took her to the Spanish encampment from which she managed to escape.[77]

Duin also included the childhood memories of Jan van Dam, whose observations have a strong sense of authenticity, precisely because they are so fragmented. He remembered Spaniards jumping into the river after the defenders covered them with molten lead poured from the town walls. He had witnessed people forced to undress by the soldiers before being killed, in order to keep the clothes clean for sale. Captured by a Spaniard who made him carry goods to the military camp, Jan burned his feet when walking barefoot over hot stones and smouldering wood in the ruined city. In the camp, a canteen woman who bandaged his wounds advised him not to flee to Gouda because of dangers on the road. His most harrowing memory was that of his Spanish captor, who had threatened to kill him several times.[78]

In Oudewater, the appearance of more detailed personal narratives in print coincided with the disappearance of the last survivors, and this seems significant. Yet the survivors had also gradually found better ways to frame their stories, possibly influenced by existing representations of the events. Memories are subject to change, and it seems likely that the imagery about Spanish cruelty, circulating ever since Hogenberg first produced his print of the Oudewater sack from the safety of distant Cologne, coloured individual memories like those of the Oudewater survivors. In his print, Hogenberg included the detail of a pregnant woman, strung up and cut open in order to kill the foetus, and this became a central feature of all subsequent images of this event.[79] The first witness testimony about the fate of this pregnant woman, however, only appeared five decades after the event, and subsequently a number of quite different versions of the story started to circulate. In 1624, Judith Adriaens testified for a notary in Utrecht that Anna van Danswijck, mother of Marrichgen and Trijntge Thonis had been hanged in her doorway.[80] On the list of survivors of 1650, Anna Pelgrums, aged eighty-two, attested that two children were cut out of her aunt's body.[81] According to Duin, Japikje Pieters had also seen a pregnant woman being hanged.[82] Duin named the woman as Aeltgen Pieters and claimed that she had been pregnant with triplets. The detail about the triplets probably served to accentuate the cruelty of the act.[83] The variation in detail suggests that Hogenberg's image had worked its way into the memory of the eye-witnesses.[84] Public remembrance and personal memory had intertwined, and were now indistinguishable.

VI

Unlike the sieges of Leiden, Alkmaar and Haarlem, the sacks of the Dutch Revolt initially triggered almost no collective commemoration. Although survivors did tell tales of their experiences, especially as they got older, it took a long time for such stories to reach the public domain. In several respects, the experiences of early modern victims of atrocities seem comparable to the survivors of modern episodes of extreme violence. Two factors can hamper the emergence of a shared memory culture. First, lasting dislocation and continued violence prevent the basic sense of closure that is needed for a commemorative community to emerge, as in the case of places like Maastricht, Zutphen and Aalst. Secondly, political circumstances can dictate silence, either because memories jar with new political realities, as happened in the Southern Netherlands, or because no consensus exists on the political events that preceded the violence, as was the case in rebel cities in the North.

A collective memory culture requires a framework that gives meaning and some purpose to the suffering. It takes time for such a framework to take shape, and for individual survivors to identify with it. In the Northern Netherlands, the emergence of a collective master narrative about the Revolt from 1600 helped this process along, because it allowed individual victims to gain a special place in the collective victimhood experienced by the Dutch. This could even result, as in the case of Oudewater, in the blanket recognition that all survivors needed support. In the Southern Netherlands, by contrast, the collective memory of the Revolt did not comprise the people's suffering under the yoke of the repressive military regime of the 1570s and 80s. Instead public memory culture in the South celebrated the victory of the true Catholic religion and the people's loyalty to their natural king.

Peter Arnade's argument that the experiences of war encouraged the strengthening of civic identities is quite correct, but this only applied in cities that also had something to celebrate, not those that experienced sacks. The existence of a canonical master narrative about the Revolt may eventually have enabled survivors of the violence to find a meaningful framework for their suffering, but there is very little evidence that the experience of terror also created or supported civic identity. Individual memories focused on pain, fear and loss, with the occasional sense of satisfaction at outwitting some soldiers. While the rousing rhetoric of anti-Spanish cruelty undoubtedly impacted on the political identity of the Dutch Republic, the survivors of that cruelty did not draw lessons for the future from their experiences – others did so for them.

NOTES

1 We researched this essay in the context of the VICI project *Tales of the Revolt: Memory, Oblivion and identity in the Low Countries, 1566–1700*, funded by the Netherlandish Organisation for Scientific Research (NWO) and Leiden University. We would also like to thank the members of the History Department of the University of Antwerp and the UCSIA Fund for their support and hospitality while we completed this article.

2 Geoffrey Parker, 'The etiquette of atrocity: the laws of war in early modern Europe', in Geoffrey Parker, *Empire, War and Faith in Early Modern Europe* (London, 2003), pp. 143–68.

3 Emanuel van Meteren, *Commentarien ofte memorien van-den Nederlandtschen staet, handel, oorloghen ende gheschiedenissen van onsen tyden, etc. mede vervattende eenige haerder ghebueren handelinghen* (Schotlandt, 1609), fol. 119r.

4 W. H. Schukking, 'Het beleg van Maastricht door Parma in 1579', *Publications de la Société Historique et Archéologique dans le Limbourg/Jaarboek van Limburgs Geschied- en Oudheidkundig Genootschap* (1952) 75–97; H. H. E. Wouters, *Grensland en bruggehoofd: historische studies met betrekking tot het Limburgse Maasdal en, meer in het bijzonder, de stad Maastricht* (Assen, 1970), pp. 250–8.

5 There is still no way to establish the number of victims. Jean-Marc Pluvrez, *Tienen 1635: Geschiedenis van een Brabantse stad in de zeventiende eeuw* (Tienen, 1985), p. 39.

6 Peter Arnade, 'The city defeated and defended: civism as political identity in the Habsburg–Burgundian Netherlands', in Robert Stein and Judith Pollmann (eds), *Networks, Regions and Nations: Shaping Identities in the Low Countries, 1300–1650*, Studies in Medieval and Renaissance Traditions 149 (Leiden 2010), pp. 195–216, at pp. 199, 200, 216.

7 Simon Schama, *The Embarrassment of Riches: An Interpretation of Dutch Culture in the Golden Age* (Berkeley, 1988), pp. 51-126; Judith Pollmann, 'Het oorlogsverleden van de Gouden eeuw', inaugural lecture (Leiden, 2008).

8 See for overviews, for example, Geoffrey Cubitt, *History and Memory* (Manchester, 2007), pp. 208-14, Astrid Erll, *Kollektives Gedächtnis und Erinnerungskulturen* (Stuttgart and Weimar, 2005), pp. 46-8, 86-90; Jay Winter, *Remembering War: The Great War between Memory and History in the Twentieth Century* (New Haven, 2006), pp. 2-69; Dominick LaCapra, *Representing the Holocaust; History, Theory, Trauma* (Ithaca, NY, 1994). For this paper, we found Aleida Assmann, *Der lange Schatten der Vergangenheit: Erinnerungskultur und Geschichtspolitik* (Munich, 2006) especially useful.

9 Paul Connerton, 'Seven types of forgetting', *Memory Studies*, 1 (2008), 59-71.

10 For example, Mark Greengrass, 'Amnistie et oubliance: Un discours politique autour des édits de pacification pendant les guerres de religion', in P. Mironneau and I. Pébay-Clottes (eds), *Paix des Armes, Paix des âmes* (Paris, 2000), pp. 113-23; Sheryl Kroen, *Politics and Theater: The Crisis of Legitimacy in Restoration France, 1815-1830* (Berkeley, 2000). See useful reflections on the working of such agreements in Ross Poole, 'Enacting oblivion', *International Journal of Politics, Culture and Society*, 22 (2009), 149-53.

11 Assmann, *Der lange Schatten*, p. 75.

12 Henri Rousso, *The Vichy Syndrome: History and Memory in France since 1945* (Cambridge, MA, 1991).

13 Assmann, *Der lange Schatten*, pp. 74-5, Winter, *Remembering War*, pp. 52-76.

14 Assmann, *Der lange Schatten*, pp. 76-8.

15 Leon van der Essen, *Kritische studie over de oorlogsvoering van het Spaanse leger in de Nederlanden tijdens de XVIe eeuw, nl. de bestraffing van opstandige steden*, Mededelingen van de Koninklijke Vlaamse academie van wetenschappen, letteren en schone kunsten, klasse der letteren 14, 1 (Brussels 1952); Parker, 'The etiquette of atrocity'. See also J.-L. Charles, 'Le sac des villes dans les Pays-Bas au seizième siècle: Etude critique des règles de guerre', *Revue internationale d'histoire militaire*, 24 (1965), 288-301.

16 See on the events of these years, for example, Geoffrey Parker, *The Dutch Revolt* (Harmondsworth, 1979).

17 In Antwerp, the mutineers joined forces with remaining loyal troops who were commanded by Jeronimo de Roda, a councillor of state who had recently been unseated by the States of Brabant. See on these events, for example, Michel Baelde (ed.), *Opstand en pacificatie in de Lage Landen: Bijdrage tot de studie van de Pacificatie van Gent. Verslagboek van het Tweedaags Colloquium bij de vierhonderdste verjaring van de Pacificatie van Gent* (Ghent, 1976).

18 *De kroniek van Godevaert van Haecht over de troebelen van 1565 tot 1574 te Antwerpen en elders*, ed. R. van Roosbroeck, Uitgaven van het Genootschap voor Antwerpsche geschiedenis, 2 (2 vols, Antwerp, 1929), vol. ii, pp. 218-19, 222-3.

19 Willem Janszoon Verwer, *Memoriaelbouck: Dagboek van gebeurtenissen te Haarlem van 1572-1581*, ed. J. J. Temminck (Haarlem, 1973), p. 16.

20 *Dagboek van broeder Wouter Jacobsz (Gualtherus Jacobi Masius) Amsterdam 1572–1578 en Montfoort 1578–1579*, ed. I. H. van Eeghen (2 vols, Groningen, 1959), vol. ii, pp. 610–11.

21 [Pieter Aertsz] *Moort-dadich verhael vande gheschiedenissen, moort ende destructie vande stede van Naerden . . . op ten i. Decembris ende andere daer aen volghende daghen* (no year, no place), p. 10. Internal evidence suggests that the text was published after November 1573. The introduction places much direct blame on Philip II, which suggests it may date from after 1580, when the rebels abandoned the fiction that they were only fighting the King's evil advisers. Parts of the text were reprinted in 1626 as 'Cort verhael van de moort ende destructie der stadt Naarden', in Gysius, *Oorspronck ende voortgang der Neder-landscher beroerten ende ellendicheden. Waerin vertoont worden, de voornaemste tyrannijen, ende andere onmenschelijcke wreetheden, die onder het ghebiedt van Philips II . . . door zijne stad-houders in 't werck ghestelt zijn, gheduyrende dese Nederlantsche troublen ende oorlogen* (Leiden, 1616), pp. 480–92.

22 See on this issue also F. Prims, 'Te herschrijven geschiedenis' F. Prims in *Antwerpiensia*, vol. 21 (Antwerp, 1951), pp. 304–9; E. I. Rooms, 'Een nieuwe visie op de gebeurtenissen die geleid hebben tot de Spaanse Furie te Antwerpen op 4 November 1576', *Bijdragen tot de geschiedenis*, 54 (1971), 31–55.

23 [George Gascoigne], *The spoyle of Antwerpe: Faithfully reported, by a true Englishman, who was present at the same* (London, 1576).

24 Van Meteren, *Commentarien*, fol. 119r.

25 Bernardino de Mendoza, 'Commentaires memorables de Don Bernardin de Mendoce, chevallier ambassadeur en France pour le Roy Catholique, des guerres de Flandres & Pays Bas depuis l'an 1567 jusques a l'an mil cinq cens soixante & dixsept . . .' (Paris, 1591), cited in P. Génard (ed.), *La Furie Espagnole: Documents pour servir à l'Histoire du sac d'Anvers* (Antwerp, 1876), p. 222.

26 As in the lists for the Spanish Fury published by the Fonds Plaisier, http://home.pi.be/~ma479346/fonds_plaisier.htm (accessed 4 August 2011).

27 Ger Luijten (ed.), *Frans Hogenberg: Broadsheets* (2 vols, Ouderkerk aan den IJssel, 2009); *The New Hollstein Dutch & Flemish Etchings, Engravings and Woodcuts, 1450–1700* (Roosendaal, 1949–), vols 61–2.

28 For example, [Gascoigne], *The spoyle of Antwerp: Warhafftige und erbermliche Zeitung von dem unmenschlichen Mord . . . so die von Antorff . . . erlitten* (no place, 1576); *Antorfische Zeitung, grüntliche und kützre Beschreibung . . . des greulichen Uberfalles, Schadens, Raub und Mord der Hispanischen Rebellen* (no place, 1577). The latter two were both translated from the French. Frederic Perrenot, Seigneur de Champaigney, who had been governor of the city recounted his experiences in *Recveils d'Aretophile* (Lyon, 1578). For other foreign accounts, see *Discovrs dv siege et prinse de la ville de Mastrich* (Paris, 1579); *Warhafftige, Vnd Erbermliche zeitung, von der grossen Blutstürtzung, der Statt Mastrich* (Cologne, 1579).

29 Pluvrez, *Tienen 1635*; See on the atrocity discourse, for example, Barbara Donogan, 'Atrocity, war crime and treason in the English civil war', *American Historical Review*, 99 (1994), 1137–66.

30 For example, Willem Baudartius, *Morgen-wecker der vrije Nederlantsche provinctien* ('Danzig', 1610); *Spieghel der ievght ofte korte kronijk der Nederlandse geschiedenissen . . . geduerende deze veertigh-jarighe oorloge* (Amsterdam, 1614); Johannes Gysius, *Oorsprong en voortgang der Neder-landtscher beroerten*. On the emergence of this discourse about the Revolt, see Pollmann, *Het oorlogsverleden*. On comparisons with the Americas, see Benjamin Schmidt, *Innocence Abroad: The Dutch Imagination and the New World, 1570–1670* (Cambridge, 2001), and on the Black Legend also K. W. Swart, 'The Black Legend during the Eighty Years War', in J. S. Bromley and E. H. Kossmann (eds), *Some Political Mythologies: Papers Delivered to the 5th Anglo-Dutch Conference*, Britain and the Netherlands 5 (The Hague, 1975).

31 As demonstrated by Thera Wijsenbeek, *Honger*, 3 Oktoberlezing (The Hague, 2006).

32 Judith Pollmann, *Herinneren, herdenken, vergeten. Het beleg en ontzet van Leiden in de Gouden eeuw*, 3 Oktoberlezing (Leiden, 2008).

33 Mia M. Mochizuki, 'The quandary of the Dutch Reformed church masters', in Arie-Jan Gelderblom, Jan L. de Jong and Marc van Vaek (eds), *The Low Countries as a Crossroads of Religious Belief* (Leiden en Boston, 2004), pp. 141–63, Marloes Huiskamp, 'De Tachtigjarige Oorlog en de Vrede van Munster in de decoratie van zestiende- en zeventiende eeuwse stadhuizen. Een verkenning', *De zeventiende eeuw*, 13 (1997), 335–47.

34 It was mostly burned when the Spanish captured the city in 1623, but the rudder was allegedly saved and is on display to this day in the Breda's Museum, www.breda-museum.org/cgi-bin/www_edit/projects/breda/scripts/breda.cgi?a=36335&code=128 (accessed 5 August 2011).

35 It was never reprinted and only survives in a single copy [Aertsz] *Moortdadich verhael*. The brief account of the sack of Mechelen that was published in *Vvarachtighe historie, ende ghetrouwe beschryuinghe vande alteratie ende veranderinghe, gheschiet inde Stadt Mechelen, ende oock vande groote Tirannye, ende onghehoorde wreetheyt vande Spaigniaerden, daer naer ghevolcht, inden Jare Xvc. LXXII* (Mechelen, 1581) was very succinct. The main aim of this pamphlet was to try and persuade the Mechelers to continue supporting the Revolt.

36 Pieter Christiaensz. Bor, *Vande Nederlantsche oorloghen, beroerten ende borgerlijcke oneenicheyden, gheduerende den gouvernemente vanden hertoghe van Alba inde selve landen* (Utrecht, 1601). Emanuel van Meteren, *Historia Belgica nostri potissimum temporis Belgii sub quator Burgundis et totidem Austriacis principibus coniunctionem et gubernationem breviter* (no place, 1598). There had been an earlier German edition but this was the first edition authorised by the author. The first Dutch edition appeared in 1599.

37 Felix Archief, Antwerp, SA R18 (1577), fol. 357r, five musicians were given wine for their contribution to the commemorative Mass. We are grateful to Marianne Eekhout who alerted us to this entry.

38 Antonius Bynaeus, *Naardens burgermoort door de Spaansche begaen op den 1/11 December 1572 vertoont op den jaarlijkschen gedenk-dagh in den jaren 1686* (Amsterdam, 1687).

39 Nettie Stoppelenburg, *De Oudewaterse moord* (no place, 2005), pp. 55–46. Someone, but we do not know who, commissioned a graphic painting of the Spanish Fury, which is now in the Antwerp Vleeshuis, AV.980.014; if it was painted for an Antwerp owner, the anti-monastic detail in the painting suggests it was painted before 1585, when the city passed into Habsburg hands and Protestants were leaving the city. Another early painting of the burning city hall is there now, but not on public display, Inv. No. 1150. We are most grateful to Marianne Eekhout and Annemie de Vos of the Vleeshuis for their information on these paintings.

40 F. de Cacamps, 'Dertig maanden uit de geschiedenis van Aalst. Juni 1579 tot December 1581', *Het land van Aalst*, 8 (1956), 117–50.

41 Pierre Bergeron, *Voyage ès Ardennes, Liège [et] Pays-Bas en 1619*, ed. H. Michelant (Liège, 1875), p. 238.

42 J. C. G. M. Jansen, 'Economische en sociale gevolgen van de val van Maastricht in 1579', in G. van Breen (ed.), *'Van der Nyersen upwaert': Een bundel opstellen over Limburgse geschiedenis aangeboden aan drs. M.K.J. Smeets bij zijn afscheid als Rijksarchivaris in Limburg* (Maastricht, 1981), pp. 127–35.

43 W. Th. M. Frijhoff, *Geschiedenis van Zutphen* (Zutphen, 2003), pp. 85–6.

44 For example, in Carolus Scribani, *Antverpia* (Antwerp, 1610); Heribertus Rosweyde, 'Kerkelijcke historie van Neder-landt, vervatende d'outheyt des gheloofs in de XVII provincien . . .', in Heribertus Rosweyde and Caesar Baronius (eds), *Generale kerckelycke historie van de gheboorte onses H. Iesv Christi tot het iaer M.DC.XXIV: Bewysende de vasten standt der H. Roomsche Kercke . . .* (2 vols, Antwerp, 1623). For example, the painting attributed to Daniel van Heil that is currently in the Deutsches Historisches Museum, Berlin Inv. No. E03/157,03/211, and the similar work by his hand sold by Christie's London on 23 April 1993 [Lot 128].

45 A list of the 101 casualties and their families was compiled by the Fonds Plaisier and can be found at http://home.pi.be/~ma479346/fonds_plaisier_7.htm (accessed 5 August 2011). A late eighteenth-century chronicler in Antwerp deplored the loss of the image to the French invaders, see Brecht Deseure 'Den ouden luijster is verdwenen'. Geschiedenis, herinnering en verlies bij Jan Baptist Van der Straelen (1792–1817)', *Belgisch Tijdschrift voor Nieuwste Geschiedenis/Revue belge d'histoire contemporaine*, 40 (2010), 517–55, at 532. We are most grateful to him for alerting us to this evidence.

46 Henk van Nierop, 'Het foute Amsterdam', inaugural lecture University of Amsterdam (Amsterdam, 2000).

47 Lambertus Hortensius, *Hortensius over de opkomst en den ondergang van Naarden*, ed. P. Hofman Peerlkamp and A. Perk (Utrecht, 1866), pp. 86–97, 101–16, 152–3.

48 Ibid., pp. 124–30.

49 *Dagboek van broeder Wouter Jacobsz*, vol. ii, p. 519.

50 Ibid., vol. ii, p. 517; Van Meteren, *Commentarien*, fol. 106v.

51 Ignatius Walvis, *Het Goudsche Aarts Priesterdom* (Delft, 1999), p. 143.

52 It was perhaps no accident that it was one of Naarden's negotiators, and the kinsman of another, who accounted in writing for their role, and for their own survival, when so many other men had died. Ibid., and Aertsz, *Moort-dadich verhael*. See also the recriminations by an anonymous Catholic chronicler from Mechelen

in his manuscript 'Discours du pillage de Malines fait le 2e Octobre 1572', published by Jan Frans Willems (ed.), *Mengelingen van historisch-vaderlandschen inhoud* (Antwerp, 1827–30), pp. 393–422. When Aalst was taken by the rebel army in 1582, a number of citizens apparently collaborated with the rebels from within the walls. During the sack, these people were spared as they were wearing the beggars' logo on their hats. F. de Cacamps, 'Vier maanden uit de geschiedenis van Aalst. 1 januari tot 23 april 1582', *Het land van Aalst*, 6 (1954), 170, 185–6.

53 Cited by Parker, 'The etiquette of atrocity', pp. 156–7.

54 Johannes Gysius, *Oorsprong en voortgang der Neder-landtscher beroerten ende ellendicheden* (Leiden, 1616), p. 544.

55 John P. Wilson, Boris Droždek and Silvana Turkovic, 'Posttraumatic Shame and Guilt', *Trauma, Violence, and Abuse*, 7 (2006), 122–41; Ashwin Budden, 'The role of shame in posttraumatic stress disorder: a proposal for a socio-emotional model for DSM-V', *Social Science and Medicine*, 69 (2009), 1032–9.

56 Gascoigne, *The Spoyle of Antwerp*, CVIIv.

57 *Wahrhafte und erbermliche Zeitung*, reprinted in Génard, *La Furie Espagnole*, pp. 572–6.

58 'Discours du pillage', p. 417. Four days after the sack of Oudewater, priests' and nuns' habits from the monasteries of Oudewater were sold in Amsterdam, see *Dagboek van broeder Wouter Jacobsz*, vol. ii, p. 519. The inhabitants of nearby Montfoort plundered burned houses in Oudewater and undressed corpses to sell the clothes. See Arnoldus Duin, *Oudewaters moord: of Waerachtig verhael van d'oudheid, belegering, in-nemen en verwoesten der geseide stad.* (Oudewater, 1669), p. 16.

59 [Aertsz] *Moort-dadich verhael*, p. 15.

60 Van Meteren, *Commentarien*, fol. 119v.

61 Survivors' accounts, for example, *Hortensius over de opkomst en den ondergang van Naarden*; Letter by Geeraert Janssen to Jacop Cool, 14 November 1576, in J. H. Hessels (ed.), *Ecclesiae Londino-Batavae Archivum* (4 vols, Cambridge, 1887–97), vol. i, pp. 145–53, and see also below. Details of how the soldiers proceeded can be gleaned from the many statements of people in Antwerp who ended up in disputes with others about ownership of plundered goods, loans made and debts incurred during the sack. Some of these are in Génard, *La Furie Espagnole*, pp. 531–71, and many other examples in the Fonds Plaisier, http://home.pi.be/~ma479346/fonds_plaisier.htm (accessed 5 August 2011) for the years after the Fury.

62 Van Meteren, *Commentarien*, fol. 119v.

63 P. C. Hooft, *Nederlandsche historien* (Amsterdam, 1656), pp. 463–4.

64 See the Fonds Plaisier, http://home.pi.be/~ma479346/fonds_plaisier.htm (accessed 5 August 2011).

65 S. J. Brison, *Aftermath: Violence and the Remaking of a Self* (Princeton, NJ, 2002); Assmann, *Der lange Schatten*, pp. 74–6; Annet Mooij en Jolande Withuis (eds), *The Politics of War Trauma: The Aftermath of World War II in Eleven European Countries* (Amsterdam, 2010), passim.

66 P. C. Hooft, *Nederlandsche historien* (Amsterdam, 1656), pp. 463–4.

67 S. J. Schmidt, 'Memory and remembrance: a constructivist approach', in Astrid Erll, Ansgar Nünning and S. B. Young (eds), *Cultural Memory Studies: An*

International and Interdisciplinary Handbook (New York, 2008), p. 192; Harald Welzer, 'Communicative memory', in ibid., pp. 285–98.

68 Pieter Christiaensz. Bor, *Nederlantsche oorloghen, beroerten, ende borgerlijcke oneenicheyden . . .* (Leiden, 1621), Book 8, fol. 121v.

69 Els Kloek, *Kenau: De heldhaftige zakenvrouw uit Haarlem (1526–88)* (Hilversum, 2001); Els Kloek, 'Heldenmoed, huwelijkstrouw en vrouweneer: Bakhuizen van den Brink en de "nijvere huisbestierster" Brecht Proosten († ca. 1592)', *Bijdragen en mededelingen betreffende de geschiedenis der Nederlanden*, 117 (2002), 307–30, at 447.

70 Pluvrez, *Tienen 1635*.

71 Duin, *Oudewaters moord*, sig. A3v.

72 Nationaal Archief, The Hague, 3.01.04.01, States of Holland, Inv. No. 333, fols 519v–520.

73 Oud Stadsarchief, Oudewater, inv. nr. 165.

74 We have searched for, but so far not found, any trace of the decision-making process or the accounts of the pensions in the States of Holland's archive.

75 Stoppelenburg, *De Oudewaterse moord*, pp. 54–6.

76 Duin, *Oudewaters moord*, sig. A1.

77 Ibid., pp. 12–14.

78 Ibid., pp. 15–16.

79 Wolfgang Cilleßen, 'Massaker in der niederländischen Erinnerungskultur: Die Bildwerdung der Schwarzen Legende', in Christine Vogel (ed.), *Bilder des Schreckens: die mediale Inszenierung von Massakern seit dem 16. Jahrhundert* (Frankfurt am Main, 2006), pp. 93–135.

80 Stoppelenburg, *De Oudewaterse moord*, p. 111.

81 Ibid.

82 Duin, *Oudewaters moord*, p. 13.

83 Ibid., p. 18.

84 Schmidt, 'Memory and remembrance', p. 193; Willem A. Wagenaar and Jop Groeneweg, 'The memory of concentration camp survivors', *Applied Cognitive Psychology*, 4 (1990), 77–87. See also Willem A. Wagenaar, *The Popular Policeman and Other Cases: Psychological Perspectives on Legal Evidence* (Amsterdam, 2005).

11

Language and conflict in the French Wars of Religion

MARK GREENGRASS

Words, like looks, can kill. If that is so, we should listen to the voices, as well as observe the actions, of those who participated in and contributed to the conflicts of the French wars of religion. Yet the history of sectarian conflict in the French wars of religion has focused more on the targets of violence, animate and inanimate, than on its vocal manifestations. In 1987, Peter Burke and Roy Porter urged that it was 'high time for a social history of language, a social history of speech, a social history of communication'.[1] This chapter explores the possibilities and problems of writing such an account for these complex events.

One of the fundamental elements of religious change in the sixteenth century was that it created a contested lexicon. Protestantism generated a 'speech-community' whose claims (to speak the truth, to be a godly community) were larger than, and different from, those speech-communities confined by localised customs or specific dialects. Its language was radicalised by the claims to speak for, and to act out, God's truth and for a reformed life, claims that were impossible to disprove and difficult to contradict, precisely because the language in which they were expressed reinforced their truth-claims. They were deployed by those who would not normally have been expected to have a voice on such matters. Their expression was allowed to those for whom, in other circumstances, it would have seemed inappropriate, offensive or seditious. Language is always a manifestation of cultural power. The force and significance accorded to words used as (or interpreted by others as) hate-speech, oaths and profanities, is a powerful indicator of the significance of language in conflictual circumstances, just as the control of words, and the deployment of oaths of peace are essential instruments of reconciliation.

Our sources are not shy about communicating the 'sound' of sectarian conflict. On the contrary, it was fundamentally noisy. In the midst of the sectarian tension in Angers on the eve of the first civil war in 1562, a monk led a crowd into the house of a prominent merchant. Finding a Protestant Bible, he speared it with his halberd and led his followers with it aloft through the main street 'exclaiming and crying out: There is the lost truth, the truth of all the devils, there is the invincible and Eternal God.' When they arrived at the Loire, he threw it in, exclaiming: 'There is the truth of all the devils drowned.'[2] At Issoudun, Protestants sang Psalms in the vineyards just outside the town, as the tocsin rang within, the prelude to the ensuing massacre.[3] An outraged woman, whose baby had been forcibly taken from her to be re-baptised by the local priest, summoned her courage to protest 'loudly that it was too wicked and altogether against her wishes; saying which, she struck the priest with all her might'.[4] That would be followed in due course by the sound of the troops of the Catholic commander St André, patrolling the streets: 'with hideous blasphemies, calling God with a sneer the Eternal, the strong, and even pronouncing execrable things against the Virgin Mary'.[5] In the midst of the sectarian insurrection in May 1562 in Toulouse, the streets were full of the 'cries and appalling lamentations of poor innocent people' caught in the storm.[6] Meanwhile, in Montauban, citizens found themselves embroiled in 'a horrible verbal dispute on the streets'.[7]

Words conveyed the voice of authority in the functioning reality of a 'face-to-face' society.[8] So, when judges from the Parlement of Toulouse left the tense scene of a forcible disinterment of the body of a suspected Protestant from a city cemetery, they were reported to have authorised verbally a Catholic assault upon Protestant protesters present with the words: 'Kill everyone, pillage everything. We are your (city) fathers; we shall be your guarantors.'[9] That, at least, was what a Protestant source believed, reckoning that the depositions of those who could testify to its having been said afterwards had been later destroyed to avoid incrimination. In Blois, the local commander used the town crier to summon Catholics 'at the king's command' with arms to the château.[10] Before dawn had begun to light the Paris sky on 24 August 1572, the Duke of Guise left the lodgings where Coligny had been executed to tell an assembled body of armed men (in the hostile testimony of the Genevan Protestant Simon Goulart): 'Courage, soldiers; we have begun well; let us go on to others, for the king commands it', repeating loudly and emphatically: 'The king commands it, it is the will of the king, it is his express will.'[11] In the political turbulence of royal minorities and bitterly contested factionalism at court, it was unclear whose word to trust. The magistrates in Caen, for example, did not know how to interpret the 'Declaration' and 'Second Declaration' issued by Louis de Bourbon, Prince of Condé in April 1562, 'concerning the captivity of the King and the Queen Mother'. They doubted the royal orders they received, despite their arriving under the royal seal.[12]

Rumour was just one of the forces subverting the 'voice' of institutionalised and legitimated authority in the wars of religion. Behind the extreme inter-personal violence was the prior, high-decibel and vocalised fears on both sides that they would shortly be the targets of such violence. Panic was diffused orally. Massacres were not premeditated, but they were predicted. In the early months of 1562, it was the 'bruit' that Protestants were preparing to 'make their [Catholic] blood run through the streets' that was the catalyst for contention.[13] At more or less the same moment, Protestants at Bourges were roused by a rumour that letters had been intercepted at Orléans to the Duke of Guise and Cardinal of Lorraine promising to exterminate the Huguenots of Berry.[14] Huguenot troops seized the city to forestall attack, marching in to the chant of Psalm 124 as their response.[15] Meanwhile the Protestants of Le Mans petitioned the king against the word on the streets that local Catholics were planning to massacre them, 'seditious words not merely voiced by the common people but in the mouths of the most notable'.[16] The news of the 'massacre' at Vassy spread (initially) by word of mouth to become a motor of sectarian tension in the month between when it occurred (1 March 1562) and the gallop of Louis, Prince of Condé's troops into Orléans (2 April 1562) to raise the standard of revolt.

The closeness of the link between fear and language lies in the expressed imagination.[17] 'Fortis imaginatio generat casum' ('a strong imagination begets the event') is the title of Michel de Montaigne's essay on the disturbing force of the psychosomatic.[18] Exemplifying how words have the power to stimulate our imaginations, and then influence our bodies, he tells the story of the gentleman of his acquaintance who entertained a large house party, letting it be known a few days later as a joke that he had fed them on baked cat: 'at which a young gentlewoman, who had been at the feast, took such a horror, that falling into a violent vomiting and fever, there was no possible means of saving her'.[19] Fear was so readily transmitted to others in the circumstances of sectarian tension, precisely because it articulated emotion, its expression in words being a constituent part of its motivation. Catholics in Metz had no real experience of what went on in Protestant *temples*, but they voiced to one another their imagined fears so readily that they became the impulse to violent actions. In the pulpit, they said, the pastor had two horns (a reflection of his *toque*?), the hour-glass was the devil's familiar and they held two suppers, one for the rich (with white bread) and one for the poor (with brown).[20] The 'common opinion' in Paris at the time of the St-Jacques 'affair' (September 1557), when a clandestine Protestant congregation in Paris was attacked, was that the Protestants had assembled for a fine banquet before putting the lights out for a sexual orgy.[21]

The language of sectarian conflict included hate-speech of all sorts. Protestant women, for example, were often subjected to verbal assaults. When the congregation in the rue St-Jacques was set upon, notable female members of the congregation were 'called whores and subjected to all sorts of insults'.[22] In Rouen, a 'rumpus' ('une noise') in the streets in May 1561 occurred between the Catholic Colaye Flament and the Protestant Jean Morel, the former calling the latter's wife 'whore, bawd, and Lutheran', before accusing Morel himself.[23] Despite the formal conclusion of hostilities after the first civil war in 1563, Huguenot women in Dijon were insulted and threatened the following year, called 'bitches' ('chiennes') and accused of offering their sexual favours freely.[24] In Troyes, the bodies of naked Huguenot female corpses were arranged with their legs splayed out to show their 'shameful parts', whilst their deriders pointed with a stick, saying to passers-by: 'that is where they bestowed their charity' (i.e. their sexual favours).[25] Threats, taunts, mockery, derision, swearing and profanation were constituent parts of sectarian violence. The distinctive Huguenot singing of metrical Psalms was turned against them by their opponents in satirical *contrafacta*.[26] At Montauban, Psalm 50 ('The mighty God, even the Lord, has spoken . . .') was the object of 'more than abominable blasphemies'.[27] In Rouen, Protestants regarded themselves as subject to 'rude songs, words and gestures and abominable lewdness'.[28] The vilification of victims included the mocking of their beliefs. In Montauban, the captain directing the despatch of Protestant victims into the river invited them to sing Psalm 137 ('By the waters of Babylon . . .').[29] At Thouars, poor Antoine Julien was disembowelled whilst still alive, his murderers mocking him: 'Ask thy God to save thee.'[30] In sham trials and parades, parodies of those elements of public life in which words played a crucial role, victims were subjected to contempt, so as to humiliate and dehumanise them. At Villeneuve-lès-Avignon, their livers were paraded around on the end of a stick to the accompaniment of the cry: 'sixpence for Huguenot tripe'.[31] At Gaillac, captured Protestants were led, with mock politeness to their relatives ('Voici ton parent'). Then, having drowned them in the river, their murderers dressed in their clothes and danced before the widows and orphans of the town with mocking laughs.[32] Johann Wilhelm von Botzheim, a German student who witnessed the massacre at Bourges in the wake of Saint-Bartholomew's Night, recalled how the house where he lodged held a party as the grizzly events took place outside on the streets: 'Everybody congratulated one another.'[33]

Oaths, threats and prophecies complemented hate-speech. As the Protestant preacher opened his Advent sermon in the clandestine preaching in Issoire in the last days of November 1560, Catholics remarked openly to one another on the storm that overtook the town 'that they said was the end of the world'.[34] Protestants in Montigny outside Metz, recalled to one another how Guillaume Farel had prophesied the troubles which eventually came to pass in their locality in a sermon years before.[35] A rumour, said to have started with a letter from the famous astrologer Nostradamus, was responsible for coming close to stimulating the sack of the city of Toulouse, which was what his letter had predicted.[36]

This evidence, however, begs the question whether the written sources at our disposal reflect what had actually been said. The reality is that 'oraliture' (speaking and hearing) and literature (writing and reading) are in a complex and contested relationship in the circumstances of conflict.[37] The *Histoire ecclésiastique des églises de France* (upon which we have drawn for the majority of our evidence so far) is a later, partisan (Protestant) source, published nearly twenty years after the events which it describes, compiled from a variety of post-facto accounts and subsequently edited in Geneva. There is barely a shred of corroborative testimony for what is claimed to have been said. The partisan nature of its testimony precluded such corroboration. The use of reported speech in post-facto accounts was the acknowledged way by which 'memorialists' of the period made events appear more immediate, emphasising agency, engagement and urgency in the same way that humanist historians placed nicely crafted speeches in the mouths of their heroes. To do so, they emphasised how they accurately reported what had been said. The Protestant *Mémoires de l'histoire de l'estat de France* (1578), edited by Simon Goulart, assured the reader in the preface that his purpose was simply to 'let those speak who had pronounced these discourses'.[38] The contemporary historian Lancelot de Voisin, sieur de La Popelinière guaranteed that he recorded what he had 'seen and heard', although he added that there were occasions when he had to take at face-value the statements of others for events where he had not been directly present.[39] Yet, when one examines closely the reported speech around the moment of the Admiral Coligny's assassination in the four near contemporary sources upon which later historians relied for their accounts, there are considerable differences as they sought to dignify and dramatise the event.[40] Accounts like the *Histoire ecclésiastique* were designed to turn the ephemeral contingency of the spoken into a historicised, albeit constructed, speech-event representing the fears of the past in a way that the present and the future could comprehend. And, beyond that evident difficulty, there is the even more imponderable fact that words in conflictual situations were almost always linked to gestures, the one reinforcing and rendering the other more menacing. Can we take such evidence seriously?

A similar complex relationship between the spoken and the written is also present when it comes to the *procès-verbaux* of a town council or representative assembly. Yet they must take us closer to the *ipsissima verba*, even though we have to read between the lines to 'hear' the implied discourse that they represent, and to imagine the gestures which accompanied it. The depositions for the Irish troubles of 1641 provide testimonies for the significance of verbal violence as an integral component within the rebellion, a verbal violence with its own logic and dynamics. Comparable material tends not to survive from the sectarian conflicts of the French civil wars. The legal system was paralysed by the military operations and, in the aftermath of conflict, the edicts of pacification formally prevented commissions of enquiry. In the twelve months between Easter 1561 and the opening of the civil war a year later, however, is a document, found in 2005 among the thousands of still-unclassified case-notes ('sacs à procès') from the Parlement of Toulouse.[41] It is an interrogation of fourteen witnesses to the sectarian events in Cahors in September and October 1561, conducted by a court usher ('huissier') in late November of that year. What can that tell us about verbal violence in that one instance?

The events in question are known to us in outline through the *Histoire Ecclésiastique*.[42] The Protestant congregation took a low profile in the small cathedral town after their minister had been arrested in 1560. At Eastertide 1561, however, some students arrived from Toulouse to continue their studies at the local university having been driven out of the Midi capital by the troubles there. That gave new momentum to the movement, especially following the arrival of a new pastor, Dominique Cestat from Montauban, and the beginning of public Protestant preaching on 15 October 1561. There had already been a violent incident on 7 September 1561 when the sacristan at the cathedral had been killed whilst ringing the bells for the feast of the Nativity the following day. There were further street clashes at the time of the annual fair in Cahors on 28 October, when some 300 Protestants used it as an opportunity to make their presence felt, singing Psalms in public and insulting priests and Catholics and ransacking the Carthusian monastery. The local magistrates made a vain effort to enforce royal ordinances preventing Protestant preaching, which in turn led to a major confrontation on Sunday 16 November, when a large group of Protestants, with a Calvinist preacher called La Faverge at their head, occupied by force an abandoned property known as the 'maison d'Auriol'. The latter belonged to a local noble family and lay on the main street, next door to the local *présidial* court and adjacent to the parish church of Notre-Dame-des-Soubirous, to which there was direct access through its garden. Once they had occupied it, the Protestants attacked, hurling stones and abuse, a funerary procession on the narrow street in front of the property. A large group of Catholics (perhaps up to 4,000–5,000) gathered after Mass in and around, bent on vengeance. In the tumult which followed, at least thirty Protestants were killed.

The fourteen witnesses in question were all Catholics. They included five labourers, a messenger-boy, a carpenter and a cutler, a nineteen-year old law-student, three priests, an attorney and a surgeon. The objective of the inquiry by Guillaume Petri, the usher in question, was not impartial. His aim was to acquire the evidence to prove that the Catholics in Cahors were not guilty of the murder of Protestant victims or disturbing the public peace, but that, on the contrary, they had been provoked, and acted in self-defence. His investigations stopped short of searching for any information relating to the deaths of the individuals in question. A *procès-verbal* attached to the dossier explained that, before he left the town on 2 December, the deputy king's attorney had required him to furnish a signed copy of all his testimonies so that the evidence would not be lost.

The testimonies document five separate 'encounters'. The first took place at an undetermined moment in the house of Antoine Bertault, a prominent Protestant in Cahors. It is recorded by his vineyard labourers, who testified to what they heard as they sat around the supper table.[43] They recorded the comings and goings of people from outside the town, and their accounts of Protestant uprisings nearby at Villefranche-en-Rouergue, at Montauban, at Moncucq, and at Sarlat in the Périgord – all towns no more than about 60 kilometres away. There heard discussions about Cahors itself, someone saying that 'they would have a [Protestant] temple in that town, whatever the judicial and town authorities decided, and that if there was resistance, they would cut the throats of those who tried to stop them'.[44] They would smash and burn the images, throw anyone who tried to turn the belfry into a strong-hold 'from the top to the bottom' and turn priests out of the pulpit.[45] One of the priests in question, Raymond Alric, documented the 'many blasphemies against the Catholic faith' which he had heard.[46] There was some loose talk about how 'they should no longer be paying taxes to the king or other temporal lords'.[47] Pierre Noguié overheard the city magistrates being derided (called with a rude pun, 'vergers'), the people saying that they 'wanted to be liberal ('liberaux') without paying any tribute, taxes or loans to the king or to the church, saying that these were all larcenies put upon the people'.[48] One of the labourers in question mentioned attempts to persuade him to attend a preaching.[49] Another recorded how he was put under pressure to have a new-born child baptised as a Protestant.[50]

Antoine Cantagrelh, another labourer also present in the Bertault house-hold, recalled an angry altercation with a Protestant student over supper. His hat was knocked off and he was slapped round the head by the student in question. The latter apparently taunted him with how old peasant 'clogs' ('esclopets') like him were not worth a halfpence. He retorted 'that the peasants and people were good folk ('gens de bien') when compared with Huguenots'.[51] Two witnesses testified to a matter of 'common fame'. One of the chamber-maids in the household had given birth to an illegitimate child by a journeyman charcoal-worker ('peyrolier').[52] Bertault had the Protestant minister marry the couple, but the chambermaid died in child-birth, leaving her child to be baptised a Protestant. No one knew where the mother was buried, and the affair had been hushed up. The witnesses in question sought to bring this Protestant household into disrepute. That domestic contention was the con-text for the more public verbal encounters which would follow.

The next set of incidents took place on the streets of Cahors on 28 October, the day of the annual fair. That was also when a Protestant preaching took place in a makeshift temple at the house of one of its prominent Protestants. Protestants were reportedly carrying firearms.[53] There were rumours that they had stacks of weapons and supporters ready to take it by force and it was common knowledge that they were raising money.[54] When the city consuls attempted to enforce royal ordinances against Protestant preaching, it resulted in violent encounters. Bertault himself seized one of the town consuls by the beard. From the window, an onlooker shouted abuse (in dialect) to the consul.[55] Etienne Raffi, the messenger-boy, reportedly heard someone say 'that they feared neither king nor magistrate'.[56] Raymond Alric, priest in charge at the parish of St Laurent, heard three Protestants agree that, 'even if it had a seal as big as his hat it would be worthless because they feared neither king nor queen'.[57] Antoine Cantagrelh, the labourer, testified with his mark that he heard them say that 'they feared 'ni roy ni roc' ('roc' being the popular term for the castle in chess, the origins of the English 'rook').[58] Etienne Raffi reported that 'they feared neither king nor magistrate'.[59] These minor differences in the memorised forms of what people had said are somewhat reassuring, a clue as to how individuals internalised what they had heard, transforming it into a form that was consonant with memory or their own forms of expression, but bearing a detectible relationship to the substance of what had been said at the time.

Rumours and taunts evidently contributed to the events of the day of the festival. The priest Gerauld Tauriac was persuaded by the rumour that the Protestants wanted to 'capture the minster' ('moustier', i.e. cathedral)' and destroy 'all that was inside'.[60] The priest Guillaume Raffi said that he 'heard say' that they called priests like him 'evil executioners, papists, idolaters, abusers'.[61] Jehan Lasalle, another priest, added that they called the pope, archbishops and bishops 'antichrists and idols'.[62] The law student, Jehan Vitalis added that he heard one of them declare that 'all goods should be in common and they should be shared amongst them all'.[63] This discourse of social levelling and political radicalism was heard elsewhere in the region. Ten days after the Cahors massacre of 16 November 1561, the baron de Fumel was assassinated in his own château, only 55 kilometres from Cahors.[64] The king's lieutenant Blaise de Monluc's *Commentaires* are about as full of supposedly recorded speech as any memoirs from this period, and he recalled in detail the outrageous things he heard, 'terribles langages et outrageuses parolles' as he moved up-country to investigate the Fumel affair.[65]

The last encounter reported by this small group of testimonies took place on the streets and in and around the parish church adjacent to 'maison d'Auriole'. The evidence allows one to construct the possible interplay between verbal and physical violence. All the witness accounts testify to the interaction between them. From the occupied house, as the funerary procession passed by on the street outside, Raymond Alric recalled how Protestants made mock wailing noises and threw stones. Other witnesses testified to the affronts to honour and status as well as religious contestation that contributed to the dynamics of confrontation. There were also those who, aware of the dangers of the situation, tried to prevent the intermixture of verbal and physical violence. Pierre Benoist, an attorney at the local *présidial* court was having breakfast with the archdeacon as this incident of the funerary procession began. He vouchsafed to the conversation around the breakfast table, leading to the archdeacon's refusal of the request from the consuls to ring the tocsin bell of the cathedral for fear of inflaming the situation still further.[66]

This small set of depositions illuminates the role of verbal violence in a local environment in one short period, emphasising how it interpenetrated domestic as well as public spaces. But it also provides some reassurance that what the 'memorialists' are trying to tell us about its role and its significance carries a degree of authenticity. Andy Wood has claimed that we can recover the voices from sixteenth-century English rebels, even if only in the trace elements of what is recorded by their antagonists, and the almost proverbial ventriloquism of it in later accounts.[67] Why should we not recover something about the disputed role of language from the fractured and incomplete record of sixteenth-century French sectarian violence?

Language is about power, and some are more skilled in the control of language than others, just as social norms accord some a greater degree of hegemony through the use of language than others. Stefano Guazzo (in his well-known Italian treatise on *Civil Conversation*, first published in a French translation by François de Belleforest in 1579) quoted the proverbial saying: 'when the rich speak, everyone is silent, but when the poor open their mouths to speak, people ask who is that who is speaking?'[68] Who is allowed to speak, in what contexts, and the extent to which what they say is regarded as worth hearing, are essential parts of the relationship between language and conflict. Guazzo's was just one of the emerging conduct books in which the conventions of politeness were extended to being prudent in one's speech, not speaking out of turn, interrupting, raising one's voice or failing to observe the norms of speaking applicably in particular social settings. French Protestants repeatedly transgressed these conventions in the period before and during the height of the sectarian hatreds. More significant in the French civil wars than the 'world turned upside down' was the 'word turned upside down': *parrhesia*, 'speaking one's mind', refusing to accept that it was wrong to speak out boldly. In the interrogations of Huguenots before clergy and magistrates, published and popularised by the French martyrologist Jean Crespin, unlearned men and women repeatedly challenged the learned, spoke out of turn, challenged those in authority, showed them verbal disrespect and argued with them

in ways that disregarded the conventions of academic debate. Jean de Crues
from Flanders, for example, was a 'simple tradesman' who, by his own account,
spoke sharply ('asses asprement') to his judge, challenging him with vernacular
Biblical citations on key issues.[69] Blind André Michel from Tournai put his
hands over his ears when confronted by his interrogators. The Jesuit fathers,
sent to reason with him, eventually became so exasperated by his behaviour
towards them that they declared him damned.[70] French Protestants en route
to their execution, and in their last dying speeches, proclaimed their beliefs
(leading to the use of the 'baillon' or ball-gag to prevent their doing so) rather
than obey the conventional behaviour of the convicted, penitent criminal.[71]
When afforded the opportunity for a dispute with Catholic priests, Protestant
pastors seized the opportunity, but aggressively and on their own terms. The
pastor at Vassy found himself confronted before his congregation in the barn
which served as a church by the Bishop of Châlons-sur-Marne on 16 December
1561. The bishop had seigneurial rights as well as diocesan jurisdiction in that
neighbourhood. But the pastor stood his ground, saying that he was in the
pulpit first, and demanding that the bishop (addressed as plain 'Monsieur')
hear him out. When the bishop interrupted him, the congregation joined
in the fun as the pastor repeatedly questioned Episcopal authority. The bishop
was forced to retired to jeering calls from the congregation ('wolf', 'fox',
'ass', 'back to school', etc.).[72] By then, Catholic homilies were often reportedly
interrupted by individuals in the congregation, arguing with them or making
hostile comments. In Rouen, a barber's journeyman stood up in a Franciscan's
sermon on the sacraments to contest his assertion that there were seven of
them. That was also a subject on the agenda for a bitter, semi-public speaking contest, held in the wake of the first edict of pacification, perhaps in
late 1563 at the château at Nantes, presided over by Jean de Bretagne, Duke
d'Etampes, king's lieutenant in lower Brittany. In the account published
by Jacques Dupré, *théologal* (diocesan theologian) of the cathedral church,
he disparaged the 'insolence' of the two pastors in question, who seized the
initiative by demanding that they pray in public and sing a Psalm before
the proceedings began.[73] The fact that they did not have a common language
of prayer became a subject of contention, even before the main theological
dispute commenced.

That challenge of the 'word turned upside down' may, at least in part,
have been responsible for the more combative and engaged sort of Catholic
preaching which emerged towards the beginning of the French wars of
religion. A distinctive change from the sedate, conservative, Latinate styles
of preaching, unrelated to the real world, it worried some contemporaries,
but attracted many more.[74] Claude Haton, a priest at Provins, was among the
latter. His diary records his impression of visiting preachers to the town, and
his assessments were those of a professional who was in regular touch with

distinguished Parisian theologians and sermonisers. In Lent 1560, he attended those of the Dominican prior from Auxerre, Pierre d'Yvolé (or 'Dyvolé').[75] Dyvolé cut an impressive figure in the pulpit with his 'huge corpulence, a squint in one eye, ruddy in complexion and plain-speaking, four-square ('droit de corps'). He had earned his reputation as a 'great exterminator of false doctrines and mighty adversary of Huguenot heretics'. A version of the sermons he gave as guest preacher in Chartres cathedral in 1558 was published years later (by Simon Vigor) in 1577. 'There are two wars going on', he told the audience in Chartres, 'one spiritual, and the other temporal'. The spiritual war is carried on by the heretics and infidels who try to corrupt the true faith. They are assisted by invisible enemies (devils) who assist them by their beguiling temptations. The result is that, here below, Satan now reigns, and holds the world in blindness. The Great Dragon (heresy) of the Book of Revelation is in their midst. Haton was impressed with the immediacy of Dyvolé's message. Even Protestants in Provins attended, if only to see if they could find an opportunity to 'accuse and impugn him if he said something contrary to the wishes of the government and its edicts'.[76] What impressed Haton was that Dyvolé put into words what people in Provins, especially in the wake of the conspiracy of Amboise, were thinking. He 'revealed entirely and in its true light, the design and purpose of the Huguenots of France, declaring it out loud . . . he predicted the evil that they would in no time at all, wreak in France, and how and in what ways they raise arms and seditions against God, the Roman Catholic religion, against the king, his state, and the public quiet of the realm'.[77] Had he not declared from the pulpit that the Huguenots aimed 'to exterminate the king and his state' and that God permitted Catholics in these circumstances (citing Abraham, Moses and David) to act in self-defence? Had not the Scriptures presaged that a royal minority was a sign of God's wrath?[78]

Political authority was dependant on a certain respect for the word, on the status of those who declared it, and the obedience of those who heard it. There was nothing harder, however, than trying to enforce that respect by means of the law. Seditious libel was not a defined category in French law, but a residual case of *lèse-majesté*, the ill-defined and broadly defined notion of treason, for which only the Ordinances of Villers-Cotteretz of 1539 provided much by way of definition in law. The same vagueness surrounded the notion of 'slander' ('injure'; or 'injure atroce', from the Roman law notion of 'injuria').[79] French lawyers distinguished three kinds of 'injure' – 'aut re, aut verbis, aut scripto' ('in act, in word, and in writing'). Actions were extensible to gestures (e.g. fixing horns upon someone's door) and were generally treated as much more serious than what was written, which was, in turn, more important than what was said. What mattered was 'calumny', and that was judged according to the intentions of the defendant in question and the demonstrable effect of the slander in terms of loss of reputation or honour. In practice, it was easy to mount a defence to the charge of verbal calumny on the grounds of provocation, and the courts were really only interested in calumny when it was reinforced by a defamatory act.

The bailiff in Provins quickly discovered that there were more immediate, political difficulties in trying to pursue a preacher for sedition. Stirred into action by Dyvolé's provocative sermon, he sought sworn testimonies of what had been said. Dyvolé returned to the pulpit the following Sunday, offering to help him with an attestation, signed in his own blood, that he had said: 'that cursed is the land and the country which has a young child for its king, and which has princes who are the disloyal companions of scoundrels!'. He had only cited the words of Holy Scripture, after all. The bailiff soon had the congregation in question openly criticising him. And when he arrived at the royal court in Fontainebleau to present his preliminary report, he was met by the imposing presence of François, Duke of Guise, who had been alerted to the case by his almoner, Nicolas Chanterene. Guise gave him a dressing down, accusing the bailiff of not being able to keep order in his own town, a humiliation to which Dyvolé would allude in his final sermon. The poor bailiff discovered that the word had acquired a moral authority and credibility that was not in his hands, or in his office, to deliver. The 'ceremonies of information', on which the French state rested so heavily for the embodiment of the 'word' were in the process of being devalued.[80]

That was the fate, too, of a sequence of royal efforts in the initial months of the minority of Charles IX, seeking to calm growing unrest by outlawing the uttering of humiliating or provocative words in public. One of the very first proclamations in Charles IX's name was to forbid the use of all kinds of verbal violence in public places on pain of death.[81] It was reinforced by separate letters missive, and then later by royal ordinances.[82] These led up to the general edict of 31 July 1561, which included a specific clause against Catholic preachers who used 'insults and words of invective' from the pulpit, and requiring them to read out an injunction before each sermon was preached. Verbal violence had become, almost overnight, a serious offence. The legal groundwork was being laid for the ambitious clauses in the edicts of pacification, from 1563 onwards, which forbad verbal insults and hate-speech in religious matters, on pain of prosecution in the royal courts. Initially, however, such an intrusion of the state into what people could say in public must have felt unfamiliar and alien, making them conscious of what they were saying (and who might record it), and where, and proposing the flimsiest of distinctions between what was 'good' and 'bad' speech.

Such a change was bound to be contested. Claude Haton provides us with an early example of someone who did just that. He recalls the Franciscan Jehan Barrier coming to preach at Provins in the wake of the July 1561 edict. From the pulpit he read out the required injunction, paused and then continued:[83]

> And so, people of Provins, what should I and other preachers in France, do? Should we obey this injunction? What would you that I should preach? The Word, says Monsieur the Huguenot, by which he means the errors of Calvin, Martin Luther, Beza, Peter Martyr and other preachers with their erroneous and cursed doctrine, condemned for a millennium by the church and by its holy and general councils as worthless, damnable and not God's word at all. To declare loud and clear that the Huguenot heretics of France are evil apostates, that they have renounced the true Catholic Church to follow their heretic ways, is that not to preach the Word? . . . Yet someone could say to me: Brother, what are you saying? You are disobeying the king's edict. You are calling Calvin and his companions . . . heretics and Huguenots. You will be prosecuted, put in prison and hanged for sedition! I reply that it is likely true, for Ahab and Jezabel put true prophets to death in their day and gave free rein to the false prophets of Baal. Brother, that's going too far, you will be hanged! Ah well, by God, that's one Franciscan hanged. They will have to hang many more; for God, through his Holy Spirit, will inspire the pillars of his church right to its foundation, and it will never be ruined until the end of the world, whatever blows befall it.

Barrier was right. There were plenty of preachers in 1561 willing to denounce openly from the pulpit what seemed to be an outrageous infringement upon their vocation, an alien intrusion by the state into their domain. In reality, there was not much in the short term that could be done to control seditious preaching when there was no diocesan licensing of preachers, almost no Episcopal authority over the preaching of those in regular orders in their diocese and a marked reluctance by urban authorities to become involved in monitoring what was said from the pulpit, more especially when preachers were only saying out loud what many of them were thinking and saying in private.

Setting the word back to rights, so to speak, in the sense of distancing language and conflict in a contested religious context, would take a generation and more. It was partly achieved through the patient efforts of the commissioners for the edicts of pacification, masters of requests and senior magistrates from the sovereign courts, accompanied by Huguenot nominees as well in the later edicts of pacification, despatched to localities to settle particular issues and disputes arising from the terms of the edicts. They applied a form of equitable jurisdiction, seeking to place within a framework of justice issues which had lain outside it.[84] Their achievement was not to magic confessional conflict away, but to relocate it in a judicial and political framework over which the king had a monopoly. That framework was dominated by written petitions, attested evidence and courtroom discussions in which the rules of verbal engagement were firmly in place. The grammar of sectarian conflict, as it were, was changed. Commissioners insisted on the proper decorum and respect to be accorded by both sides to one another. They enforced the terms of the edict against those who slandered one another on religious grounds in the street. When the commissioners Le Cirier and Lamoignon arrived in Amiens in August 1563, one of their early measures was to issue instructions in the king's name that no one was to 'offend one another in deed or word' on the grounds of religion.[85] When Michel Larchie verbally assaulted a Protestant on the streets of the city in contravention of their ruling, he was fined 20s.[86] A potter called Jehan Guiot brought a suit before them for having been called a 'Huguenot' and won himself 20s in compensation from his accuser.[87] The government of the Regent Catherine de Médicis offered a collective and individual right of remonstrance to Protestants at the royal court as a way of short-circuiting rumours and libels, a right that was maintained, albeit uncertainly, throughout much of the wars of religion and beyond. For Queen Catherine, as for her chancellor Michel de l'Hospital and other notables, peace could only be fostered by talking, by which they meant replacing war with words, language being a God-given human capability, on which civil society (as Stefano Guazzo had insisted) ultimately rested.[88] Commissioners required written evidence to be submitted for their consideration. Simply verbal assertions would not do. Arguments against where to site a Huguenot cemetery or place of worship had to be couched not in theological, still less eschatological, language, but in terms of the mundane (the risks to the security of the town and the state, etc.).

The commissioners would not have succeeded, however, if similar processes were not at work elsewhere in the French polity. One of the effects of the edicts of pacification and the recovery of royal authority was the re-establishment of the 'word' of local magistrates, consuls and bailiffs and their progressive distanciation from sectarian language and deeds.[89] The opportunities for verbal violence were reduced by taking the situations which might give rise to them off the streets and into the council chambers. There, representatives of the contending faiths could agree 'pacts of friendship', incongruous amidst the continuing civil wars, but aimed at protecting a local community from the dangerous conflicts coming from without. How they swore is a vignette of the oral rupture which had occurred as a result of the sectarian conflicts. It was typically not on the basis of an 'oath' ('serment') since an oath, sworn on the Holy Scriptures, before an image of the crucifixion, in the presence of a priest and solemnised by a Mass was no longer credible. Where, as at Lectoure, there was an oral agreement, Protestants made their testimony 'to the living God, raising their hands' ('au Dieu vivant, levant leurs mains'). More generally, they were called 'agreements' ('accord'; 'entente'; 'contrat'; 'confédération') and were signed, witnessed by notaries and sealed by a handshake or exchange of pledges. Although there were probably more of these 'pacts' than we are currently aware of, they remained limited in time and space.[90] Often agreed verbally among leaders of local communities, their aim was to shore up local solidarity against the divisive effects of rumour and verbal violence, and all those that might seek to 'instrumentalise' them. The dominant language was that of 'friendship'. At Millau, in September 1572, the two communities swore to one another to be 'neighbours and friends, loving and cherishing one another'.[91] At nearby St-Affrique, Protestants and Catholics agreed that same month 'between inhabitants and citizens [that] there would be peace, concord, love and friendship'. At Annonay, inhabitants agreed among themselves in October 1567 not to 'shout abuse at or offend one another' ('s'entre injurier ni offenser') whilst at Caen, that same month, their pact committed them not to 'offend one another in word or deed, not to provoke in any way, not to distribute false rumours, handbills or placards tending towards any sort of riot or sedition'.[92] In south-west France, the inhabitants of Grenade-sur-Garonne agreed in mid-May 1562, as news of the bloody insurrection in Toulouse reached them, that all those preaching in the town ('ministres', 'prebstres' and 'moynes') should moderate the language that they used in the pulpit whilst they committed one another to 'live and behave together in good peace, union and concord, as brethren and good citizens'.[93]

Consistorial Protestantism perhaps played its part as well in rendering the word once more into a social stable and less conflictual medium. Consistories were concerned to the point of obsession with the need to bridle the human tongue and its capacity to undermine the godly society through blasphemy or slander. The evidence from the detailed examination of the scattered surviving consistorial registers suggests an intrusive concern for what was said, both in private and in public, matched by a language of censure.[94] Huguenot magistrates in cities like Castres and Pau found themselves 'speaking the king's language' as they collaborated in the enforcement of the edicts of pacification, or heard the cases coming on appeal before the bi-confessional legal tribunals, established by the edicts of pacification.[95] Meanwhile, Huguenot pastors willingly engaged in formal, organised inter-confessional 'conferences', with Catholic theologians and polemicists. In part, the inheritors of the medieval 'disputatio', such verbal confrontations adopted the rules of academic disputation. Like a game of chess, the latter restricted the game to professional players, and constrained them to play by its rules. These rules did not preclude participants from adopting polemical strategies to undermine their opponents – verbal intimidation, *ad hominem* arguments and ridicule – as well as the well-established techniques of demonstrating non sequiturs, or undermining the evidence or relevance adduced by one's opponents.[96] In part, jousting tournaments in which opponents had the opportunity to inflict intellectual damage upon one another, they also served to domiciliate controversy, taking it off the streets and into a more neutral, gentrified space in which there were social conventions as well as ground rules for the handling of argument.

The social conventions were dictated by the locations of the conferences, and the audiences before which they took place.[97] They were often held in college precincts, or in the salons of prominent nobles. Catholic churches or Protestant temples were never used, since they did not provide the necessary neutral terrain on which a conference necessarily had to proceed. The audience was by invitation and from a literate background. It was often, by mutual agreement, a restricted one. Jean de l'Espine, for example, only agreed to participate in the 1566 conference in Paris if it was 'in the presence of a few people'. Gentien Hervet took part in a conference at Gravant in the Orléanais on the understanding that there would only be 'two or three honest folk present, with the books to hand'. It was, he said, 'to be feared otherwise that there might be some unrest stirred up among the people (who one could not negotiate with as one might like)'.[98] The conferences often included well-born women as well as men, who participated, or at least intervened, by way of questions, interjections or encouragement. It was generally the decision of the moderator to bring the proceedings to a conclusion. Both sides knew that the proceedings would, in due course, probably be published. The occasion for the conference was often a well-publicised conversion or abjuration, especially of an aristocratic lady. In July 1566, one such conference took place in the hotel of the Duke of Nevers in Paris, its occasion being the conversion to Protestantism of the Duke of Montpensier's daughter, who had married the Duke of Bouillon.[99] At least a hundred people attended the week-long joust between Arnaud-Guillaume Barbaste, Jeanne d'Albret's almoner and Guillaume Ruzé, royal confessor and tutor to the Duke of Montpensier's son, and their various companions. Some attended to surprise them, some with their gibes, others with their insults, and others with their threats.[100] On the sixth day of the conference, the duke of Nevers declared that the proceedings had taken long enough and that the debates should thereafter continue in writing, his secretary acting as the intermediary. The 1609 conference between the Huguenot controversialist and pastor at Paris/Charenton, Pierre Du Moulin and the noted 'conferencier' Père Jean Gontier took place in Paris at the house of Monsieur de Liembrune, attended by a room 'pleine de Dames', invited there by Madame de Mazencourt. Marguerite Hurault de l'Hospital, Baronne de Salignac, even took the place of Gontier towards the end of the conference, and tried to impress Du Moulin with her patristic learning. The wife of Monsieur de Liembrune sat in a corner and burst into tears when the debate grew tense.[101]

The ground-rules for the conferences were established by those of academic disputations. These were sometimes arranged in advance, those for the conference in July 1566 in Paris taking a week of preliminary negotiations to set up. They included the number of participants, the subjects to be debated, the means of recording the debates, and the books that each side were allowed to consult. Sometimes both sides agreed to abide by rules of politeness. At Orléans in 1563, the theologians involved in a conference agreed to 'confer without obstinacy or bitterness'. There was often a deliberate attempt to distinguish a 'conference' from the normal cut and thrust of religious polemic, if only in the pretention that the exercise has as its objective the discovery of a truth that both sides could agree on. That objective, of course, was unrealisable. Yet it was the reason why there was a strict codification of the engagements, and therefore the limitation of the capacity of either side to do damage to the other.

The oral memory of the verbal violence of the French civil wars, however, lived on, embalmed in a marginalised popular culture in which it became 'folksonomised' and 'euphemised'. The Huguenot chants and Catholic *contrefacta* would be remembered, and sung in the seventeenth century. The physical violence of the civil wars would be remembered in local speech-forms. Around Argentan, if someone had been violently killed, it was said that they had been 'sent to Carlat', a speech-memory of a Protestant sergeant-at-arms, Jaubert Bastide, who had been murdered there in 1562. At Tours, the massacres were recalled in the form of euphemisms: 'Take him to see Monsieur du Pont, Monsieur de la Riviere, Monsieur de la Mare'.[102] 'Laschez la grande levrière' became a proverbial expression, meaning 'to go all out', first used in the early 1560s to describe the proscription of Huguenots from French towns and countryside.[103] 'Vive la Croix!' lived on in the Toulouse verbal memory-bank into the seventeenth century as the oral touchstone for that same proscription, commemorated in a tablet in marble on the house of the capitouls (its municipal officials) by order of the Parlement, its edict cried out round the city each year and accompanied by a solemn procession. The memory of verbal conflict was the hardest of all memories to eradicate in the seventeenth century.

NOTES

1 Peter Burke and R. Porter (eds), *The Social History of Language* (Cambridge, 1987), p. 1.
2 Georg Baum and Edouard Cunitz (eds) *[ascrib: Théodore de Bèze]*, *Histoire ecclésiastique des églises réformées du Royaume de France* (3 vols, Paris, 1883–9) (henceforth 'HE'), vol. ii, p. 651 ('crians et hurlans: Voilà la verité perdue, la verité de tous les diables, voilà le Dieu le fort, l'Éternel'; 'Voilà la verité de tous les diables noyée').
3 Ibid., vol. ii, p. 598.
4 Ibid., vol. ii, p. 603 ('à haute voix que cela estoit trop villain & qu'elle n'en vouloit point, & disant cela, frappe le prestre de toute sa puissance').

5 Ibid., p. 604 ('avec horribles blasphèmes, appelans Dieu par risée l'Éternel & le fort, & mesmes desgorgeans choses execrables contre la vierge Marie').

6 Ibid., vol. iii, p. 18 ('il n'y avoit que cris & lamentations espouvantables des pauvres innocens').

7 Ibid., vol. iii, p. 87 ('un horrible débat par les rues').

8 For the continuing significance of the 'face-to-face' society in early modern Europe, and a (controversial) view of its gradual attenuation, see Rudolf Schlögl, 'Vergesellschaftung unter Anwesenden: Zur Kommunikativen Form des Politischen in der vormodernen Stadt', in Schlögl (ed.), *Interaktion und Herrschaft: Die Politik der frühneuzeitlichen Stadt* (Konstanz, 2004), pp. 9–59; Schlögl, 'Kommunikation und Vergesellschaftung unter Anwesenden: Formen des Sozialen und ihre Transformation in der Frühen Neuzeit', *Geschichte und Gesellschaft*, 34 (2008), 155–224; Schlögl, 'Politik Beobachten: Öffentlichkeit und Medien in der Frühen Neuzeit', *Zeitschrift für Historische Forschung*, 35 (2008), 581–616. Cf. Adam Fox, *Oral and Literate Culture in England, 1500–1700* (Oxford, 2000).

9 HE, vol. iii, p. 5 ('Tués tout, pillés tout: nous sommes vos pères, nous vous garentirons').

10 Ibid., vol. ii, p. 681.

11 Simon Goulart, 'Relation du massacre de la Saint-Barthélemy', in L. Cimber and F. Danjou (eds), *Archives curieuses de l'histoire de France* (Paris, 1835), series 1, vol. vii, p. 122 ('"Courage, soldats; nous avons heureusement commencé; allons aux autres, car le Roy le commande." Et répétoit souvent à haute voix ces paroles: "Le Roy le commande, c'est la volonté du Roy, c'est son exprès commandement"'). Cf. Barbara B. Diefendorf, *Beneath the Cross: Catholics and Huguenots in Sixteenth-Century Paris* (New York and Oxford, 1991), p. 99; Denis Crouzet, *La nuit de la Saint-Barthélemy: un rêve perdu de la renaissance* (Paris, 1994), p. 409.

12 HE, vol. ii, p. 834 ('qu'en telle diversité de bruits semés par la France, mesmes sous le nom de monsieur le Prince de Condé, touchant la captivité du Roy & de la Royne mere, on ne se doit si legerement avancer à recevoir tous mandemens, quelques apparences de marques & sceaux qu'ils ayent, veu le bas aage d'iceluy, & qu'on maintient que sa volonté est forcée').

13 HE, vol. ii, p. 426 ('le bruit que ceux de la Religion les menaçoient de faire couler leur sang par les rues').

14 Ibid., vol. ii, p. 578.

15 Psalm 124 (in the Clément Marot metrical version): 'Or, peut bien dire Israel maintenant, / Si le Seigneur pour nous n'eust point esté / Si le Seigneur nostre droit n'eust porté / Quand tout le monde à grand fureur venant / Pour nous meurtrir dessus nous s'est iecté'.

16 HE, vol. ii, p. 615 ('Et n'estoient ces propos seditieux entre le commun peuple seulement, mais en la bouche des plus grands, c'est-à-dire des plus mutins').

17 Mathilde Bernard, *Ecrire la Peur à l'époque des guerres de Religion: Une étude des historiens et mémorialistes contemporains des guerres civiles en France (1562–1598)* (Paris, 2010), p. 14.

18 Michel de Montaigne, *Les Essais*, ed. Pierre Villey (2 vols, Paris, 1921), vol. i, chapter 21.

19 Ibid., p. 131.

20 HE, vol. iii, p. 560.

21 Ibid., vol. i, p. 120 (pour faire un beau banquet, et puis paillarder pesle mesle les chandelles estainctes').

22 Ibid., vol. i, p. 143.

23 Denis Crouzet, *Les guerriers de Dieu: la violence au temps des troubles de religion vers 1525–vers 1610* (2 vols, Paris, 1990), vol. i, p. 244.

24 AM Dijon, D63 (8 March 1564). I am grateful to Luc Racaut for this reference.

25 See Penny Roberts, 'Peace, ritual and sexual violence during the Religious Wars', in Graeme Murdock, Penny Roberts and Andrew Spicer (eds), *Ritual and Violence: Natalie Zemon Davis and Early Modern France*, Past and Present Society Supplement, No. 7 (Oxford, 2012), pp. 86–7.

26 Judith Pollmann, 'Hey ho, let the cup go round! Singing for reformation in the sixteenth century', in Heinz Schilling and Istvan György Tóth (eds), *Religion and Cultural Exchange in Europe, 1400–1700* (Cambridge, 2007), pp. 294–316. At Gien, for example, Protestants were grossly offended in 1562 by the 'infinis blasphèmes' of their opponents, singing 'certains couplets des Psaumes de David, avec risée & moqueries de Dieu' (HE, vol. ii, p. 534).

27 HE, vol. iii, p. 119. The Marot text: 'Le Dieu, le fort, l'Eternel parlera . . .' was transposed into: 'Le Dieu le fou . . .'.

28 HE, vol. ii, p. 784 ('chansons, paroles, gestes impudiques & paillardises abominables').

29 Ibid., vol. iii, p. 84.

30 Crouzet, *Guerriers de Dieu*, vol. i, p. 253 ('un pierou . . . le foye des huguenots').

31 Ibid., vol. i, p. 256.

32 Ibid., vol. i, p. 298.

33 Charles Read, 'La Saint-Barthélemy à Orléans, racontée par Joh. Wilhelm von Botzheim, étudiant allemand, 1572', *Bulletin de la société de l'histoire du protestantisme français*, 21 (1871), 351 ('tous se félicitaient, se rejouissaient d'avoir enrichi leurs demeures . . . et de les avoir en outre occis presque tous').

34 Crouzet, *Guerriers de Dieu*, vol. i, p. 178.

35 HE, vol. iii, p. 529.

36 HE, vol. iii, p. 59.

37 Peter Burke and Roy Porter (eds), *Language, Self and Society* (Cambridge, 1991), p. 5.

38 Cited Cécile Huchard, *D'encre et de sang: Simon Goulart et la Saint-Barthélemy* (Paris, 2007), p. 12.

39 Ibid.

40 The four accounts in question (the *Vita Colinii*; the *Stratagème, our la ruse de Charles IX* [Capilupi]; the *Reveille-Matin*; and the *Mémoires de l'Estat sous Charles IX*) are compared in Ibid., pp. 218–21.

41 Daniel Rigaud (ed.), *L'insurrection protestante à Cahors en 1561* (Cahors, 2006) (henceforth 'Rigaud').

42 HE, vol. i, pp. 462–3.

43 Rigaud, pp. 41–5 (testimony of Antoine Resinbault), 45–51 (Pierre Noguié), 55–61 (Antoine Cantagrelh).

44 Ibid., p. 47.

45 Ibid., p. 47; cf testimony from Estienne Raffi, p. 64.

46 Ibid., pp. 51–5.

47 Ibid., p. 58.

48 Ibid., p. 47; cf the deposition of Antoine Cantagruelh, p. 58.

49 Ibid., p. 46.

50 Ibid., p. 43.

51 Ibid., p. 56.

52 Ibid., pp. 46–7; cf. p. 52 and p. 67.

53 Ibid., p. 77 (testimony of Me Bernard Baldi, priest at the parish church of Notre Dame de Sobiros).

54 Ibid., pp. 56–8; p. 65.

55 Ibid., p. 56 ('ung viech d'ase pour vous' – that is, 'a donkey's prick for you').

56 Ibid., p. 65 ('qu'ilz ne creignioient roy ne magistratz').

57 Ibid., p. 53 ('que l'ons porroit pourter ung seel que feust si grand que leur chapeau car ilz ne craignoient ny roy ny royne').

58 Ibid., p. 59.

59 Ibid., p. 65.

60 Ibid., p. 76.

61 Ibid., p. 88 ('meschans borreaulx, papistes, ydolatres, abuseurs, etc'); identical depositions from Me Jehan Vitalis, a scholar (p. 89) and Me Jehan Lasalle (p. 95).

62 Ibid., p. 92.

63 Ibid., p. 89 ('que tous les biens sont comungs et que les fault partir entre tous').

64 Serge Brunet, 'De l'Espagnol dedans le Ventre!'. Les catholiques du Sud-Ouest de la France face à la Réforme (Paris, 2007), pp. 50–62.

65 Blaise de Lasseran-Massencôme de Mon[t]luc, Commentaires (Paris, 1626), vol. 5, p. 4.

66 Rigaud, pp. 61–4.

67 Andy Wood, The 1549 Rebellions and the Making of Early Modern England (Cambridge, 2007), chapter 3.

68 Etienne (Stefano) Guazzo, La civile conversation, divisée en quatre livres, trans. François de Belleforest (1609, Paris), book 2, fol. 172v ('ce qui est signifié par cette sentence qui dit que lors que le riche parle, chacun se taist, mais le pauvre, ouvrant la bouche pour parler, on demande qui est celuy qui parle').

69 Daniel Benoît (ed.), Jean Crespin: Histoire des Martyrs persecutez et mis a mort pour la verité de l'Evangile . . . (from 1619 edition) (3 vols, Toulouse, 1885–1888), vol. ii, p. 80.

70 Ibid., vol. ii, p. 214.

71 David Nicholls, 'The theatre of martyrdom in the French reformation', Past and Present, 121 (1988), 49–73.

72 Recounted in Discours entier de la persécution et cruauté exercée en la ville de Vassy (1564), in M. Michaud and M. Poujoulat (eds), Nouvelle Collection des Mémoires (Paris, 1839), vol. vi, pp. 478–80.

73 Jacques du Pré, Conference avec les ministres de Nantes en Bretaigne (Paris, 1564), fols. 8–9 ('l'insolence d'aucuns Ministres de conferer auecques eulx . . . nous ne voulons suivre leur version Françoise, ny Maroter & Bezer [references to Clément Marot and Théodore de Bèze, but also crude double entendres: "marotter" and "baiser"] auecques eulx . . .').

74 Larissa Juliet Taylor, *Soldiers of Christ: Preaching in Late Medieval and Reformation France* (New York, 1992); Larissa Juliet Taylor, *Heresy and Orthodoxy in Sixteenth-Century Paris: François Le Picart and the Beginnings of the Catholic Reformation* (Leiden, 1999).

75 Laurent Bourquin (ed.), *Mémoires de Claude Haton* (4 vols, Paris, 2001–7) (henceforth 'Haton'), vol. i, pp. 171–6.

76 Haton, vol. i, p. 171.

77 Ibid., vol. i, p. 172.

78 Ibid., p. 172 ('Que maudit soit le jeune roy qui gouverne la terre de France! ... Que malheureuse est la terre et le pays qui ont ung jeune enfent pour leur roy, et qui ont des princes qui soyent larrons ni compaignons des larrons.').

79 Emily Butterworth, *Poisoned Words: Slander and Satire in Early Modern France* (London, 2006).

80 Michèle Fogel, *Les cérémonies de l'information dans la France du XVIe au XVIIIe siècle* (Paris, 1989).

81 *Edict du Roy, par lequel il défend à toutes personnes d'entrer en débat, de prendre querelles et de se reprocher aucunes choses les uns aux autres pour le faict de la religion, sur peine de la vie* (Orléans, 1561) – Bibliothèque Nationale de France (henceforth BNF), Rés. F. 1984.

82 *Lettres missives du Roy Charles neufviesme de ce nom, contenantes certaines deffenses pour le faict de la Religion* (Paris, 1560 [Old Style, i.e. 1561]), issued Fontainebleau, 15 February 1561, with explicit prohibition 'à toutes personnes, de quelque estat, qualité ou condition qu'ils soyent, qu'ils n'ayent d'icy en auant, en quelque sorte que ce soit, à disputer, contendre by debatre aucunement entre eulx pour le faict de la Religion, ny à ceste raison se reprocher, iniurier, ne irriter l'vn l'autre de parolles ne de faict ...' (BNF, F 46821(9)); also *Ordonnance du Roy* (Fontainebleau, 3 April 1561) (BNF Fz2232); *Lettres patentes du Roy envoyées à Monsieur le Bailly d'Orléans ...* (Fontainebleau, 19 April 1561) (BNF F 46821(20)).

83 Haton, vol. i, pp. 262–3.

84 Penny Roberts, 'Religious pluralism in practice: the enforcement of the edicts of pacification', in Keith Cameron, Mark Greengrass and Penny Roberts (eds), *The Adventure of Religious Pluralism in Early-Modern France* (Bern, 2000), pp. 31–43; Jérémie Foa, 'Making peace: the commissioners for enforcing the pacification edicts in the reign of Charles IX (1560–1574)', *French History*, 18 (2004), 253–74.

85 AC Amiens, AA 14 fol. 208v, cited in Jérémie Foa, 'Preuves et épreuves: La politisation des conflits confessionnels au début des guerres de Religion', in Olivia Carpi and Philippe Nivet (eds), *Guerre et Politique en Picardie aux époques moderne et contemporaine* (Amiens, 2007), p. 14.

86 Ibid.

87 Ibid., p. 20.

88 Denis Crouzet, *Le haut coeur de Catherine de Médicis* (Paris, 2005), esp. pp. 232ff (on the 'magic of the language of concord'); *La sagesse et le malheur: Michel de l'Hospital, chancelier de France* (Paris, 1998), pp. 364–448 ('l'herméneutique d'un prince de vertu').

89 Olivier Christin, *La paix de religion: L'autonomisation de la raison politique au XVIe siècle* (Paris, 1997).

90 Ibid., pp. 122–32; also Olivier Christin, 'Pactes d'amitié et républicanisme urbain: quelques villes françaises devant la biconfessionalité', in Heinz Duchhardt and Patrice Veit (eds), *Krieg und Frieden im übergang vom Mitterlalter zur Neuzeit: Theorie, Praxis, Bilder* (Mainz, 2000), pp. 157–66; Olivier Christin, ' "Peace must come from us": friendship pacts between the confessions during the Wars of Religion', in Ruth Whelan and Carol Baxter (eds), *Toleration and Religious Identity: The Edict of Nantes and its Implications in France, Britain and Ireland* (Dublin, 2003), chapter 5.

91 Cited by Jérémie Foa, 'Les usages de l'amitié: serments d'obéissance et pactes d'amitié entre protestants et catholiques au début des guerres de religion', in *HAL-SHS [open internet ressource: Institut des Sciences de l'Homme, Lyon]* (Lyon, 2005), p. 9 and references, http://halshs.archives-ouvertes.fr/halshs-00006742/en/ (accessed 18 January 2012).

92 Ibid., p. 10.

93 Jérémie Foa, 'Quelques mots d'amour entre catholiques et protestants du Sud-Ouest au temps des guerres de religion', *Moreana*, 45 (2008), 33–44, at 36.

94 Raymond A. Mentzer, Françoise Moreil and Philippe Chareyre, *Dire l'Interdit: The Vocabulary of Censure and Exclusion in the Early Modern Reformed Tradition* (Leiden, 2010).

95 Amanda Eurich, ' "Speaking the king's language": the Huguenot magistrates of Castres and Pau', in Raymond Mentzer and Andrew Spicer (eds), *Society and Culture in the Huguenot World, 1559-1685* (Cambridge, 2002), pp. 117–38; Stéphane Capot, *Justice et religion en Languedoc au temps de l'édit de Nantes: La chambre de l'édit de Castres (1579-1679)* (Paris, 1998).

96 Jérémie Foa, 'Le miroir aux clercs: Les disputes théologiques entre catholiques et réformés au début des guerres de Religion', in Vincent Azoulay and Patrick Boucheron (eds), *Le mot qui tue: L'histoire des violences intellectuelles de l'Antiquité à nos jours* (Seyssel, 2008), pp. 130–46.

97 I have not been able to consult the unpublished doctoral thesis of Isabelle Hentz-Dubail, 'De la logique à la civilité: disputes et conférences des guerres de religion (1560–1610)' (Ph.D. thesis, Université de Grenoble III, 1999).

98 Cited Foa, 'Le miroir aux clercs', p. 134.

99 *Actes de la dispute & conference tenue à Paris, és mois de Iuillet, & Aoust, 1566, entre deux doctevrs de Sorbonne, & deux Ministres de l'Eglise reformee . . .* (Strasbourg, 1566).

100 Ibid., p. 16 'pour les estonner, aucuns par leurs brocards, autres par leurs iniures, autres par leurs menaces'.

101 [Jean Gontery], *Véritable narré de la conférence entre les sieurs Du Moulin et Gontier [Gontery], secondé par Madame la baronne de Salignac, le samedi onzième d'avril 1609, avec la response du sieur Du Moulin aux lettres du sieur Gontier au Roy sur le sujet de ceste conférence, en laquelle response sont XVII semandes audit Gontier . . .* (1609). Cf. Jacques Pannier, *L'Eglise Réformée de Paris sous Henri IV* (Paris, 1911), ch. 5.

102 HE, vol. ii, p. 697.

103 Ibid., p. 685.

12

How to make a successful plantation: colonial experiment in America

KAREN ORDAHL KUPPERMAN

England's leaders believed that in planting colonies abroad they had the opportunity to create more perfect versions of their own society. These colonies would then both reflect back onto the Old World, opening the way for England to rectify corruption that had crept in there, and offer a demonstration model of a better civil society that people in colonised regions would emulate. The creation of successful versions of English society in novel contexts required virtue, and plantations were always fore-grounded as attempts to carry the blessings of Christianity and its companion, civility, to savage, unreconstructed populations. In short, a principal goal of colonisation, as presented by English promoters in the later sixteenth and early seventeenth centuries, was the increase of virtue in the world.

In order to create successful colonies, planners should have reflected in a systematic way on the forms and foundations of local society in England, and the web of clientage and patronage woven together by mutual obligation that made it function as well as it did. Promoters of American colonies always had one eye on Ireland and on the poor record of England's plantation attempts there. In fact, many were or had been investors in Irish ventures. Because they assumed a mutuality of interests among colonists and investors, and because they assumed everyone involved would have the same desire to see the overall plan succeed, promoters were always dismayed when problems arose. Indeed, all of England's early attempts to plant colonies foundered and most ultimately failed. The first response to problems, on both sides of the Atlantic, was to blame them on personal inadequacy: the wrong sort of people had been sent to the colonies, while the investors back home were venal rather than high-minded, according to analysts. As they tried to figure out why colonies did not thrive, analysts always construed failure as a result of human weakness. The men and women charged with doing the work were always, in retrospect, deemed deficient in character. For all kinds of reasons, critics saw them as inadequate representatives of the very society whose cultural riches they were expected to communicate.

As promoters tried to assign reasons for this inadequacy, the most common answer concluded that the rank and file colonists were drawn from the wrong elements of English society. They were, as promoters of every American region said again and again, 'the very scum of the Land'. The Virginia Company claimed early on that the 'idleness and bestial slouth, of the common sort' led to failure and despair. Captain Ralph Lane, governor of Ralegh's Roanoke colony, wrote to Sir Philip Sidney complaining about the 'wylde menn of myne owene nacione'. At the end of his life, Captain John Smith castigated the Virginia Company: 'Much they blamed us for not converting the Salvages, when those they sent us were little better, if not worse.'[1]

By the time Smith summed up his lifetime of analysing the problems of the American colonies, that view had become conventional wisdom, due in part to his own persuasive books. Sir Francis Bacon reflected on the experience of colonisation in 'Of Plantations', which appeared in the third edition of his *Essays or Counsels, Civill and Morall*, published in 1625. As he wrote, 'It is a Shamefull and Unblessed Thing, to take the Scumme of People, and Wicked Condemned Men, to be the People with whom you Plant.' Not only would their idleness and mischief sap the colony's strength, but also they would 'be quickly weary' and then discredit the plantation at home by their reports.[2]

Colonists also saw the plantations' problems as the result of human failure, but they argued that the true deficiency lay with the leadership. Colonists argued that the men of rank, those supposed to set the standard, were the worst of all, and some in England agreed with that. Smith himself turned the charge of virtue deficiency back on the promoters:

> we did admire how it was possible such wise men could so torment themselves and us with such strange absurdities and impossibilities, making Religion their colour, when all their aime was nothing but present profit, as most plainly appeared by sending us so many Refiners, Gold-smiths, Jewellers, Lapidaries, Stone-cutters, Tabacco-pipe-makers, Imbroderers, Perfumers, Silke-men, with all their appurtenances, but materialls, and all those had great summes out of the common stocke.

Bacon also argued that the expectation of immediate financial gain caused the greatest harm to the project of colonisation.[3]

Virtue emerged as the central issue in every critique of England's colonial efforts. It was a truism that without virtuous people you could not construct a plausible version of English society abroad, and everyone agreed that whatever glue held English society together at home seemed to dissolve when people moved from there. So, given that virtue was apparently not a quality inherent in human nature (or at least English nature), how would colonial sponsors elicit virtuous behaviour?

The first answer had been to select the right kind of people, but that seemed to be impossible. Even those who appeared virtuous at home often turned out otherwise in the colonies. Robert Cushman, who promoted the separatist puritan colony at Plymouth in New England, heard of 'many men gone to that other Plantation in Virginia', men who in England had 'seemed very religious, zealous, and conscionable' but who now 'are become meere worldlings'.[4] Even in puritan Massachusetts Bay, Governor John Winthrop wrote to his wife, 'heere are some persons who never shewed so much wickednesse in England as they have doone heer'.[5] As they analysed their problems, colonial promoters were forced to think about the fundamentals of England's social and political system. England certainly did not lack challenges to the standing order, but leaders saw these as unusual, and mechanisms existed for their resolution. They assumed that a kind of mutuality held English society together, and cast the challenges at home in terms of restoration of that mutuality.[6] Many commentators pictured the beehive as the ideal society. In the hive, every bee knew his role and did it without question, even at the cost of life itself. Selfishness was unknown in the hive and that is how it should be in human relations.[7] The problem was how to achieve this ideal state, and the emerging consensus argued that the solution lay in good government.

The Rev. William Crashaw preached a sermon before the commanders of the great fleet that set out, with a new charter, to renew the Virginia colony in February 1609. In this 'New-yeeres Gift to Virginea', Crashaw argued that virtue is not innate, but rather the product of wise and effective rule. Rather than dwelling on the defects of the early colonists, he urged his listeners to:

> looke into Gods booke, and see who kept with David, and were the beginners of the kingdom of Judah: "There gathered unto David all men that were in trouble, and all that were in debt, and all that were vext in minde: and David was their prince and they were in all about foure hundred." See for their number but foure hundred, and for their qualitie, who were they? three sorts: first, men that had done some trespasses against the lawe, and therefore were in trouble: secondly, such as were in debt and could not pay: thirdly, such as were malcontents at the proceedings of the State in the times of Saul, and discontented at his government. A strange kinde of people, and a poore number (a man would thinke) to be the founders and reformers of such a kingdome.[8]

Like many of his contemporaries, Crashaw implied that the root of the problem lay in England, which also needed reformation. He argued that

> the very excrements of a full and swelling State, if they be removed out of the fat and feeding ground of their native countery, and from the licentiousnesse and too much libertie of the States where they have lived, into a more bare and

barren soile, as every country is at the first, and to a harder course of life, wanting pleasures, and subject to some pinching miseries, and to a strict course of
governement, and severe discipline, doe often become new men, even as it were
cast in a new mould, and become good and worthie instruments and members
of a Common-wealth.

He concluded by pointing again to the 'infallible testimonie' of David's followers,
and the 'base churls' who ridiculed them.[9]

Where Crashaw pointed to the Bible, George Donne, the soldier-son of the
poet, referred to Matteo Ricci's description of the effects of good government
in contemporaneous China: 'Riccius the jesuite, discoursing the prosperity of
China, yields the Reason of it, There is not a Beggar nor an Idle person in it.'[10]

For transatlantic plantations, once faith in innate virtue was given up, the
way to create a hive-like colony seemed obvious: iron control. Migrants would
simply be forced into virtue. In early Virginia, after three disastrous years,
the company authorised the institution of martial law simultaneously with the
publication of Crashaw's sermon. The use of martial law over civilian populations became a flashpoint issue in England, so it is remarkable that the Virginia
Company actually arranged for the code's publication in London, possibly to
reassure investors and the public generally that the colony was being brought
to order.[11]

On the first page, the company made it clear that the institution of martial
law did not rely on the whim of one governor. The laws were introduced
as 'Articles, Orders, and Lawes, Divine, Politique, and Martiall, for the Colony
in Virginea, first established by Sir Thomas Gates, Knight, Lieutenant Generall,
the 24. of May 1610. exemplified and approved by the Right Honourable
Sir Thomas West Knight, Lord Lawair, Lord Governour and Captaine
Generall the 12. of June 1610. Againe exemplified by Sir Thomas Dale Knight,
Marshall, and Deputie Governour, the 22. of June 1611.'[12] Both Dale and
Gates were veterans of the religious wars in the Netherlands, and Dale had
also served in Ireland; thus, they both had experience of martial law and its
implementation. William Strachey, who had been the company's secretary
in Virginia and who saw the code into publication, called Dale 'our present
Ethnarches', a term commonly used for the governors the Romans set over
Jewish provinces.[13] David Konig argues that the administration of justice
under Dale's laws emulated the practice of conciliar administration in the
North of England and in Wales and before that in 'England's marchland
experience in Ireland'; frontier regions required different methods.[14] The major
difference lay in the population over whom the laws extended. In Virginia,
only those in the English plantation were subject to the code; the indigenous
population remained under their own government.

The *Lawes Divine, Morall, and Martiall* lay out the blueprint for the exact
behaviour required to make an English society function well. In his preface

to the Virginia Company, Strachey asked for patience, saying that much of the code would seem 'auncient and common' to the knowledgeable.[15] But the Virginia Company's instructions to Sir Thomas Gates gave him very broad latitude to shape his government and even to depart from their instructions if he believed conditions on the ground warranted it. They also encouraged him to 'proceede rather as a chauncelor than as a judge, rather uppon the naturall right and equity then uppon the nicenes and letter of the lawe which perplexeth in this tender body ... so that a summary and arbitrary way of justice discreetely mingled with those gravities and fourmes of magistracy as shall in your discrecion seeme aptest for you and that place, wilbe of most use both for expedicion and for example'. Gates's instructions, Konig argues, were 'a magna carta for baronial tyranny'. Even in civil war conditions in England, as Barbara Donagan demonstrates, the authorities imposed martial law on civilian populations reluctantly, considering its imposition 'exceptional and unfortunate'. The commissions were strictly limited; most ran for only a few months.[16]

Religion, the first element in a good society, was the first topic taken up in the *Lawes Divine, Morall and Martiall*. The code required attendance at divine service twice a day on weekdays, with ministers to preach sermons on Sundays and Wednesdays. Blasphemy or denial of the Trinity brought the death penalty. Nor was outward conformity enough: according to the code, every man or woman in the colony had to 'give an account of his and their faith, and religion, and repaire unto the Minister, that by his conference with them hee may understand, and gather, whether heretofore they have beene sufficiently instructed, and catechized in the principles and ground of Religion'. Those with an insufficient grasp of religious principles were required 'to repaire often unto him, to receive therein a greater measure of knowledge'.[17]

The 'Articles, Orders, and Lawes, Divine, Politique, and Martiall' occupy the first nineteen pages of Strachey's book. They defined punishments for a variety of crimes from murder and stealing to criticising the Virginia Company, running away to the Indians or dishonest trading. They also sought to create behaviour that would produce liveable conditions. Launderers and laundresses (the code assumed both men and women would do these jobs) were not to

> throw out the water or suds of fowle cloathes, in the open streete, within the Pallizadoes or within forty foote of the same, nor rench, and make cleane, any kettle, pot, or pan, or such like vessell within twenty foote of the olde well, or new Pumpe: nor shall any one aforesaid within lesse then a quarter of one mile from the Pallizadoes, dare to doe the necessities of nature, since by these unmanly, slothfull, and loathsome immodesties, the whole Fort may bee choaked, and poisoned with ill aires.

Colonists were required to keep their houses and the street in front 'sweete and cleane', and their beds 'three foote at least from the ground, as he will answere the contrarie at a martiall Court'. The martial law section repeated the requirement that beds be at least three feet above ground level several times, noting that sleeping on or near the ground 'hath bin the losse of many a man'.[18]

Although presented separately, considerable overlap existed between the 'Articles, Orders, and Lawes' and the martial laws. The first two pages of the martial law section referred back to the preceding articles and specified that violations and crimes committed under the 'Civill and Politique Lawes' just enumerated 'are no lesse subject to the Martiall law, then unto the Civill Magistrate'. This statement reiterated a point already made clear in the way punishments for violations of the law and their adjudication had been expressed in the laws for colonists. For one thing, the stipulated punishments were extremely harsh. Many crimes, from blasphemy to embezzlement to the killing of any breeding animals, even if the animals were the property of the offender, carried the death penalty. Defalcation of duty, especially when it endangered the colony's food supply, provoked similar sanctions:

> What man or woman soever, shall rob any garden, publike or private, being set to weed the same, or wilfully pluck up therin any roote, herbe, or flower, to spoile and wast or steale the same, or robbe any vineyard, or gather up the grapes, or steale any eares of the corne growing, whether in the ground belonging to the same fort or towne where he dwelleth, or in any other, shall be punished with death.

Those guilty of repeat violations of rules, from failure to attend twice-daily church services to short-changing weight on baked and cooked goods would be sent to 'the gallies' for terms of six months to three years. A 'martiall court' set the punishment for many other infractions, including dumping washwater in the fort or failing to work a full day.[19]

Ignorance of the law would be no excuse. The final stipulation in 'Articles, Orders, and Lawes' directed ministers to 'read all these lawes and ordinances, publikely in the assembly of the congregation' weekly before catechism on Sundays. Failure to do so would result in 'his entertainment checkt for that weeke'.[20]

The following fourteen pages of purely martial laws were presented in the first person. Although the 'I' who enunciated these laws, 'appertaining only to martiall discipline', was not identified in the text, the frequently reiterated date of 22 June 1611 for their initiation ties them to Dale. David H. Flaherty argues that Dale drew on the code promulgated by the earl of Leicester in the Netherlands in 1585 and employed by the earl of Essex in Ireland in 1599.[21] The published code endorsed by the earl of Essex is far simpler and briefer.[22] Dale's laws, apparently reflecting the inexperience of the company he governed, spelled out the duties of each rank and the responsibilities of captains, lieutenants, sergeants and corporals, both to their superior officers and to the men serving under them.[23]

As in other codes, the Virginia laws concerned maintaining the chain of command and preventing any failure in duty. The punishment for drawing one's sword in a garrison town or camp was loss of the right hand. Any soldier who 'shall give offence to the Indians' in such a way as to have 'beene cause of breach of their league, and friendship, which with so great travaile, desire, and circumspection, we have or shall at any time obtaine from them without commission so to doe, from him that hath authoritie for the same, shall be punished with death'. The same punishment applied to any soldier who 'negligently' set fire to an Indian's house, religious temple or granary, or who mistreated or ransacked Indians through whose territory the English marched or even with whom the English were at war. As with the civil code, these regulations were to be read out weekly.[24]

In the implementation of these martial laws, as in those for civilians, stated requirements overlapped, and the soldiers worked alongside colonists. Captain John Smith, the last governor under the first charter, required men of all ranks to cooperate for the general good. Drawing on the common metaphor of the beehive, he warned 'the drones' that his own labour provided the benchmark by which the daily accomplishments of others would be judged, and the punishment for falling short involved banishment until the offender indicated a willingness to work. The martial laws that replaced his rule similarly directed soldiers and officers to contribute their labour to the ongoing work of establishing the colony. All colonists, soldiers or civilians would begin and end the workday at the sound of the drum.[25]

Dale's enunciation of the martial laws constantly framed them in the religious purpose of the colony, and England's larger strategic goals. He recurred again and again to the proper roles of elite and rank and file, and the need for all to have security in their stations. He sought to make the 'worthier and better sort understand how well it shall become their Honours, birthes, breedings, reputations, and faithes, to do their bests, and emulously to actuate in this worke, the utmost of their cleerest powers of body and mind, where the travaile of both is so deerly valued, & highly interpreted by al good and wise men'. Reflecting accusations that had already marred life in Virginia, Dale reminded those in command that they must not allow 'wasting the stocke, commodities and provisions of the store . . . and so leave the poore Souldier and Labourer, miserably pilled, oppressed and starved'.[26] While, the 'life of a poor Souldier' was precious, 'how much more pretious his soule', and it was the captain's duty to ensure behaviour that protected both. Ensigns were advised to treat 'inferiours . . . with faire perswasion and all gentlenes, and sweetnes of command'. And each 'privat soldier' was counseled to work hard to do his part in the great work: 'There be many men of meane descent, who have this way attained to great dignity, credit, and honor.' Dale himself began life as a common soldier, so this sentiment reflected his personal experience.[27]

In enumerating the responsibilities of leaders from the marshall to the corporals, Dale took the opportunity to explain again the union of civil and military authority. Like Crashaw, he pointed to the Bible and the organisation of a new polity, citing the Israelites' departure from Egypt 'to make their plantation in the land of Promise'. The 'first and great commander over the Colony of the Children of Israel appointed Captains over Tribes and hundreds for the wars, and Elders to sit upon the bench, (whilest unto himselfe all great causes whether civil or military were brought to direct and determine . . .)'. The multitude of problems that arose in new societies required such a stream-lined mode.[28]

With the martial laws in place, Dale wrote to the Earl of Salisbury in 1611 suggesting that the Virginia Company should now give up trying to find worthy people, and send men who could be compelled to function well through 'severe discipline'. Specifically, Dale recommended that the company should simply make a contract with the government to dispatch all men under judicial sentence of death for the next three years, and offered an unusual justification: 'thus doth the Spaniard people his Indes'. The 'diseased and crased bodies' of the colonists already in Virginia did not constitute good candidates for rectification, even with the laws now in effect. He asked the company to ship 2,000 such men in two separate lots; if they came with provisions to sustain them over the first six months, then Dale promised that the colony would be so well established as to not require further support from home.[29]

The Virginia Company did not take him up on this suggestion, and in fact only small numbers travelled to the colony during the martial law period. Thus, analysts returned to the central problem of virtue, and the even more fundamental question: what are the elements of virtue? Martial law might force a certain level of behaviour, but iron control would not foster the innovation and initiative required to make a success of the venture in the absence of a commodity to be gained in trade with the Indians. Nor could the kind of web of mutuality on which local society ran in England emerge within such a system. Just forcing people to conform to a set of rules, even if it had been possible, would not be enough. For a plantation to succeed, virtue had to include a willingness to innovate, even to take risks. American colonies required develop-ment of new products, crops processed in ways previously unknown on both sides of the Atlantic. Innovation and iron control were ill-suited partners.

Fortunately, for the Virginia colony, iron control never proved possible in the early modern context, and as some colonists moved away from the fort, they began to experiment. Nature also cooperated. A devastating drought had settled on the region just before the foundation of the colony in 1607, but it had lifted by 1614 when John Rolfe started to see success in his efforts to produce a less harsh – and more marketable – tobacco crop than the native variety. Tobacco became Virginia's gold, but it is a voracious consumer of labour and requires taking the long view for the eighteen months between planting and sale.[30]

The kind of innovation represented by Rolfe's experiments with tobacco involved a whole new conception of the Virginia experiment. The original scheme hoped for some readily realisable source of wealth, either through trade with the Indians or through finding a valuable commodity that migrants could pick up and bring home. A small, self-sustaining, largely male settlement would be ideal for this purpose and a military model for such a group seemed logical. Company members may have hoped for a trading station such as those maintained by the Levant or East India Companies, in which people would be rotated home after a tour of duty to be replaced by others. In such a station, the company itself would be the only landowner and the men worked for the company.

The tobacco model – or any kind of agricultural production – required a programme the Virginia Company had sought to avoid at all costs: transfer of labour across the Atlantic, with the expectation that the migrants would consider their move permanent. In addition to the expense involved in such a plan, it also required a fundamentally different relationship between company and settlers. So, the Virginia Company was back where it started: the company needed to be able to send a critical mass of colonists to support new crops and to ensure that they would work productively for the common good. This is where the innovation occurred, a genuine conceptual breakthrough after a decade of failure and thrashing around. How did the company accomplish this? It seems clear that it involved listening to people on the ground to some extent, although there was no open acknowledgement of this fact. Rolfe travelled to England in 1616 with his wife Lady Rebecca, aka Pocahontas, and he may have been one of the people whose experience informed company deliberations.

However it happened, the Virginia Company came up with a dramatically changed vision of colony design and especially of how to solve the virtue conundrum. The answer centred on the concept of devolution, relinquishment of control rather than its intensification. In what came to be known as the headright system, the company offered all who came to the colony fifty acres in something close to freehold once they completed their term of servitude. Those who paid for someone else's passage would receive fifty acres per head. The headright for servants did not last long, although many former servants did become landowners, but it continued in Virginia's sibling colony of Maryland until 1681.

Land did not mean much, though, unless you had a family to pass it on to, so the company also took steps at the same time to send over suitable women to be wives for the planters. The company noted how, 'By long experience we have found that the Minds of our people in Virginia are much dejected, and their hearts enflamed with a desire to return for England only through the wants of the comforts without which God saw that Man could not live contentedly, no not in Paradise.' It would prove impossible 'tie and root the Planters' minds to Virginia' without 'the bonds of wives and children'.[31] It had long been a commonplace in England that a farmer without a wife would not be successful. As Thomas Tusser argued, a man must have his wife with him, 'husbandrie otherwise speedeth not well'.[32]

Land also did not mean much if it could be taxed out from under you, so the company directed the planters to hold a General Assembly, with delegates from all the plantations. This assembly meted out obligations for the public works and dealt with other matters. The company's instructions for all these institutional changes came to be known as the Great Charter. The professional military men all exited the colony as a result of all these changes, with defence placed in the hands of a planter militia. Gates and Dale actually applied for and received remuneration from the Dutch States General for all the while they had been in Virginia, as they had been on leave from their appointments in the Netherlands the entire time.[33]

Now, with this new Magna Carta in place, the colony began to grow dramatically, although the death rate for newcomers, mainly from English malaria, continued to be high. The first Africans famously appeared in the colony in 1619 – in a letter to Sir Edwin Sandys, John Rolfe mentioned the first meeting of the Assembly and news of the colonists' trading food supplies for a Dutch ship's cargo of '20. and odd Negroes'.[34] They were probably not the first Africans in Virginia; early in 1620 census of the Virginia plantations recorded thirty-two Africans, seventeen women and fifteen men.[35] Slavery as it was later defined did not yet exist in the Chesapeake, and some of these Africans lived to achieve their freedom, but they served much longer terms than English indentured servants, who provided the bulk of the labour during the first decades.[36]

The sudden growth of the colony, with tobacco plantations spreading on the best land along Virginia's highways – the rivers that run from the bay to the mountains in the west – forced the Indians to react. On 22 March 1622, the Pamunkeys and their client tribes attacked the plantations in what became known then as the Massacre of 1622. They meant to attack all of them simultaneously, but some were spared – a sign of the complicated relationships already growing up. A decade of warfare ensued. The Indians' great attack of 1622 actually freed planters of oversight from London, and the colony took off in the atmosphere of devolution.[37] Two years later the crown instituted quo warranto proceedings and the company lost its charter. Under royal control, the planters largely ran their own colony. Given hard times in England in the decades of the 1620s and 1630s, those who organised the trade in servants found people willing to take up their offers.

The formation of the Massachusetts Bay Company, a decade after the development of the new design in Virginia, resulted in the massive migration of puritans to New England between 1630 and 1640. Throughout the 1610s and 1620s, Captain John Smith found his true calling as a theorist of colonisation, and he wrote many books drawing the lessons of the Virginia experience. He pointed out the breakthrough made by the Virginia Company and explained why it mattered. In his final book, *Advertisements for the Unexperienced Planters of New England, Or Any where* (1631), he advised the Massachusetts Bay leaders 'not to stand too much upon the letting, setting, or selling those wild Countries, nor impose too much upon the commonalty . . . for present gain'. Giving immigrants land, for 'him and his heirs for ever', would ensure their commitment to the colony and make it a success.[38]

Smith's message was definitely heard. The founders of Massachusetts had clearly read his books and they actually quote him without attribution. The design of every colony henceforth – whether the puritan colony in New England or the Roman Catholic colony in Maryland a few years later – followed the same plan: widespread land ownership, family formation and some form of representative government.

There was one remarkable exception to this pattern – the colony of Providence Island, founded at the same time and with the same colonist profile as Massachusetts Bay, on an island off the coast of Nicaragua. Many Providence Island Company members also sponsored the northern colony, but they thought of it as a holding action; the Caribbean, where they thought the Spanish were ripe for elimination, provided the real focus of interest. These men were the great lay puritans of England: Robert Rich, 2nd earl of Warwick and his cousin, Sir Nathaniel Rich, John Pym, Lord Saye and Sele, Sir Benjamin Rudyerd, Lord Mandeville (soon to be earl of Manchester), Sir Gilbert Gerrard and Lord Brooke. They had studied the record as much as anyone; many were veterans of the Virginia Company and other ventures. But they rejected the conclusions drawn by everyone else. They ascribed previous failure to inadequate supervision and, rather than devolution, they chose the path of micro-management.

The Massachusetts founders made their emigration contingent on taking the charter with them; they actually turned the company charter into their government, free of interference from home. All heads of families became landowners. The Providence Island colonists came from the same kind of carefully selected middling puritan families as went to Massachusetts; the mayor of Banbury, Henry Halhead, for example, went with a group of his citizens. Yet in Providence Island, no colonist was allowed to be a landowner: all were tenants, and at first they were tenants at halves. They had no say in choosing their government, which was selected by the company in London and headed by a professional military man. Ministers were appointed from London and the company greeted with hostility the attempt by some colonists to create a gathered congregation.

What makes this all so remarkable is that the Providence Island Company leaders subsequently led England into Civil War in opposition to Stuart arbitrary rule a little more than a decade later. The year before the creation of the Providence Island Company, Sir Nathaniel Rich argued in his speech against the Forced Loan in 1628, 'No propriety [property], no industry; no industry, all beggars; no propriety, no valor; no valor, all in confusion.'[39] Company members would make such points repeatedly when the Long Parliament assembled.

So, how could they have gone so wrong in planning a government for their colony? It was not that company members forgot about the centrality of property, rather they pointed out that Providence Island was *their* property. By implication, the planters were still clients as they had been in England, all bound together by their devotion to the great goal. The company's micromanagement was a token of their commitment of both time and money to the project and they assumed colonists would value that properly. Establishing a colony, however, composed principally of people committed to the more radical forms of Protestantism proved tricky. In Providence Island, as in Massachusetts, colonists fought over the proper avenue to a godly life. This should not have surprised the investors, but it did. As Sir Benjamin Rudyerd wrote to Governor Philip Bell,

> We well hoped (according to our Intentions) That we had planted a Religious Colony in the Isle of Providence, instead whereof we find the root of bitterness plentifully planted amongst you, an industrious supplanting one of another, and not a Man there of Place (a strange thing to consider) but he doth both accuse, and is accused; these are uncomfortable fruits of Religion.[40]

Virtue apparently dissolved in the colonies.

Providence Island was never a success. The assumption of company members that the sustained commitment of the colonists to mutual goals would carry them through proved wrong. The development of crops in the subtropical environment required experimentation and innovation far beyond that needed in North America. Many years would pass before the planters developed the necessary expertise, and investors learned through bitter experience that colonists would need to be sustained in the meantime. Investors drew on all their contacts, including East India Company resources, to provide a steady stream of slips, seeds and plants to the island, but the colonists never produced a commercially viable crop. Over the years, the desperate planters acquired a large number of enslaved Africans, probably people who had escaped from slavery under the Spanish and been recaptured by Moskito Coast Indians. By 1635, the colony's population of Africans outnumbered those from Europe, the first English colony to achieve this distinction. Barbados would not arrive at these proportions until decades later. Also in 1635, the Providence Island Company won the right to issue letters of marque, which helped investors to recoup some of their outlay. But, given that the colony lay 'in the heart of the Indies & the mouth of the Spaniards', becoming a base for privateers spelled its doom.[41] The third Spanish attack ousted the settlers in 1641, just as a series of events that would lead to civil war in England diverted investors' attention nearer home.

Providence Island Company leaders were heavily involved in England's response to the Irish rebellion of 1641, alongside many puritan colleagues from the Massachusetts colony. In response to the Irish uprising, an impoverished government attempted to field a force funded by private investment, the same mode by which England planted American colonies. Parliament decreed that investors would be paid in the 'many millions of acres of the rebels lands of that kingdom which go under the name of profitable lands'. John Pym worked to get investors from among his parliamentary colleagues, while Lord Brooke was named commander in chief of the forces.

As the gathering crisis in England increasingly diverted attention away from Ireland, the Providence Island investors made one last attempt to keep their patent rights alive in the western Caribbean. In stark contrast to the avalanche of publications associated with other English colonies, no books appeared about the Providence Island colony because the investors retained tight control over the population and the administration. Now, in 1643, a pamphlet surfaced, apparently sponsored by these same investors. It lacked a title page, so authorship and date are uncertain and it may have been intended for relatively private circulation, but the land it described closely corresponds to descriptions of the Moskito Coast by Providence Islanders.

This pamphlet, *Certaine inducements to well minded people, who are heere straitned in their estates or otherwise or such as are willing out of noble and pub[l]ique principles, to tran[s]port themselves, or servants, or agents for them into the West-Indies, for the propagating the Gospell, and increase of trade*, recommended the kind of ownership and control repeatedly opposed by the company, even in the face of insistent demands from the colony. Speed was clearly of the essence. The pamphlet offered six acres within the proposed town and sixty acres elsewhere for every person who went or was sent, provided they arrived within two months of the first landing. Those who arrived within six months would get four acres in town and a fifty-acre holding elsewhere. Those who arrived in the first year but after the first six months would get thirty acres as well as a town lot. An investment of £100 would earn 500 acres. The pamphlet promised a headright for servants, who would get land and a town lot when their indenture expired. This unrealistically precise timetable bespeaks a continued desire to micromanage, but if the Providence Island investors had been willing to offer land in this way at an earlier stage, the trajectory of the colony might have been very different.

Although the drama of civil war forced leaders in America to take sides over the next several years, it also provided an opening for the colonists to develop their own economies and various social regimes. English migration to Massachusetts largely ended with the outbreak of war in England, but the population continued to grow dramatically through natural increase. After the civil war, the migrant stream to all the colonies would comprise British – from Scotland and Ulster – and European dissenters. Before the 1670s, the English government made little effort to control or even to find out much about what was going on across the ocean. Devolution worked in America: the qualities that added up to virtue in the eyes of English leaders emerged most effectively when people laboured and innovated for themselves.

The virtue conundrum rebounded back on England, even with the godly in control. Henry Halhead, leader of the substantial civilian colonists in Providence Island, wrote an impassioned attack on enclosures, published posthumously in 1650. *Inclosure Thrown Open: or Depopulation Depopulated, not by Spades and Mattocks, but by the Word of God* opened with a quotation from Ezekiel 4.1: 'So I returned and considered all the oppressions that are done under the Sun; and behold the tears of such as were oppressed, and they had no comforter. And on the side of their oppressors there was power; but they had no comforter.' Halhead wrote that enclosers worked by convincing common people that they would be three times better off following the enclosure of the land; they did not realize the truth until they had lost their rights. Halhead, comparing himself to a man ringing the fire bell because he has 'seen and felt the danger of it', argued that Parliament ought to rectify these wrongs; instead that body, now under puritan control, was full of enclosers.[42] The lessons of America now needed to be brought home.

NOTES

1 Virginia Company, *A True and Sincere Declaration of the Purpose and End of the Plantation Begun in Virginia* (London, 1610), p. 10; Ralph Lane to Sir Philip Sidney, 12 August 1585 in David Beers Quinn (ed.), *The Roanoke Voyages, 1584–1590* (2 vols, London, 1955), vol. i, pp. 204–6, at p. 204; John Smith, *Advertisements for the Unexperienced Planters of New-England, or Any-Where* (London, 1631), p. 5.
2 Bacon, *Essays or Counsels, Civill and Morall* (London, 1625), pp. 198–204, at pp. 198–9.
3 Smith, *Advertisements*, pp. 4–5; Bacon, *Essays*, pp. 198–9.

4 Robert Cushman, *A Sermon Preached in Plimmoth in New-England* (London, 1622), p. 11.

5 John Winthrop to Margaret Winthrop, 23 July 1630, in *Winthrop Papers* (6 vols, Boston, 1931–), vol. ii, p. 303.

6 Michael J. Braddick, *State Formation in Early Modern England, c.1550–1700* (Cambridge, 2000); Steve Hindle, 'The political culture of the middling sort in English rural communities, c.1550–1700', and Andy Wood, ' "Poore Men Woll Speke One Daye": plebeian languages of deference and defiance in England, c.120–1640', in Tim Harris (ed.), *The Politics of the Excluded, c.1500–1850* (Houndmills and New York, 2001) pp. 67–98.

7 Karen Ordahl Kupperman, 'The Beehive as a Model for Colonial Design', in Kupperman (ed.), *America in European Consciousness* (Chapel Hill, 1995), pp. 272–92.

8 William Crashaw, *A Sermon Preached in London before the Right Honourable the Lord Lawarre* (London, 1610), sig. E3v–F.

9 Ibid. De la Warr himself did not go out to Virginia until 1610, and the sermon was published in that year. The winter of 1609–10 was the infamous 'starving time' in Virginia. The pamphlet's running head was 'A New-yeeres Gift to Virginea'.

10 T. H. Breen (ed.), 'George Donne's "Virginia Reviewed": a 1638 plan to reform colonial society', *William and Mary Quarterly*, 3rd series, 30 (1973), 462. Ricci's work was published in 1615 and republished by Samuel Purchas in his *Purchas His Pilgrimes*. See Matteo Ricci, *China in the Sixteenth Century: The Journals of Matthew Ricci, 1583–1610*, trans. J. Louis and S. J. Gallagher (New York, 1953); Jonathan D. Spence, *The Memory Palace of Matteo Ricci* (New York, 1984).

11 See William A. Nelson, *The Common Law in Colonial America*, vol. 1, *The Chesapeake and New England, 1607–1660* (Oxford, 2008), pp. 14–18.

12 William Strachey, *For the Colony in Virginea Britannia: Lawes Divine, Morall and Martiall, etc.* (London, 1612), p. 1.

13 Ibid., sig. A3v. On the term ethnarches, see the *Oxford English Dictionary*.

14 D. T. Konig, 'Colonization and the common law in Ireland and Virginia', in James A. Henretta, Michael Kammen and Stanley N. Katz (eds), *The Transformation of Early American History: Society, Authority, and Ideology* (New York, 1991), pp. 70–92; and ' "Dale's Laws" and the non-common law origins of criminal justice in Virginia', *American Journal of Legal History*, 26 (1982), 354–75, esp. 363. For a similar argument see Peter Charles Hoffer *Law and People in Colonial America* (Rev. edn, Baltimore, 1998), pp. 15–16.

15 Strachey, *Lawes Divine, Morall and Martiall*, sig A2v. See Konig, ' "Dale's Laws" and the non-common law origins'.

16 Virginia Company, 'Instruccions, orders and constitucions by way of advise sett downe, declared and propounded to Sir Thomas Gates, Knight, Governor of Virginia', in D. B. Quinn *et al.* (eds), *New American World: A Documentary History of North America to 1612* (5 vols, New York, 1979), vol. v, p. 213; Konig, 'Colonization and the common law', p. 83; Barbara Donagan, *War in England, 1642–1649* (Oxford, 2008), pp. 171–6.

17 Ibid., 3–5, 16. Several pages of punishments for crimes and illegal trading come between the requirement to be present at church and the inquiry into colonists' religious knowledge.

18 Ibid., pp. 12–13, 65, 74.

19 Ibid., pp. 1–19, quotes 14–5, 20–1.

20 Ibid., p. 19.

21 Ibid., pp. 20–1; D. H. Flaherty, 'Introduction', in William Strachey, *For the Colony in Virginea Brittania: Lawes Divine, Morall and Martiall* (Charlottesville, 1969), p. xxvi.

22 Robert, Earle of Essex and Ewe, *Lawes and Orders of Warre, Established for the Good Conduct of the Service in Ireland* (1599?).

23 On the growing need for enlarged military discipline in seventeenth-century English military campaigns, see Wayne E. Lee, *Barbarians and Brothers: Anglo-American Warfare, 1500–1865* (Oxford, 2011).

24 Strachey, *Lawes Divine, Morall and Martiall*, pp. 28, 32–4. See also p. 41 on desecrating temples 'be they sacred or prophane'.

25 Ibid., pp. 53, 61, 69; Smith, *The Generall Historie of Virginia, New-England and the Summer Isles* (London, 1624), pp. 83–7.

26 Strachey, *Lawes Divine, Morall and Martiall*, pp. 35, 39.

27 Ibid., pp. 56, 66, 80. On Dale's career, see the biography of him by Darrett Rutman in the American National Biography.

28 Strachey, *Lawes Divine, Morall and Martiall*, p. 47.

29 Sir Thomas Dale to the President and Counsell of the Companie of Adventurers and Planters in Virginia, 25 May 1611, in Alexander Brown (ed.), *The Genesis of the United States* (2 vols, Boston, 1891), vol. i, pp. 489–94; Dale to the Earl of Salisbury, 17 August 1611, ibid., pp. 501–8, at pp. 503, 507.

30 D. W. Stahle *et al.*, 'The lost colony and Jamestown droughts', *Science*, 280 (1998), 564–7. On tobacco cultivation and processing, see T. H. Breen, *The Mentality of the Great Tidewater Planters on the Eve of Revolution* (rev. edn, Princeton, 2001).

31 Virginia Company, 'A Coppie of the Subscription for Maydes', 16 July 1621, Ferrar Papers, Magdalene College, Cambridge partially reprinted in David R. Ransome, 'Wives for Virginia, 1621', *William and Mary Quarterly*, 3rd series, 48(1991), 3–18, at 7. Company discussions of the need to send women colonists are in S. M. Kingsbury (ed.), *Records of the Virginia Company* (4 vols, Washington, DC, 1906–35), vol. i, pp. 256, 268–9, 391, 566; vol. ii, p. 394; vol. iv, pp. 82, 265, 521. On this campaign, see Lois G. Carr and Lorena S. Walsh, 'The planter's wife: the experience of white women in seventeenth-century Maryland', *William and Mary Quarterly*, 3rd series, 34 (1977), 542–71; Kathleen M. Brown, *Good Wives, Nasty Wenches, and Anxious Patriarchs: Gender, Race and Power in Colonial Virginia* (Chapel Hill, 1996), pp. 24–7, 80–7. On the importance of women on English farms and changing gender roles in the seventeenth century, see Allan Kulikoff, *From British Peasants to Colonial American Farmers* (Chapel Hill, 2000), pp. 27–38.

32 Thomas Tusser, *Five Hundreth Pointes of Good Husbandrie* (London, 1585), p. 120; on this literature, see Susan Cahn, *Industry of Devotion: The Transformation of Women's Work in England, 1500–1660* (New York, 1987), chapter 4.

33 E. B. O'Callaghan (ed.), *Documents Relative to the Colonial History of the State of New-York* (15 vols, Albany, 1856–1887), vol. i, pp. 2–3, 9–10, 16–21.

34 John Rolfe to Sir Edwin Sandys, in Kingsbury (ed.), *Virginia Company Records*, vol. iii, p. 243; Engel Sluiter, 'New light on the "20. and Odd Negroes" arriving in Virginia, August 1619', *William and Mary Quarterly*, 3rd series, 54 (1997), 395–98; John Thornton, 'The African Experience of the "20. and Odd Negroes" Arriving in Virginia in 1619', 3rd series, 55 (1998), 421–34.

35 'Coppie of the totall sums of the generall Muster of Virginia 1619', in David R. Ransome (ed.), *The Ferrar Papers, 1590–1790* (Microfilm, Wakefield, 1992), reel i, 159. William Thorndale has argued that the census was collected in March 1619, but Martha McCartney has recently demonstrated conclusively that the date is Old Style, so that the census was actually done in March 1620. See William Thorndale, 'The Virginia census of 1619', in *Magazine of Virginia Genealogy*, 33 (1995), 60–161 and Martha W. McCartney, 'An early Virginia census reprised', *Quarterly Bulletin of the Archaeological Society of Virginia*, 54 (1999), 178–96.

36 T. H. Breen and Stephen Innes, *'Myne Owne Ground': Race and Freedom on Virginia's Eastern Shore, 1640–1676* (New York, 1980).

37 Konig, 'Colonization and the common law in Ireland and Virginia, 1569–1634', in Henretta, Kammen and Katz (eds), *Transformation of Early American History*, pp. 90–2.

38 Smith, *Advertisements*, p. 23.

39 British Library (BL), Stowe MS 366, fols. 20v–21. On the career of the Providence Island Company and its colony, see Karen Ordahl Kupperman, *Providence Island, 1630–1641: The Other Puritan Colony* (Cambridge, 1993).

40 Bermuda Archives, Acc. 51, Rudyerd to Gov. Bell, 1633.

41 This description came from the first governor, Capt. Philip Bell in a letter to Sir Nathaniel Rich, March, 1629, printed in Vernon A. Ives (ed.), *The Rich Papers: Letters from Bermuda, 1615–1646* (Toronto, 1984), pp. 319–21.

42 Henry Halhead, *Inclosures Thrown Open*, with preface by Joshua Sprigge (London, 1650), A2, pp. 1, 4–6, 8, 11–12, 15–17.

13

An Irish Black Legend?
1641 and the Iberian Atlantic*

IGOR PÉREZ TOSTADO

On 12 October 1642, Edward Wilson reported to the Commission for the Despoiled Subject in Dublin the massacre of one hundred people, 'men women and children' in Aghalow (co. Tyrone),

> some whereof they killd with swords others they hanged others they shott to death, others they hung vpp by the armes thumbs and with theire swords did hack them to see how many blowes they would endure before they died and others they knockt in the head with hatchetts

After this gruesome description, Wilson ended his statement by referring to 'men of creditt', who allegedly told him 'that the Rebells said . . . that the king of spaine should be theire kinge, and druncke his health in the house of a scotchman whome they first murthered'.[1]

The 1641 depositions and other contemporary manuscript and printed sources relating to the rebellion contain plenty of references, on all sides, to the Spanish monarchy, still the champion of the Catholic cause on the continent. Not surprisingly, Spanish activities in Ireland and Britain, both real and imaginary, received enormous attention. This awareness of the Spanish monarchy as rival, model and anti-model, influenced developments during the 1641 rebellion, as well as its long-term effects.

The origins of the violent events of the 1640s lay in the harsh transformations suffered by Ireland, and the changing attitudes from the mid-sixteenth century between the native Irish, the Anglo-Irish (or Old English), the English crown and the new, mainly Protestant, settlers. These developments have been linked to the upheavals associated with the Reformation, the formation of the modern state and the readjustment of political power between England, Scotland and Ireland.[2] This interpretation has been enriched by a broader archipelagic perspective, part of a general historiographic trend in search of more integrated explanations to the early modern history of Britain and Ireland.[3] As a result, historians of the war in Ireland for the most part now focus on the complex and multidimensional context of 'War of the Three Kingdoms', rather than seeing the conflict as a mere appendix to the English Civil War.[4] Similarly, scholars such as David B. Quinn, Hugh Kearney and Aidan Clarke, have established parallels between the processes of colonisation in Ireland and North America.[5] This perspective stresses the impact of the European experience with the peoples of the New World in reshaping the English attitude towards the native Irish.[6] Jane Ohlmeyer, Tadhg Ó hAnnracháin and Micheál Ó Siochrú, among others, explore the links with similar developments on the European continent.[7] This approach has led to the exploitation of new sources significant to Irish history in foreign archives, while also avoiding the pitfalls of an exceptionalist approach to the past.[8] In all these processes, much attention has been paid to Hiberno-Iberian relations.[9]

The violence involved in the transformation of early modern Ireland received renewed attention in the last decade, thanks mainly to the efforts coordinated by David Edwards, Pádraig Lenihan and Clodagh Tait, who first labelled the memory of 1641 in Ireland as a 'Black Legend' in their edited volume, *Age of Atrocity*.[10]

Connecting the Hispanic dimension of events in 1641 and the birth of an Irish 'Black Legend' comparable to the classical 'Spanish Black Legend' requires further reflection on the meaning of violence. Elizabeth Stanko's conceptualisation of violence demonstrates its definition to be both fluid and mutable.[11] Christopher Taylor explores the meaning of violence on a number of different levels: the imaginary, the discursive and the real. The 'imaginary' level is composed of different fuzzy cultural codes and non-verbalised icons or images, shared by most members of a community. These are codified intuitively and cannot be directly translated into discourse (and thus studied by historians). Nonetheless, they form an implicit body of knowledge that reflects the deep-seated fears and desires of a group. The 'discourse' level of violence is formed by verbalised elements around which the social actors organise their aims and goals and act in order to obtain them. This language enables individuals and groups to verbalise the ideologies of their friends and foes, and explain the pragmatic goal of each of their actions. The violence of the 'real' level has biological and psychological consequences over its victims in the form of physical or psychological abuse or even death. This last level communicates with the other two, increasing the social meaning of the violent actions.[12]

The interaction between these three levels is constant and fluid, and explains partly the mutable nature of violence. The discursive material, once verbalised as ideological affirmations and narratives, may become so common that it begins to affect the unconscious. Ideas once explicitly stated and openly discussed, gradually become tacit and implicit, transforming and incorporating onto the imaginary level of violence. During an outbreak of extreme violence, when all limits evaporate, many of the ideas usually not verbalised receive expression. Explosive events, therefore, such as the 1641 rebellion in Ireland, are extremely important in order to understand the whole early modern period. On the one hand, the deeper fears, implicit ideas and hidden conflicts and desires of those participating in the rebellion and repression, which lie below the surface of ideology and formal discourses, get verbalised and explicit. On the other, the experience of real violence and its outcome reshaped the mindset of the populations in Britain and Ireland, together with those of the Spanish monarchy, which served as both rival and model in the creation of a modern state and an Atlantic empire.[13]

In this relationship of implicit fears, discourse and explicit violence between Ireland, England and the Spanish monarchy, 1641 marks a turning point in which the implicit gets articulated and becomes public, while the actual violence opens new avenues of discourse.[14] Which role did the Spanish monarchy play in this process? First, the Spaniards, their king and their Catholicism held a special place in the nightmares of the hegemonic group in Ireland, disproportionate to their actual role in the rising. Second, the violence in Ireland can be better understood as an interpretation of the treatment offered in Spain to the converted Muslim population, the Moriscos.

The courts of Madrid and Brussels deployed an important influence in Britain and Ireland in the years preceding the outbreak of the War of the Three Kingdoms. Three Spanish legates in London and a group of officials headed by the Lord Deputy of Ireland, Thomas Wentworth, negotiated intensely in order to reach an agreement to provide the Stuart Crown with soldiers and money to contain its Scottish crisis.[15] Although the two sides failed to reach an agreement, and no Spanish army crossed the channel, the lengthy negotiations artificially prolonged the life of the army created by Wentworth in Ireland to assist the king in Scotland, creating an important destabilising element in the British political scene. The Irish exiles in the Spanish Monarchy were, on their own terms, extremely active in the years prior to 1641. It is impossible, however, to gauge the real involvement of the monarchy in their schemes due to the disappearance of the private archive of the count-duke of Olivares, King Philip IV's favourite.[16] Nonetheless, the fervent negotiations at the Spanish court illustrate the maturity of the exiled community by this time and the emergence of their distinct point of view on the affairs of Britain and Ireland.[17]

At this critical juncture, rebellions broke out in Catalonia and Portugal in 1640, which strongly affected Spanish influence in both Britain and Ireland. These two conflicts escalated into full wars, and thus became unexpected drains for the already exhausted military and financial resources of the Spanish Monarchy. The new contests, closely connected to the ongoing war with France, especially on the Catalan front, reduced the attention and resources available for the Irish struggle. In response, the Irish exiles and the envoys of the Catholic confederates carried an unprecedented public campaign of information, both at court and beyond, aimed to obtain support and resources for their cause. To do so, they interpreted the causes and the outbreak to the rebellion for a continental Catholic audience.

It was not difficult to find the necessary intellectual resources for that operation. First, much of the intellectual effort made in the continent by exiles was linked to religious and educational institutions in the Spanish Monarchy, particularly to the colleges aimed at the training of the clergy. Thus, they were able to draw examples and parallels with internal examples of the Spanish monarchy, especially with the Moriscos, which could spur local identification. On the other hand, an important part of the intellectual efforts carried on in these continental institutions aimed to support the cause of the insular Catholics and to convince the authorities of the Spanish monarchy on their moral and religious duty to support the Catholic exiles by all possible means.[18]

On 1642, Irish pamphlets were printed in the Iberian presses, aiming to offer their point of view to the reasons why they had taken arms, as good subjects, in defence of their King and religion, and against the aggression of the English Parliament over their rights, liberties and properties (specially through the plantations).[19] The gazettes that circulated in the court of Madrid sided heavily with the Irish Catholics in arms. The first published reports spoke of a complete success of the rising, although they later reduced this to an almost complete dominion of the island.[20] The reaction of the gazettes in the Spanish Netherlands was favourable to the Irish rising, according to the repeated complaints presented by Henry de Vic, the English agent in Brussels to the governor, the marquis of Velada.[21]

These attitudes in the presses of the Spanish monarchy did not differ from other reports being published in Rome, which were characteristic for the amount of detail offered.[22] In Portugal, which was in rebellion to the Spanish monarchy, newsletters also reported the almost immediate and complete success of the Irish rising.[23] In Lisbon, the local Irish community made an important effort to transfer swiftly their loyalties to the new Braganza dynasty, comparing the experience of the Irish Catholics with the English Protestants with that of the Portuguese with their Castilian neighbours.[24] However, newsletters in Barcelona, which had also rebelled against the crown authority, reproduced documents arriving from London, referring to Irish affairs, such as the transcription of the adventurer's act and discourses of the king to the English Parliament on Ireland, but without further comment.[25]

The credentials presented publicly by the deputies of the confederation to Philip IV focused on the connections between Ireland and the Spanish kingdoms, and more concretely between the Irish Catholics, now risen in arms, and Philip IV, 'the greatest king of the world', which they had loyally served for a long time and whom they regarded as their protector in spite of the efforts by the French monarch to occupy that position.[26] Past military services in the Spanish armies were reminded, pointing out the loyalty of the Irish in all the wars of the seventeenth century, and the many thousands of Irish who had died in the service of the Spanish king, which they numbered as forty thousand, many of them lords.[27]

When addressing written discourses to the Count-Duke of Olivares, the representatives of the confederation referred proudly to the Spanish ascent of the Irish nation, in order to obtain his support and royal intercession.[28]

The answer of the Spanish monarchy to the effort carried out in the presses and the court was of qualified and limited support, understandable in the pressing internal and external military situation of the crown.[29] A general sympathy and positive attitude towards the Irish cause was clearly appreciable, both at the royal Alcazar and beyond. The terms and ideas expressed by the Irish confederates were assumed and reproduced almost exactly in internal debates of the state councillors.[30] This positive disposition, only tarnished by the depredations carried out by the Basque corsairs on merchantmen trading and carrying supplies to Ireland, was as present in the Spanish monarchy as in all Catholic Europe, where no public performance, discourse or publication can be found directly criticising the Irish rising.[31]

From the Irish side, the positive attitude towards the Spanish monarchy was not empty rhetoric used by the exiled intelligentsia aimed solely to obtain weapons, money and political support for the rising. The depositions, which were never aimed for a Spanish audience, show symbolic and discursive acts from which a general positive attitude from the Irish rebels towards the Spanish monarchy can be inferred.

In the deposition of Edward Wilson, symbolic acts or discourses in favour of the king of Spain were reported to be delivered by the rebels. Simon Wesnam reported a priest 'who saide that the Englishe did gouerne this kingedome with a most tiranicall gouernement worse the any Nation in Europpe and did applaud the spanishe gouernment'.[32] The rebels at Duncanon, reported George Burne, 'sayd alsoe that thenglish Lawes were greivous and intoller-able, And that the spaniards would take England'.[33] It was also believed by the deponents that, in addition to the support being sent officially by Philip IV, 'that the Clergie of Spaine had already contributed 5000 Armes and powder for a whole yeare', as Robert Maxwell is reported to have heard.[34]

General sympathy was claimed to be mutual and the Irish connected them-selves to a Spanish or Portuguese ancestry. Furthermore, links and parallels were also drawn between the enemies of both sides. In the case of the Irish rebels, these were 'the puritanos', a term used in the documents published in the Spanish monarchy to refer to the English Parliament and radical Protestantism. These *puritanos*, instead of being solely compared with the external Protestant rival of the Habsburgs, most notably the Dutch, were also equated to the internal enemy of the monarchy, the Moriscos.

The year 1641 was not the first occasion in which a Morisco metaphor was used in the Irish context. From the planters' and English administrators' perspective, such as Matthew de Renzy or Edmund Spenser, a comparison with the Moriscos had been used to advocate the material dispossession and cultural absorption of the Gaelic Irish or 'white moores', as they were referred to by Chichester.[35] The parallelisms made by the New English between the Gaelic Irish and the Spanish Moriscos have allowed to perfect the understanding of the mindset of the colonisers. Ciaran O'Scea has analysed the way in which the Spanish administration treated the expulsion of the Moriscos and the reception of the Irish exiles in a radically different way.[36] However, less is known on the reasons and context of the Catholic Irish comparison of the Protestant settlers with the Moriscos. At a first glance, it could seem that Irish Catholic pamphleteers and activists wished to obtain the empathy of the Spanish monarchy, showing themselves in the same position as the Spanish monarchy had found itself thirty years before.

However, two reasons lead us to think that this comparison with the Moriscos was a serious and profound question within seventeenth-century Ireland, which had to do more with the idea of justifying undiscriminating collective punishment or a massacre, as termed in the documentation, than with obtaining continental support. The first is that the only place where the comparison between the English settlers and the Moriscos was used in print was Lisbon in 1644, and in a publication in Portuguese.[37] The war of the Alpujarras provoked the resettling of the Moriscos in lower Andalusia and New Castile, not affecting Lisbon or Portugal. It is bizarre that, if it was attempted to be used as a merely rhetorical argument, that it was not used in the places, such as Seville, which had had more difficulty in integrating the Moriscos expelled from Granada.[38] The second and most important reason is that, beyond the publications and discourses in the Spanish monarchy, the debate and comparison with the Moriscos was used in Ireland itself in the same terms, as it is shown by the depositions. The statement by Henry Jones, the dean of Kilmore who headed the commission in charge of collecting the evidence of the violence exerted against the Protestants in 1641, referred strikingly to similar events.[39] The parallels among these two equally partisan but radically opposed documents add more weight to the hypothesis first presented by Michael Perceval-Maxwell of the real existence of a meeting reported by Jones in Multyfarnham, county Westmeath, in which the objectives of the incoming rebellion were discussed.[40] Although not referring explicitly to this particular meeting, the Portuguese publication referred to several secret wider and smaller meetings of nobles, clergymen and bishops and consultations among them in order to define the objectives of the rising.[41]

According to Jones, the leaders of the conspiracy had been sharply divided on 'what course showld be taken with the English and all other that were found to be protestants'. Those in favour of banishing them but respecting their lives, put the example:

of the King of Spaines expelling out of Granada & other parts of his dominions the Moores to the number of many hundreds of thousands; all of them beeing dismisssed with there lives, wives & children & with some part also of there goodes. That this merciful proceeding redounded much to the honour of Spaine; whereas the slaughter of so many Inocents would have laid an everlasting blemish of cruelty on that State.[42]

Those who replied to this argument also berated the way in which the Spanish monarch had acted:

the effect [of banishing the moriscos] shewed him moste vnmerciful not only to his owne dominions but to all chrestendom besides. That this was evident in the greate & excessive charge that Spaine hath since that time beene put vnto by those Moores & there posterity to this day. All Christendom also hath & doth still groane vnder the miseries it doth suffer by the Pyracies of Algiers, Sally, & the like denns of theeves.[43]

From this point of view, the conclusion drawn from the experience of the Spanish moriscos was 'that all this might have been prevented in a fewe houres worke by a general Massacre'.[44] Thus, the Irish rebels had to learn from this lesson:

how dangerous the like expelling of the English might prove to this kingdom. That these robbd & banished men might againe returne with swordes in there handes, . . . would prove farre more cruel, & be more earnest in prosecution of there revenge, then any strangers not in there owne persons injured & newly sent over out of England could be.[45]

Ready not to repeat the mistake made by the king of Spain, 'a general Massacre was the safest & readiest way for freeing the kingdom of any such feares'.[46]

The difference between the narrative of Henry Jones and the publication in Lisbon was that the latter conceded that the women and children who surrendered on terms, should be allowed, following natural law, to quit the country.[47] The works of Henry Jones, especially his 1642 publication *A Remonstrance of Divers Remarkable Passages Concerning the Church and Kingdom of Ireland*, together with John Temple's 'The Irish rebellion', became the first elements to shape the protestant interpretation of events of 1641.[48] These texts represent the reverse of the triumphalist teleology of a national English narrative of greatness based on steady resistance to Romanism.[49] They were linked necessarily to a victimologic fear of, and anxiety about, internal rising, foreign invasion and general massacre, which shall be called here the hegemon nightmare.[50] This nightmare was projected over the interpretation of events in 1641, and thus the fears of the hegemon group surfaced, mixed with the description of the atrocity stories of the Thirty Years' War which circulated in Britain and Ireland.[51]

Although there were medieval precedents for religious massacres, starting with the Crusades and following through the Middle Ages, according to Joseph Pérez, the idea of the internal barbarian and thus of the massacre consolidated during the wars of religion of the early modern period.[52] Due to its centrality, the social and cultural anxiety in Renaissance Britain and Ireland has attracted the attention of both historians and literary critics.[53] However, the way in which the Spanish monarchy was connected to this hegemon nightmare has not received much attention, in spite of the abundance of sources such as the depositions and contemporary prints, where it is a recurrent subject.

Deponents linked their experience of violence at the hand of rebels with a wider continental plot. For example, Richard Castledine frequently heard that the Catholic powers of the continent, the pope, the emperor and the kings of France and Spain, would send an army to 'rute out and vtterly destroy all the purytantes out of both kingdomes' and restore Charles I to his complete regal authority.[54] Similar stories were told by Arthur Culme about the rooting out of 'all the protestantes in Europe' by the continental Catholic powers.[55] Luce Spell had heard merchants speaking of Spain sending an army to England 'with the helpe of Catholicks there [to] putt all the puritans and protestants to the sword'.[56] Patrick O'Brian even knew that the king of Spain had promised 15,000 soldiers.[57] A similar plan for a Spanish landing was reported by Nathaniell Higginson.[58] John Mountgomery estimated the number of expected soldiers arriving from Spain at 15,000 plus arms and payment.[59] Thomas Crant reported that eight Spanish vessels with soldiers and ammunition had appeared in Carlingford,[60] while George Cottingham reported that 'the seas were full of spanish & ffrench shippinge'.[61] Anne Bullinbrooke even heard news of the Spaniards having landed and captured Dublin.[62] Martha Culme was told of 40,000 Spaniards landing in Ulster.[63]

The deponents who spoke of the Spanish monarchy feared harsh collective punishment, even genocide. John Montgomery concluded that an invading Spanish army would put to the sword 'protesants or others that wold not goe to Masse'.[64] According to Anne Bullinbrooke, the rebels would 'leave neithr scottish nor English in Ireland' before taking Philip IV of Spain as their new king.[65]

The presence of the Spanish monarchy together with the Catholic Irish in the hegemon nightmares in Britain and Ireland meant that there was a transmission of negative qualities between them. Elements and narratives of the violence of the Thirty Years' War had already been transferred to an Irish context, as Cope has pointed out.[66] As the war finally engulfed all the kingdoms of the Stuart crown, it also provided the actual experience of massacres and extreme collective violence within English society.[67] Interesting comparisons were also drawn in England between the rising in Catalonia and that of Ireland.[68] Even negative attributes of unruly women in sixteenth-century Ireland were transferred to the Catholic Irish in 1641.[69]

These processes of transferences worked also in the opposite sense: negative elements attributed to the Spanish monarchy, referred to by historians under the term the 'Spanish Black Legend', were also transferred to the Irish.[70] In this translocation, elements of negative identification were exchanged or homogeneised through the interpretation of three elements: the Catholic Irish (understood as the internal enemy of the *status quo* and based on contemporary examples of the Thirty Years' War), the Spanish monarchy (interpreted as the main external enemy and colonial rival deeply intermingled in its attributes to the Irish) and the native Americans (the new colonial subjects of the crown on whose interpretation the negative attitudes towards both the Irish and Spaniards interplayed).

In the early modern period, the myth of the Spanish descent of the inhabitants of Ireland was used as a weapon by those who opposed the expansion of English rule and sought foreign protectors based on ancient blood and religious links, and by the new settlers, who were either sceptical of this Irish origin-myth, or it was appropriated in order explain and justify, in Irish terms, the contemporary process of re-colonisation.[71] From a religious perspective, contemporary British writers equally regarded both Irish and Spaniards as 'Demonic others'.[72] The Muslim medieval past of the Iberian Peninsula and its ancient links with Ireland meant that the polarised and antipathetic representation of the Muslims in general and Turks in particular had strong synthetic and interchangeable negative characteristics.[73] This interchangeability is also clear in Spenser's interpretation of the Irish. According to Claire Carroll, Spenser and others constructed the inferior category of Irish through non-European ethnic identity 'alternatively Scythian, African, or Moorish'. It is far from surprising, therefore, that Cranford's *Tears of Ireland* considered the 'cruelties and tortures' of the Irish rebels to exceed 'all parallel, unheard off among Pagans, Turks, or Barbarians'.[74]

The English frequently used comparisons with the New World in order to understand the relationship between Ireland and the Spanish monarchy. During the sixteenth and early seventeenth centuries, a positive transfer of good character traits occurred between the native Americans and the Protestants, based on the trials and sufferings of both at the hands of Catholics, both Spanish and Gaelic Irish. The publication in 1642 of Cranford's infamous *Teares of Ireland* and the subsequent translation in 1656 of Bartolomé de las Casas's *Brevissima relación de la destrucción de las Indias* under the title

The Tears of the Indians make this connection evident.[75] The model for this comparison was clearly Dutch. Benjamin Schmidt points out that the end of the Twelve Years' Truce witnessed the publication of new editions of las Casas in the United Provinces (five in 1620 alone), renamed *Mirror of Spanish Tyranny*. Starting in the 1620, a popular account of the history of the Dutch revolt, *Mirror of the Spanish Tyranny Committed in the Netherlands*, accompanied these translations, unambiguously connecting events in the New World and in the Netherlands.[76] Events in Ireland in the 1640s, therefore, reflected contemporary transformations affecting the mentalities across Europe.[77]

Similarly, there is a reason why the study of connections between Ireland and America needs to have a consolidated historiography.[78] In this relationship, early optimistic hopes for the cultural and religious transformation of both Irish and Native Americans into good British subjects through the positive influence of settlers dispersed among them were soon disappointed. James VI and I described the native Americans as 'beastly Indians, slaves to the Spaniards, refuse of the world, and as yet aliens to the holy covenant of God'.[79] The king's point of view proved not far removed to that of the English expansionists, who oftentimes based their interpretation of the American natives on their previous experiences in Ireland, which, in turn, were influenced by Spanish writers on America, such as Las Casas and Oviedo.[80]

The period between the 1620s and the 1640s witnessed the emergence of a much more pessimistic view on the nature of people, with the Native Americans and Gaelic Irish seen as beyond hope of integration. In this process of progressive degradation, the accusation of cannibalism, 'the ultimate hallmark of barbarism', makes its first appearance.[81] Cranford's account of the 1641 rebellion portrays the Irish Catholics as more cruel than the cannibals, 'O Sun, to behold the inhumane cruelties and beastly usages of these unheard of Cannibals.'[82] First in America and then in Ireland, colonists grew accustomed to living under a constant fear of attack, which materialised later into accusations of massacres. After the restoration, the Catholic cleric John Lynch attributed the famous comparison between Ireland and the Spanish American colonies (and implicitly between England and Spain) to the earl of Thomond: 'Ireland is another India for the English, a more profitable India for them than ever the Indies were to the Spaniards', which as, Jane Ohlmeyer points out, 'recaptures the reality of Ireland's colonial position for much of the early modern period'.[83]

The incorporation of a Spanish perspective to the 1641 equation offers a new approach to contextualising and understanding the stereotypes and discourses at the core of the symbolic and real violence of the rebellion and its aftermath. This link provides further information to locate the Irish experience in its contemporary European and the Atlantic contexts. A change at this time in the discourse linked to alleged atrocities served to impose a new *status quo* which justified collective punishment and domination. In response, historians involved in the construction of a nation based on a common historical heritage, in both Ireland and Spain, have felt the urge to continue a polemic, often reduced to a monologue inherited from the seventeenth century.

An isolated study of the Black Legend, be it Spanish or Irish, leads to circular arguments and counter arguments. However, a comparative and connected study can show new light on the birth and evolution of stereotypes and their use in order to justify power relations. Rather than a comparative study of negative attributes, an interconnected history of the Irish Black Legend is still to be done. This new approach, emanating from the study of information, such as the depositions, will certainly shed new light over the process of integration, subordination and exclusion in the early modern states and empires.[84] This perspective on the shared Black Legend, extended to the contemporary period in the writings of historians and polemicists, offers new understanding of a partisan, victimist and exceptionalist historical discourse in both Ireland and the Hispanic world.

NOTES

* This text has been elaborated thanks to the funding offered by the following research groups to which the author belongs: *Hispanofilia, La proyección política de la Monarquía Hispánica (I): aliados externos y refugiados políticos (1580–1610)*, Proyecto HAR2008-01107 of the Ministerio de Ciencia e Innovación, *Proyección Política y Social de la Comunidad Irlandesa en la Monarquía hispánica y en la América Colonial de la Edad Moderna (siglos XVI–XVIII)* Proyecto HAR2009-11339 (subprograma HIST), *Afinidad, violencia y representación: el impacto exterior de la Monarquía Hispánica* Proyecto HAR2011-29859-C02-02 and *Nuevos productos atlánticos, ciencia, guerra, economía y consumo en la España del Antiguo Régimen, el caso andaluz (1492–1824)* proyecto de excelencia HUM5330 of the Junta de Andalucía.

1 Trinity College Dublin (TCD), MS 839, fols 025r–025v, Deposition of Edward Wilson, 12 October 1642, 1641 Depositions Project, online transcript December 2009, http://1641.eneclann.ie/ (accessed 3 August 2010).

2 See S. E. Ellis and S. Barber (eds), *Conquest and Union: Fashioning the British State, 1485–1725* (London, 1995); C. Brady, *The Chief Governors: The Rise and Fall of Reform Government in Tudor Ireland* (Cambridge, 1994); C. Lennon, *Sixteenth-Century Ireland: The Incomplete Conquest* (Dublin, 1994); A. I. Macciness, 'The multiple kingdoms of Britain and Ireland: the "British problem"', in B. Coward (ed.), *A Companion to Stuart Britain* (Oxford, 2003), pp. 3–25; T. Barnard, 'The making of Greater Britain and Ireland', in Coward (ed.), *A Companion to Stuart Britain*, pp. 26–44.

3 N. Canny, 'Irish, Scottish and Welsh responses to centralisation, c.1530–c.1640: a comparative perspective', in A. Grant and K. I. Stringer (eds), *Uniting the*

Kingdom? The Making of British History (London, 1995), pp. 147–69; N. Canny, 'Writing early modern history: Ireland, Britain and the wider world', *Historical Journal*, 46(3) (2003), 723–47; D. Edwards, 'A haven of popery: English Catholic migration to Ireland in the age of plantations', in A. Ford and J. McCafferty (eds), *The Origins of Sectarianism in Early Modern Ireland* (Cambridge, 2005), pp. 95–126; J. Morrill, 'The British Problem, c.1534–1707', in B. Bradshaw and J. Morrill (eds), *The British Problem, c.1534–1707: State Formation in the Atlantic Archipelago* (London, 1996), pp. 1–38; K. Bottingheimer, 'Kingdom and colony: Ireland in the Westward Enterprise, 1536–1660', in K. Andrews, N. Canny and P. Hair (eds), *The Westward Enterprise: English Activities in Ireland, the Atlantic, and America 1480–1650* (Liverpool, 1978), pp. 45–64; A. Williamson, 'Patterns of British identity: "Britain" and its rivals in the sixteenth and seventeenth centuries', in G. Burgess (ed.), *The New British History: Founding a Modern State 1603–1715* (London, 1999), pp. 138–73; B. Bradshaw, 'The English Reformation and identity formation in Ireland and Wales', in B. Bradshaw and P. Roberts (eds), *British Consciousness and Identity: The Making of Britain, 1533–1707* (Cambridge, 1998), pp. 43–111.

4 Canny, 'Writing early modern history', pp. 729–30 makes J. C. Beckett the father of the concept 'War of the three kingdoms'. It is important to stress the importance of the perspective provided by the collective volume J. Ohlmeyer (ed.), *Ireland from Independence to Occupation* (Cambridge, 1995); J. Morrill, 'The war(s) of the three kingdoms', in G. Burgess (ed.), *The New British History: Founding a Modern State, 1603–1715* (London, 1999), pp. 65–91; M. E. Daly, 'Recent writings on modern Irish history: the interaction between past and present', *Journal of Modern History*, 69(3) (1997), 517; R. Armstrong, *Protestant War: The 'British' of Ireland and the Wars of the Three Kingdoms* (Manchester, 2005); P. Lenihan, *Confederate Catholics at War, 1641–1649* (Cork, 2001); M. Perceval-Maxwell, 'Ireland and the monarchy in the early Stuart multiple kingdom', *Historical Journal*, 34(2) (1991), 279–95.

5 See note 4 above. The major works of D. B. Quinn have been appraised and analysed in N. Canny and K. O. Kupperman, 'The scholarship and legacy of David Beers Quinn, 1909–2002', *William and Mary Quarterly*, 60(4) (2003), 843–60.

6 See K. Andrews, N. Canny and R. Gillespie (eds), *The Westward Enterprise: English Activities in Ireland, the Atlantic and America, 1480–1650* (Liverpool, 1978); C. Brady and P. Hair (eds), *Natives and Newcomers: The Making of the Irish Colonial Society, 1534–1641* (Dublin, 1986) and N. Canny, *The Elizabethan Conquest of Ireland: A Pattern Established 1565–76* (Hassock, 1976).

7 See especially J. Ohlmeyer, 'Ireland independent: confederate foreign policy and international relations during the mid-seventeenth century', in J. Ohlmeyer (ed.), *Ireland from Independence to Occupation* (Cambridge, 1995), pp. 89–111; T. Ó hAnnracháin, *Catholic Reformation in Ireland: The Mission of Rinuccini, 1645–1649* (Oxford, 2002); M. Ó Siochrú, *Confederate Ireland: A Constitutional and Political Analysis* (Dublin, 1999); M. Ó Siochrú (ed.), *Kingdoms in Crisis: Ireland in the 1640s* (Dublin, 2001); B. Hazard, *Faith and Patronage: The Political Career of Flaithrí Ó Maolchonaire, c.1560–1629* (Dublin, 2010).

8 See the essays collected in C. Brady (ed.), *Interpreting Irish History: The Debate on Historical Revisionism, 1938–1994* (Dublin, 1994); Also B. Walker, *Dancing to History's Tune: History, Myth and Politics in Ireland* (Belfast, 1996); H. Howe, *Ireland and Empire: Colonial Legacies in Irish History and Culture* (Oxford, 2000), pp. 76–106; K. Whelan, 'The revisionist debate in Ireland', *Boundary 2*, 31(1) (2004), 184–94.

9 Many of these efforts have been collaborative: T. O'Connor (ed.), *The Irish in Europe* (Dublin, 2001); T. O'Connor and M. A. Lyons (eds), *Irish Migrants in Europe after Kinsale* (Dublin, 2003); T. O'Connor and M. A. Lyons (eds), *Irish Communities in Early Modern Europe* (Dublin, 2006); T. O'Connor and M. A. Lyons (eds), *The Ulster Earls and Baroque Europe: Refashioning Irish Identities, 1600–1800* (Dublin, 2010); D. M. Downey and J. Crespo MacLennan (eds), *Irish–Spanish Relations through the Ages* (Dublin, 2008); H. Morgan (ed.), *The Battle of Kinsale* (Cork, 2006); E. García Hernán, M. A. de Bunes Ibarra and O. Recio Morales (eds), *Irlanda y la Monarquía Hispánica: Kinsale 1601–2001, Guerra, Política, Exilio y Religión* (Madrid, 2002); E. García Hernán and O. Recio Morales (eds), *Extranjeros en el Ejército: Militares Irlandeses en la Sociedad Española* (Madrid, 2007); I. Pérez Tostado and E. García Hernán (eds), *Irlanda y el Atlántico Ibérico: Movilidad, Participación e Intercambio Cultural (1580–1823)* (Valencia, 2010).

10 C. Tait, D. Edwards and P. Lenihan, 'Early modern Ireland: a history of violence', in D. Edwards, P. Lenihan and C. Tait (eds), *Age of Atrocity: Violence and Political Conflict in Early Modern Ireland* (Dublin, 2007), pp. 12–13.

11 E. A. Stanko, 'Conceptualising the meaning of violence', in E. A. Stanko (ed.), *The Meanings of Violence* (London and New York, 2003), p. 3.

12 C. C. Taylor, 'Visions of the "oppressor" in Rwanda's pre-genocidal media', in N. A. Robins and A. Jones (eds), *Genocide by the Oppressed: Subaltern Genocide in Theory and Practice* (Bloomington and Indianapolis, 2009), pp. 124–5.

13 See J. H. Eliott, *Empires of the Atlantic World: Britain and Spain in the Americas* (New Haven, 2006); J. Hart, *Comparing Empires: European Colonialism from Portuguese Expansion to the Spanish–American War* (New York, 2003), pp. 79–107; J. Hart, *Contesting Empires: Opposition, Promotion and Slavery* (New York, 2005), pp. 11–41.

14 J. C. Scott, *Domination and the Art of Resistance: Hidden Transcripts* (New Haven, 1990).

15 J. H. Elliott, 'The year of the three ambassadors', in H. Lloyd-Jones, V. Pearl and B. Worden (eds), *History and Imagination: Essays in Honour of H. R. Trevor-Roper* (London, 1981), pp. 161–81.

16 F. Troncarelli and I. Pérez Tostado, 'A plot without "cappriccio": Irish utopia and political activity in Madrid, 1639–1640', in Downey and Crespo MacLennan (eds), *Irish–Spanish Relations*, pp. 123–36; F. Troncarelli, *La Spada e la Croce: Guillén Lombardo e l'Inquisizione in Messico* (Roma, 1999); R. Crewe, 'Brave New Spain: an Irishman's independence plot in seventeenth-century Mexico', *Past and Present*, 207 (2010), 53–87.

17 J. I. Casway, 'Gaelic Macabeanism: the politics of reconciliation', in J. Ohlmeyer (ed.), *Political Thought in Seventeenth-Century Ireland* (Cambridge, 2000), pp. 176–88.

18 J. J. Ruiz Ibáñez, 'Inventar una monarquía doblemente católica: Los partidarios de Felipe II en Europa y su visión de la hegemonía española', *Estudis: Revista de Historia Moderna* (2008), 87–109.

19 Biblioteca Nacional de Lisboa (hereafter BNL), reservados, 4249//34, *Manifesto de los principales cavalleros católicos del condado de Galway* (Barcelona: Iayme Romeau, 1642).

20 See, for example, Real Academia de la Historia (hereafter RAH), Ms. 9/3663, fol. 57 'Relacion verdadera de las famosas Vitorias . . .'; RAH, Ms. 9/3663 'Relacion verdadera de la Insigne vitoria que los catolicos del Reyno de Irlanda . . .' fol. 42 (1642).

21 The National Archives (hereafter TNA), State Papers 77 (hereafter SP 77), vol. 31, fols 150–1 and 171–2.

22 Biblioteca Apostolica Vaticana (hereafter BAV), vol. 5253, fols 106–9 and 110–3.

23 BNL, reservardos, vol. 3960, Carta de treinta de otubre de Paris . . . (1642); BNL, H. G. 6777//16V 'Relaçam dos sucecssos do reyno de Irlanda . . .' (1646).

24 *Mercurius ibernicus que relata algunos casos notables que sucedieron en Irlanda, después que tomó las armas por defender la religión Catholica* ([Lisbon?] 1645).

25 BNL, Reservados 4249//39, 'Relacio verdadera de las festas fetas al naxement de un fill del gran Turch' (1642).

26 Archivo General de Simancas (hereafter AGS), Estado (hereafter E), legajo (hereafter leg.) 2525, Credential letters of the Irish deputies. See in the same folder the documentation submitted by the deputies and the letter of James Talbot to Philip IV.

27 AGS, E., leg. 2525, Letter of the Province of Munster to Philip IV (1642).

28 AGS, E., leg. 2525, Letter of James Talbot to the count Duke of Olivares (September of 1642).

29 O. Recio Morales, *España y la Pérdida del Ulster: Irlanda en la Estrategia Política de la Monarquía Hispánica (1602–1649)* (Madrid, 2003), pp. 158–218.

30 AGS, E., leg. 2057, 'Consulta of the Council of State, 30th of May 1641'.

31 G. D. Burtchaell and J. M. Rigg (eds), *Historical Manuscripts Commission Report on Franciscan Mss: Preserved at the Convent, Merchants' Quay, Dublin* (Dublin, 1906), pp. 223, 228–9.

32 TCD MS 833, fols 204r–6v, Deposition of Symon Wesnam, 22 July 1642, 1641 Depositions Project, online transcript December 2009, http://1641.eneclann.ie/ (accessed 3 August 2010).

33 TCD MS 839, fols 038r–039v, Deposition of George Burne , 12 January 1644, 1641 Depositions Project, online transcript December 2009, http://1641.eneclann.ie/ (accessed 3 August 2010).

34 TCD MS 809, fols 5r–12v, Deposition of Robert Maxwell, 22 August 1642, 1641 Depositions Project, online transcript January 1970, http://1641.tcd.ie/ (accessed 3 August 2010).

35 J. Ohlmeyer, ' "Civilizinge of those rude partes": colonization within Britain and Ireland, 1580s–1640s', N. Canny (ed.), *Oxford History of the British Empire, Vol. 1: The Origins of Empire* (Oxford, 2001), pp. 126–7 and 135–7; On Matthew de Renzy's view, see N. Canny, *Making Ireland British* (Oxford, 2001), pp. 176–7 and B. Mac

Cuarta, 'A planter's interaction with Gaelic culture: Sir Matthew de Renzy, 1577–1634', *Irish Economic and Social History*, 20 (1993), 1–17; B. Fuchs, 'Spanish lessons: Spenser and the Irish Moriscos', *Studies in English Literature*, 42(1) (2002), 50; B. Fuchs, 'Conquering islands: contextualizing the Tempest', *Shakespearean Quarterly*, 48(1) (1997), 51–52; B. Fuchs, 'Learning from Spain: the case of the Irish Moriscos', in B. Rajan and E. Sauer (eds), *Imperialisms: Historical and Literary Investigations, 1500–1900* (New York, 2004), pp. 33–52.

36 C. O'Scea, 'Caracena: champion of the Irish, hunter of the Moriscos', in Morgan, (ed.), *The Battle of Kinsale,* pp. 229–39.

37 BNL, Reservados, 95//4V, ff. 131–140v.

38 K. Ingram, 'Introduction', in K. Ingram (ed.), *The Conversos and Moriscos in Late Medieval Spain and Beyond* (Leiden, 2009), pp. 18–19.

39 On Jones, see J. Cope, 'Fashioning victims: Dr. Henry Jones and the plight of Irish protestants, 1642', *Historical Research*, 74(186) (2001), 370–91.

40 M. Perceval-Maxwell, *The Outbreak of the Irish Rebellion of 1641* (Montreal, 1994), pp. 237–8; also M. Ó Siochrú, 'Catholic confederates and the constitutional relationship between Ireland and England, 1641–1649', in Brady and Ohlmeyer (eds), *British Interventions in Early Modern Ireland*, p. 212; R. Clifton, ' "An indiscriminate blackness?": massacre, counter-massacre and ethnic cleansing in Ireland, 1640–1660', in M. Levine and P. Roberts (eds), *The Massacre in History* (New York, 1999), p. 112.

41 See above, note 38.

42 Statement by Henry Jones relating to the rebellion, TCD MS 840, fols 32r–32v, 1641 Depositions Project, online transcript January 1970, http://1641.tcd.ie/ (accessed Friday 6 August 2011).

43 Ibid.

44 Ibid.

45 Ibid.

46 Ibid.

47 See above, note 38.

48 H. Jones, *A remonstrance of Divers Remarkable Passages Concerning the Church and Kingdom of Ireland* (London, Godfrey Emerson, 1642); K. M. Noonan, ' "Martyrs in Flames": Sir John Temple and the Conception of the Irish in English martyrologies', *Albion*, 36(2) (2004), 223–55; S. Achinstein, 'Texts in conflict: the press and the Civil War', in N. Keeble (ed.), *The Cambridge Companion to Writing of the English Revolution* (Cambridge, 2001), pp. 50–68.

49 E. Curran, *Roman Invasions: The British History, Protestant anti-Romanism, and the Historical Imagination in England, 1530–1660* (Newark and London, 2002), pp. 253–4.

50 Following the definition offered by A. Jones, 'On the genocidal aspect of certain subaltern uprising: a research note', in Robins and Jones (eds.), *Genocide by the Oppressed*, p. 52.

51 On the relation of Irish narratives with German atrocity stories, see J. Cope, *England and the 1641 Irish Rebellion* (Woodbridge, 2009), pp. 101–3.

52 J. Pérez, *La Légende Noire de l'Espagne* (Paris, 2009), pp. 75–7.

53 See the essays collected in V. P. Carey and U. Lotz-Heumann (eds), *Taking Sides? Colonial and Confessional Mentalites in Early Modern Ireland* (Dublin, 2003); K. N. Noonan, ' "The cruel pressure of an enraged, barbarous people": Irish and English identity in seventeenth-century policy and propaganda', *Historical Journal*, 41(1) (1998), 151–77; J. Gibney, *Ireland and the Popish Plot* (Houndsmill, 2009), pp. 5–27.

54 TCD MS 833, fols 115r–116v, Deposition of Richard Castledine, 19 July 1642, 1641 Depositions Project, online transcript December 2009, http://1641.eneclann.ie/ (accessed 3 August 2010).

55 TCD MS 833, fols 127r–132v, Deposition of Arthur Culme, 9 May 1642, 1641 Depositions Project, online transcript December 2009, http://1641.eneclann.ie/ (accessed 3 August 2010).

56 TCD MS 834, fols 006r–007v, Deposition of Luce Spell, 5 February 1642, 1641 Depositions Project, online transcript December 2009, http://1641.eneclann.ie/ (accessed 3 August 2010).

57 TCD MS 835, fols 082r–083v, Deposition of Patrick O'Brian, 29 January 1642, 1641 Depositions Project, online transcript December 2009, http://1641.eneclann.ie/ (accessed 3 August 2010).

58 TCD MS 835, fols 117r–118v, Deposition of Nathaniell Higginson, 7 January 1642, 1641 Depositions Project, online transcript December 2009, http://1641.eneclann.ie/ (accessed 3 August 2010).

59 TCD MS 834, fols 130r–135v, Deposition of John Mountgomery, 26 January 1642, 1641 Depositions Project, online transcript December 2009, http://1641.eneclann.ie/ (accessed 3 August 2010).

60 TCD MS 832, fols 212r–219v, Deposition of Thomas Crant, 13 February 1642, 1641 Depositions Project, online transcript December 2009, http://1641.eneclann.ie/ (accessed 3 August 2010).

61 TCD MS 834, fols 106r–107v, Deposition of George Cottingham, 4 March 1642, 1641 Depositions Project, online transcript December 2009, http://1641.eneclann.ie/ (accessed 3 August 2010).

62 TCD MS 839, fols 030r–030v, Deposition of Anne Bullinbrooke, 22 December 1642, 1641 Depositions Project, online transcript December 2009, http://1641.eneclann.ie/ (accessed 3 August 2010).

63 TCD MS 834, fols 111r–111v, Deposition of Martha Culme, 14 February 1642, 1641 Depositions Project, online transcript December 2009, http://1641.eneclann.ie/ (accessed 3 August 2010).

64 TCD MS 834, fols 130r–135v, Deposition of John Mountgomery, 26 January 1642, 1641 Depositions Project, online transcript December 2009, http://1641.eneclann.ie/ (accessed 3 August 2010).

65 TCD MS 839, fols 030r–030v, Deposition of Anne Bullinbrooke, 22 December 1642, 1641 Depositions Project, online transcript December 2009, http://1641.eneclann.ie/ (accessed 3 August 2010).

66 Cope, *England and the 1641 Irish Rebellion*, p. 95.

67 B. Donagan, 'Codes of conduct in the English Civil War', *Past and Present*, 118 (1998), 65–95; B. Donagan, 'Atrocity, war crime and treason in the English Civil

War', *American Historical Review*, 99(4) (1994), 1137–66; W. Coster, 'Massacre and codes of conduct in the English Civil War', in Levine and Roberts (eds), *The Massacre in History*, pp. 89–105.

68 W. S. Maltby, *The Black Legend in England: The Development of Anti-Spanish Sentiment, 1558–1660* (Durham, 1971), p. 113.

69 W. Palmer, 'Gender, violence and rebellion in Tudor and early Stuart Ireland', *Sixteenth Century Journal*, 23(4) (1992), 699–712.

70 R. García Cárcel, *La Leyenda Negra: Historia y Opinión* (Madrid, 1997); B. Aram, *Leyenda Negra y Leyendas Doradas en la Conquista de América: Pedrarias y Balboa* (Madrid, 2008), pp. 28–35.

71 W. Maley, *Nation, State and Empire in English Renaissance Literature, Shakespeare to Milton* (New York, 2003), pp. 76–80.

72 D. Shugen, 'Irishmen, aristocrats and other white barbarians', *Renaissance Quarterly*, 50(2) (1997), 495; N. Johnston, *Devil and Demonism in Early Modern England* (Cambridge, 2006), pp. 40, 227; Tait, Edwards, Lenihan and Pádraig, 'Early modern Ireland: a history of violence', p. 27; C. Cannino, 'The discourse of Hell: Paradise Lost and the Irish rebellion', *Milton Quarterly*, 32(1) (1998), 15–23; C. Carlton, *Going to the Wars: the Experience of the British Civil Wars, 1638–1651* (London, 1992), p. 62.

73 N. Matar, *Turks, Moors and Englishmen in the Age of Discovery* (New York, 1999), pp. 106–107; N. Canny, 'The ideology of English colonization: from Ireland to America', *William and Mary Quarterly*, 30(4) (1973), 586.

74 J. Cranford, *The Teares of Ireland* (London, 1642), p. 3.

75 See Anonymous: *Lacrimae Germaniae or, the Teares of Germany* (London: I. Okes, 1638); P. Vincent, *The Lamentations of Germany* (London: E. G., 1638); B. de Las Casas, *The Tears of the Indians* (London: J. C., 1656); Cope, *England and the 1641 Irish Rebellion*, p. 95, note 28, shows more parallels between the three kind of sources.

76 B. Schmidt, *Innocence Abroad: the Dutch Imagination and the New World, 1570–1670* (Cambridge, 2001), pp. 188–97.

77 G. Scammell, 'On the discovery of the Americas and the spread of intolerance, absolutism and racism in early modern Europe', *International History Review*, 13(3) (2011), 502–21.

78 See Canny, 'Writing early modern history', pp. 734 and ff.

79 Quoted by A. T. Vaughan, 'From white man to redskin: changing Anglo-American perceptions of the American Indian', *American Historical Review*, 87(4) (1982), 929.

80 J. Ohlmeyer, 'Seventeenth century Ireland and the New British and Atlantic histories', *American Historical Review*, 104(2) (1999), 459 and ff; J. McGurk, 'The pacification of Ulster, 1600–3', in Edwards, Lenihan and Tait, *Age of Atrocity*, pp. 119–29. See the reply of R. Rapple 'Writing about violence in the Tudor kingdoms', *Historical Journal*, 54(3) (2011), 837–8.

81 C. Carroll, 'Representation of women in some early modern English tracts on the colonization of Ireland', *Albion*, 25(3) (1993), 389–90; R. Takaki, 'The tempest in the wilderness: the racialization of savagery', *Journal of American History*,

79(3) (1992), 893–5; Canny, 'The ideology of English colonization', pp. 587, 593–4; B. Sandberg, 'Beyond encounters: religion, ethnicity and violence in the Atlantic world', *Journal of World History*, 17(1) (2006), 17–18.

82 Cranford, *The Teares of Ireland*, pp. 77–78.

83 Jane Ohlmeyer, 'A laboratory for empire?: early modern Ireland and English imperialism', in K. Kenny (ed.), *Ireland and the British Empire* (Oxford, 2004), p. 26.

84 N. Robins, *Native Insurgencies and the Genocidal Impulse in the Americas* (Bloomington and Indianapolis, 2005), pp. 142–53.

14

Afterword
Settler colonies, ethno-religious violence and historical documentation: comparative reflections on Southeast Asia and Ireland

BEN KIERNAN

In the early modern period, extreme violence often accompanied conflict in disparate regions of the world. In Tibet, the Fifth Dalai Lama cracked down hard on rebels. In 1660, he issued these orders:

> Make the male lines like trees that have had their roots cut;
> Make the female lines like brooks that have dried up in winter;
> Make the children and grandchildren like eggs smashed against rocks;
> Make the servants and followers like heaps of grass consumed by fire...
> In short, annihilate any traces of them, even their name.[1]

In Southeast Asia, too, between 1590 and 1800 specific groups of Christians, Muslims and Buddhists all perpetrated genocidal massacres against others and even against members of their own communities.[2] Religious demarcations sometimes worked in tandem with quests for land and power to divide people who may or may not have been ethnically different.

Yet ethnic difference also served as a motivation for extreme violence. Cultural collisions were common in an age of conquest and a scramble for territory. As maritime European powers expanded, land-based Asian empires grew as well. English expansion in Ireland and elsewhere in the sixteenth and seventeenth centuries occurred in the same era as the rise of new Southeast Asian dynasties, which achieved major territorial reach in Burma, Siam, Viet Nam and Java. Many of these conquests were extremely violent. Early in the sixteenth century, Iberian conquistadors used genocidal massacres in the name of religion as a route to power in the New World, and some of their successors tried in the same way again in Cambodia in the 1590s.[3] In the 1640s, the Javanese monarch Amangkurat I slaughtered over 5,000 of his kingdom's

Islamic teachers and their families. And in the 1750s, the conquering Burmese monarch Alaung-hpaya conducted ethnic massacres and destruction of the Buddhist monkhood of the defeated Mon kingdom.[4]

Throughout these varied regions of the world, subjugated peoples contested domination of their communities, settler occupation of their lands or seizure of their resources. They, too, often adopted violent means to launch their own new kingdoms, regain lost kingdoms, or purify threatened realms of unsuitable people or ideas. For instance, while imperial monarchs in Java and Burma slaughtered political, religious or ethnic opponents to extend or stabilise their control, rulers of the smaller Mon and Khmer kingdoms in lower Burma and Cambodia, for their part, conducted genocidal massacres to reverse territorial losses or eliminate encroaching settlers. In most of these cases, even supposedly pacifistic Buddhists, for instance, deployed their faith to attack and massacre their neighbours. Examining such distant cases of ethno-religious violence during the broad historical era of the early modern conflicts in Ireland may illuminate some of the transnational contexts for the political and territorial quests that often lay behind murderous wars.

In Southeast Asia after 1450, the 'Age of Commerce' created vast trading fortunes and opportunities.[5] Some groups got in the way. Yet even over several centuries in this large area of the world, cases of genocidal massacres were not the norm but in fact quite exceptional. Ethnic politics certainly intensified but still fell short of full polarisation, even though war and killing were common enough as new dynasties expanded and sought political and cultural uniformity. Universalist Islamic and Buddhist aspirations, regional loyalties, personal patronage, dynastic claims over myriad subject peoples, and a good deal of intermarriage, all served to limit ethnic violence to some extent. Some of those factors might already be familiar to readers of earlier chapters of this book.

I shall turn here to how a possibly global phenomenon played out in two regions of eighteenth-century Southeast Asia. In the Burmese and Cambodian deltas, indigenous farmers clashed with perceived outsiders settling on their land. Students of seventeenth-century Ireland may again recognise some common themes.[6]

I

In the vast, polyethnic region that was pre-modern Burma, its three major groups, Burmans, Mons and Shans, spoke different languages but all practiced Theravada Buddhism and wet-rice cultivation. The long Irrawaddy River linked Burma's two main regions: the northern, upland interior, inhabited largely by Burmans and Shans, and the southern delta and coastal regions, home of Mons, Burmans and Karens.

In 1598, an expanding northern dynasty took the Mon capital Pegu in the south, and then moved the capital upriver to Ava. Ethnicity, along with regionalism, now began to entail a political loyalty.[7] Burman–Mon competition for land and resources on the southern frontier led rival groups to seize on ethnic markers as symbols of difference in the interest of more effective group mobilisation.[8] From 1635, Burmans gained total control of the northern court and began to associate Burman ethnicity with religious orthodoxy, even against fellow Theravada Buddhists such as the Shans and Mons, whose distinct languages and hairstyles they now highlighted as alien.[9]

In the 1660s, as Burman farmers moved south into the Irrawaddy delta and the northern Ava court replaced local Mon officials with Burman appointees, Mons revolted. Dutch observers wrote that the Mons of Pegu 'at present are tormented above all others' and predicted that they 'would in all probability put to death the Burmans'. But by the mid-eighteenth century, Mons were reduced to only 60% of the delta's population.[10] Along with Burman settlers came Karens from the east.[11]

Mons increasingly saw themselves as a people subjected to alien rule. Finally, in 1740, they rebelled twice. High taxation was a major initial grievance. The Ava court briefly re-established control, but in a second revolt in November 1740, Karens and Mons assassinated Ava's Burman appointee. They acclaimed a Karen leader, Smin Dhaw, as king of a once again independent Pegu. Smin Dhaw quickly sent 10,000 Mon and Siamese troops to take the Ava-controlled port of Syriam (see 'Siriao' on map). On 4 December 1740, Pegu's army entered Syriam 'in tumult and violence', wrote the English East India Company's agent there. The victorious commander quickly issued orders to all Europeans 'to keep at home'.[12]

The victorious Pegu forces wanted no witnesses to their bloody occupation of Syriam. A week or two later, Smin Dhaw wrote to the English representative to explain what his army had done in the city. In his letter, the new king of Pegu complained first of 'the very great oppressions the poor Peguers formerly labour'd under by the Buramore [Burma] government and the massacre [the latter had] intended on the casts of people called Siamers and Peguers'. Smin Dhaw then explained that 'having advice that the Burmar Prince of Syrian design'd to take and imprison all the Peguers, Siamers, Tavays and all strangers [Europeans] and resolved to burn them by treachery, I Samentho [Smin Dhaw] was obliged to send my soldiers to kill all the governing Burmars that were in Syrian; and as now the said governing Burmars are destroyed'.[13] Corroboration of this reached British Madras the next month. After eighty years of Burman rule, the report said, 'the Natives tired with Cruelty Rose upon 'em and killed 7 or 8,000 Burmars in Syrian only, wholly owing to a Struggle for Liberty'. In the aftermath of this massacre, the British learned, '[t]he port of Syrian is Quiet'.[14]

Smin Dhaw insisted he wanted peace.[15] But conflict continued. The English agent claimed: 'I saved the lives of above two thousand Burmars and have since been endeavouring by all means to regulate and moderate the Government.' Smin Dhaw's forces marched north. A British agent reported that they 'will not rest' till they had conquered Ava.[16] Indeed, Smin Dhaw's successor, an ethnic Shan who vowed to restore the sixteenth-century Pegu kingdom,[17] finally did capture Ava in 1752. The revived Mon kingdom, led first by a Karen and then a Shan, had temporarily triumphed.

But a new Burman leader, Alaung-hpaya (1714–60), quickly gathered strength. After the fall of Ava, he later recalled, 'the Mon rebels carried off people, selling and reselling them as slaves'.[18] In his own campaigns, Alaung-hpaya spared Burman prisoners of war, but he executed Mon captives. Determined to become the universal Buddhist monarch, he distributed a prophetic letter from Sakka, the king of the second Buddhist heaven, dated 9 April 1756: 'He shall exalt the Faith . . . the Mons and Shans shall serve him.'[19]

Alaung-hpaya attacked the Mon capital in 1756. After a year-long siege, Pegu fell on the morning of 7 May 1757. According to a Mon account, Alaung-hpaya's army razed the city and massacred the garrison, 'with bodies piled so high in the gates that people within the city could not escape'.[20] The victors also slaughtered Mon civilians, especially the Buddhist monkhood, many of whom had led the resistance.[21] Another Mon chronicle asserts that 'Alaungpaya took revenge on the Mons . . . He flung most of them including over 3,000 monks [under] the elephants, killing them all.'[22] The northern Burman kingdom had finally subdued the southern Irrawaddy delta.

II

In the sparsely settled, largely brackish flood lands of the Mekong delta, competition for rice land and resources from around the turn of the eighteenth century increasingly plagued relations between local Khmers (Cambodians), who were Theravada Buddhists, and Vietnamese settlers, whose eclectic culture included elements of Mahayana Buddhism, Confucianism, Daoism, spirit cults and, in some cases, Christianity. The southern Vietnamese kingdom of Đàng Trong, known to Europeans as Cochinchina, was expanding southward down the coast. It intervened militarily in Cambodia five times between 1658 and 1700.[23] About 40,000 Vietnamese households had independently settled near the Mekong delta by the start of the eighteenth century.[24] From its capital upriver at Udong, the Cambodian court claimed the delta region, inhabited mostly by Khmers, and contested further Vietnamese encroachment. Vietnamese assisted the Khmer prince Ang Im to gain the Cambodian throne in 1700, and to regain it in 1714. Four years later, a Siamese invasion from the west forced Ang Im's court to pay tribute to Siam.[25]

After a decade of peace, massive violence exploded in 1731. French missionaries in the Mekong delta reported witnessing a genocidal Cambodian attack, led by a self-proclaimed Buddhist monk, on the Đàng Trong-controlled port of Hà Tiên: 'People say that the war originated because of a certain woman who claimed to be the daughter of their god sent to punish the excesses of the Cochinchinese against the Cambodians, magic is mixed up in it and a great deal of prestige. She raised a considerable army of Cambodians . . . thus armed and protected by several mandarins [they] marched against the Cochinchinese and made an enormous carnage of them[;] they counted more than ten thousand of them lost as they were not at all ready to oppose her.' From there the genocidal massacres spread. '[T]hus they ravaged all the provinces of the south of Cochinchina, putting all to fire and blood, killed the great mandarin of the place called Say Gon [Saigon], and burned down the fine church of a Franciscan father.' Yet, 'They were not content with this. They killed all those [Cochinchinese] that they found in Cambodia, men, women and children.'[26] Đàng Trong armies responded with two unsuccessful attacks on Cambodia in 1731–32.[27] The Khmer court at Udong retained control of most of the Mekong delta.[28]

In 1750, the Khmer king Ang Snguon (r. 1749–55) escalated the killing in a new outbreak of genocide. A French missionary in Cambodia reported that war 'raged more than ever' there, and that ethno-political conflict with Đàng Trong had produced more massacres of Vietnamese. 'It is also war outside, against the Cochinchinese who are not far away . . . There have been great cruelties on both sides. The Cambodians have massacred all the Cochinchinese that they could find in the country, including three mandarins; several Christians were caught up in this murder . . . At first they took no prisoners, but killed all those they could find. Now they are sent as slaves to the king of Siam, to repay him for the help he has given to the king of Cambodia.'[29]

A few months later, another missionary, Monsieur d'Azema, identified the author of this massacre as King Ang Snguon himself. '[L]ast year the king had his son, who had been at the court of Cochinchina, killed on some suspicion of rebelling against him.' Then at the end of July 1750, it was Ang Snguon who launched the attacks on every Vietnamese residing in Cambodian territory, including the delta; 'he gave orders or permission to massacre all the Cochinchinese who could be found, and this order was executed very precisely and very cruelly; this massacre lasted a month and a half; only about twenty women and children were spared; no one knows the number of deaths, and it would be very difficult to find out, for the massacre was general from Cahon to Ha-tien, with the exception of a few who were able to escape through the forest or fled by sea to Ha-tien'. Of Cambodia's 'numerous' Vietnamese residents, d'Azema reported finding no survivors, 'pagan or Christian'.[30]

D'Azema was also able to observe other Cambodian authorities' approval of this 'general massacre'. In Phnom Penh, 'the great mandarin of this place, who is the first after the king, and who governs everything', summoned the missionary for an audience. It was only then, and from d'Azema, that the mandarin learned that Đàng Trong had expelled the Christian missionaries there 'on almost the same day' that Cambodia had commenced the mass killing of Đàng Trong residents in its own territory. Although Cambodia had proved unreceptive to Christian proselytisation, the Khmer mandarin quickly pointed to Đàng Trong's expulsions of missionaries as justification for the massacres. D'Azema reported with apparent surprise: 'He even told us that God was punishing the Cochinchinese for their iniquities, and especially for the impieties committed against our holy religion.' The Khmer mandarin offered to have a painting done of a European priest with 'his foot on the throat' of a Vietnamese.[31] D'Azema added that other 'pagans of the kingdom, king, princes, great and small', also took the news of Đàng Trong's mistreatment of missionaries and burning of churches as justification for their own massacres of Vietnamese. Cambodian Buddhist mandarins 'raised their hands to the sky saying that God is just, that he had used them [the Cambodians] to avenge us [Christians]' against the Vietnamese.[32]

Outbreaks of genocidal violence in early modern Southeast Asia fall into several categories. Expanding land-based indigenous kingdoms could resort to extermination, like Alaung-hpaya's massacres of Pegu's ethnic Mon monkhood in 1752–60. But rulers of vigorous smaller kingdoms were equally capable of selecting members of an encroaching ethnic group for annihilation. Threatened by settlement, conquest, internal division or all three, the Mon monarch in 1740 and the Khmer king in 1750 each ordered precisely targeted genocidal massacres. Whether genocidal massacres did happen in any particular case depended on deliberate decisions made by specific leaders, who may or may not have chosen to manipulate ethnic or religious tensions. And whether the evidence of that survives can be a matter of chance. These cases from Southeast Asia demonstrate that historical circumstance and context can yield compelling evidence of what transpired, and of the intent of the perpetrators.

III

It is fruitful to juxtapose these Southeast Asian examples with William J. Smyth's close 'cultural geography' of the events in Ireland in 1641.[33] We might investigate whether eighteenth-century Mon and Khmer cultivators in the Irrawaddy and Mekong deltas perceived their actions against Burman and Vietnamese outsiders in ways similar to the Irish rebels – in Smyth's words, as a war 'about restoring rights to ancestral lands', about 'access to adequate resources and livelihoods' and against 'further displacement'. For instance, the 'violent reaction' of Mon and Khmer rebels seems to have been provoked by a similar fear of being 'totally overwhelmed' by 'great numbers' of 'newcomers', and, in particular, of the 'impact of new immigrant communities being established in what they saw as *their . . . countrysides'*. The two southeast Asian uprisings also contain echoes of the earlier Irish example of a 'war spurred on by prophecies', and of an attempt at the 'erasure of English culture and its symbols – the wiping out of the cultural capital of the coloniser'. The Irish experience also prefigures the participation of women leaders, including their role 'in advocating war and executions', at least in the case of the 1731 Cambodian violence that was led by 'a certain woman who claimed to be the daughter of their god'. Perhaps in the Mekong delta, too, an 'extraordinary world' had emerged in which 'women could recreate themselves'. It is instructive to read the Lords Justices and Council of Ireland explaining in 1642 the killing of Irish women, on the grounds that 'many women' were 'manifestly very deep in the guilt of this rebellion, and, as we are informed, very forward to stir up their husbands and kindred to side therein'.[34]

A comparative look at the 1641 events, as detailed in Smyth's chapter, also tells us many things that we don't know and may never know about the material nature of the Mon and Khmer predicaments. Historians of Southeast Asia are yet to uncover much specific evidence about the overall numbers of Burman and Vietnamese newcomers in the two deltas, about the extent and proportion of settler landholdings there or about gender ratios among the settlers. By contrast, Smyth shows that in the Irish case the 1641 depositions and other contemporary evidence can yield rather rich data on all these key issues. But even given the relative paucity of the Southeast Asian manuscript sources, it is possible that they have yet to be fully exploited in the light of such comparative insights. Several other points Smyth makes are worth pursuing in a search for recurring factors that may indicate a likelihood of violence against settlers. That outcome, he writes, was common in Ireland in 1641 under certain geographic and demographic conditions: first, in 'an exposed salient or island of English/Protestant settlement in a dominant Irish area', and, second, 'where the settlers were well represented but outnumbered by c. two-to-one'. It might still be possible to retrieve that kind of data from existing sources on the Irrawaddy and Mekong delta conflicts (especially in the latter case, given the rather rich compilations assembled by Vietnamese authors in the eighteenth and nineteenth centuries), and, if so, to investigate whether or not the patterns of settlement and violence were similar to those in Ireland a century earlier.

Only now are the 1641 depositions becoming 'universally accessible' and open to discussion, as Aidan Clarke shows in his chapter in this volume. The combination of the depositions' unique content, including eye-witness accounts that Nicholas Canny calls 'so clinical in detail as to be entirely plausible', and the 350-year interval before their complete and accurate publication, raises three important issues for historical analysis of secret or long-suppressed archival collections.[35] These issues are in some ways complementary, sometimes contradictory, yet all three are possibly universal in the study of mass violence and its recurrence.

First, historical silence and forgetting, the concealment or erasure of evidence of violent crimes and the pain they cause, facilitates impunity. This is not just a legal matter. Unashamed or unpunished perpetrators, and their followers or successors, are more likely to repeat such deeds. The importance of full disclosure and open access to the evidence is critical, and not only for historians.

Second, violence or suffering inflicted on individuals or a community, *especially* when conducted with impunity, often becomes seared into that community's memory, even when silenced or subconsciously suppressed. Later, traumatic memories may well propel victims or their sympathisers or successors back onto the historical stage to wreak a new and vengeful contribution to a continuing cycle of violence. In 1675, Samuel Gorton, an elderly English settler in Rhode Island, pleaded with Governor Winthrop of Massachusetts not to start a new cycle by launching a war against Indians in New England. As a warning, Gorton explained the 1641 violence in Ireland as a long-delayed response to the earlier Elizabethan conquest. He wrote to Winthrop: 'I remember the time of the warres in Ireland (when I was young, in Queen Elizabeth's days of famous memory), when much English blood was spilt by a people much like unto these [Indians] . . . And after these Irish were subdued by force, what treacherous and bloody massacres have they attempted is well knowne.'[36] Sadly, the Puritan forces ignored Gorton's advice about the lesson of 1641, and, within months, they perpetrated genocidal massacres of previously non-hostile Narragansett Indians in Rhode Island.[37] These intertwined seventeenth-century cases illustrate my first two points: the contributions to continuing violence of both recidivist perpetrators and vengeful victims.

Third, the 1641 depositions may fairly be characterised, without casting any doubt on their accuracy, as an example of a 'single-purpose' archive, rather than the product of general documentation of routine official or other activity. As Clarke notes, in 1641–47 the clerical Commission for the Despoiled Subject collected all 3,500 depositions pursuant to a very specific 'official duty' – 'registering the losses of despoiled Protestants'. These depositions include 1,860 'sworn statements of Protestant refugees taken by a group of eight clergymen, headed by Henry Jones, acting on the authority of three successive commissions issued by the Dublin government' in 1641–42. To these were added 1,600 'similar statements from English Protestants' taken in Munster in 1642–43 'under the authority of a special commission' that was also apparently 'modelled on the original commission'.[38] Such an assembly of targeted depositions was not unique in that era, but it is clear that this enterprise was conducted to a specific purpose. Joseph Cope points out that the depositions 'simply do not preserve the pauses, clarifications or leading questions that may have occurred in this context, much less the practical ramifications of the power imbalance between witnesses and examiners'.[39] Moreover, Catholics were rarely asked to contribute their testimony.[40] Canny has described the depositions as 'a body of material which is emotional and which seeks to represent Irish Catholics in the worst possible light'.[41]

Single-purpose archives by definition do not record the full context. For example, none of the depositions details the brutal atrocities committed by the English Protestant planter Sir Charles Coote, military governor of Dublin in 1641–42.[42] Evidence of his violence survives only in other sources and archives. According to a manuscript account written in the 1650s, 'that human blood sucker Sir Charles Coote gave his opinion once in the Councell table in Dublin, before those Comotions, that all the Irish women should be deprived of their papps, and the men gelded, to render the one incapable of future generation and the other of nurishinge'.[43] In early December 1641, seven Catholic lords of the Pale complained that Coote had urged the Lord Justices and Council 'to execute upon those of our religion a generall massacre'. A few weeks later, these lords reiterated that Coote had even 'offered to performe . . . a generall massacre upon all of our religion . . . had the Council consented thereunto'.[44] On 22 December, the seven Catholic lords wrote again to the Lords Justices and Council in reference to 'Some words mentioned in our former Letters which Wee were informed Sir Charles Coote should have spoken att Councell Board', and noting now that 'the bitter effects that followed are a Cleere proofe of Sir Charles his Intencions against professors of our Relligion and a further motive to con[vince?] us in the Assurance that such words Issued from him'. The lords then went on to list Coote's actions: 'Wee beheld [with] noe small affright the Inhumane Acts perpetrated upon the Inhabitants of the County of Wicklow . . . [and] the late massacre of Santry and also Mr Kings house and whole substance burnt by Sir Charles Coote'.[45] The next month, the rebel commander General Preston also denounced 'the cruell proceedings of our enemies by destroying by fire and sword, men, women, and children, without regard had to age or sex'.[46]

These partisan views are partly corroborated in the contemporary account of the Lords Justice themselves, who described their troops' activities in strikingly similar language. They wrote on 7 June 1642: 'We have hitherto where we came against the rebels, their adherents, relievers, and abettors, proceeded with fire and sword, the soldiers sometimes not sparing the women and sometimes not children.'[47] In his 1682 work, *An Impartial Collection of the*

Great Affairs of State, John Nalson wrote: 'I have heard a Relation of my own, who was a Captain in that Service, Relate, that no manner of Compassion or Discrimination was shewed either to Age or Sex, but that the little Children were promiscuously Sufferers with the Guilty, and that if any who had some grains of Compassion reprehended the Soldiers for this unchristian Inhumanity, they would scoffingly reply, *Why? Nits will be Lice*, and so would dispatch them.'[48] In a long manuscript composed in 1711, Nicholas Plunkett levelled more charges that are precise. He wrote that in November 1641 the Lords Justices, Sir William Parsons and Sir John Borlase, had issued orders to Sir Charles Coote and others 'that these souldiers should kill the catholick People without distinction of age or sex. And when the question was put to Sir William Parsons in particular, whether women and children were to be killed? He answered, that not one of the Irish must be spared, who was grown a span long. Upon this, Partyes marched out. Sir Charles Coot was ordered to go first to the County of Wicklow: where he performed such barbarous murthers (that tis a horror to name them) upon men, women and children, sitting quietly at home in their poor Cabbins, minding their little country affayrs . . . The children and grandchildren of these massacred men and women, have at this day a Liveing History of this Cannibal's butchery in the said County.'[49]

A digital search of the 1641 depositions for information relating to these charges was unresponsive. That is hardly surprising. Although Sir Charles Coote was killed in action on 7 May 1642, his sons Charles jnr. and Chidley played continuing roles not only in the fighting but also in assembling some of the depositions on Protestant suffering, partly in order to claim compensation for their family's losses.[50] There is even evidence of Sir Charles himself, before his death, suppressing evidence from a deposition in March 1642.[51] Nonetheless, selectivity or omissions of this kind do not address the question of the collection's accuracy – only its purpose and comprehensiveness.

Researching this single-purpose archive took me forward to the Cambodia of the 1970s. Some key points to be made about archival collections that document violence or repression may extend even to the present day. When the Vietnamese armed forces overthrew the Pol Pot regime in January 1979, they uncovered a secret prison and its previously unknown archive. The latter notably contained a special category of documents, over 4,000 'confessions', also created for a single purpose. But in most ways, the archive of the prison that the Khmer Rouge regime called 'S-21' is very different from the 1641 depositions. From 1976 to 1979, the S-21 jailers not only assembled these 'confessions' in a highly selective manner, they extracted them under torture or the threat of torture. The confessions total in various drafts perhaps 100,000 pages of handwritten and typed autobiographical accounts (often including the torturers' marginal notes in red ink), as well as other Khmer-language documents detailing the torture methods used, and also including tables, charts, ledgers and extensive lists of victims whom the prison commandant had ordered to be 'smashed' (*komtech*, here meaning 'kill').[52] The documentation of the terror is conclusive even if none of the prisoner-authors survived to tell the story of how they had been compelled to write their 'confessions'. The Khmer Rouge murdered all but a dozen of the approximately 14,000 inmates of S-21, apparently including every single one of the 4,000 prisoners whose confessions are extant. As David Chandler has written, there are real questions about the purpose of this S-21 archive 'when its contents were kept secret, so much of the material was untrue, and all of the prisoners were killed'.[53]

Interpreting the confessions themselves has been a challenge. Nearly all the prisoner-authors wrote fantastical 'admissions' that they had been spies or agents of the US Central Intelligence Agency, the Soviet KGB or the Vietnamese communists (and quite often all three simultaneously). To the satisfaction of their S-21 torturers, this proved that they were 'traitors' who deserved execution. But the concern was more about getting the prisoners to commit such confessions to paper, than about their specific content. It is not at all clear that the CPK's security police, the *Santebal*, ever believed these accusations, of which of course it was the real author. Rather, S-21's preordained purpose was to subdue and execute its prisoners. That involved assembling an archive of lies, that the jailers conjured up and the prisoners penned before their execution.

Yet there is more to the confessions than the guilt they proclaim. The documents are structured as lengthy autobiographies, which served not only to humiliate their authors, but also to detail their links to their political colleagues, who then became Santebal suspects and so would also be arrested. For the torturers, the charge of membership in a supposed 'CIA-KGB-Vietnamese' network clearly *did* require at least some evidence, which in turn required detailed career histories. In outline only, these are largely reliable. In the case of nearly every prisoner, the dates, places, positions, military or political units, and associates listed in their confessions appear to be authentic, drawn from the prisoner's own memory. This is true even though the content is often ludicrous, particularly accounts of supposed conspiratorial conversations. The structure of the autobiographies does provide an extremely rich source of evidence for an institutional history of the Communist Party of Kampuchea (CPK), indeed, for a unique 'inside story'. I doubt that accessible archives of any other political group in Southeast Asia (possibly even currently inaccessible archives) would provide anything close to comparable information about the party's organisation. The historical data are so informative and detailed that two commentators have even suggested that 'the archive was assembled to provide the Party Centre with raw material for a massive, unwritten history of the Party . . . The model that Pol Pot and his colleagues were following, it seems, was the *History of the Communist Party of the Soviet Union*, as published in 1939'.[54]

In fact, the Khmer Rouge displayed little interest in reading or writing and certainly none in publishing historical works.[55] Stalin put on public show trials for many of the innocents he murdered, but Pol Pot's victims simply disappeared into deathly silence. The confessions themselves also consign the political history of the CPK to obscurity. Indeed, that was their purpose. Proving that the prisoners were simply 'traitors' meant denying them any chance to explain their dissidence or their actions. In fact, the torturers often required prisoners to make declarations that they had no reason for dissent, beyond membership of a conspiratorial network, or sometimes, sexual depravity. One jailer instructed a prisoner to confess his 'sexual activities with your own child in detail'. The prisoner courageously wrote to Pol Pot denying the charge and defending his young daughter's honour, but the letter was suppressed.[56] Few prisoners were allowed to present any evidence of genuine disagreement or political dissidence. The confessions contain almost no hint, memory or discussion of alternative policies or indigenous opposition. Their precise purpose was indeed to conceal any evidence of such a history within the CPK by accusing the prisoners of foreign subservience, and documenting the allegation with their tortured assent.

Thus, what the archives do not tell us is as important as what they do. Perhaps more so, in this case, if other evidence demonstrates that authentic dissidence did exist. A need to cover it up might in turn explain the existence of S-21. It would tell us why the regime was determined to arrest and kill so many people: to obliterate internal disagreement by both forcing the dissidents to erase it from their own histories, and then killing them.

The truth, then, depends on examining other evidence. We must avoid concluding from the confessions alone that no genuine dissidence existed, as Elizabeth Becker did when she asserted that the S-21 archives 'show' that 'the entire Party was implicated and involved in "Pol Potism"'.[57] That is like saying the 1641 depositions demonstrate that no Irish Catholics suffered violence at English or Protestant hands. Worse, offering the confessions as proof of the absence of substantial policy disagreement is to ignore the limitations on human expression in a death camp. That would be to concede yet another success to the totalitarian CPK system. The system was successful in eliminating dissidence in any action (by striking it from the party) and on paper (from the confessions). Historiography should not mimic its successes.

Especially in single-purpose archives, the absence of evidence cannot constitute evidence of absence. For instance, after the Santebal executed the prominent leftist intellectual Tiv Ol, it then arrested his wife Leng Sim Hak, also a CPK member, who had spent the previous two years running a Phnom Penh hospital. Grasping at straws to stay alive in S-21, Leng Sim Hak omitted from her autobiographical 'confessions' any mention of her having led, two years earlier, a CPK Women's Association delegation to Hanoi before the official Khmer Rouge declaration of war on Vietnam. Not only would this information have quickly sealed her fate, but her torturers would also have required confessions of her alleged recruitment in Hanoi by Vietnamese intelligence or the KGB. As it was, her torturers seem to have been unaware of the trip but condemned her to death anyway, concluding: 'The important thing is that she was with her husband throughout.'[58] That is no evidence of the couple's treason, *or* of their supposed agreement with CPK policies.

A single-purpose collection is possibly much easier to generate than the more conventional archives. But such a concentration of documentation is also much easier to hide or destroy. The Khmer Rouge regime created S-21 in total secrecy. Its existence was unknown even to most members of the ruling CPK, until that regime fell. The archive's purpose was secret collection, not public dissemination. Indeed, when the CPK regime faced defeat by the Vietnamese, Pol Pot's deputy Nuon Chea ordered the S-21 commandant, Duch, to destroy the archive. Duch stayed behind for several hours after Vietnamese forces entered Phnom Penh that morning, but, instead of destroying the archives, he preferred to murder the few remaining prisoners.[59] When he later rejoined his colleagues on the Thai border, Duch told a furious Nuon Chea that he had failed to burn the prison's archives before his flight.[60] The cover-up had failed; the documentary evidence of their massive crimes survived. In 2010, Duch was found guilty of crimes against humanity, while Nuon Chea is facing charges of genocide.

Even without destruction of its contents, a single-purpose archive is also easier to discredit, if only because its selectivity and partisan omissions are likely to stand out. Canny shows that this problem contributed to the long neglect of the 1641 depositions: 'Instead of countering it with an interpretation of their own, those who were uneasy with Temple's version of events strove to discredit the authority on which it was based by asserting that the 1641 depositions were so biased in their reportage that they could not be admitted as evidence.'[61] Thomas Fitzpatrick challenged this view in 1903 but for decades his research was not investigated.[62]

As Canny points out, 'despite these apparent biases this Protestant testimony cannot be ignored, because it represents the only detailed evidence of what happened in Ireland in and after October 1641'. And this evidence is not only unique but also more nuanced than might have been expected. Many deponents and commission officials not only detailed the suffering of Protestants, but also took pains to identify their attackers, and therefore often 'recorded the gist of the justifications for the onslaught offered to them by their assailants', making it possible for historians 'to suggest explanations for the involvement of different social elements from within the Irish Catholic community'.[63]

It is thus possible to document some of Sir Charles Coote's actions even though in the 1640s apparently not a single deponent denounced any of his crimes. For instance, when the Cromwellian High Court of Justice gathered a further series of testimonies in 1652–54, the Dublin butcher Robert Neale testified that 'about Christmas [1641] after Sir Charles Coote cominge into the County of wickloe and haveinge there killed som of the Irish *Rebells* the Irish gave out that they would be revenged of the English'. And in detailing the circumstances of their brutal retaliation, Capt. Cahir of Wicklow added that 'upon Sir Charles Cootes first marching into the County of wickloe, it beinge reported in that Contry that an woman one of the Irish woman of the Rebells partie was by his Comand hanged', an Irish rebel leader arrested two Englishmen, marched them to the site, 'and finding for Certaine that the saide woman had beene hanged', ordered the two prisoners to be hanged on the same spot.[64]

In his 1735 biography of the Duke of Ormonde (1610–1688), Thomas Carte described 'the executions, which Sir Charles Coote had ordered in the County of Wicklow, among which, when a soldier was carrying about a poor babe on the end of his pike, he was charged with saying, that *he liked such frolicks*'. Carte went on to assert that this violence had political implications, as it created the impression that the authorities had 'determined to proceed against all suspected persons in the same undistinguishing way of cruelty'. That then 'served either for an occasion, or pretence', for those Catholic lords of the Pale already mentioned to 'put themselves with their followers in a posture of defence', by joining forces with the Gaelic Irish rebels in the Confederacy.[65]

Of course, Coote was not the only perpetrator of anti-Irish violence. In the 1650s, additional examinants also told the Cromwellian High Court of Justice of the 'generall Murder' of Catholics at Island Magee and Carrickfergus in early 1642. One examinant reported that 'they and the rest of the Irish were forced to shelter themselves in houses and that they were taken out and murthered but how or by whom he cannot declare'.[66] Several other possible witnesses were also questioned about 'the murther Comitted upon the Irish in Iland Magee in the beginninge of the Rebellion'.[67] In the 1650s, the High Court of Justice even executed a number of Scots for these massacres of Catholic Irish.[68]

In 1682, John Nalson charged certain 'half-faced Historians' with having 'concealed some things and palliated others'. He asserted that 'the Cruelty of the Rebels' in Ireland during the 1640s had been 'strange and barbarous', but he also lamented that 'on the other side there is not the least mention of any Cruelty exercised upon the Irish'. Nalson also pointed out that 'so to deny or smother matters of fact, so easily to be proved, even by many Protestants still alive', only undermines the truthful accounts of the 'inhumane Cruelties' of Catholic violence against Protestants.[69] Conversely, over 350 years Ireland has discovered that suppressing or ignoring thousands of depositions that detail crimes against Protestants was no answer either to bias in the viewpoints that archive contains.

By a brutal stroke of luck, the documentation of Khmer Rouge violence escaped the perpetrators' attempt to consign it to oblivion. It is now evidence in genocide prosecutions under international criminal law. But the work of its historical interpretation has barely begun. Like the 1641 depositions, it must be analyzed alongside other sources of evidence.

NOTES

1 rGyal-dbang lnga-pa, *Rgya-Bod-Hor-Sog-gi* . . . (Xining, 1993), p. 225, quoted in Elliot Sperling, ' "Orientalism" and aspects of violence in the Tibetan tradition', in Thierry Dodin and Heinz Räther (eds), *Imagining Tibet: Perceptions, Projections, and Fantasies* (Boston, 2001), pp. 317–18.

2 For definitions of genocide and genocidal massacres, see Ben Kiernan, *Blood and Soil: A World History of Genocide and Extermination from Sparta to Darfur* (New Haven, 2007), pp. 10–15.

3 See, for instance, Gabriel de San Antonio, *Breve y verdadera relacion de los successos del reyno de Camboxa* (Valladolid, 1604); Mak Phoeun, *Histoire du Cambodge de la fin du XVIe siècle au début du XVIIIe* (École française d'Extrême-Orient (EFEO), Paris, 1995), pp. 66–91.

4 An analysis of these three cases may be found in Kiernan, *Blood and Soil*, pp. 133–56.

5 Anthony Reid, *Southeast Asia in the Age of Commerce, 1450–1680* (2 vols, New Haven, 1988–93).

6 For an early comparable exercise, see R. B. Smith, 'England and Vietnam in the fifteenth and sixteenth centuries: an essay in historical comparison', in C. D. Cowan and O. W. Wolters (eds), *Southeast Asian History and Historiography* (Ithaca, 1976), pp. 227–45.

7 William J. Koenig, *The Burmese Polity, 1752–1819* (Ann Arbor, 1990), pp. xiii, 6–7; Victor Lieberman, *Strange Parallels: Southeast Asia in Global Context, c.800–1830*, vol. I, *Integration on the Mainland* (Cambridge, 2003), p. 135.

8 Victor Lieberman, personal comment; and his 'Ethnic politics in eighteenth-century Burma', *Modern Asian Studies*, 12 (1978), 455–82, at 463.

9 Lieberman, *Strange Parallels*, vol. i, pp. 198–201, 136–7.

10 Lieberman, 'Ethnic politics', pp. 463, 465, and *Strange Parallels*, vol. i, pp. 203, 199, 204.

11 Koenig, *Burmese Polity*, pp. 9–11; Victor Lieberman, *Burmese Administrative Cycles* (Princeton, 1984), p. 189.

12 Jonathan Smart (Syriam) to Fort St George (Madras), 17 March 1740/41, in *Records of Fort St. George. Letters to Fort St. George 1681/82–1744/45* (29 vols, Madras, 1916–33), vol. xxvi, pp. 35–7, at p. 36. Victor Lieberman kindly provided a copy of this letter.

13 Smart to Fort St George, 23 December 1740, and 'Translation of the letter from King Sementho [Smin Dhaw] to Mr. Smart', delivered 21 December 1740, in *Records of Fort St. George: Letters to Fort St. George 1681/82–1744/45*, vol. xxvi, pp. 8–9. Lieberman kindly provided copies; see his 'Ethnic politics', pp. 463–64.

14 British Library, London, India Office Records, Correspondence with India (Examiner's Office), E/4/4, Abstract of Letters Received from 'Coast' and 'Bay' 1734–44, 'Fort St George General dated 31th Janry 1740', p. 332.

15 'Translate of the Letter from King Sementho to Mr. Smart', delivered to Syrian, 21 December 1740, p. 9.

16 Smart to Fort St. George, 17 March 1740/41, *Letters to Fort St. George 1681/82–1744/45*, vol. xxvi, pp. 35–6.

17 Arthur Phayre, *History of Burma* (London, 1883; repr. Bangkok, 1998), p. 145.

18 Lieberman, *Burmese Administrative Cycles*, pp. 230–1.

19 Lieberman, 'Ethnic politics', pp. 464 note 22, 473, 479; *Burmese Administrative Cycles*, pp. 236–7, 249, 244; Koenig, *Burmese Polity*, p. 13, cites Alaung-hpaya's 'open appeals to Burman ethnic chauvinism'.

20 *Phongsawadan mòn phama* ('Annal of the Mon of Burma'), in *Prachum phong-sawadan phak thi 1*, History Series, part 1 (Bangkok, 1963), vol. ii, p. 112, translation from the Thai kindly supplied by Kennon Breazeale. Lieberman, *Burmese Administrative Cycles*, p. 248.

21 Lieberman, 'Ethnic politics', pp. 473, 476–7; *Strange Parallels*, vol. i, pp. 184, 199–200; Phayre, *History of Burma*, p. 166.

22 British Library (BL), London, MS Oriental 3464, pp. 148–50. This is a Burmese translation of a Mon history of Pegu by the Monk of Athwa, probably composed in the late 1760s, according to Victor Lieberman, who kindly supplied a copy. Translation from the Burmese by U. Khin Maung Gyi.

23 Mak Phoeun, *Histoire*, pp. 294–410, dates the first five Vietnamese military interventions at 1658–1700.

24 Choi Byung Wook, *Southern Vietnam under the Reign of Minh Mang (1820–1841): Central Policies and Local Response* (Ithaca, 2004), p. 165.

25 Lieberman, *Strange Parallels*, vol. i, p. 411, says there were thirteen Vietnamese interventions by 1772, which would include eight in the eighteenth century (see note 23, above). However for the period 1700–1730, Sok mentions Vietnamese involvement only in 1714, in assisting Ang Im to regain the throne: Khin Sok, *Le Cambodge entre le Siam et le Viêtnam (de 1175 à 1860)* (EFEO, Paris, 1991), p. 36.

26 Missions Etrangères de Paris (MEP) [136], vol. 739, Pierre du Puy du Fayet, Jean de Antoine de la Court and Charles Gouge, to the Directors, 26 July 1732, pp. 925–30. Translation by Nola Cooke, who very kindly supplied her detailed notes from the MEP archives. See also Lieberman, *Strange Parallels*, vol. i, p. 412.

27 Khin Sok, *Le Cambodge entre le Siam et le Vietnam*, p. 36.

28 Mak Phoeun, 'La frontière entre le Cambodge et le Viêtnam du XVIIe siècle à l'instauration du protectorat français présentée à travers les chroniques royales khmères', in Pierre-Bernard Lafont (ed.), *Les Frontières du Vietnam* (Paris, 1989), pp. 139–40.

29 M. Piguel to Mgr. Lefebvre, 8 April 1751, in Adrien Launay, *Histoire de la Mission de Cochinchine 1658–1823, Documents Historiques, vol. II, 1728–1771* (Paris, 1924), p. 368.

30 M. d'Azema to M. de Noëlène, undated, quoted in M. J. B. Maigrot to Mgr. de Martiliat, 16 September 1751, and d'Azema to Directeurs du Séminaire des M.-E., Cambodge, 20 June 1757, in Launay, *Histoire de la Mission de Cochinchine 1658–1823*, vol. ii, pp. 365–73, at pp. 366, 370; Khin Sok, *Le Cambodge entre le Siam et le Vietnam*, p. 37.

31 D'Azema to De Noëlène, undated, and Piguel to Lefebvre, 8 April 1751, in Launay, *Histoire*, pp. 365–6, 368.

32 D'Azema to Directeurs du Séminaire des M.-E., Cambodge, 20 June 1757, Launay, *Histoire*, pp. 370–1.

33 Chapter 5.

34 Lords Justices and Council to His Majesty's Commissioners for the Affairs of Ireland, 7 June 1642, in *Calendar of the Manuscripts of the Marquess of Ormonde*, new series (Historical Manuscripts Commission, 8 volumes, London, 1902–20), vol. ii, pp. 130–1.

35 Nicholas Canny, 'What Really Happened in Ireland in 1641?', in Jane Ohlmeyer (ed.), *Ireland from Independence to Occupation 1641–1660* (Cambridge, 1995), p. 28.

36 Samuel Gorton to Winthrop, 11 September 1675, quoted in Francis Jennings, *The Invasion of America: Indians, Colonialism, and the Cant of Conquest* (New York, 1975), p. 312.

37 Kiernan, *Blood and Soil*, pp. 236–41.

38 Aidan Clarke, 'The 1641 Depositions', in Peter Fox (ed.), *Treasures of the Library, Trinity College Dublin* (Dublin, 1986), pp. 111–22, at pp. 120, 112, 114. For the numbers of depositions I draw on Clarke's chapter in this volume. See also Trinity College Dublin (TCD) MS 809, 'Deposition of Henry Jones', 3 March 1642, fos 1r–4v: TCD, 1641 Depositions Project, http://1641.tcd.ie/deposition.php?depID<?php echo 809001r001?> (accessed 22 June 2011).

39 Joseph Cope, *England and the 1641 Irish Rebellion* (Woodbridge, Boydell Press, 2009), p. 35.

40 Noting 'a few exceptions', Kenneth Nicholls cites several Protestant depositions that document atrocities committed 'against the Irish'; see Nicholls, 'The other massacre: English killings of Irish, 1641–2', in David Edwards, Pádraig Lenihan and Clodagh Tait (eds), *Age of Atrocity: Violence and Political Conflict in Early Modern Ireland* (Dublin, 2007), pp. 176–91, at p. 180.

41 Canny, 'What Really Happened in Ireland in 1641?', p. 27.

42 Robert Armstrong, 'Coote, Sir Charles', in James McGuire and James Quinn (eds), *Dictionary of Irish Biography* (9 vols, Cambridge, 2009), vol. ii, pp. 827–8; Cope, *England and the 1641 Irish Rebellion*, p. 68 note 63. On Coote's atrocities, see also 'R. S.', *A Collection of Some of the Murthers and Massacres committed on the Irish in Ireland Since the 23d of October 1641* (London, 1662), p. 15; Thomas Carte, *An History of the Life of James, Duke of Ormonde* (3 vols, London, 1735–36), vol. i, pp. 242, 244–5; Clodagh Tait, ' "The just vengeance of God"; reporting

the violent deaths of persecutors in early modern Ireland', and Kevin Forkan, 'Inventing a Protestant icon: the strange death of Sir Charles Coote, 1642', in Edwards, *Age of Atrocity*, pp. 141–4, 204–18; Aidan Clarke, *The Old English in Ireland, 1625–42* (Dublin, 2000), pp. 177–8, 186, 189–90, 200, 225, 231; Micheál Ó Siochrú, *Confederate Ireland 1642–1649: A Constitutional and Political Analysis* (Dublin, 1999), p. 24; Ó Siochrú, *God's Executioner: Oliver Cromwell and the Conquest of Ireland* (London, 2008), pp. 15, 26; Robert Armstrong, *Protestant War: The 'British' of Ireland and the Wars of the Three Kingdoms* (Manchester, 2005), pp. 17, 21–2; M. Perceval-Maxwell, *The Outbreak of the Irish Rebellion of 1641* (Montreal, 1994), p. 245.

43 TCD MS 846, 'R. S.', *An Aphorismicall Discovery of Treasonable Faction*, chapter 6, paragraph 52, p. 8. See also the printed version in John T. Gilbert (ed.), *A Contemporary History of Affairs in Ireland from 1641 to 1652* (3 vols, Dublin, 1879), vol. i, p. 32.

44 Fingal and six other Pale lords to the Lords Justices from the Hill of Taragh, 7 December 1641; and, Confederate Peers to Nobility and Gentry of Galway, 29 December 1641; in Richard Bellings, 'The Irish Confederation and War, 1641–1642' [c.1670], in John T. Gilbert, (ed.), *History of the Irish Confederation and the War in Ireland* (7 vols, Dublin, 1882–91), vol. i, pp. 38–9, 244–45. Consistent with this, Coote is reported to have ordered his troops to kill Irish Catholic men, women and even children 'more than a span long', and in the face of his officers' objections, he is alleged to have retorted: 'Kill the nits and you will have no lice.' Sean O'Callaghan, *To Hell or Barbados: The Ethnic Cleansing of Ireland* (Dingle, 2000), p. 45. See also Peter Beresford Ellis, *Hell or Connaught: The Cromwellian Colonisation of Ireland 1652–1660* (Belfast, 1975), pp. 19–20; Thomas Fitzpatrick, *The Bloody Bridge, and Other Papers Relating to the Insurrection of 1641* (Dublin, 1903), pp. 160–1.

45 TCD MS 840, Pale lords at Tara to the lords justices and council, 22 December 1641, fos 39r–40v, http://1641.tcd.ie/deposition.php?depID<?php echo 840039r022?> (accessed 30 June 2011).

46 General Preston to the earl of Clanricarde, 18 January 1642, in Carte, *History of the Life of James, Duke of Ormonde*, vol. iii, p. 120.

47 Lords justice and council to his majesty's commissioners for the affairs of Ireland, 7 June 1642, in *Calendar of the Manuscripts of the Marquess of Ormonde*, vol. ii, pp. 130–1.

48 John Nalson, *An Impartial Collection of the Great Affairs of State* (2 vols, London, 1682–83), vol. ii, p. vii. In his memoir of the 1640s wars in Ireland, the earl of Castlehaven asserted that 'there have been great cruelties committed upon the *English* . . . But the truth is, they were very bloody on both sides, and tho' some will throw all upon the *Irish*, yet 'tis well known who they were that used to give *orders* to their parties, sent into enemies' quarters, to spare neither man, woman, nor child', James Touchet, earl of Castlehaven, *The Earl of Castlehaven's Memoirs: or, his Review of the Late Wars of Ireland, with his own Engagement and Conduct therein*, ed. Charles O'Conor (Waterford, 1753), p. 19 (italics original).

49 National Library of Ireland, MSS 476–7 [Nicholas Plunkett], 'A Light to the Blind; whereby they may see the dethronement of James the Second, King of England, with a brief Narrative . . . Anno 1711', vol. i, pp. 69–71 (chapter 6, paragraph 25).

50 TCD MS 831, 'Examination of John Boyes', taken before Charles Coote, 3 February 1645, fos 109r–109v, http://1641.tcd.ie/deposition.php?depID<?php echo 831109r101?>, MS 815, 'Deposition of Isacke Sands', fos 180r–181r, http://1641.tcd.ie/deposition. php?depID<?php echo 815180r260?>, and the depositions of Coote's tenant Gefferey Corbett, MS 815, fos 318r–318v, http://1641.tcd.ie/deposition.php?depID<?php echo 815318r381?>, and Coote's agent John Bourke, MS 833, fos 223r–223v, http://1641. tcd.ie/deposition.php?depID<?php echo 833223r163?> (all accessed 2 July 2011); MS 814, 'Deposition of Chidley Coote', fos 204r–216v, http://1641.tcd.ie/deposition. php?depID<?php echo 814204r129?> (accessed 30 June 2011).

51 Fitzpatrick, The Bloody Bridge, pp. xxviii–xxix.

52 Anthony Barnett, Ben Kiernan and Chanthou Boua, 'Bureacracy of death: documents from inside Pol Pot's torture machine', New Statesman (2 May 1980), cover and pp. 668–76.

53 David P. Chandler, Voices from S-21: Terror and History in Pol Pot's Secret Prison (Berkeley, 1999), p. 49.

54 Chandler, Voices from S-21, pp. 50 (citing S. Heder), p. 105.

55 For a secret, unpublished 'Abbreviated lesson on the history of the Kampuchean revolutionary movement', see Pol Pot Plans the Future: Confidential Leadership Documents from Democratic Kampuchea, 1976–1977 (New Haven, 1988), pp. 213–26.

56 'Planning the past: the forced confessions of Hu Nim', translation in Pol Pot Plans the Future, pp. 266, 281–2, 289, 293–5, 297, 308; Chandler, Voices from S-21, pp. 157–9.

57 Elizabeth Becker, 'Cambodia Blames Ousted Leader, Not Party', Washington Post (2 March 1983), p. A12.

58 Ben Kiernan, The Pol Pot Regime: Race, Power and Genocide in Cambodia under the Khmer Rouge, 1975–1979 (New Haven, 1996), pp. 124, 159ff., 355, 464.

59 Kiernan, The Pol Pot Regime, p. 452.

60 'You are stupid', Nuon Chea raged at Duch. Jean-Claude Pomonti, 'Le "repentir" d'un tortionnaire khmer rouge', Le Monde (3 September 1999); see also Nic Dunlop and Nate Thayer, 'The confession', Far Eastern Economic Review (2 May 1999).

61 Canny, 'What Really Happened in Ireland in 1641?', p. 25.

62 'It is a fault perhaps common to all . . . to treat of the depositions as of equal merit or demerit throughout. The fact is that – as I would appraise them – they are of every degree of merit from worthlessness upwards', Fitzpatrick, The Bloody Bridge, 166.

63 Canny, 'What really happened in Ireland in 1641?', p. 27.

64 TCD MS 811, 'Examination of Robert Neale', 14 September 1652, fos 191r–192v, http://1641.tcd.ie/deposition.php?depID<?php echo 811191r136?>, and 'Examination of Cahir alias Charles Birne', 8 October 1652, fos 205r–206v, http://1641.tcd.ie/ deposition.php?depID<?php echo 811205r143?>, (both accessed 2 July 2011).

65 Carte, History of the Life of James, Duke of Ormonde, vol. i, pp. 242, 244–5.

66 TCD MS 838, 'Examination of Owen Magee', 31 May 1653, fos 220r–220v, http://
1641.tcd.ie/deposition.php?depID<?php echo 838220r267?> (accessed 22 June 2011).
For independent evidence of this massacre, see Nicholls, 'The other massacre:
English killings of Irish, 1641–2', in Edwards, *Age of Atrocity*, pp. 180–1; Michael
McCartan, 'The Cromwellian High Courts of Justice in Ulster, 1653', *Seanchas
Ard Mhacha*, 23 (2010), 91–161, esp. 95–7.

67 TCD MS 838, 'Examination of William Elsinor', fos 207r–207v [http://1641.tcd.ie/
deposition.php?depID<?php echo 838207r258?>; TCD MS 838, 'Examination of
Robert Boyd', fos 137r–137v http://1641.tcd.ie/deposition.php?depID<?php echo
838137r196?>; TCD MS 838, 'Examination of Margrett Lowrye', fos 234r–234v
http://1641.tcd.ie/deposition.php?depID<?php echo 838234r282?> (all accessed
22 June 2011).

68 McCartan, 'The Cromwellian High Courts of Justice in Ulster, 1653'.

69 Nalson, *Impartial Collection*, vol. ii, p. vii.

Index

1641 depositions
  anthropological analysis 10–11, 71,
    84–7
  bias in 3–4, 80–3, 134–5, 261–3, 266
  centenary of 2, 44
  collection of 1–2, 10–11, 42–3, 136,
    261–2
  compared with equivalent English
    evidence 135–6
  content of 2–3, 42–3, 135–6, 260–1
  controversy surrounding 2, 3–4,
    11–12, 71, 134–5
  descriptions of attacks 75–80, 137–44,
    236
  evidence of rebels' Spanish
    sympathies 240
  extracts used in *Remonstrance* 38–9,
    40, 42, 120, 242
    and untitled sequel to 40–1, 42, 47
  fatalities reported *see* fatalities
  fear of continental plot in 243
  geographical analysis of 10, 71–83, 259–60
  linguistic analysis of 5
  and orality 8–9, 39, 84, 136, 201
  presented to Trinity College 2, 44
  as propaganda 2, 4, 58, 81, 120–1
  publication of *see* 1641 Depositions
    Project
  as single-purpose archive 3, 134–5,
    261–3, 266
  social class of deponents 74, 146
  sworn and unsworn testimonies 1–2,
    39, 44, 45–6
  use as historical source 5, 43–9, 61,
    134–5
1641 Depositions Project 4–5, 11–12, 37,
  260–1

Aalst 176, 179, 181
Aberdeen University 4
'Abstract' (anon.) 98–9, 103–5
Aertz, Pieter 179, 181, 183–4
Aghalow 236
Alaung-hpaya 255, 257, 259
Alba, Duke of *see* Álvarez de Toledo,
  Fernando, Duke of Alba
Aldridge, William 47
Alkmaar 179, 180, 186, 189
Alric, Raymond 203, 204, 205
Álvarez de Toledo, Fernando, Duke of
  Alba 176, 178–9
America (De Bry) 58
Americas, the 9–10, 19–22, 52–4, 57–9,
  62–6, 84–6, 219–32, 237, 244–5, 261
Amussen, Susan 29
Anderson, Lee 21
Ang Snguon 258
anthropology 10–11, 71, 84–7, 135
  cultural 23
  of violence 11, 136–7, 143

Antrim, County 72, 74, 75, 83, 101, 104
Antrim, Earl of *see* MacDonnell, Randal, Earl of Antrim
Antwerp 176, 179, 181, 182, 183, 184–5
Ardee 76
Armagh, County 7, 48, 72, 74, 76, 78, 101, 104, 106
Armstrong, Robert 80
army 96–8, 99–100, 102, 103–4, 105–7, 108, 118; *see also* Laggan army; martial law; Scottish Covenanter Army
Arnade, Peter 176–7, 190
articles of war 156, 160
Arts Humanities Research Council (AHRC) 4, 5
Asia 254–60
Assmann, Aleida 177, 178
atrocities
    defining term 7, 154–5, 156, 178
    distinguished from violence 7, 136, 154–5, 156, 169
    and geography 164–5
    and intent 154, 159–62, 166
    against the Irish 83, 262–3, 267
    by the Irish 76–8, 83, 137–44
    narratives of 9, 57–9, 63, 84, 185–7, 243
    and propaganda 157–9, 167–9, 176, 180, 186
    in Southeast Asia 254–9, 263–6
    in the Thirty Years War 7, 19, 153–69, 243
    see also genocide; massacre; violence
Aughanure 89
Augher 76
Austria 27

Bacon, Sir Francis 220
Bailyn, Bernard 22
Bandon 80
barbarism 52, 55, 56–60, 62–6, 134, 140, 244; *see also* propaganda; rhetorical representations; stereotyping
Barcelona 8, 115, 116, 117–19, 127, 128, 239
Bardon, Jonathan 46

Barrier, Jehan 208–9
Barry, David, Earl of Barrymore 122
Barrymore, Earl of *see* Barry, David, Earl of Barrymore
Beccari, Bernadino 115
Becker, Elizabeth 265
Beckett, J.C. 46
beheadings 134, 138, 139–40
Bell, Philip 230
Belturbet 39, 141, 142
Benburb, battle of 124, 127
Bertault, Antoine 203, 204
bible
    desecration of 79, 139, 141, 142–3
    Old Testament 134, 143
    Revelations 146, 155
Bingham, Thomas 139
Birr 76, 89
Blayney, Robert 106
Boate, Arnold 56–7
Boate, Gerald 56–7
Bohemian Revolt 158, 159
Bor, Pieter 181, 186
Borlase, Sir John 263
Bourbon, Louis de, Prince of Condé 24, 198, 199
Bourges 199, 200
Boyle, Richard 102
Bradshaw, Brendan 32
Brady, Thomas 28
Braganza, Duke of 119
Breda 180
Brereton, Robert 139
Brereton, Sir William 75
British identity 4, 80
Brooke, Lord *see* Greville, Robert, Lord Brooke
Brussels 238
Buddhism 254, 255–6, 257
Bullingbrooke, Anne 243
Burke, John 121
Burke, Myles 103
Burke, Peter 197
Burke, Sir Theobald 103
Burke, Ulick, Earl of Clanricard 118–19, 122
Burke clan 107

Burma 254, 255–7, 259–60
Burne, George 134, 240
Butler, Lady Ann 2–3
Butler, James 41, 122, 128, 267
Bysse, Philip 2, 47

Caen 198, 211
Cahors riots 9, 202–5
Cambodia 254, 255, 257–60, 263–6
Cambridge University 4, 5
cannibalism 22, 58, 59, 167, 245
Canny, Nicholas 6, 9, 52–67, 84, 134,
    137, 145, 261, 262, 266
Cantagrelh, Antoine 203, 204
Carleton, Charles 19
Carlow, County 72, 99, 102
Carlow town 89
Carrickfergus 104, 267
Carroll, Claire 244
Carroll, Stuart 28–9
Carte, Thomas 267
cartography 10, 71, 87
Cary, Henry, Lord Falkland 104, 105
Castile 8, 115, 116–17, 119, 126–8
Castledine, Richard 243
Castlehaven, Earl of see Touchet, James,
    Earl of Castlehaven
castration 78, 140
Catalonia 116–19, 125, 126, 128, 238, 244
Catholic Confederation 120, 123–4, 125,
    127, 128, 239–40, 267
Catholic identity 8, 79, 91, 157–8
Catholic/Protestant conflict, as
    Europe-wide issue 55–6, 146,
    157–8, 239, 240–1, 243
Cavan, County 39, 72, 75, 89, 104, 106,
    141, 142
Cecil, Robert, Earl of Salisbury 226
Certaine inducements to well minded
    people (pamphlet) 231–2
Chandler, David 264
Charles I 60, 108, 116, 118, 120, 121, 123,
    125, 127
Charles II 124
Charles IX of France 208
Chichester, Sir Arthur 97, 98, 101, 241
Chichester, Sir Edward 104

children, violence against 61, 62, 83, 179,
    180, 184, 188, 262–3
churches, desecration of 72, 79–80, 86,
    141–3, 259
Civil Conversation (Guazzo) 205
civilian militias 161–2, 166
civil war see English Civil Wars; French
    Wars of Religion
Clanricard, Earl of see Burke, Ulick,
    Earl of Clanricard
clan structures 89
Clare, County 72
Clarendon, Earl of see Hyde, Edward,
    Earl of Clarendon
Clark, Stuart 27
Clarke, Aidan 6, 7, 37–49, 81, 115, 146,
    237, 260, 261
Clendinnen, Inga 25–6
Clifton, Robin 83, 90
clothing see dress style
Clotworthy, Sir John 38
Cochinchina 257–8
Codrington, Robert 118
Cole, Sir William 104
Coligny, Gaspard de 198, 201
collective memory 84, 177–8, 180–1,
    189–90, 261
colonial violence 20–2, 26, 53–4, 84–7,
    88
colonialism 9–10, 20–2, 26, 52–67, 84–8,
    91, 219–32, 237, 244–5, 254–5
Columbian quincentenary 20–2
commemoration 8, 177–8, 180–2, 187, 189
Commentaries (Monluc) 204
Commission for the Despoiled Subject
    1–2, 136, 143, 236, 261–2
    Remonstrance 38–9, 40, 42, 120, 242
    untitled sequel to 40–1, 42, 47
    see also 1641 depositions
Communist Party of Kampuchea (CPK)
    264–6
comparative history 6, 10, 71, 259–60
compensation claims 43, 143, 178, 186–8
'Concerning Ireland' memorandum 105
Condé, Prince of see Bourbon, Louis
    de, Prince of Condé
conferences (Catholic/Protestant) 211–13

Connacht 72, 75, 76, 83, 98, 99, 103, 107, 108, 109; *see also individual counties*
Connolly, Sean 46
Coote, Sir Charles 83, 104, 108, 123, 262-3, 267
Cope, Joseph 244, 262
Corbin, Alain 141
Corish, Patrick 46
Cork, County 72, 76, 80
Cork city 72, 80
corpses, mutilation of 76, 78, 140, 141, 166
Cottingham, George 243
Coughlan clan 89
Counter-Reformation 88, 121
Courts of Justice *see* High Courts of Justice
Cranford, James 244, 245
Crant, Thomas 243
Crashaw, William 221-2, 226
Crespin, Jean 205-6
Crouzet, Denis 23-4, 30
crowd actions 23, 135, 138, 146-7; *see also* popular violence
Cullen, L.M. 75
Culme, Arthur 243
Culme, Martha 243
CULTURA 5
cultural anthropology 23
culture *see* English culture; Indian culture; Irish culture; memory: culture of
Cushman, Robert 221

Dale, Sir Thomas 222, 224-6, 228
Danvers, Thomas 107
Davells, Thomas 107
Davies, Sir John 88
Davis, Natalie 23, 25
deaths *see* fatalities
De Bry, Theodore 58
Declaration of the State of the Colony (Waterhouse) 9, 59, 63-6
Declaration on the rise and progress of the grand rebellion (English Commons) 41-2

dehumanisation 31, 52, 66, 137, 138, 200; *see also* othering
Denmark 160
De Renzy, Matthew 241
Derry, County 72, 75, 80, 101
Derry city 75
Desan, Suzanne 25
desecration
    of the bible 79, 139, 141, 142-3
    of churches 72, 79-80, 86, 141-3, 259
    of graveyards 79-80, 141
Devereux, Robert, Earl of Essex 224
diaspora *see* Irish diaspora
Disart Castle 139, 140
Disputatio Apologetica de Iure Regni Hiberniae (O'Mahony) 124-5
divine intervention 143-4, 159, 182, 183, 186-7, 258
Domenico à Jesu Maria 159
domestic violence 29
Donagan, Barbara 223
Donegal, County 72, 78, 80, 99, 102, 103, 106
Donne, George 222
Down, County 72, 74, 75, 81, 104
Down Survey 10, 72
dress style 86, 89, 145, 256
drownings 7, 39, 48, 76, 134, 143, 200
Droysen, Gustav 154
Dublin 72, 80
Dublin, County 83
Dublin Castle 1, 41, 61, 105
Duch, Comrade 266
Dungarvan 102
Dunyveg Castle 101
Dupré, Jacques 206
Dutch Revolt 8, 176-90
Dyvolé, Pierre 207, 208

Ecclesiastical History of Ireland (Warner) 44
Edwards, David 10, 17-18, 95-110, 139, 237
Eikonoklastes (Milton) 42
Elias, Norbert 28
Elizabeth I 60, 96
Elizabethans and the Irish (Quinn) 52-3
Ellis, Steven 32

England 29, 98, 116, 119, 121, 137, 144,
    146–7, 180, 238
English Civil Wars 19, 20, 124, 144, 153,
    165, 230, 232, 237
English culture 87–8
English language 81, 136, 145
English law 144–5
Enniskillen 104
Enniskillen Castle 104
Esmond, Sir Lawrence 104, 106–7
Essen, Leon van der 178
Essex, Earl of see Devereux, Robert,
    Earl of Essex
ethnic identity 80, 86
Europe
    Catholic/Protestant conflict in 9,
        55–6, 146, 157–8, 239, 240–1, 243
    Ireland as European 59, 66, 236–46
    Irish colleges in 85, 88, 239
    Irish diaspora in 87, 88, 98
    mock trials in 144
    pamphlets published in 115–29
    see also Denmark; Dutch Revolt;
        Flanders; France; French Wars
        of Religion; Germany; Italy;
        Netherlands; Spain; Thirty Years
        War
exposure 40, 42, 43, 48, 49, 76
expulsions 40, 62, 76, 78
'Extraordinary News' (pamphlet) 117–18,
    127

Falkenberg, Dietrich von 168
Falkland, Lord see Cary, Henry, Lord
    Falkland
family names 89
Fanon, Franz 88
Farnese, Alessandro, Duke of Parma
    176, 181
fatalities
    geographical distribution 76–8
    of the Irish population 83, 90, 262–3,
        267
    methods of killing 48, 138–40
    numbers reported per deponent 81
    quantifying 7, 37–8, 40, 41–9, 81, 91, 179
    see also atrocities; genocide; massacre

fear 81–3, 199, 242–4
    of invasion 10, 103, 108, 242–3
Ferdinand II, Holy Roman Emperor
    155, 157, 158, 159
Fermanagh, County 78, 79, 81, 104, 106,
    142
Fethard Castle 142
Fethard-on-Sea 79
Fidelis of Sigmaringed 159
Fiennes, William, Lord Saye and Sele 229
FitzMaurice, Patrick, Baron of Lixnaw
    122
Fitzpatrick, Thomas 266
Flaherty, David H. 224
Flanders 99, 178
Foster, R.F. 46
France 9, 20, 22–4, 29, 38, 59, 99, 103, 116,
    119, 160, 180, 197–213, 238
Francis, Duke of Guise 198, 199, 208
Franciscans 26, 128, 145, 206
Frankfurt on the Oder 168
Frederick V, Elector Palatine 158
French Wars of Religion 23–4, 29, 56,
    59, 160, 197–213
Fudge, Erica 138
Fullerton, Sir James 96

Galway, County 107
Galway city 72, 118–19, 120, 140
Gardiner, Samuel 45, 46
Gascoigne, George 179, 183
Gates, Sir Thomas 222, 223, 228
general massacre 38, 40, 41, 45, 48, 81,
    242, 262
genocide 154, 155, 164, 243, 254–9, 266;
    see also atrocities; massacre
geography 10, 71–83, 87, 164–5, 259–60
Germany 20, 24–5, 116, 153–4, 155, 156,
    180
Gerrard, Sir Gilbert 229
ghosts 58, 143, 164
Giraldus Cambrensis 57, 62
Girard, René 27
Gomez de Blas, Juan 126, 127
Gorey 104
Gorton, Samuel 261
Goulart, Simon 201

Grandison, Viscount *see* St John,
    Sir Oliver, Viscount Grandison
graveyards, desecration of 79–80, 141
Great Charter 10, 228
Greengrass, Mark 8–9, 28, 155, 197–213
Gregory, Brad 24, 30, 31
Greville, Robert, Lord Brooke 229, 231
Grimmelshausen, H.J.C. von 162
Guazzo, Stefano 205
guilt 178, 183
Guise, Duke of *see* Francis, Duke of
    Guise
Gustavus Adolphus 155, 158, 159, 167–9
Guzmán, Gaspar de, Count-Duke of
    Olivares 116, 127, 238, 240

Haarlem 179, 180, 186, 189
Habsburg monarchy 8, 98, 116, 126,
    176, 241
Halberstadt, Christian von 164, 165
Halhead, Henry 229–30, 232
Hamilton, Sir Frederick 83
hangings 40, 48, 58, 76, 106, 138, 185,
    267
Hardwick, Julie 29
Hart, Jeffrey 21
hate-speech *see* verbal abuse
Haton, Claude 206–7, 208–9
headright system 227, 232
hearsay 39, 40, 44, 48–9, 58, 81, 146;
    see also rumour
hegemon nightmare 242–4
Henry II 59–60
heroism 177, 178, 185, 186
Hickson, Mary 45–6
Higginson, Matthew 243
High Courts of Justice 2, 43, 267
Hill, Moses 105
Histoire ecclésiastique 201, 202
Historiae Catholiciae Iberniae
    Compendium (O'Sullivan Beare)
    121
historiography
    and orality 201
    and violence 6, 17–22, 30–3
history
    comparative 6, 10, 71, 259–60

and memory 4, 5, 12, 17–20, 22, 32
    mythico- 10, 84, 91
History of England (Gardiner) 45
*History of England in the Eighteenth
    Century* (Lecky) 45, 46
History of Great Britain (Hume) 44
*History of the Rebellion and Civil-war
    in Ireland* (Warner) 44
*History of the Rebellion and Civil Wars
    in England* (Clarendon) 43
*History of the Rebellion and Civil Wars
    in Ireland* (Clarendon) 43
Hogenberg, Frans 180, 183, 188–9
honour 156–7, 160, 165, 205, 208
Hopton, Sir Arthur 116
Horowitz, Donald 136, 137, 138, 140, 141
hostage-taking 184
Huizinga, Johan 28
Hume, David 44
humiliation 78, 86, 87, 88, 137, 139, 140,
    166, 200, 264
Hyde, Edward, Earl of Clarendon
    37–8, 43

iconoclasm 143, 166; *see also* desecration
identity *see* British identity; Catholic
    identity; ethnic identity; Irish
    identity; military identity;
    Protestant identity
Impartial Collection, An (Nalson)
    262–3, 267–8
Inchiquin, Baron of *see* O'Brien,
    Murrough, Baron of Inchiquin
Inclosure Thrown Open (Halhead) 232
Indian culture 86
Initium, Incrementa et Exitus (O'Daly)
    124
intent 154, 159–62, 166
invasion
    fear of 10, 103, 108, 242–3
    planned 104, 105
Irish colleges 85, 88, 239
Irish culture 88–90
Irish diaspora 87, 88, 98
'Irish Docquet Book' (Wentworth) 106
Irish identity 8, 80, 88–90, 91
Irish language 81, 87, 88, 89, 123, 136

Irish Manuscripts Commission 4
Irish Privy Council 98, 101
Irish Rebellion, The (Temple) 9, 42, 45,
    59–63, 65–7, 81, 83, 242
Irish Research Council for the
    Humanities and Social Sciences
    (IRCHSS) 4
Ironmongers' Company 101
Islam 26, 163, 238, 244, 254, 255
Island Magee 43, 267
Italy 115, 239

Jacob, Sir Robert 98, 100–1
James VI and I 96–7, 98, 245
Japan 254–5
Java 254, 255
João IV of Portugal 124
Johann Georg, Elector of Saxony 160
Jones, Henry 1–2, 39, 47, 120, 241–2, 261
Jones, Jane 3
judicial violence 24–5, 29, 138, 140, 141,
    224–5
Julianstown 41
just war, concept of 156–7

Kaiser, Michael 157
Kaplan, Benjamin 27
Karens 255, 256
Kavanagh clan 89
Kearney, Hugh 237
Keating, Geoffrey 88
Khmelnytsky Uprising 6, 19
Khmer Kingdom 255, 257–60
Khmer Rouge 263–6
Kiernan, Ben 3, 6, 254–68
Kildare, County 72, 79
Kilkenny, County 72, 76, 105, 106–7,
    109, 140
Kilkenny city 104, 120, 127, 128, 141, 143
killings see fatalities
Killybegs 103
King's County see Offaly, County
kingship 89
Kinsale 80
Konig, David 222, 223
Kuijpers, Erika 8, 176–90
Kupperman, Karen 9–10, 219–32

Laggan army 80, 83
Lamentations of Germany (Vincent)
    153
Lamport, William 126
land
    competition for in Asia 256, 257
    given to planters in America 227–8,
        231–2
    identification with 87, 90
Lane, Ralph 220
language 5, 197–213, 255, 256; see also
        English language; Irish language
'Language and Linguistic Evidence in
        the 1641 Depositions' project 5
Laois, County 72, 76, 80, 99, 105, 107,
        139, 142
Las Casas, Fra Bartolomé 57–8, 244–5
Lawes Divine, Morall, and Martiall
    (Strachey) 222–5
Lawliss, William 141
Lecky, W.H. 45, 46
legitimacy 6, 7, 8, 23, 135–6, 143, 145–6,
        155, 157–8, 162, 165
Leicester, Earl of see Sidney, Robert,
        Earl of Leicester
Leiden 179, 180, 186 ,189
Leinster 72, 75, 76, 79, 81, 83, 99, 102,
        104, 106–7, 108, 109; see also
        individual counties
Leipzig Convention 167, 168
Leitrim, County 40, 48, 76, 78, 81, 89, 103
Leng Sim Hak 265–6
Lenihan, Pádraig 17–18, 237
Leslie, David 120
Limerick, County 72, 76, 79, 81
Limerick city 72, 107
Lindner, Evelin G. 87
Lisbon 8, 115, 116, 119–26, 128, 239, 241
Lismore 142
Lisnagarvey 76, 80
livestock, destruction of 57, 74, 144
Lixnaw, Baron of see FitzMaurice,
        Patrick, Baron of Lixnaw
Loftus, Sir Arthur 108
London 116, 119, 120, 238
Londonderry 75
Londonderry, County 72, 75, 80, 101

Longford, County 76, 103, 104
lordships 89, 97
Loughrea 107
Louis XIII of France 160
Louth, County 72, 106
Louvain 88
Love, Walter 39
Low Leinster 102
Lurgan 80

Maastricht 176, 179, 181–2, 183, 186
McAleese, Mary 11
MacColla, Alasdair 124
MacCormack, Sabine 24
MacDonnell, Randal, Earl of Antrim 118
MacDonnell clan 89, 101
MacGovern clan 104
MacMahon, Hugh 38, 123
MacMahon, Ross Boy McBrian Sariagh 106
MacMahon clan 89, 99
MacMurragh Kavanagh clan 89
Madrid 104, 105, 118, 119, 238, 239
Magdeburg, sack of 7, 153–4, 160, 161, 163, 164, 166, 167–9
Maguire, Sir Connor 99
Maguire clan 89, 104
Malkki, Lissa 84
Manifiesto de Los confederados Catolicos de Irlanda (pamphlet) 127
Mantua 165
mapping see cartography
Martel, H.E. 22
martial law 9–10, 97, 101, 103–4, 106, 166, 222–6
martyrdom 24, 56, 65, 121, 154, 178
Maryland 227, 229
masculinity 136
Massachusetts Bay 221, 229, 231, 261
Massachusetts Bay Company 229
massacre
    in the Dutch Revolt 176
    in the English Civil Wars 165
    general 38, 40, 41, 45, 48, 81, 242, 262
    and intent 154, 159–62, 166
    and premeditation 7, 37–8, 39, 40, 61, 154–5, 199

and propaganda 157–9, 167–9, 176, 180
    scale of 7, 37–8, 40–9, 81
    in Southeast Asia 254–9
    in the Thirty Years War 164, 165–6, 168–9
    use of term 6–7, 38, 154–5
    see also atrocities; genocide; Magdeburg, sack of; Pequot massacre; St Bartholomew's Day Massacre; Virginia massacre
Mass-going 72, 79
Maximilian I, Duke of Bavaria 157, 160
Maxwell, Robert 41–2, 240
Mayo, County 72, 81, 99, 103, 145
Meath, County 72, 76
Mechelen 176, 178, 179, 181, 182, 183
Memoires de l'histoire de l'estat de France (Goulart) 201
memory
    collective 84, 177–8, 180–1, 189–90, 261
    culture of 176–7, 180–1, 182, 189–90
    and history 4, 5, 12, 17–20, 22, 32
    and trauma 81, 136, 176–8, 182, 183, 187–8, 261
memory texts 83
Mendoza, Bernadino de 179–80
mentalité model of violence 6, 18, 22–5, 26, 30–1, 32
mercenaries 154, 163–4
Mercers' Company 101
Mercurius Ibernicus (pamphlet) 122–3
Mervyn, Sir Audley 43
Metz 199, 200
Mexico 126
military identity 166
Milton, John 42, 48
mockery see humiliation; verbal abuse
mock trials 144–5, 200
Monaghan, County 72, 75, 104, 106, 142
Mon Kingdom 255–7, 259–60
Monluc, Blaise de 204
Montaigne, Michel de 199
Montauban 198, 200, 203
Morgan, Hiram 7–8, 115–29

Moriscos 238, 239, 241–2
Morrill, John 18
Moryson, Fynes 88
Mountgomery, John 243
Mountrath 142
Muchembled, Robert 28
Mullaghmast 54
Multyfarnham 120, 241
Munroe, Robert 128
Munster 1, 2, 42, 47, 72, 75, 76, 81, 83,
    98, 99, 102, 103–4, 108, 109, 262;
    see also individual counties
murders see fatalities
mutilation 107, 138, 141
  of corpses 76, 78, 140, 141, 166
mutiny 176, 179
mythico-history 10, 84, 91

Naarden 176, 179–80, 181, 182, 183–4
Nalson, John 262–3, 267–8
name-calling see verbal abuse
naming conventions 89
nationalism 4, 20, 116, 119, 154
Native Americans 9, 20–2, 26, 52–4,
    57–8, 59, 63–6, 84–6, 228, 244–5,
    261
Neale, Robert 267
Neubrandenburg 160, 168
Netherlands 8, 57, 176–90, 222, 239, 245
New British History 52–3
New Ross 106, 140
Newry 109
Nicandro (Olivares) 116
Nicholls, Kenneth 83
Nine Years War 55–6, 96, 100
Nirenberg, David 26–7, 28
Nördlingen 160
Nostradamus 200–1
Nuon Chea 266

O'Brennan clan 106
O'Brian, Patrick 243
O'Brien, Barnabas, Earl of Thomond
    122, 245
O'Brien, Murrough, Baron of Inchiquin
    80, 122, 124
O'Byrne clan 89, 109

O'Cahan clan 89, 101
O'Carroll clan 89
O'Connolly, Owen 38, 61, 62, 65
O'Connor, Teige 109
O'Cullinane, Owen 105
O'Daly, Dominic 124, 125
O'Doherty, Sir Cahir 96
O'Donnell, Hugh, Earl of Tyrconnell
    119, 126
O'Doran clan 107
Offaly, County 72, 76, 79, 81, 99, 107,
    141
'Of Plantations' (Bacon) 220
Ó hAnnrancháin, Tadhg 237
Ohlmeyer, Jane 1–12, 237, 245
O'Kennedy clan 89
O'Lawlor clan 107
Olivares, Count-Duke of see Guzmán,
    Gaspar de, Count-Duke of
    Olivares
O'Mahony, Cornelius 124–5, 126
O'Maloney, John 142
Ó Mealláin, Toirdhealbhach 81
O'Molloy clan 89
O'Mulvaney, Patrick 105
O'Neill, Eoghan Rua 89, 120, 121, 123,
    124, 125, 127–8
O'Neill, Hugh 100, 126
O'Neill, John 117
O'Neill, Sir Phelim 41, 89, 120, 127
O'Neill, Sean 105
O'Neill clan 89, 101
orality 8–9, 39, 84, 136, 137–8, 197–213
O'Reilly, Mulmory McPhilip 106
O'Reilly, Philip McShane 106
O'Reilly clan 89
Orléans 199, 213
Ormond, Earl of see Butler, James
Ormonde, Duke of see Butler, James
O'Rourke clan 89
O'Scea, Ciaran 241
Ó Siochrú, Micheál 1–12, 237
O'Sullivan Beare, Philip 121
othering 52, 80, 87, 143, 145, 163, 244,
    256; see also dehumanisation
O'Toole clan 89
Oudewater 176, 179, 181, 182, 186–9

pacts of friendship 210–11
Paisley, Ian 12
Palmer, William 244
pamphlets 7–8, 83, 115–29, 153, 155, 180,
    231–2, 239
Paris 117, 198, 199, 212–13
Parker, Geoffrey 129, 178
Parma, Duke of *see* Farnese, Alessandro,
    Duke of Parma
Parrie, John 142
Parsons, Sir William 263
partisans 161–2
peer pressure 166
Peisley, William 108
Pequot massacre 53–4
Perceval-Maxwell, Michael 241
Pérez, Joseph 243
Pérez Tostado, Igor 8, 236–46
performative violence 11, 134–47
Peru 24, 84–6
Petty, Sir William 45, 72, 75, 81, 90;
    see also Down Survey
Philip IV of Spain 105, 116, 119, 124, 238,
    239–40
Piggott, John 78, 140
Piggott, Martha 78, 140
Piggott, William 139
place names 89, 145
Plantation of Ulster (Robinson) 46,
    74–5
plantations
    America 9–10, 53, 63–6, 219–32, 245,
        261
    Ireland 10, 53, 56, 60, 99, 100–1, 104,
        107, 245
plundering 162–3, 164, 166, 176, 179
Plunkett, Nicholas 263
Plunkett, Richard 109–10
Plymouth, New England 221
Pol Pot regime 263–6
political engagement 11, 135, 146–7
Pollmann, Judith 8, 176–90
popular violence 11, 23, 27–8, 135, 138,
    146; *see also* crowd actions
population sizes 74–5, 90–1
Portadown Bridge 7
Porter, Roy 197

Portugal 8, 115, 116–17, 119–26, 128, 238,
    239, 241
Powerscourt 141
pre-emption 137
pregnant women, violence to 58, 78,
    164, 186, 189
premeditation 7, 37–8, 39, 40, 61,
    154–5, 199
Prendergast, Simon 106–7
Preston, Thomas 121, 123
print media 7–8, 83, 115–29, 146, 153,
    155, 169, 179–80, 181, 239
Privy Council *see* Irish Privy Council
propaganda
    and the 1641 depositions 2, 4, 58, 81,
        120–1
    in the Dutch Revolt 176, 180, 186
    in Iberian pamphlets 7–8, 120–1, 128
    in the Thirty Years War 7, 157–9, 167–9
    see also rhetorical representations;
        stereotyping
prophecy 89, 137, 200–1, 260
prosecutions 2, 43
Protestant/Catholic conflict, as
        Europe-wide issue 9, 55–6, 146,
        157–8, 239, 240–1, 243
Protestant identity 4, 91, 157–8
Protestant ministers, violence against
        79, 101, 139, 142, 143
Providence Island 229–32
Provins 206–9
psalms 139, 144, 200, 202
punishment 29, 138, 140, 141, 178, 223,
    224–5
Pym, John 229, 231
Pynnar, Nicholas 75

Queen's County *see* Laois, County
Quinn, D.B. 52–3, 67, 237

Radcliffe, Sir George 109
ransoming 179, 184–5
rape 134, 136, 166, 176, 184, 186
Rathlin Island 54
Razin rebellion 6, 19
Reformation 79, 157, 236
Relaçam dos successos (pamphlet) 123–4

Relaçam Sumaria (pamphlet) 121–2
Relacion verdadera de la insigne Vitoria (pamphlet) 126
Relacion verdadera de las felizes vitorias (pamphlet) 127–8
Remonstrance (Commission for the Despoiled Subject) 38–9, 40, 42, 120, 242
    untitled sequel to 40–1, 42, 47
'Remonstrance' (Wentworth) 108–9
representations *see* rhetorical representations
revenge 1, 56, 63, 83, 87, 104, 158, 161, 166, 168–9, 202, 261
rhetorical representations
    of Catholics 53, 54, 57–8
    of the Irish 52–3, 54–60, 62–3, 66–7, 134, 140, 244–5
    of Native Americans 52–3, 58–9, 63–6, 67, 244–5
    of Protestants 145
    of the Spanish 57–8, 244–5
    see also othering; propaganda; stereotyping
Rhode Island 261
Ricci, Matteo 222
Rich, Sir Nathaniel 229, 230
Rich, Robert, Earl of Warwick 229
Riches, David 11, 136, 137, 143, 145
Rinuccini, GianBattista 124, 125
ritual 23, 26, 27, 78, 84, 89, 135, 138–46
Robinson, Philip 46, 74–5
Rolfe, John 227, 228
Rome 115, 239
Roper, Lyndal 24–5
Roscommon, County 72
Rouen 200, 206
Rudé, George 23
Rudyerd, Sir Benjamin 229, 230
Ruff, Julius 28
rumour 74, 81, 137, 199, 200–1, 203, 204, 211; *see also* hearsay

S-21 archive 263–6
sacking (of cities) 160–1, 165, 168–9, 176–80, 181–4, 189, 256–7; *see also* Magdeburg, sack of

St Bartholomew's Day Massacre 20, 28, 38, 59, 200
St John, Sir Oliver, Viscount Grandison 97, 101
St Leger, Sir William 83, 109
Sale, Kirkpatrick 20–1
Salisbury, Earl of *see* Cecil, Robert, Earl of Salisbury
Sandberg, Brian 22
Sandys, Sir Edwin 228
savageness *see* barbarism
Saye and Sele, Lord *see* Fiennes, William, Lord Saye and Sele
Schiller, Friedrich 153–4
Schmidt, Benjamin 245
Scotland 53, 56, 66, 91, 99, 116, 124, 126–7, 129, 238
Scottish Covenanter Army 80, 108
Seville 117, 126, 127, 128, 241
sexual depravity 58, 199, 265
sexual humiliation 78, 86, 140, 200
sexual violence 134, 136, 166, 176, 184
Shagan, Ethan 6, 12, 17–33
shame 178, 183
Shans 255, 256, 257
Sharp, John 142
Shepard, Alexandra 29
Siam 254, 257
Sidney, Sir Philip 220
Sidney, Robert, Earl of Leicester 120, 224
Silverman, Lisa 24
Simms, Hilary 7, 48
Simplicissimus (Grimmelshausen) 162
single-purpose archives 3, 134–5, 261–6
Slacke, Edward 142
slavery 19, 22, 228, 231
Sligo, County 83, 109
Sligo town 78, 140
Smin Dhaw 256–7
Smith, John 220, 225, 229
Smith, Leslie 129
Smyth, William 6, 10–11, 71–91, 259–60
social class 74, 146
socio-cultural interaction model of violence 6, 18, 25–30, 31
solidarity 166, 177–8

Spain 8, 26–7, 55–8, 84–6, 98–9, 103, 104, 105, 115–19, 126–9, 236–46
Spanish fury 176, 179, 181, 182, 183, 184–5
spectres see ghosts
speech see orality
Spell, Luce 243
Spenser, Edmund 57, 88, 241, 244
Spierenburg, Pieter 30
stabbings 78, 101, 138
Stanko, Elizabeth 237
starvation 42, 43, 48–9, 76
Stearne, John, Bishop of Clogher 2, 44
stereotyping 8, 49, 84, 123, 157–9, 244, 245; see also propaganda; rhetorical representations
Strabane 75
Strachey, William 222–5
strategic violence 137, 155, 162
stripping 40, 41, 62, 72, 76, 78, 86, 137, 142, 186, 188
superstition 58, 143–4, 164
surrender 165, 168, 176, 178–9, 182
symbolism see desecration; performative violence; ritual

Tait, Clodagh 17–18, 139, 141, 237
Takaki, Ronald 21
Taylor, Christopher 237
Teares of Ireland (Cranford) 244, 245
Temple, Sir John 9, 42, 45, 59–63, 65–7, 81, 83, 242
Tesaran 141
Thailand see Siam
Thirty Years War 7, 19, 20, 28, 56, 153–69, 180, 243–4
Thomond, Earl of see O'Brien, Barnabas, Earl of Thomond
Thompson, E.P. 23
Tibet 254
Tienen 176, 180, 186
Tilly, Count of see Tserclaes, Johann, Count of Tilly
Tipperary, County 72, 76
Tiv Ol 265
tobacco 227, 228
torture 24, 86, 105, 138, 176, 184, 185, 263–6

Touchet, James, Earl of Castlehaven 123
Toulouse 198, 201, 202, 211, 213
Toulouse, Parlement of 198, 202, 213
trauma
  and memory 81, 136, 176–8, 182, 183, 187–8, 261
  psychological effects 185
Trinity College Dublin 2, 4, 5, 11, 44
Tserclaes, Johann, Count of Tilly 160–1, 168
Tusser, Thomas 228
Tyrconnell, Earl of see O'Donnell, Hugh, Earl of Tyrconnell
Tyrone, County 72, 74, 80, 81, 101, 105, 106, 236
Tyrone, Earl of see O'Neill, Hugh; O'Neill, John; O'Neill, Sean

Ukraine 6, 19
Ulbricht, Otto 28
Ulster 41–2, 56, 72, 74–6, 79, 80, 81, 83, 99, 100–1, 103–6, 108; see also individual counties
United States see Americas, the
Urban VIII, Pope 117, 121
urban expansion 82, 87
Utrecht 182, 186, 188

Van Haecht, Godevaert 179
Van Meteren, Emanuel 179, 181, 184
Vane, Sir Henry 99, 106
Vassy 199, 206
verbal abuse 137–8, 199–200, 203, 204–5, 208–10, 211
Vietnam 254, 257–9, 263, 266
Vincent, Philip 153
violence
  against children 61, 62, 83, 179, 180, 184, 188, 262–3
  anthropology of 11, 136–7, 143
  colonial 9–10, 20–2, 26, 53–4, 84–7, 88
  decline of 28
  distinguished from atrocity 7, 136, 154–5, 156, 169
  domestic 29
  and historiography 6, 17–22, 30–3

violence (*continued*)
  against the Irish population 3, 134–5,
    261–3
  judicial 24–5, 29, 138, 140, 141, 224–5
  and legitimacy 6, 23, 137, 143, 145–6,
    155, 157–8, 162, 165
  meaning of 237–8
  mentalité model 6, 18, 22–5, 26, 30–1,
    32
  and memory 81, 136, 176–8, 182, 183,
    261
  performative 11, 134–47
  popular 11, 23, 27–8, 135, 138, 146
  pre-emptive 137
  against Protestant ministers 79, 101,
    139, 142, 143
  as punishment 29, 138, 140, 141, 178
  and ritual 23, 26, 27, 78, 84, 138–46
  sexual 134, 136, 166, 176, 184
  as social practice 157
  socio-cultural interaction model 6,
    18, 25–30, 31
  strategic 137, 155, 162
  verbal 137–8, 199–200, 203, 204–5,
    208–10, 211
  against women 20, 29, 58, 78, 83,
    136, 164, 179, 180, 184, 186, 189,
    262–3
  see also atrocities; fatalities; genocide;
    massacre
Virginia, Co Cavan 89
Virginia, USA 9–10, 59, 63–6, 221–9
Virginia Company 9–10, 220, 222–3,
  226, 227–9
Virginia massacre 9, 59, 63–6, 228
virtue 220–2, 230, 232
Voisin, Lancelot de 201

Walcott, Judith 38
Wallenstein, Albrecht von 159, 160
Walter, John 11, 134–47
Ware, Sir James 104
Waring, Thomas 2, 42
Warner, Ferdinando 44–8

Warwick, Earl of *see* Rich, Robert,
  Earl of Warwick
Waterford, County 72, 76, 102, 142
Waterford city 72, 102
Waterhouse, Edward 9, 59, 63–6
Wenman, Sir Thomas 108
Wentworth, Sir George 108
Wentworth, Thomas 54, 75, 95, 99–100,
  105–9, 238
Wesnam, Simon 240
West, Sir Thomas 222
Westmeath, County 72, 241
Wexford, County 43, 72, 79, 99, 102,
  104, 106–7, 140, 142
Whitchurch 143
Wicklow, County 72, 83, 99, 102, 107,
  109, 141, 262–3, 267
William of Orange 176, 186
Willoughby, Sir Francis 107
Wilson, Edward 236, 240
Wilson, Peter 6–7, 19, 153–69
Windsor, Sir William 104
Winthrop, John 221, 261
witch hunts 19–20, 24–5, 27
witness accounts
  of the 1641 rebellion *see* 1641
    depositions
  of the Cahors riots 202–5
  of the Dutch Revolt 177, 179–80, 181,
    187–9, 245
women
  and heroism 185, 186
  role in rebellion 88, 90, 260
  shipped to Virginia colony 10, 228
  violence against 20, 29, 58, 78, 83,
    136, 164, 179, 180, 184, 186, 189,
    262–3
Wood, Andy 27–8, 205
world view *see mentalité*
Würzburg 167, 169

Yucatán 26

Zutphen 176, 178, 179, 181, 182

Lightning Source UK Ltd.
Milton Keynes UK
UKOW02f1859220315

248238UK00001B/4/P